The Cambridge Companion to the Modern German Novel

The Cambridge Companion to the Modern German Novel provides a wide-ranging introduction to the major trends in the development of the German novel from the 1890s to the present. Written by an international team of experts, it encompasses both modernist and realist traditions, and also includes a look back to the roots of the modern novel in the *Bildungsroman* of the late eighteenth and nineteenth centuries. The structure is broadly chronological, but thematically focused chapters examine topics such as gender anxiety, images of the city, war and women's writing; within each chapter, key works are selected for close attention. Unique in its combination of breadth of coverage and detailed analysis of individual works, and featuring a chronology and guides to further reading, this *Companion* will be indispensable to students and teachers alike.

D0061278

THE CAMBRIDGE
COMPANION TO

THE MODERN
GERMAN NOVEL

EDITED BY
GRAHAM BARTRAM

CAMBRIDGE
UNIVERSITY PRESS

CAMBRIDGE UNIVERSITY PRESS
Cambridge, New York, Melbourne, Madrid, Cape Town, Singapore,
São Paulo, Delhi, Dubai, Tokyo

Cambridge University Press
The Edinburgh Building, Cambridge CB2 8RU, UK

Published in the United States of America by Cambridge University Press, New York

www.cambridge.org
Information on this title: www.cambridge.org/9780521483926

First published 2004

A catalogue record for this publication is available from the British Library

Library of Congress Cataloguing in Publication data
The Cambridge companion to the modern German novel / edited by Graham Bartram.
        p.   cm. – (Cambridge companions to literature)
        Includes bibliographical references and index.
    ISBN 0 521 48253 4 (hardback) – ISBN 0 521 48392 1 (paperback)
1. German fiction – 19th century – History and criticism.   2. German fiction – 20th
        century – History and criticism.   3. Bildungsroman.
            I. Bartram, Graham. 1946–   II. Series.
                    PT771.C36   2004
            833′.9109–dc22   2003058436

        ISBN 978-0-521-48253-0 Hardback
        ISBN 978-0-521-48392-6 Paperback

Transferred to digital printing 2010

CONTENTS

CONTENTS

NOTES ON CONTRIBUTORS

LYNN ABRAMS is Professor of Gender History at the University of Glasgow. She has published widely in the field of German women's and gender history. She is the author of *The Making of Modern Woman: Europe 1789–1918* (2002) and co-editor with Elizabeth Harvey of *Gender Relations in German History* (1996)

ALAN BANCE is Emeritus Research Professor of German at the University of Southampton. He is former Germanic Editor of the *Modern Language Review* and past President of the Conference of University Teachers of German in Great Britain and Ireland. His books include *Theodor Fontane: the Major Novels* (1982), and (as editor) *Weimar Germany: Writers and Politics* (1982) and *The Cultural Legacy of the British Occupation in Germany* (1997). His translation of a volume in the new Penguin Freud series appeared in 2002 under the title *Wild Analysis*, and he is currently translating Brigitte Hamann's 'Winifred Wagner oder Hitlers Bayreuth'. He is also working on projects on Ödön von Horváth and on the theme of war and society in twentieth-century Germany.

DAGMAR BARNOUW is Professor of German and Comparative Literature at the University of Southern California. Among her more recent publications are *Germany 1945: Views of War and Violence* (1997) and *Naipaul's Strangers* (2003). Her latest book, *Feared Memories: the Uses of Remorse in Postwar Germany and America*, is due to appear in 2004.

GRAHAM BARTRAM is Lecturer in German Studies and former Associate Dean (Postgraduate and Research) in the Faculty of Arts and Humanities at Lancaster University. His co-edited books include *Brecht in Perspective* (1982), *Culture and Society in the GDR* (1984), *Walter Benjamin in the Postmodern* (1994) and *Reconstructing the Past: Representations of the Fascist Era in Postwar European Culture* (1996). He is currently working on a study of Hermann Broch's *Die Schlafwandler*.

RUSSELL A. BERMAN is Walter A. Haas Professor in the Humanities at Stanford University. His publications include *Between Fontane and Tucholsky* (1983), *The Rise of the Modern German Novel* (1986), *Modern Culture and Critical Theory* (1989), *Cultural Studies of Modern Germany* (1993) and *Enlightenment or Empire: Colonial Discourse in German Culture* (1998). In 1997 he was awarded the Cross of Merit of the Federal Republic of Germany. He is currently at work on a project on literary history.

ELIZABETH BOA is Emeritus Professor of German at the University of Nottingham. She has published *The Sexual Circus: Wedekind's Theatre of Subversion* (1987), *Kafka: Gender, Class, and Race in the Letters and Fictions* (1996) and *Heimat – a German Dream: Regional Loyalties and National Identity in German Culture 1890–1990* (2000, co-author Rachel Palfreyman), and co-edited *Women and the Wende: Social Effects and Cultural Reflections of the German Unification Process* (1994, with Janet Wharton) and *Anne Duden: a Revolution of Words* (2003, with Heike Bartel). She has also published numerous essays in feminist criticism on German literature from the eighteenth century to the present.

MICHAEL BUTLER is Emeritus Professor of Modern German Literature at the University of Birmingham and has been awarded the Cross of Merit of the Federal Republic of Germany. He has published widely in the areas of twentieth-century German literature and society and contemporary German-Swiss society, culture and literature. His books include *The Novels of Max Frisch* (1976) and *The Plays of Max Frisch* (1985); he has also edited *Rejection and Emancipation: Writing in German-speaking Switzerland 1945–1991* (1991), *The Narrative Fiction of Heinrich Böll: Social Conscience and Literary Achievement* (1994), *The Making of Modern Switzerland 1848–1998* (2000) and *The Challenge of German Culture* (2000).

STANLEY CORNGOLD is Professor of German and Comparative Literature at Princeton University. Among his books are *The Fate of the Self: German Writers and French Theory* (1986; revised edition 1994), *Franz Kafka: the Necessity of Form* (1988), *Borrowed Lives* (with Irene Giersing) (1991) and *Complex Pleasure: Forms of Feeling in German Literature* (1998). He has edited a critical edition of Kafka's *Metamorphosis* (1996); his new study of Kafka entitled *Lambent Traces* appears in 2004; and he is preparing a critical edition of *Selected Stories of Franz Kafka*.

ALLYSON FIDDLER is Professor of German and Austrian Studies at Lancaster University. Her publications, mainly on women writers, include *Rewriting Reality: an Introduction to Elfriede Jelinek* (1994), and she has recently co-edited (with W. E. Yates and John Warren) a volume entitled *From Perinet to Jelinek: Viennese Theatre in its Political and Intellectual Context* (2001).

PATRICIA HERMINGHOUSE is Fuchs Professor Emerita of German Studies at the University of Rochester. She has written widely on nineteenth- and twentieth-century German literature, the social contexts of women's writing, and German émigrés in nineteenth-century America. Editor of the textbook anthology *Frauen im Mittelpunkt* and a volume of translated writings by Ingeborg Bachmann and Christa Wolf, she also edited two volumes on GDR literature and, more recently, *Gender and Germanness: Cultural Constructions of Nation* (1998) as well as an anthology of *German Feminist Writings* from the seventeenth century to the present. She co-edited the *Women in German Yearbook* from 1995 to 2002.

PAUL MICHAEL LÜTZELER is Rosa May Distinguished University Professor in the Humanities at Washington University in St Louis. He has published nine books on German and European literature from the eighteenth to the twentieth century, including *Die Schriftsteller und Europa. Von der Romantik bis zur Gegenwart* (1992), and (as editor) *Deutsche Romane des 20. Jahrhunderts. Neue Interpretationen* (1983) and *Spätmoderne und Postmoderne. Beiträge zur deutschsprachigen Gegenwartsliteratur* (1991). He is the editor of the works of Hermann Broch and the author of the biography *Hermann Broch* (1985) that appeared in German, English, Spanish and Japanese. He is a regular reviewer for the German weekly *DIE ZEIT* and has been awarded the German Cross of Merit and the Austrian Cross of Honour in Arts and Sciences.

MICHAEL MINDEN is Senior Lecturer at the University of Cambridge and Fellow of Jesus College. He has published essays on a wide range of German prose, poetry and drama from 1750 to the present, and on the cinema of the Weimar Republic. His most recent book is *The German Bildungsroman: Incest and Inheritance* (1997), and he is co-editor (with Holger Bachmann) of *Fritz Lang's 'Metropolis': Cinematic Visions of Technology and Fear* (2000). He is currently working on a cultural history of German literature.

PHILIP PAYNE is Professor of German Studies at Lancaster University. His books include *Robert Musil's Works, 1906–1924: a Critical Introduction* (1987) and *Robert Musil's 'The Man without Qualities': a Critical Study* (1988). In 1989 he was awarded the Robert Musil Medal by the City of Klagenfurt, Austria. His most recent publication is a translation of Musil's diaries.

BURTON PIKE is Professor Emeritus of Comparative Literature and German at the Graduate School of the City University of New York. He is author of *The Image of the City in Modern Literature* (1981), and has edited and co-translated (with Sophie Wilkins) Robert Musil's *The Man Without Qualities* (1995). He has also published translations of other works by Musil, and of Goethe's *The Sorrows of Young Werther*; further translations have appeared in a number of literary journals.

J. H. REID is Professor Emeritus of Contemporary German Studies at the University of Nottingham. He is co-editor of the *Kölner Ausgabe der Werke Heinrich Bölls* (2002–), and author of *Heinrich Böll: a German for his Time* (1987), *Writing without Taboos: the New East German Literature* (1990) and numerous articles on postwar German literature.

RITCHIE ROBERTSON is Professor of German at Oxford University and a Fellow of St John's College. His books include *Kafka: Judaism, Politics, and Literature* (1985), *Heine* (1988), *The 'Jewish Question' in German Literature, 1749–1939: Emancipation and its Discontents* (1999), and (as editor) *The Cambridge Companion to Thomas Mann* (2002).

RONALD SPEIRS is Professor and Head of the Department of German Studies at the University of Birmingham. He has published numerous articles on modern German literature, society and culture. Among his books are *Bertolt Brecht* (1987) and (with Beatrice Sandberg) *Franz Kafka* (1997), and he has co-edited and translated writings by Friedrich Nietzsche (*The Birth of Tragedy and Other Writings*) (1999) and Max Weber (*Political Writings*) (1994).

ANTHONY WAINE is Senior Lecturer in German Studies at Lancaster University. He has published widely on German literature and culture in the twentieth century, particularly Brecht, Seghers and Martin Walser; among his books are *Martin Walser: the Development as Dramatist 1950–1970* (1978) and *Martin Walser* (1980). He is currently working on a study of modern German writing and the impact of popular culture.

PREFACE

A *Companion to the Modern German Novel* faces the daunting task of covering, in a relatively limited space, a period of German culture, from about 1880 to the present, in which the novel genre has displayed an extraordinary richness and variety of form, and has also played a key part in articulating German as well as Austrian and Swiss-German experiences of the social and political upheavals of the long twentieth century. This volume tries to do justice both to stylistic diversity and experimentation, including the provocative innovations of modernism, and to the novel's role as witness (albeit always a partial and imaginative one) to the sometimes overwhelming events of the age. In choosing works for inclusion we have attempted to strike a balance between eclecticism and selectivity, and also between detailed discussion of individual texts and broader accounts of literary and cultural developments. The balance has been struck differently in different chapters: readers will find some largely or entirely devoted to one or two writers (e.g. chapter 5 on Kafka), while others focus on broader trends or, in many cases, adopt a combination of the two approaches. Each chapter relates the novels it studies to their socio-political or cultural context, but in chapter 2 Lynn Abrams gives a social historian's overview of the whole period, with its continuities but also its major political turning-points of 1918, 1933, 1945 and 1989. Chapters are dovetailed with each other as far as possible and cross-refer to each other where this is helpful, but there has been no attempt to impose the straitjacket of a single critical perspective on the book as a whole; indeed, one of its purposes is to illustrate a range of approaches to the understanding and interpretation of modern German fiction.

The structure of the *Companion* is broadly chronological, but each chapter is organised around a central theme, and in two (chapter 8 on 'Images of the city', and chapter 14 on the depiction of the 'little man' in novels by Fallada, Böll and Walser) the development of a *topos* is followed from the early decades of the twentieth century into the post-1945 period. In an attempt to highlight the different emphases of other German-speaking national cultures, chapter 7 focuses on the Austrian 'classical modernist' novel of the early 1930s and chapter 16 on postwar Swiss and Austrian writing, though Austrian texts are also studied in detail elsewhere. Two further chapters (9 and 17) are devoted to women's writing, in the Weimar Republic and the 1970s and 1980s respectively, though texts by women of course feature in other chapters too.

For part of chapter 6, and briefly too in chapter 4, we look back, beyond the main timespan covered by the *Companion*, to the modern German novel's roots in the tradition of the *Bildungsroman* ('novel of education/ maturation'), in particular Goethe's late eighteenth-century masterpiece *Wilhelm Meisters Lehrjahre*. Apart from these retrospectives, chapters 3 to 7 show the transition from the 'social realism' of the late nineteenth century to the flowering of modernism in Germany, and in the Austro-Hungarian Empire and its post-1918 successor states, in the first three decades of the twentieth century; chapters 10 and 11 examine novels of the First World War, produced during the war and in its long aftermath, and the novel during the Third Reich; the remaining chapters (12 to 18) cover the second half of the twentieth century, beginning with the 'coming to terms with' the Nazi (and later, GDR) past, and concluding with a wide-ranging survey of the German novel in the 'postmodern' present.

In a volume such as this it is inevitable, particularly given its thematic structure, that some important writers will receive regrettably scant treatment or will be omitted altogether. Here this is the case with (among others) the Austrians Joseph Roth (*Radetzky-Marsch*), Elias Canetti (*Die Blendung*) and Thomas Bernhard; the Swiss Friedrich Dürrenmatt (particularly his three detective novels from the 1950s); the late 1920s novels of Erich Kästner, including the internationally famous children's book *Emil und die Detektive* (1929); the historical novels of Lion Feuchtwanger; the works of Alfred Andersch; the not uninteresting (though currently neglected) output of 'mainstream' GDR authors such as Hermann Kant and Erwin Strittmatter; and the powerfully haunting fictions of the late W. G. Sebald. The *Companion*'s 'Chronology' (pp. xiv–xxii), which notes the publication dates of the novels we discuss, also includes some of these 'excluded' items, so that readers interested enough to research further might at least have a starting-point for their investigations.

This project has had a lengthy gestation, and I owe a great debt of gratitude to all who have collaborated on it: first to the contributors, for their enthusiasm and patience, their willingness to accommodate cuts to their chapter-length, and above all for the skill and care with which they have addressed the interests of both the general reader and the seasoned *Germanist*; second to my editors at Cambridge University Press, Katharina Brett, Linda

Bree and Rachel de Wachter, for their unfailing encouragement and support over the years. Allyson Fiddler, Claire Hadfield and Ritchie Robertson have read draft chapters and provided helpful comments and suggestions. I am particularly grateful to Anne Payne who during the final stages of compilation has hunted down innumerable bibliographical data, carried out meticulous corrections, and helped me finally banish the nightmare of misbehaving computer files; and to her husband and my colleague Phil, who from the outset has always been on hand with advice and support, and who has more recently given invaluable and unstinting help with the editing of some of the *Companion*'s chapters. Last but not least my thanks and appreciation go to Kay McKechnie for her careful and sensitive editing of the final typescript.

CHRONOLOGY

Political events refer to Germany, unless Austria or Switzerland is specifically mentioned.

1210	Wolfram von Eschenbach, *Parzival*
1554	Jörg Wickram, *Der Knabenspiegel*
1669	Grimmelshausen, *Der abenteuerliche Simplicissimus Teutsch*
1767	Christoph Martin Wieland, *Agathon*
1774	Johann Wolfgang von Goethe, *Die Leiden des jungen Werthers*
1795 (–1796)	Johann Wolfgang von Goethe, *Wilhelm Meisters Lehrjahre*
1798	Ludwig Tieck, *Franz Sternbalds Wanderungen*
1799	Friedrich Hölderlin, *Hyperion*
1802	Novalis, *Heinrich von Ofterdingen*; Jean Paul, *Titan*
1809	Johann Wolfgang von Goethe, *Die Wahlverwandtschaften*
1819	Arthur Schopenhauer, *Die Welt als Wille und Vorstellung*
1854 (–1855)	Gottfried Keller, *Der grüne Heinrich* (first version)
1855	Gustav Freytag, *Soll und Haben*
1857	Adalbert Stifter, *Der Nachsommer*
1871	Germany unified under Kaiser Wilhelm I (King of Prussia) and Chancellor Bismarck. Universal manhood suffrage introduced for Reichstag elections.
1872	Friedrich Nietzsche, *Die Geburt der Tragödie*
1878	Anti-socialist legislation introduced, in force until 1890. Friedrich Nietzsche, *Menschliches, Allzumenschliches I*
1880	Friedrich Nietzsche, *Der Wanderer und sein Schatten. Menschliches, Allzumenschliches II*
1882	Friedrich Nietzsche, *Die fröhliche Wissenschaft*
1883	Friedrich Nietzsche, *Also sprach Zarathustra I* and *II*
1884	Friedrich Nietzsche, *Also sprach Zarathustra III*
1885	Friedrich Nietzsche, *Also sprach Zarathustra IV*

1886	Friedrich Nietzsche, *Jenseits von Gut und Böse*
1887	Friedrich Nietzsche, *Zur Genealogie der Moral*
1888	Accession of Kaiser Wilhelm II. Theodor Fontane, *Irrungen Wirrungen*
1890	Bismarck resigns. Theodor Fontane, *Stine*
1891	Theodor Fontane, *Unwiederbringlich*
1892	Theodor Fontane, *Frau Jenny Treibel*
1894	Heinrich Mann, *In einer Familie*
1895	Sigmund Freud and Josef Breuer, *Studien über Hysterie*; Theodor Fontane, *Effi Briest*; Gabriele Reuter, *Aus guter Familie*
1896	Helene Böhlau, *Das Recht der Mutter*; Theodor Fontane, *Die Poggenpuhls*
1898	Theodor Fontane, *Der Stechlin*
1900	Sigmund Freud, *Die Traumdeutung*; Heinrich Mann, *Im Schlaraffenland*
1901	Gustav Frenssen, *Jörn Uhl*; Thomas Mann, *Buddenbrooks*
1902	Hugo von Hofmannsthal, *Ein Brief*
1903	Otto Weininger, *Geschlecht und Charakter*
1906	Robert Musil, *Die Verwirrungen des Zöglings Törleß*; Lulu von Strauss und Torney, *Der Hof am Brink*
1910	Expressionist movement (intellectuals, artists, writers) gains momentum. Ida Boy-Ed, *Ein königlicher Kaufmann*; Rainer Maria Rilke, *Die Aufzeichnungen des Malte Laurids Brigge*; Hermann Löns, *Der Wehrwolf*
1912	Thomas Mann, *Der Tod in Venedig*; (–1914) Franz Kafka writes *Amerika*
1914	Outbreak of the First World War, greeted with some enthusiasm in Germany and the Austro-Hungarian (Habsburg) Empire. Switzerland remains neutral. Franz Kafka writes *Der Process*
1915	Franz Kafka, *Die Verwandlung*
1916	Walter Flex, *Der Wanderer zwischen beiden Welten*; Georg Lukács, *Theorie des Romans*; Franz Kafka, 'Das Urteil'
1917	November: revolutionary unrest among soldiers and sailors. Growing politicisation of Expressionist movement
1918	Defeat of Germany and Habsburg Empire. Collapse of Kaiserreich, proclamation of Weimar Republic as parliamentary democracy. Disintegration of Habsburg Empire, foundation of independent Republic of Austria. Heinrich Mann, *Der Untertan*

1919	Versailles Treaty allocates guilt for war to Germany and imposes massive reparations. Continuing left-wing revolutionary movements. Hermann Hesse, *Demian*
1920	Right-wing Kapp putsch defeated by general strike. Ernst Jünger, *In Stahlgewittern*
1922	Franz Kafka writes *Das Schloß*
1923	Munich Beer Hall putsch (Hitler, Ludendorff) defeated. Hyperinflation peaks.
1924	Germany's finances stabilised; increasing political stability. Expressionism runs out of steam. Thomas Mann, *Der Zauberberg*; Robert Musil, *Drei Frauen*
1925	'Neue Sachlichkeit' (New Objectivity, New Sobriety) becomes new cultural slogan. Lion Feuchtwanger, *Jud Süß*; Franz Kafka, *Der Prozeß* (posth.)
1926	Abortion law reformed. Franz Kafka, *Das Schloß* (posth.)
1927	Hermann Hesse, *Der Steppenwolf*; Franz Kafka, *Amerika* (posth.); Arnold Zweig, *Der Streit um den Sergeanten Grischa*
1928	Vicki Baum, *stud. chem. Helene Willfüer*
1929	Wall Street stock market crash hits German economy; worsening depression and spiralling unemployment. Thomas Mann awarded Nobel Prize for Literature. Vicki Baum, *Menschen im Hotel*; Werner Beumelburg, *Sperrfeuer um Deutschland*; Alfred Döblin, *Berlin Alexanderplatz*; Hans Henny Jahnn, *Perrudja*; Erich Kästner, *Emil und die Detektive*; Erich Maria Remarque, *Im Westen nichts Neues*
1930	Werner Beumelburg, *Gruppe Bosemüller*; (–1932) Hermann Broch, *Die Schlafwandler*; Lion Feuchtwanger, *Erfolg*; Robert Musil, *Der Mann ohne Eigenschaften* (Book 1); Franz Schauwecker, *Aufbruch der Nation*
1931	Marieluise Fleißer, *Mehlreisende Frieda Geier* (see also 1975); Erich Kästner, *Fabian*; Irmgard Keun, *Gilgi – eine von uns*; Gabriele Tergit, *Käsebier erobert den Kurfürstendamm*
1932	Hans Fallada, *Kleiner Mann – was nun?*; Hugo von Hofmannsthal, *Andreas oder die Vereinigten* (posth. written mainly 1912–13); Irmgard Keun, *Das kunstseidene Mädchen*; Joseph Roth, *Radetzky-Marsch*
1933	German unemployment tops 6 million. National Socialists (Nazis) seize power. Public burning of banned books. Austria: Parliamentary government ceases. Lion Feuchtwanger, *Die Geschwister Oppenheim*; Thomas Mann, *Die Geschichten*

Jaakobs; Robert Musil, *Der Mann ohne Eigenschaften* (portion of Book 2)

1934   Thomas Mann, *Der junge Joseph*

1935   Werner Bergengruen, *Der Großtyrann und das Gericht*; Elias Canetti, *Die Blendung*; Heinrich Mann, *Die Jugend des Königs Henri Quatre*

1936   Thomas Mann, *Joseph in Ägypten*; Jan Petersen, *Unsere Straße*

1937   Ödön von Horváth, *Jugend ohne Gott*; Irmgard Keun, *Nach Mitternacht*

1938   *Anschluß* (annexation) of Austria by Nazi Germany. Heinrich Mann, *Die Vollendung des Königs Henri Quatre*

1939   Outbreak of Second World War. Ernst Jünger, *Auf den Marmorklippen*

1940   Lion Feuchtwanger, *Exil*

1941   Nazi policy against Jews turns into systematic genocide.

1942   Anna Seghers, *Das siebte Kreuz*

1943   Hermann Hesse, *Das Glasperlenspiel*; Thomas Mann, *Joseph der Ernährer*; posthumous publication of remainder of Robert Musil's *Der Mann ohne Eigenschaften*

1944   Lion Feuchtwanger, *Simone*

1945   Germany defeated by Allies; collapse of Nazi regime; July: Potsdam Conference divides Germany and Austria into Allied zones of occupation (American, British, French, Soviet). Berlin (in Soviet zone) also divided into four occupied sectors. Four Allies initially agree goals of de-Nazification, demilitarisation and democratisation. Hermann Broch, *Der Tod des Vergil*

1946   Germany: increasing economic and political divergence of Western (US/British/French) and Eastern (Soviet) zones of occupation. Hermann Hesse awarded Nobel Prize for Literature.

1947   Thomas Mann, *Doktor Faustus*

1948   Western Allies integrate their three zones and implement currency reform.

1949   May: Federal Republic of Germany (FRG) founded as pluralist parliamentary democracy in three Western zones, with Bonn as capital and including West Berlin as one of its *Länder*. September: Konrad Adenauer (CDU) (conservative Christian Democratic Party) becomes chancellor. October: German Democratic Republic (GDR) founded as embryo socialist state (not recognised by FRG or any other Western government) in Soviet zone, with capital in East Berlin and SED (Socialist Unity Party) led by Walter Ulbricht entrenched as dominant political force.

1950   Decade of *Wirtschaftswunder* (economic miracle) begins in FRG.

1951   Heinrich Böll, *Wo warst du, Adam?*; Friedrich Dürrenmatt, *Der Richter und sein Henker*; Wolfgang Koeppen, *Tauben im Gras*

1952   Friedrich Dürrenmatt, *Der Verdacht*

1953   Heinrich Böll, *Und sagte kein einziges Wort*; Wolfgang Koeppen, *Das Treibhaus*

1954   Max Frisch, *Stiller*; Wolfgang Koeppen, *Der Tod in Rom*

1955   Austrian Treaty recognises Austria as independent unified state.

1957   Alfred Andersch, *Sansibar oder Der letzte Grund*; Max Frisch, *Homo Faber*

1958   Ingeborg Bachmann, *Der gute Gott von Manhattan*; Friedrich Dürrenmatt, *Das Versprechen*

1959   Heinrich Böll, *Billard um halb zehn*; Günter Grass, *Die Blechtrommel*; Uwe Johnson, *Mutmassungen über Jakob*

1960   Martin Walser, *Halbzeit*; Peter Weiss, *Der Schatten des Körpers des Kutschers*

1961   August: Under Soviet protection, GDR authorities build fortified Berlin Wall between Eastern and Western sectors to cut off flow of GDR citizens to the West. Günter Grass, *Katz und Maus*; Uwe Johnson, *Das dritte Buch über Achim*

1963   FRG: Ludwig Erhard (CDU) replaces Adenauer as chancellor. Beginning of Frankfurt Auschwitz Trial (–1965). Thomas Bernhard, *Frost*; Heinrich Böll, *Ansichten eines Clowns*; Günter Grass, *Hundejahre*; Erwin Strittmatter, *Ole Bienkopp*; Christa Wolf, *Der geteilte Himmel*

1964   Max Frisch, *Mein Name sei Gantenbein*; Hermann Kant, *Die Aula*; Alexander Kluge, *Schlachtbeschreibung*

1965   Wolfgang Hildesheimer, *Tynset*

1966   FRG: Growing economic-political crisis; CDU government replaced by CDU–SPD (Social Democrat) 'Grand Coalition' led by former Nazi Kurt Georg Kiesinger. Heinrich Böll, *Ende einer Dienstfahrt*; Martin Walser, *Das Einhorn*

1967   FRG: Beginning of radical left student movement and 'extra-parliamentary opposition'. Thomas Bernhard, *Verstörung*

1968	*Kursbuch* articles proclaim 'death of literature'. Siegfried Lenz, *Deutschstunde*; Christa Wolf, *Nachdenken über Christa T.*
1969	FRG: 'Grand Coalition' ousted by SPD-led coalition under Willy Brandt, whose *Ostpolitik* seeks better relations with communist Eastern Europe, inc. GDR. Günter Grass, *örtlich betäubt*; Peter Handke, *Die Angst des Tormanns beim Elfmeter*; Irmtraud Morgner, *Hochzeit in Konstantinopel*
1970	Thomas Bernhard, *Das Kalkwerk*; Uwe Johnson, *Jahrestage I*
1971	GDR: Stalinist leader Walter Ulbricht replaced by Erich Honecker, more favourable to rapprochement with West and initially promising more freedom to GDR writers. Ingeborg Bachmann, *Malina*; Heinrich Böll, *Gruppenbild mit Dame*; Uwe Johnson, *Jahrestage II*; Dieter Kühn, *Ich Wolkenstein*
1972	'Basic Treaty' regularises relations between FRG and GDR; mutual recognition as separate states. Heinrich Böll awarded Nobel Prize for Literature. Volker Braun, *Das ungezwungne Leben Kasts. Drei Berichte*; Günter Grass, *Aus dem Tagebuch einer Schnecke*; Peter Handke, *Der kurze Brief zum langen Abschied*; Peter Handke, *Wunschloses Unglück*; Hermann Kant, *Das Impressum*; Martin Walser, *Die Gallistl'sche Krankheit*
1973	Barbara Frischmuth, *Das Verschwinden des Schattens in der Sonne*; Max von der Grün, *Stellenweise Glatteis*; Wolfgang Hildesheimer, *Masante*; Uwe Johnson, *Jahrestage III*; Peter Schneider, *Lenz*; Karin Struck, *Klassenliebe*; Günter Wallraff, *Ihr da oben, wir da unten*; Martin Walser, *Der Sturz*
1974	FRG: Chancellor Willy Brandt resigns, replaced by Helmut Schmidt (also SPD). Heinrich Böll, *Die verlorene Ehre der Katharina Blum*; Stefan Heym, *5 Tage im Juni*; Irmtraud Morgner, *Leben und Abenteuer der Trobadora Beatriz*
1975	Thomas Bernhard, *Korrektur*; Volker Braun, *Unvollendete Geschichte*; Marieluise Fleißer, *Eine Zierde für den Verein* (= rev. edn of 1931 *Mehlreisende Frieda Geier*); Max Frisch, *Montauk*; Elfriede Jelinek, *Die Liebhaberinnen*; Alice Schwarzer, *Der kleine Unterschied und seine großen Folgen*; Verena Stefan, *Häutungen*; Karin Struck, *Die Mutter*; Peter Weiss, *Die Ästhetik des Widerstands* (vol. 1)
1976	GDR: Biermann Affair (regime-critic Biermann stripped of his citizenship and exiled; numerous GDR intellectuals

protest and many subsequently leave the GDR). Nicolas Born, *Die erdabgewandte Seite der Geschichte*; Peter Handke, *Die linkshändige Frau*; Martin Walser, *Jenseits der Liebe*; Gabriele Wohmann, *Ausflug mit der Mutter*; Christa Wolf, *Kindheitsmuster*

1977   Kidnappings and murders of prominent figures by terrorist Red Army Faction. Günter Grass, *Der Butt*; Jutta Heinrich, *Das Geschlecht der Gedanken*; Edgar Hilsenrath, *Der Nazi & der Friseur*; Brigitte Schwaiger, *Wie kommt das Salz ins Meer?*; Maxi Wander, *Guten Morgen, du Schöne*

1978   Ingeborg Bachmann, *Der Fall Franza; Requiem für Fanny Goldmann* (posth. fragments); Peter Weiss, *Die Ästhetik des Widerstands* (vol. II)

1979   Nicolas Born, *Die Fälschung*; Volker Braun, *Das ungezwungne Leben Kasts* (with additional fourth part); Max Frisch, *Der Mensch erscheint im Holozän*; Peter Handke, *Langsame Heimkehr*; Stefan Heym, *Collin*; Helga Novak, *Die Eisheiligen*; Ruth Rehmann, *Der Mann auf der Kanzel*; Martin Walser, *Seelenarbeit*; Christa Wolf, *Kein Ort. Nirgends*

1980   Günter Grass, *Kopfgeburten oder Die Deutschen sterben aus*; Helmut Heißenbüttel, *Textbücher 1–6*; Elfriede Jelinek, *Die Ausgesperrten*; Adolf Muschg, *Baiyun oder Die Freundschaftsgesellschaft*; Brigitte Schwaiger, *Lange Abwesenheit*; Gerold Späth, *Commedia*; Martin Walser, *Das Schwanenhaus*

1981   Paul Nizon, *Das Jahr der Liebe*; Peter Weiss, *Die Ästhetik des Widerstands* (vol. III)

1982   FRG: SPD-led government ousted by CDU-led coalition under Helmut Kohl. Ralph Giordano, *Die Bertinis*; Christoph Hein, *Der fremde Freund*; Aysel Özakin, *Die Preisvergabe*; Martin Walser, *Brief an Lord Liszt*

1983   Elfriede Jelinek, *Die Klavierspielerin*; Uwe Johnson, *Jahrestage IV*; Bodo Kirchhoff, *Zwiefalten*; Irmtraud Morgner, *Amanda. Ein Hexenroman*; Sten Nadolny, *Die Entdeckung der Langsamkeit*; Aysel Özakin, *Die Leidenschaft der Anderen*; Christa Wolf, *Kassandra*

1984   Christoph Ransmayr, *Die Schrecken des Eises und der Finsternis*

1985   Volker Braun, *Hinze-Kunze-Roman*; Patrick Süskind, *Das Parfum*; Martin Walser, *Brandung*

1986	Jurek Becker, *Bronsteins Kinder*; Thomas Bernhard, *Auslöschung. Ein Zerfall*; Günter Grass, *Die Rättin*; Gert Hofmann, *Veilchenfeld*; Barbara Honigmann, *Roman von einem Kinde*; Uwe Timm, *Der Schlangenbaum*
1987	Barbara Frischmuth, *Über die Verhältnisse*; Anna Mitgutsch, *Die Züchtigung*; Aysel Özakin, *Der fliegende Teppich. Auf der Spur meines Vaters*; Rafik Schami, *Eine Hand voller Sterne*; Gabriele Wohmann, *Der Flötenton*; Christa Wolf, *Störfall. Nachrichten eines Tages*
1988	Günter Grass, *Zunge zeigen*; Gert Hofmann, *Vor der Regenzeit*; Christoph Ransmayr, *Die letzte Welt*; Gerold Späth, *Barbarswila*; TORKAN, *Tufan. Brief an einen islamischen Bruder*; Martin Walser, *Jagd*
1989	October: reforming Soviet leader Mikhail Gorbachev visits East Berlin for GDR fortieth anniversary celebrations. 9 November: the Berlin Wall is breached. Edgar Hilsenrath, *Das Märchen vom letzten Gedanken*; Elfriede Jelinek, *Lust*; Aysel Özakin, *Die blaue Maske*; Rafik Schami, *Erzähler der Nacht*
1990	3 October: (Re-)unification of Germany. Bodo Kirchhoff, *Infanta*; Michael Krüger, *Das Ende des Romans*; Sten Nadolny, *Selim oder Die Gabe der Rede*; Andreas Neumeister, *Salz im Blut*; Emine Sevgi Özdamar, *Mutterzunge*; W. G. Sebald, *Schwindel. Gefühle*; Christa Wolf, *Was bleibt*
1991	Barbara Honigmann, *Eine Liebe aus nichts*; Robert Menasse, *Selige Zeiten, brüchige Welt*; Aysel Özakin, *Die Vögel auf der Stirn*; Martin Walser, *Die Verteidigung der Kindheit*
1992	Ulla Berkéwicz, *Engel sind schwarz und weiß*; Herta Müller, *Der Fuchs war damals schon der Jäger*; Emine Sevgi Özdamar, *Das Leben ist eine Karawanserei*; Rafik Schami, *Der ehrliche Lügner*; Robert Schindel, *Gebürtig*; Peter Schneider, *Paarungen*
1993	Jeannette Lander, *Jahrhundert der Herren*; Urs Richle, *Mall oder Das Verschwinden der Berge*; W. G. Sebald, *Die Ausgewanderten*; Verena Stefan, *Es ist reich gewesen. Bericht vom Sterben meiner Mutter*; Martin Walser, *Ohne einander*
1994	Peter Handke, *Mein Jahr in der Niemandsbucht*; Sten Nadolny, *Ein Gott der Frechheit*; Peter Weber, *Der Wettermacher*
1995	Günter Grass, *Ein weites Feld*; Josef Haslinger, *Opernball*; Paul Nizon, *Die Innenseite des Mantels*; Christoph

A NOTE CONCERNING TRANSLATIONS AND BIBLIOGRAPHICAL DATA

To make this *Companion* as useful as possible to non-German speakers, all quotations from German texts are given in English translation (which may be accompanied by the German original). In the introductory chapter 1, novel titles are mainly given in English translation; thereafter, they appear in both German and English on their first mention in a particular chapter. Where a novel's English title is italicised, it is that of a published translation (normally the first), and is followed by the date of the translation's appearance. Thus, a reference to '*Der Zauberberg* (1924; *The Magic Mountain*, 1927)' indicates that the German original appeared in 1924, followed by its English translation three years later.

Bibliographical details of the main texts studied are either provided in a chapter's endnotes or precede the suggestions for further reading appended to each chapter. To economise on space, items of secondary literature mentioned in the endnotes are not repeated in the 'Further reading' list.

I

GRAHAM BARTRAM

The German novel in the long twentieth century

> Most people relate to themselves as storytellers.
> (Robert Musil, *The Man Without Qualities*, p. 709)

What kind of scope and limits should a *Companion to the Modern German Novel* set itself? What in particular do we mean by 'modern'?

One approach would equate 'modern' with 'contemporary', and thus focus on the novel in the here-and-now, in 'our era' – whether that era be relatively narrowly defined as the period since the *Wende* (turning-point) of German unification in 1989–90, or more broadly as the six decades following the collapse of Nazi Germany at the end of the Second World War. Both 1945 and 1989 mark important cultural as well as socio-political breaks in the continuum of German history, and there exists a considerable body of scholarly literature devoted to the development of the novel in these periods – as well as in the decades into which they are subdivided.[1] To anchor ourselves purely in the 'now' would however make for a viewpoint that is inherently unstable, as well as lacking a longer-term historical perspective, and a *Companion* constructed around it would fairly soon be overtaken by events.

There are, however, two other understandings of the 'modern', both of which are anchored more firmly in historical time. Both of them are also highly pertinent to the development of the European novel in general, and the German novel in particular.

The first of these definitions refers to the (still ongoing) period of history known as the 'modern age', whose emergence went hand in hand with Europe's gradual transition, between about 1500 and 1800, from a predominantly feudal to a predominantly bourgeois society. This transition encompassed a multiplicity of factors, economic, social and political, among them the emergence of manufacture, the growing competition from the mercantile and subsequently capitalist middle classes to the power of the aristocracy, and the increasing ascendancy of the nation-state over the dynastic ordering of societies. Of primary concern here, however, is its ideological dimension: what might be termed the 'spirit of modernity' was characterised by a series of challenges, ranging from Protestantism to scientific enquiry, to the dominant and hitherto all-embracing theological worldview of the Catholic Church; and it culminated, in the mid to late eighteenth century, in the Enlightenment's proclamation of the universal values of critical rationality and the freedom of the individual.

Now, if there is any one genre of literature whose development can be linked to this 'modern age', and in particular to the ethos of bourgeois individualism that emerged in the Enlightenment era, it is that of the novel, whose focus on the changing relationship between the individual and the social world equips it to play a vital role in these modernising societies' discourses about themselves and in their imaginings of their futures. The genre has in fact a far longer history: as Margaret Anne Doody has reminded us, European literature (among others) possesses a rich and sprawling tradition of narrative fiction that reaches back to Greek and Roman antiquity, encompassing both 'fantasy' and 'realism' and at times blurring the distinction between the two.[2] It is however in the modern age, and especially the age of Enlightenment, that the novel in its 'realistic' mode becomes one of the primary vehicles for the expression of the new individualism, offering as it does an ideal means of exploring consciousness introspectively, while also depicting the conscious individual in his/her interaction with the surrounding world.[3] The German novel however provides a particular inflection to this interplay between individual and society. As Russell Berman suggests in chapter 6 of this book, the 'novel of (self-)cultivation' (*Bildungsroman*) that came to the fore in Germany in the latter half of the eighteenth century, and which represents that society's major contribution to the classical phase of the European novel,[4] was marked by a distinctive inwardness, a tendency to retreat from real engagement with the social sphere, that partly reflected a recoiling from politics in the aftermath of the French Revolution and the Terror, but was also nurtured by the relative economic and political 'backwardness' of a nation then still divided into innumerable quasi-feudal kingdoms, dukedoms and other territories large and small.[5] This feature of the classical *Bildungsroman*, typified by the conclusion to Goethe's *Wilhelm Meister*, was in turn given a radical twist in the Romantic variant of the genre, which opened itself up to include elements of fantasy, myth and fairy-tale, but in which (as Ritchie Robertson points out in chapter 4) an intensified inwardness or idealising solipsism held sway: the Romantics' aesthetic vision of a 'poeticisation of reality' all too often meant that the world depicted in the novel became little more than the objectification of the hero's dreams and desires. All in all, however, we can see the widely diverse fiction of the period 1770–1830 as having established a variety of narrative modes, ranging from the realistic to the mythical/fantastical, that were henceforth to be at least potentially available to German novel writers, through the nineteenth century (in which an increasingly socially oriented *Bildungsroman* became dominant, the Romantic imagination more marginal), and on into the twentieth.[6]

Within the broadly defined modern era whose time-span roughly coincides with the rise of the novel genre, we can however locate a second, more circumscribed notion of the 'modern'; and it is on this latter that the main framework of the present *Companion* is based. The 'modern German novel' is, in a nutshell, the novel since the advent of moder*nism*: a deep-seated and long-term shift in western high culture, which in Germany began – somewhat later than in other European countries such as France – around 1880, which reached its peak (and produced its most monumental works) in the two decades 1913–33, and which over the last thirty years or so has experienced a partly contradictory prolongation under the banner of postmodernism (the subject of Paul Michael Lützeler's concluding chapter 18). Modernism, as Russell Berman shows, was first and foremost a cultural crisis that put in question some of the founding beliefs (in rationality, 'truth', progress and the integrity of the self) that underpin the modern era. (In Germany its key spokesman was the philosopher Friedrich Nietzsche, whose late nineteenth-century deconstruction of these beliefs has been taken up nearly a century later by the theorists of the postmodern.) But the modernist era also ushered in what the historian Eric Hobsbawm has termed the 'Age of Extremes' – a series of man-made upheavals and catastrophes which, beginning with the First World War of 1914–18, transformed the social and political landscape of Europe (as well as of many other parts of the globe) almost beyond recognition.[7] It hardly needs saying that Germany – key participant in the First World War and effective initiator of the Second; cradle (together with Austria) of Nazism, one of the two totalitarian systems that fought for domination in the mid twentieth century; divided after 1945 between a capitalist West and communist East – was at the centre of these upheavals throughout the 'short twentieth century' that Hobsbawm describes. Our *Companion* therefore sets out to show how the German novel has, over the last one hundred and thirty years, developed a range of strategies, forms and themes, both modernist and otherwise, in its attempt to articulate and come to grips with the profoundly destabilising impact that these 'internal' and 'external' forces have had on modern Europe's traditional understandings of individual and social identity.

The origins of Austrian and German modernist culture lie in the traditionally hierarchical, superficially stable pre-First World War society of the Habsburg and Wilhelmine Empires with their semi-autocratic political systems, within which however were fermenting the social divisions and conflicts described by Lynn Abrams in chapter 2.[8] While admittedly some of the weightiest modernist novels – Thomas Mann's *The Magic Mountain* (chapter 6) or Hermann Broch's *The Sleepwalkers* (chapter 7) for example – were completed in the 1920s or early 1930s, thus in the aftermath of the débâcle of 1914–18, their authors, together with other modernist writers such as Musil and Hofmannsthal, had grown up amidst the apparently still intact social traditions of the prewar era. As a consequence, their cultural and aesthetic values were shaped through and through by a complex tension between fragmentation and wholeness: between the seeming order of pre-1914 institutions and the threat of disintegration lurking underneath, but also between the exposure of that disintegration, and a longing for an ideal harmony and integrity that could be embodied in the structures of the work of art itself. Key to the modernist novel's impact on the society of its day, however, was its gesture of provocation and rupture. As Musil points out through his hero Ulrich, 'most people relate to themselves as storytellers': our own – supposedly non-fictional – narratives of our lives, with deeply ingrained ideas of development through time and goals to be reached (but also maybe tragedies and disappointments), are one of our main defences against the fear that existence may be nothing but disorder and pointlessness. Modernists saw traditional fiction as encouraging its readers to cling on to their comforting but illusory notions of meaning and progression; and in parallel with Ulrich's realisation that his own life has in fact lost that sense of meaningful sequence that 'most people' still have, Musil his creator sets about undermining his readers' complacency by drawing them from the outset into a narrative that breaks radically with the established stylistic and structural conventions of nineteenth-century realism.

Modernism's breaking of nineteenth-century realism's contract between writer and reader took many forms, often involving subject-matter (the articulation of previously taboo aspects of sexuality, for example) as much as structure and style; linking them all was the modernist movement's much broader tendency to identify artistic creation and the realm of the aesthetic as a sphere apart from, and in permanent opposition to, the smugly materialistic values of contemporary bourgeois society. Chapters 3 to 8 of the *Companion* not only show the development of modernist fiction out of the social-realist novel of the late 1880s and 1890s, but also demonstrate something of the remarkable stylistic and thematic diversity of these modernist texts, some of which still tower, alongside James Joyce's *Ulysses* and Marcel Proust's *A la recherche du temps perdu*, like distant peaks over the landscape of twentieth-century European literature. In chapter 3 Alan Bance traces the trajectory from Fontane's *Effi Briest*, with its combination of poetic imagination, carefully balanced ironies and still intact depiction of Wilhelmine society, via Thomas Mann's foregrounding of aesthetic awareness and social pessimism in *Buddenbrooks*, to the almost despairing social and political satire of Heinrich Mann's *Man of Straw*, in which the threadbare fabric of realism is shot through with elements of caricature and self-critical theatricality. In the first of three chapters in the *Companion* dealing with the themes of sexuality and gender (see also chapters 9 and 17), Ritchie Robertson's investigation of gender anxiety in texts ranging from Musil's *Törless* to Hesse's *Steppenwolf*, Hofmannsthal's *Andreas* and Jahnn's *Perrudja*, focuses on depictions and questionings of masculinity, and highlights Jahnn's novel as a neglected masterpiece of gay literature. Chapter 5 is devoted to Kafka, whose allegorical representations of modernity and the tragi-comic situation of the endlessly self-justifying individual have become one of the defining myths of twentieth-century culture. Together with readings of *The Trial* and *The Castle* (showing in the former case just how wide of the mark Orson Welles's self-indulgently pathos-laden film version was), Stanley Corngold offers an illuminating revaluation of *The Man Who Disappeared (America)*, an earlier work that paradoxically displays a more postmodern aspect to Kafka's writing than his later modernist ones. In chapter 6, Russell Berman presents Thomas Mann's *The Magic Mountain*, with its experiments in time and its ironic, ultimately humanistic critique of warring ideologies, as the simultaneous culmination and subversion of the *Bildungsroman* tradition; while chapter 7 examines the equally, if not more ambitious attempts by the Austrians Hermann Broch (*The Sleepwalkers*) and Robert Musil (*The Man Without Qualities*) to forge the novel into an aesthetic-cum-intellectual entity capable of taking the measure of, and itself measuring up to, the cultural crisis of the age. Finally, in the last of the *Companion*'s chapters devoted largely to modernism, Burton Pike's wide-ranging survey of the image of the city shows how, in such early twentieth-century works as Rilke's *The Notebooks of Malte Laurids Brigge*, Thomas Mann's *Death in Venice* and (later) Döblin's *Berlin Alexanderplatz*, the urban setting exchanges the specificity and concrete detail of the nineteenth-century text for an increasing abstraction that makes it the vehicle for a wide range of symbolic and metaphorical significances.

In 1936, a few years after the appearance of the first part of *The Man Without Qualities*, in which the modernist consciousness shared by author and protagonist had subverted narrative conventions so to speak 'from within', an essay entitled 'The Storyteller' by the German-Jewish philosopher and intellectual Walter Benjamin registered the crippling impact that the *external* events of the previous twenty years had had on people's ability to narrate their lives:

Experience has fallen in value. . . . With the World War a process began to become apparent which has not halted since then. Was it not noticeable at the end of the war that men returned from the battlefield grown silent – not richer, but poorer in communicable experience? . . . Never has experience been contradicted more thoroughly than strategic experience by tactical warfare, economic experience by inflation, bodily experience by mechanical warfare, moral experience by those in power. A generation that had gone to school on a horse-drawn carriage now stood under the open sky in a countryside in which nothing remained unchanged but the clouds, and beneath these clouds, in a force-field of destructive torrents and explosions, was the tiny, fragile human body.[9]

War, the collapse of the Kaiserreich and the 1923 inflation crisis between them swept away the old, confining yet reassuring social order that had given birth to modernism, and, in so doing, ushered in the final phase of the 'classical' modernist novel. Alongside the great retrospective works of Mann, Broch and Musil, modernism's aesthetic challenge to bourgeois society mutated in the 1920s into the politicised literature of the left-wing avant-garde (in particular the theatre of Bertolt Brecht); its stylistic innovations, though henceforth available to writers who wished to make use of them, inevitably lost the 'shock of the new'. If anything, it was the Nazi and Stalinist dictatorships, with their forcible reimposition (in right-wing and left-wing variants) of a conservatively 'German' or (socialist) 'realist' aesthetic, that helped to give a kind of afterlife to what they burned and banished as (respectively) 'decadent' or 'formalist'; in the second half of the twentieth century, it was to be the culturally conservative society of post-Nazi Austria that produced the confrontational modernism of a Thomas Bernhard or an Elfriede Jelinek, and the German Democratic Republic's state-imposed orthodoxy of 'socialist realism' that helped in part to provoke the exuberant modernist-cum-postmodernist imagination of an Irmtraud Morgner (see the discussion by Patricia Herminghouse in chapter 15 and Allyson Fiddler in chapter 17).

Meanwhile, in the late 1920s and early 1930s, there emerged a new generation of younger writers whose values and attitudes had been predominantly formed not by the prewar conventions of Wilhelmine society but by the Weimar Republic's much more open social and cultural conflict between tradition and modernity. Strikingly 'modern' – to a reader in the early twenty-first century – are the women writers Vicki Baum, Gabriele Tergit, Irmgard Keun and Marieluise Fleißer, who came to the fore against the background of the partial, and highly controversial, emancipation of women in the 1920s, and who are discussed by Elizabeth Boa in chapter 9. While variously appropriating modernist techniques (for example, the late modernist principle of montage also used by Alfred Döblin in his *Berlin Alexanderplatz*) to embody the fragmentation and cultural diversity of 1920s society and to puncture the nevertheless still potent ideologies of social 'wholeness', they combine these techniques with elements of naturalism and realism in the construction of distinctively feminine, sometimes feminist perspectives that seem to have little to do with the overwhelmingly male-dominated enterprise of modernism, and, if anything, look forward to a later, postmodernist aesthetic. Scarcely had these modern feminine voices made themselves heard, however, than they were repressed or exiled by the Nazi dictatorship with its vehemently anti-feminist ideology; and although authors such as Anna Seghers and Irmgard Keun made important contributions to literary resistance to the Third Reich (see Ronald Speirs's discussion in chapter 11), it was not until the 'second wave' women's movement of the 1970s and 1980s that women writers, some of whom played an active part in the rediscovery of their 1920s predecessors, were to re-emerge with a distinctive, and this time much more highly politicised voice.

Even when not explicitly 'political' in its intentions, the 1920s women's writing discussed in chapter 9 inevitably took on a political charge in the polarised force-field of the tradition-versus-modernity conflicts of the 1920s. The same was equally, if not even more the case with the war novels presented by Michael Minden in chapter 10, their stances ranging from the traditional idealising patriotism of Walter Flex to the subtly nuanced humanism of Arnold Zweig, from the brutally modern nationalism of Ernst Jünger to the equally modern indictment of war in Remarque's *All Quiet on the Western Front*. What is also clear, in a way that seems partly to belie Walter Benjamin's statement on the numbed 'silence' of the soldiers returning from the unprecedented horrors of trench warfare, is that a writer like Remarque was indeed able, albeit from a distance of over ten years, to articulate persuasively the reality of what he, and hundreds of thousands of others, had been through. A bestseller that effectively bridged the gulf between 'high' and popular culture, and, as Michael Minden shows, abandoned many of the structural conventions of traditional narrative in order to be adequate to what it was depicting, *All Quiet on the Western Front*, with its overriding claim to 'authenticity', signals what was to become one of the most important – but also most problematic – roles of the German novel in the turbulent twentieth century: that of what has been termed 'witness literature',[10] conveying to contemporaries and documenting for posterity a reality that is sometimes hard or even unbearable to imagine.

A similar claim of 'authenticity' could also be made for the novels of the 'little man' discussed by Anthony Waine in chapter 14. Beginning with Hans Fallada's bestseller of the 1929–33 Depression, *Little Man – What Now?*, and resuming after the Second World War with the novels of Heinrich Böll and, later, Martin Walser, this subgenre documents with imaginative empathy and often naturalistic detail the lives of ordinary people who, like Remarque's soldiers, albeit in a less extreme situation, see themselves largely as the passive objects of social forces they have no hope of controlling. (We are here indeed a long way from the 'educational' aspirations of the *Bildungsroman*, even in its modernistically self-ironising form.) Fallada's hero Johannes Pinneberg is representative of man in modern mass society, and his fate had its real-life parallels in many countries of the industrialised world in the early 1930s; at the same time, as Ralf Dahrendorf has pointed out, Fallada's deeply sympathetic portrayal of his protagonist's feelings of frustration and powerlessness provides us with a telling insight into the mentality of the masses of ordinary Germans who were about to succumb to the threats and blandishments of the National Socialists.[11]

Literature as direct and truthful witness to contemporary events could not be published within the Third Reich. As Ronald Speirs's chapter 11 shows, however, fiction written during the twelve years of the Hitler regime – in many cases by writers in exile – deployed a wide range of different forms and styles, from the 'exemplary' historical novels of Heinrich Mann to the 'eye-witness' account of Nazi Germany in Irmgard Keun's *After Midnight*, in implicit or explicit opposition to the dictatorship. *Youth without God*, by the Austrian (or more properly Austro-Hungarian) Ödön von Horváth, shows us, through the morally 'unreliable' voice of its first-person narrator, the insidiously corrupting pressure of totalitarianism on the uncommitted though well-meaning individual; Anna Seghers's *The Seventh Cross* is perhaps the most celebrated example of the politically committed resistance novel, whose humanist values are combined with a multi-perspectival (and thus intrinsically anti-totalitarian) structure in an open attack on the supposed omnipotence of the Nazi terror apparatus. At the same time, the omnipresent censorship within Germany and later Austria meant that in some cases, allegorical or quasi-mythical novels that *were* allowed by the Nazis (Bergengruen's *A Matter of Conscience*, Ernst Jünger's *On the Marble Cliffs*) were mistakenly endowed by the readers with a 'coded' anti-Hitler message that the author had not in fact intended.

In the years and decades following the 1945 defeat of Germany (including annexed Austria) and the collapse of the Nazi regime, the ways in which German-speaking novelists went about making sense of reality were marked, perhaps more starkly than they had ever been, by the divergent world-political fates of the different German-speaking states: Austria; German-speaking Switzerland (an ethnic entity within the Swiss confederation); and Germany itself, divided from 1945 until 1990 into a Soviet-dominated socialist state in the East, and a pluralist–capitalist West. Austria and Switzerland had long nourished distinctive national-cultural identities that in Austria's case had become more pronounced following the unification of Germany, excluding Austria, under Prussian dominance in 1871: in literature, this positioning outside the powerhouse of Germany but within the multilingual Habsburg Empire had engendered *inter alia* a peculiarly Austrian emphasis on the theme of *language*, its inadequacies but also its creative potential, that became particularly prominent in the modernist era (e.g. Hofmannsthal's *Ein Brief*), and was to be resumed by writers such as Peter Handke in the second half of the twentieth century. In the aftermath of 1945, however, the policies of the victorious Allies, acting now as occupying powers, further accentuated pre-existing national-cultural differences. On the one hand, the western half of divided Germany was made to confront, and feel responsible for, the crimes of the Nazi era, so that the task of *Aufarbeitung der Vergangenheit* or *Vergangenheitsbewältigung* ('coming to terms with the past') became, as Dagmar Barnouw shows in chapter 12, an overwhelming though virtually unfulfillable imperative. (The socialist GDR meanwhile neatly dissociated itself from Nazism as a product of capitalism in crisis.) Austria on the other hand was allowed to retain its unity as a nation-state and to consider itself the 1938 victim of Nazi aggression; hence the post-1945 survival there of a relatively intact and fairly complacent 'conservative' culture. Neutral Switzerland, finally, remained apparently morally and politically unscathed by whatever accommodations it had had to make with Nazi Germany during the war years. It was thus no coincidence that while in the 1950s West German novelists such as Heinrich Böll were struggling to find language and narrative structures adequate to convey the chaotic, sometimes blackly comic, horror of their war experiences (e.g. Böll's *And Where Were You, Adam?*), it was the Swiss author Max Frisch who with his 1954 novel *Stiller* began to explore the existential conflicts of personal identity that, as Michael Butler points out in chapter 16, only found more general entry into German literature with the 'New Subjectivity' of the 1970s.

The GDR, unlike the preceding Hitler regime, possessed novelists such as Anna Seghers who were not only endowed with considerable creative powers but who, as communists or left-wing socialists, were in basic sympathy with the Marxist (if not the Leninist) principles of the Soviet-backed Socialist Unity Party (SED), and who had in many cases made a conscious choice to settle in the GDR rather than in the FRG after their years of exile. Writers were seen by the Party as essential ideological allies in the creation of a new, socialist consciousness, and were in many cases generously subsidised; in exchange, however, published works, subject to a multilayered process of censorship that all too easily became self-censorship, had to conform to the Stalinist literary orthodoxy of 'socialist realism', originally enunciated by

Zhdanov in 1934. This prescribed formulaic and all-too-predictable structures for the novel, often involving a (usually proletarian) hero or heroine
encountering superable obstacles on the road to a socialist goal: a kind of
banalised *Bildungsroman*, in fact. Chapter 15 shows how a new generation
of writers coming to prominence after the building of the Berlin Wall in
1961 – in particular Christa Wolf with *Divided Heaven* – began a process
of chipping away at this deadening orthodoxy, introducing subject-matter
and narrative structures that created spaces for individual rather than so-
cialised subjectivity – Wolf's 'subjective authenticity' – and increasingly for
penetrating critiques of GDR society. In her study of works by Wolf, Irmtraud Morgner, Volker Braun, Christoph Hein and Stefan Heym, Patricia
Herminghouse shows how the GDR's 'critical Marxists', engaged to the end
with their state's professed goals and its manifest shortcomings, turned the
novel into a vital 'public space' in which between the lines, but also increasingly openly (cf. Braun's mockery of the censors), social issues received an
airing that they were denied elsewhere in the state-controlled media.

In the GDR the link between the novel and politics was (for the writer)
an unavoidable given; in the other German-speaking countries, particularly
West Germany, the 1960s witnessed a politicisation of culture that culminated in the neo-avantgardiste proclamation of the 'death of literature' in the
midst of the student movement of 1967–9, followed (according to a not altogether implausible literary-historical narrative) by a pendulum-swing into
the 'New Subjectivity', with its focus on the private and the personal, in the
1970s and early 1980s. Three of the chapters covering these decades – J. H.
Reid's discussion of literature and commitment in novels by Böll, Grass and
Weiss, Michael Butler's investigation of the 'rediscovery of the self' in Frisch
and Handke, and Allyson Fiddler's study of women's writing in the 1970s
and 1980s – make clear however that any periodisation based on a straightforward opposition between the 'personal' and the 'political', and between
politics and aesthetics, is bound to be a crass oversimplification. Political
interventions by novelists can in fact take one of two different, though in-
terrelated, forms. On the one hand, a prominent writer may exploit his/her
public reputation as an intellectual figurehead by contributing directly to
political debate and taking an active part in party-political campaigning – as
Thomas Mann did in the 1920s, and as Günter Grass has done from the late
1960s onwards. This extra-literary political activity is however quite distinct from the novelist's other opportunity for intervention: the much more
subtle and wide-ranging means that the novel itself has at its disposal to
affect its readers' consciousness and their political awareness. Firstly, the
novel in its social-realist mode can show and bring to life dimensions of a
society's experience, past and present, that its readers had hitherto ignored

or repressed, and can thereby bring about a shift, however imperceptible, in the internalised reality framework that forms a context for political awareness and political beliefs. The literature of *Vergangenheitsbewältigung*, of coming to terms with the past, is critically dependent on such revelation or recuperation of forgotten or repressed experience. Secondly, however, the novel's introspective exploration and representation of consciousness, together with its ability to focus on the social microcosm of family life and close personal relationships, equip it ideally to represent that *identification* of the 'personal' with the 'political' that is a central concern not only of the West German women writers who openly proclaimed it in the 1970s, but also of their East German contemporaries (see chapters 15 and 17), of Max Frisch and Peter Handke (chapter 16), and indeed also of the novelists of the 'little man' – Fallada, Böll and Walser – discussed by Anthony Waine in chapter 14. And thirdly, as the 'classical' modernist Robert Musil and his latter-day successors such as Peter Handke have demonstrated, the novelist can use the very medium of the genre – language – in imaginative and self-reflexive play, to subvert and explode the routinised thought-patterns and unquestioned clichés – what Handke has termed 'all the apparently unquestionable images of reality'[12] – in which the ideological assumptions of his or her readers are fixed, or, like Verena Stefan (chapter 17), to explore the potential of a newly invented 'feminine' vocabulary to challenge the dominant discourses of patriarchy.

In all three of the socially/politically committed novels of the years 1963–81 examined in detail by J. H. Reid in chapter 13, the theme of the National Socialist past looms large in the politics of the present. Particularly in the context of the student movement of 1967–9 (the background to Grass's *Local Anaesthetic*), the accusation of witting or unwitting complicity in Nazi crimes became part of a frontal attack by a younger generation on the values and authority of its parents. But this literature of indictment, subsequently mutating into the often self-indulgently psychologising *Väterbücher* ('[anti-] father-books') of the late 1970s and early 1980s, was but one moment in a long drawn-out process of 'coming to terms with the past' which, beginning in the 1950s and continuing to the present, has been dogged at every turn by the overwhelming difficulty of the enterprise. While Günter Grass's picaresque *Tin Drum*, published in Germany in 1959, achieved a *succès de scandale* by rubbing its readers' noses simultaneously in the Nazi past and in its own taboo-breaking Rabelaisian excesses, it was, suggests Barnouw, the earlier but far less well-known trilogy of novels by Wolfgang Koeppen, *Pigeons on the Grass*, *The Hothouse* and *Death in Rome*, that had in quieter and subtler fashion initiated a truly serious probing of the social and political legacy of the Hitler era.

As Paul Michael Lützeler shows in chapter 18, the last thirty years, under the cultural ascendancy of the postmodern, have witnessed a luxuriant diversification of voices, themes and locations (both chronological and geographical) in the German novel. With the abandonment of classical modernism's striving for 'totality' within the work of art, and of the construct of the representative hero, have come an increasing globalisation and multiculturalism, reflected both in the non-European settings of novels such as Grass's *Show Your Tongue*, and in the important contribution of Turkish, Iranian and Arabian authors (e.g. Aysel Özakin, TORKAN, Rafik Schami) to contemporary German fiction. The postmodern culture of Germany's recent past has been shaped by local as well as global factors: the disintegration of the Soviet Union's hegemony over Eastern Europe, followed by the collapse of the Soviet Union itself, not only redefined the geopolitical landscape and destabilised the familiar left–right polarities of world-political debate, but also led to Communist East Germany's being absorbed by its western counterpart, as the 'two states of the German nation' (Basic Treaty, 1972) became one. And, as Dagmar Barnouw points out in the concluding part of chapter 12, this further twist to the saga of German national-political identity in the long twentieth century has meant for Germans, and particularly the citizens of the former GDR, yet another past to be 'mourned' and retrospectively 'completed'.

Partly in response to these seismic shifts, the post-*Wende* epoch of the late twentieth and early twenty-first centuries has produced, alongside the self-consciously postmodern works of mythological or historiographical pastiche discussed by Lützeler, a profusion of narratives that from this latest historical vantage-point seek once again to connect Germany's present and future to the 'real', if imperfectly recollected, history of the last fifty years or more. Ranging from the picaresque black humour of Michael Kumpfmüller's *The Adventures of a Bed Salesman*, through the bleak evocation of a post-1989 Europe in Christoph Hein's *Willenbrock*, to the recall of previously forgotten German suffering in Grass's *Crabwalk*, from the renewed confrontation of issues of Holocaust-related guilt and responsibility in Bernhard Schlink's *The Reader* to the painstakingly detailed, disconcertingly factual-cum-fictional recreation of the lives of the exiled and deracinated victims of history in W. G. Sebald's *The Emigrants* and *Austerlitz*, the literature of *Vergangenheitsbewältigung* has entered a new phase. Above all, with a work like Grass's *Crabwalk*, whose first-person narrative and multiple time-frames are structured round the sinking of the German refugee ship *Wilhelm Gustloff* in the Baltic in 1945 with the loss of 9,000 lives, the contemporary novel is beginning to open up dimensions of past experience that had previously been taboo. As the late W. G. Sebald pointed out in the recently translated essay 'Air-war and literature', German literature since 1945 has up to now been almost devoid of accounts of the devastation wrought on German cities and populations in the last stages of the Second World War.[13] This silence was in part eloquent testimony to an overwhelming psychological and political legacy of the Nazi era: the tacit assumption by Germans that any public depiction or discussion of their own suffering in the war might be interpreted (rightly or wrongly) as an attempt at partial self-exculpation for the crimes committed under the Hitler regime. The time seems now to have come when the German novel is able to acknowledge the indivisibility of human pain and grief, and in so doing to relate the narratives of German history and German identity increasingly to the wider context of our precarious global future.

NOTES

1. On the novel after 1945, see for example Keith Bullivant (ed.), *The Modern German Novel* (Leamington Spa, 1987), Peter Demetz, *After the Fires: Recent Writing in the Germanies, Austria and Switzerland* (New York, 1986); on the 1970s and 1980s, Keith Bullivant, *Realism Today: Aspects of the Contemporary West German Novel* (Leamington Spa, 1987); on the 1980s, P. M. Lützeler (ed.), *Spätmoderne und Postmoderne. Beiträge zur deutschsprachigen Gegenwartsliteratur* (Frankfurt am Main, 1991), and Arthur Williams, Stuart Parkes and Roland Smith (eds.), *Literature on the Threshold: the German Novel in the 1980s* (New York, Oxford and Munich, 1990). Other items, including studies of the post-1989 period, are listed under 'Further reading' below.
2. Margaret Anne Doody, *The True Story of the Novel* (New York, 1997). For an earlier study of the long and broad tradition of European realism, see Erich Auerbach, *Mimesis* (New York, 1953).
3. See Ian Watt, *The Rise of the Novel: Studies in Defoe, Richardson and Fielding* (London, 1957); and, more recently, David Lodge, *Consciousness and the Novel* (London, 2002).
4. See Franco Moretti, *The Way of the World: the 'Bildungsroman' in European Culture* (London, 1987).
5. The 'apolitical' bent of the German educated middle class at this time is a well-established cliché, and like all such clichés, is only partially true. For a head-on challenge to it, see David Blackbourn, *The Fontana History of Germany, 1780–1918: the Long Nineteenth Century* (London, 1997), pp. 40–3.
6. For studies of the *Bildungsroman* and the German novel tradition, see the 'Further reading' listed at the end of chapter 6.
7. Eric Hobsbawm, *Age of Extremes: the Short Twentieth Century 1914–1991* (London, 1994).
8. On the historical conjuncture that gave birth to modernism, see Perry Anderson, 'Modernity and revolution', *New Left Review*, no. 144 (March/April 1984), 96–113.

9. 'The Storyteller: reflections on the works of Nikolai Leskov' (1936), in Walter Benjamin, *Illuminations*, ed. with an Introduction by Hannah Arendt (London, 1973), pp. 83–109 (pp. 83–4) (translation slightly modified).

10. Timothy Garton Ash, 'Truth is another country', *Guardian Review*, 16 November 2002, pp. 4–6.

11. Ralf Dahrendorf, 'The little man's view' (review of *Little Man – What Now?*, trans. Susan Bennett), *TLS*, 4 October 1996, p. 14.

12. Peter Handke, 'Ich bin ein Bewohner des Elfenbeinturms' (1967), in Handke, *Ich bin ein Bewohner des Elfenbeinturms* (Frankfurt am Main, 1972), pp. 19–28 (p. 20).

13. This piece, based on lectures given in Zurich in 1997, is published in W. G. Sebald, *On the Natural History of Destruction* (London, 2003), pp. 1–105. On the same topic, see the article by Peter Schneider, 'In [sic] their side of World War II, the Germans also suffered', *The New York Times*, 18 January 2003.

FURTHER READING

Beitter, Ursula E. (ed.), *Literatur und Identität. Deutsch-deutsche Befindlichkeiten und die multikulturelle Gesellschaft* (New York, Bern and Frankfurt am Main, 2000)

Brockmann, Stephen, *Literature and German Reunification* (Cambridge, 1999)

Bullivant, Keith (ed.), *Beyond 1989: Re-reading German Literary History Since 1945* (Providence and Oxford, 1997)

Fischer, Sabine, and Moray McGowan (eds.), *Denn du tanzt auf einem Seil. Positionen deutschsprachiger MigrantInnenliteratur* (Tübingen, 1997)

Hillebrand, Bruno, *Theorie des Romans. Erzählstrategien der Neuzeit*, 3rd edition (Stuttgart and Weimar, 1993)

Midgley, David (ed.), *The German Novel in the Twentieth Century: Beyond Realism* (Edinburgh and New York, 1993)

Watanabe-O'Kelly, Helen (ed.), *The Cambridge History of German Literature* (Cambridge, 1997)

2

LYNN ABRAMS

Contexts of the novel: society, politics and culture in German-speaking Europe, 1870 to the present

The relationship between cultural production and power politics in Germany, and to a lesser extent in the rest of German-speaking Europe, has often been uneasy, characterised by reluctant accommodation if not by tension and mutual distrust. Whilst it has often been said that German intellectuals, including writers, emphasised the superiority of the spirit (*Geist*) over politics, denying the reality of Germany's socio-political development, it is undeniable that from the cultural philistinism of the Wilhelmine state to the postmodern aesthetics of the present day, German culture, and not least literary output, has rarely remained indifferent to, and has often existed in a state of tension with, the prevailing political authority. The following discussion of the major social and economic developments and politically transformative moments in the modern history of German-speaking Europe (Austria is treated as an independent state but part of the wider German cultural nation) will, I hope, provide a contextual background against which not only the writers considered in this volume, but also their readers, should be understood. The leitmotiv running through this brief historical panorama is the disjuncture between society and culture on the one hand, and politics on the other.

The newly unified Germany of Bismarck and Wilhelm II could be characterised as a society in the process of coming to terms with the disruptive forces unleashed by industrialisation. Unity was essentially a political configuration which created a nation-state centred upon the economic and political might of Prussia and excluding largely agrarian, Catholic Austria, which left Austrian Germans as the most unified national grouping within the Habsburg Empire but, at the same time, lacking a homeland. By contrast, German speakers in Switzerland, which had existed as a federal state since 1848, consented to their inclusion in a constitutional republic which emerged as an exceptional and long-lasting model of consensual federalism.

Political unification gave a fillip to economic development and by the turn of the century industry was providing employment for around 40 per cent of the labour force. Germany, and Austria on a lesser, more regional scale, were rapidly becoming urbanised; cities like Hamburg saw their population double and treble in a few decades and what were formerly villages became new industrial towns seemingly overnight. This transformation from a pre-dominantly agrarian to an industrial economy was accompanied by major changes to social structure. The Germany of 1871, newly unified in political terms, might at first sight be said to have displayed a significant degree of cul-tural unity, largely owing to the predominance of the German language, but it was profoundly disparate in terms of almost any other indicator – religion, ethnicity, law codes, level of industrialisation and so on. Modernisation en-compassed a wide range of phenomena: industrial development, urbanisa-tion, the emergence of mass politics, the spread of education, the rise of a class-conscious proletariat, the growth of a sophisticated bourgeoisie, and the beginning of a reappraisal of gender relations. These multifaceted pro-cesses of change imparted a heterogeneity to the new German Empire which the governing elites did little to come to terms with.

Indeed, Imperial Germany was a paradox. Germany did not assume the true identity of a nation-state for several decades. A common language and culture provided an inadequate cement for the fissures opened up by indus-trial growth. Whilst Germany's economy developed with astonishing speed, this occurred within a political and constitutional framework which was pseudo-democratic and, in many respects, authoritarian. Such contradic-tions were at the heart of the German Empire. Whilst the introduction of universal manhood suffrage in Reichstag elections (1871) inaugurated the era of mass political participation and the formation of popular political parties such as the Catholic Centre Party and the Social Democratic Party, the Reichstag had limited powers, could be dissolved by the Kaiser on the recommendation of the chancellor and in effect was little more than a talk-ing shop. With the initiation of the masses into the political system came the formation of pressure groups such as women's organisations, trade unions, peasant leagues and nationalist associations whose activities served to high-light the disjuncture between a modernising society and a static political system. The political system of the Habsburg Empire was even less well de-veloped, some would say chaotic. Until 1882 only 6 per cent of the adult male population could vote for up to fifty political groupings in indirect elections to the Austrian parliament (Reichsrat).

Imperial Germany was a society in a profound state of unease, manifested in a series of confrontations between the state and so-called *Reichsfeinde* (enemies of the state) as well as more subterranean tensions in the field of labour relations and sexual politics. In the 1870s and 1880s Catholics, socialists and ethnic minorities were made objects of discrimination and suppression. Whole communities were made to feel they did not belong in the new Germany; identification with the nation state was not compatible with Catholicism, socialism or membership of another cultural or ethnic group. Alongside heavy-handed legislative repression like the Falk Laws of the *Kulturkampf* (literally 'struggle for civilisation', referring to the anti-Catholic campaign), the *Sozialistengesetz* (law outlawing socialist activities) and the language laws which prohibited the use of languages other than German in schools attended by Poles, Danes and French speakers, more insidious attempts to perpetuate the social structure, legitimate the new German state and impose a uniform culture were enacted through the education system, the armed forces and the Protestant Church. A three-fold strategy in domestic policy amounting to repression, indoctrination and manipulation had to be pursued by the ruling elites if, in the wake of political and economic unification, the forces of democracy and modernisation were to be repelled. By the 1890s it was clear that all such strategies had succeeded in doing was sweeping problems under the carpet. In the era following the resignation of Bismarck in 1890, tensions surrounding labour relations and sexual politics dominated the domestic agenda. Following the economic depression of 1873–8 and the anti-socialist legislation of 1878–90 the organised labour movement had consolidated and increasingly found a niche in the German political system. But beyond the SPD and the trade unions the labour movement had developed a powerful and all-embracing cultural and educational network. The working classes had come of age and were making themselves felt in the political arena.

Industrialisation also prompted a questioning of traditional gender roles. Imperial Germany was undoubtedly a patriarchal society. Women were second-class citizens under the law; they had no political representation and, until 1908 in Prussia, they were forbidden to engage in political activities. For most middle-class women marriage was the only route to economic security, and the future was grim for those who did not enter into a marriage contract. However, beginning in the 1860s, but gathering force in the 1880s and 1890s, middle-class women, who were denied access to equal education and the professions at a time when men of the same social class were achieving greater status and prosperity, started openly to challenge the patriarchal nature of bourgeois society.

In the cultural sphere conflict and tension were to an extent subsumed by intellectual and creative impulses centred upon Austria and especially Vienna. In the realms of music, art and literature as well as the social and medical sciences, Vienna was Europe's intellectual and cultural capital through the nineteenth century and arguably until the 1920s. A number of modernist movements, such as the Vienna Secession in the field of visual art and psychoanalysis pioneered by Freud, originated here. However, this Viennese culture was not specifically a Germanic culture; it was inclusive of all nationalities and ethnic groups – most notably Jews, who formed around 10 per cent of the Viennese population in 1880, and from whom many of its leading artists, musicians and writers were drawn.

German society underwent a process of progressive pluralisation in the decades prior to the First World War, as a variety of socio-cultural milieux began to establish their presence, often by means of separate cultural networks – for example, for Catholics, Poles, socialists, women and youth – but at the same time it also became more polarised. The gap between the social classes, between the sexes, between the state and society became larger, and this in turn prompted the ruling elite to engage in increasingly desperate strategies to stave off political change. These attempts, consisting of aggressive nationalism, imperial conquest and military aggrandisement, culminated in 1914 in the outbreak of war. For a time in 1914 it appeared that Germany had indeed come together as a nation state, as the Kaiser's appeal for a civil truce (*Burgfriede*) appeared to be heeded, but this was later revealed as a false identity. Similarly, in the Habsburg Empire all national groups greeted the war with some enthusiasm, whilst Switzerland confirmed its neutrality. Social tension and political disintegration were temporarily concealed by an impressive facade of monarchical splendour and military power. It was said that Germans had 'the intoxicating illusion that the social rifts of the past had disappeared'. But war brought only a temporary national consensus, and as it dragged on the polarisation of society became increasingly evident on the home and the combat fronts.

Germany's experience of 'total war' shattered what had only been a fragile consensus in 1914. As a consequence of war-weariness, a longing for peace, but above all anger and resentment at the ruling classes who had failed to implement any democratic change, German workers joined the revolutionary unrest initiated by soldiers and sailors in November 1917. The end of the war likewise brought corresponding dramatic change to the Habsburg Empire. While throughout the war all nationalities had fought together in the Imperial army, the peace settlement recognised the Austro-Hungarian people's right to self-determination. By 1918, nationalist pressures were such that the Habsburg Empire disintegrated, leaving Austrian Germans to fashion the independent Republic of Austria from 'a field of ruins'.[1]

Within the intellectual and artistic community the experience of war had been traumatic and was judged to be a massive waste of life; a mood summed up by Erich Maria Remarque in *All Quiet on the Western Front* (discussed by Michael Minden in chapter 10). For those on the left the revolution appeared to offer hope of a root-and-branch transformation of German political and social institutions. But although many artists and writers, particularly in the avant-garde Expressionist movement, were inspired to produce some of their most radical and political work during the revolutionary period, the dominant mood was negative; while railing against the undemocratic old regime there was a palpable sense of disappointment with the so-called 'revolution from above'.

Admittedly, the new regime of the Weimar Republic initially appeared to satisfy the demands of many of those who had been alienated by the Kaiserreich. However, a progressive constitution, incorporating proportional representation, universal suffrage, an elected president and a cabinet responsible to parliament, was not sufficient to deal with the pressing problems facing peacetime Germany. An immediate crisis resulted from the Versailles Treaty, which imposed on Germany the burden of guilt for the war, a substantial loss of territory and massive reparations. But in addition to this, and the further problems caused by demobilisation, the Weimar Republic (like the new Austrian Republic) was cursed with chronic economic instability, accompanied by a series of seismic social and cultural changes. These were to have a profound effect on the nature of cultural life and cultural production during the system's brief existence.

The Weimar Republic is often used as a byword for cultural modernity, and it is certainly the case that in the broadest socio-cultural sense Germany in the 1920s had modernised to an extent that affected all spheres of everyday life. The most obvious manifestation of modernisation was the emergence of a parliamentary political system, but it was in the economic and socio-cultural spheres that modernity had its greatest impact. By the 1920s Germany was a fully fledged industrial society characterised by rationalisation of production, division of labour, technological advance and a fairly well-developed bureaucracy and administrative support structure. At the same time modernisation encompassed urbanisation, with great emphasis on the city as the fulcrum of cultural life, and the redefinition of gender relations, entailing the 'emancipation' of woman from the constraints of Imperial ideology. Finally, modernisation during the Weimar Republic was associated with cultural modernism, the rejection of traditional beliefs and aesthetic standards and the production of an alternative culture which often had a radical political edge. It is clear that many of these trends were already in train before the war, and it is also the case – as Russell Berman points out in chapter 6 – that the whole relationship between modernisation and cultural modern*ism* was a complex and in some ways contradictory one. Nevertheless it is true that Weimar and modernity seemed to go hand in hand.

The rationalisation of industry – a process dramatised by Fritz Lang in his modernist cinematic masterpiece, *Metropolis* – was not achieved without the concomitant rationalisation of everyday life, and especially the domestic sphere. Rationalised domesticity was, however, only possible in the new housing estates in the city suburbs where middle-class women, aided by some technical advances in the home, may have been able to run an efficient household *and* fulfil the reproductive demands placed on them by a state desperate to redress the demographic imbalance caused by the casualties of war. However, rationalised industry was heavily dependent upon female labour, as were the rapidly developing service and consumer industries which employed women as clerks, typists and department store assistants. These women were the so-called 'New Women' of Weimar's cities; single, independent, emancipated and the ultimate expression of Weimar modernity. Their lives, aspirations and inner conflicts were in turn captured by a new generation of women writers who came to prominence in the late 1920s, and who form the focus of Elizabeth Boa's discussion in chapter 9 of this book.

The appearance of the 'New Woman' seemed to suggest gender relations were undergoing some form of redefinition. Whilst birth control was not entirely freely available it did permit many couples from the middle classes to have smaller families and enjoy a kind of suburban domesticity based on a companionate marriage. Moreover, in the cities the rationalisation of sexuality, involving taboo-breaking attempts to promote sensible and 'natural' sex, led some to hope for more fundamental legislative reform. They were to be disappointed, inasmuch as Paragraphs 175 and 218 of the Criminal Code, outlawing homosexuality and abortion respectively, were never repealed. Nevertheless, conservative sexual morality was questioned as homosexuality was increasingly brought into the public sphere, and in the field of commercial entertainment liberated sexuality was on public display. On the other hand, conservative voices were not silenced. The official reinforcement of the ideology of maternity, which cast women in a primarily domestic role, was supported by a range of pressure groups who exhorted women to devote themselves to family and home, to service the nation through motherhood and efficient housewifery. The public image of the new woman, while providing an alternative female model by challenging traditional femininity, also provoked a reactionary backlash which came to fruition in the National Socialist 1930s.

While the modernity of Weimar may not have resulted in women's emancipation, the emergence of cities – specifically Berlin, Vienna and Zurich – as European cultural centres as well as the focus for a variety of trends associated with modernity, such as liberated sexuality, modern transport and commercial entertainment, is undeniable. The city was both praised and vilified for embodying the spirit of the times. While cities like Berlin and Munich represented liberation, the metropolis was simultaneously blamed for inducing alienation and the loss of individual identity. The city also fostered the idea of the mass: mass sporting events, mass entertainment, mass consumption, mass political rallies and mobilisation made possible by new means of mass communication and transport. Finally, the city of the 1920s fostered Weimar cultural modernism, which embraced what was known as the *Neue Sachlichkeit* (New Objectivity), a coming to terms with the new reality of this technological, rationalised mass society. In the realm of popular culture it seemed as if the cult of Americanism had eclipsed traditional German culture via the cinema, popular music and dance.

The Weimar Republic could not withstand the cumulative impact of modernisation on the economy, politics and society. The Republic's 'sick economy' – characterised by industrial stagnation, lack of investment and structural mass unemployment – was unable to pay for the progressive welfare policies, was unable to meet the expectations of young people who regarded themselves as the 'superfluous generation', and could only contribute to the increasing polarisation of society and politics. The Republic came under sustained attack from left and right. On the left, the socialists and Communists bitterly criticised the capitalist economy that was to lead to six million unemployed by 1933. On the right, conservatives and nationalists attacked the moral debauchery, political weakness and social welfare provision of a regime they had never wholeheartedly supported. It was this combination of social, economic and political crisis, arguably a crisis of industrial class society as a whole, that proved the undoing of the Republic and the point of departure for the National Socialists.

Just as soon as the Nazis had seized power in 1933 they set about consolidating their position by means of a process of *Gleichschaltung* (forcing into line) which took the form of the purging of political opponents, the destruction of the labour movement, the assertion of power at the regional and local level and the attempt to coerce the German people to conform to the Nazi *Weltanschauung*. Steps towards the creation of the *Volksgemeinschaft* (people's community) were taken in all spheres of everyday life in order to create a harmonious society 'resting on bonds of blood, on a common destiny and a common political faith, to which class and status conflicts are essentially foreign',[2] in contrast to the polarisation that had characterised both the Imperial and Weimar regimes. This was carried out through indoctrination using the education system, the media, and Nazi organisations such as the Hitlerjugend (Hitler Youth) and its female equivalent, the Bund deutscher Mädel, as well as through the transformation of social experience. However, it is far from certain whether the Nazis did achieve the classless, let alone harmonious, society. Indeed, it is more likely that they created new tensions around issues of race and loyalty to the Party, while they were unable to break down traditional forms of identity such as those based on class, religion, or region.

National Socialism's social-revolutionary agenda was highly contradictory. It simultaneously espoused modern and anti-modern sentiment; revolutionary in a political sense, at the level of the transformation of society it was inconsistent. While putting forward an anti-urban, anti-industrial, anti-feminist vision, at the same time it can be argued that Nazi Germany was the apotheosis of the modern, technological state. The only consistent policy was that of extreme racist nationalism, and it is the commitment to racial 'purity' that was the only truly revolutionary element of National Socialism.

One element of the *Volksgemeinschaft* was to be the achievement of egalitarianism on the basis of loyalty to the Party and talent. Nazi society was to be characterised by upward mobility and equal opportunity, although of course only those who qualified for membership of this society – the 'racially pure', the ideologically sound, the social conformists, those who were willing to serve the nation – were permitted access to the first rung of the ladder. An increasingly broad range of persons were excluded, among them Jews, criminals, beggars, gypsies, 'asocials', the physically and mentally disabled, rebellious youth. And of course this society of upward mobility rewarded those who saw their future was with the Party. Membership of the NSDAP opened up opportunities for advancement, in the professions, the civil service and in the Party itself, especially for those from less privileged social backgrounds who frequently took the place of someone who had been removed on the grounds of racial origins or political unreliability.

On the surface, the appearance of conformity in Nazi society suggests the objective success of the *Volksgemeinschaft*, but two factors must be borne in mind: the relative economic stability of the peacetime years and the degree of coercion and terror practised at every level of society. In 1933 the Nazis had comprehensively dismantled the labour movement: active socialists and Communists were rounded up, the trade unions were replaced by the Deutsche Arbeitsfront and strikes were made illegal. A massive job-creation programme, as well as rearmament and the introduction of schemes like the Reich Labour Service for young men wiped out unemployment, while other schemes like *Kraft durch Freude* (Strength through Joy) provided at least some workers and their families with their first taste of holidays and active leisure opportunities. However, there was no fundamental restructuring of the relationship between capital and labour, and as Dick Geary writes, 'the inequalities of wealth, property ownership and life chances that continued to exist in Nazi Germany make it difficult to speak of any kind of fundamental change in social structure'.[3]

The Nazi attitude towards the role of women appeared to be unequivocal; women were primarily mothers of the nation's children and supporters and carers of husbands and soldiers. Indeed, the Nazis promised to 'emancipate women from emancipation'. Yet, when it came to the practical implementation of policy in the 1930s and especially during the war, we can identify major contradictions inherent in the attempt to combine what has been called the 'protective repression' of women with a policy of preparation for war and territorial expansion. The 'primacy of biology' came into conflict with the 'primacy of economics'. Pronatalist policies aimed at Aryan women in the form of marriage loans, financial and symbolic rewards for large families, combined with the prohibition of abortion and artificial birth control, were initially coupled with the expulsion of women, especially so-called *Doppelverdiener* (double earners, i.e. women whose husbands were employed), from the labour force. Serious contradictions, however, were always present which were highlighted in the late 1930s and again during the war when labour shortages necessitated female recruitment into industry. Throughout the period a twin-track policy was pursued, consisting of official rhetoric (a conservative policy of returning women to the home), and practical steps to ensure differentiation amongst women – primarily determined by race and class – which in practice meant that women of the working class were directed towards factory employment and middle-class women were encouraged to return to the home.

A social revolution in the sense of a fundamental restructuring of primary social relations – those of gender and class – thus appears not to have taken place, but at the same time there appears to have been widespread conformity to the regime and limited resistance. This is as true of the cultural sphere as of any other. The whole cultural domain was increasingly controlled by the Ministry of Propaganda and Enlightenment headed by Joseph Goebbels. The Nazis are infamous for their cultural philistinism and their total rejection of any form of cultural activity which smacked of modernism. While the burning of books of banned authors in 1933 was the most powerful symbolic rejection of intellectual culture, other acts designed to repudiate all that was associated with Weimar and the degenerate modernist trends in art, such as the staging of the exhibition entitled 'Entartete Kunst' (degenerate art), informed the public that modernism was alien to the German *Volk*. The response of many authors and artists was emigration overseas, while others practised what has been called 'innere Emigration', or self-censorship and silence (see Ronald Speirs's discussion in chapter 11). Indeed the concept of *innere Emigration* can usefully be applied to the mass of the German people who did not actively resist the regime but did not passively conform either. What Detlev Peukert has described as the 'atomisation of everyday life', a 'retreat into isolated, depoliticised privacy' which took the form of the destruction of traditional social bonds and their replacement by mass mobilisation and the 'stage-management of public life', resulted in a 'loss of the capacity for social action'.[4] The removal of civil liberties for all citizens meant opposition was always difficult.

The Nazis replaced the profoundly polarised Weimar society with a society characterised by a different set of fissures, most notably determined by race and loyalty to the Nazi Party. The racial revolution began with the systematic discrimination against Jews, progressed to the attempt to exclude Jews from 'normal' life, and was later to culminate in the Holocaust: the extermination of millions of Jews in the death camps. At each stage, this monstrous project depended for its 'success' on a compliant administrative and policing structure as well as the absence of opposition from the majority of the population. Very many Germans did risk their lives to protect Jews of their acquaintance, but the terrorism enacted against the Jewish population combined with the aforementioned destruction of independent collective organisation effectively emasculated ordinary citizens.

In 1938, Hitler and his entourage were greeted by huge crowds and evident enthusiasm when they triumphantly moved into Austria in the wake of what is known as the *Anschluß* (union) of the two countries. The growth of the Austrian Nazi movement had paralleled that of its larger German brother. The Austrian Republic had effectively come to an end in 1933 with the cessation of parliamentary government, but those Austrians who favoured a closer union with their larger neighbour had not anticipated what in essence became annexation and the attempted destruction of Austrian identity with the coordination of the two political systems and, subsequently, of their social, economic and racial policies. In contrast, National Socialism attracted few followers in Switzerland, where opposition to Nazism was expressed in the form of transnational and multiparty affirmation of the federal state.

The National Socialist regime reached its apogee during the course of the Second World War. It was then, under cover of wartime measures, that anti-Jewish policy turned into full-scale genocide and the German and Austrian peoples were plunged into five years of total war for which they were unenthusiastic and ill-prepared. A war fought on several fronts placed huge burdens on the population and for most urban as well as rural dwellers, this period was a struggle for survival. Those in towns and cities endured night after night of aerial bombing; in the east, millions left their homes and fled west in fear of the invading Russian troops. Defeat was a relief for most as it signalled the end of the war, the end of the regime of terror, and the end of years of national trauma. In 1945 the German population was in a state of physical and psychological collapse.

In 1945 the fate of Austria and Germany lay in the hands of the Allies. Both were ruined, economically, physically, socially and some would say morally too. *Stunde Null* (Zero Hour) was a pertinent description for the state of the nation. 'Germany seemed mute and culturally sterile after its relapse into barbarism.'[5] More than three million German and 250,000 Austrian soldiers were dead, a further one and three-quarter million were prisoners of war and more than half a million civilians had lost their lives. In addition, the displacement of people from their homes during the war and afterwards resulted in a tremendous movement of population: those who had been separated from their families and the ten million evacuated from bombed cities tried to return home; refugees and expellees from Eastern Europe flooded into Germany, and prisoners of war were slowly repatriated. The four Allied powers initially agreed on general principles to guide the future administration, such as demilitarisation, decentralisation, democratisation and de-Nazification. In a joint statement they announced their 'inflexible purpose to destroy German militarism and Nazism and to ensure that Germany will never again be able to disturb the peace of the world'. It was the Allies' stated determination to 'wipe out the Nazi Party, Nazi laws, organisations and institutions, remove all Nazi and militaristic influence from public office and from the cultural and economic life of the German people'. Similar policies were pursued in Austria with the entire country under Allied – primarily Soviet – occupation. But despite these stated aims the agreement to zones of occupation resulted in quite different policies being pursued in each zone. The distinctive policies in the Soviet zone of Germany presaged the eventual division of that country in 1949, a fate narrowly avoided in Austria, although it was not until 1955 that the Allied powers gained Soviet consent to the Austrian Treaty which recognised Austria as a 'sovereign, independent and democratic state'.

Stunde Null also implied a fresh start. Germany could begin again with a clean slate, abandoning traditions such as Prussian militarism and undemocratic government, and begin to rebuild a society utterly bankrupted by the Nazis and the war. In almost all respects, East and West adopted different official scripts and increasingly the two economies, societies and cultures diverged. In what became the German Democratic Republic (GDR) energetic attempts were made to create a uniform socialist personality within a secular state based on the doctrine of Marxism–Leninism, which was inculcated through the schools, the workplace and cultural production. In the Federal Republic, on the other hand, a more pluralistic political and artistic culture obtained which tolerated alternative and critical standpoints. Yet, the degree to which these two states can be regarded as separate and the extent to which East and West Germans regarded their divided nation as asymmetrical are more complex issues.

From an objective standpoint the two states were built on entirely different lines. The command economy, socialist political system, secular society
and official cultural uniformity of the East appeared to contrast sharply with
the capitalist economy, consumer society, liberal-democratic political culture
and cultural diversity of the West. The differences were also soon apparent
in terms of standards of living. While both states could legitimately boast
economic success stories in the first two decades following the 1948 currency
reforms, the *Wirtschaftswunder* (economic miracle) in the West clearly benefited ordinary citizens in terms of living standards, and especially the ability
to afford and purchase consumer goods. Indeed, the appearance of such un-
rationed goods in western stores came to symbolise the growing differences
between the two societies. Throughout the 1950s, 1960s and 1970s, almost
all groups in West Germany saw their living standards improve. The Federal
Republic was becoming more prosperous, but at the same time it was less
egalitarian, and it was the numerous *Gastarbeiter* ('guest workers') – around
two million by the early 1970s – who formed a new underclass.

One factor contributing to the Federal Republic's economic success was
the supply of cheap labour it received from the GDR. Early on, the Soviet
occupiers had introduced radical land and property reform measures and
the socialisation of industry, promptly disinheriting large numbers of its
citizens, many of whom fled to the West, along with large numbers of young
skilled people in search of better career prospects. Despite engineering its
own economic success story, and despite keeping prices for basic goods,
transport and housing artificially low, the GDR could not support living
standards comparable with the West. To compensate somewhat, the GDR
government pursued a policy termed 'calculated emancipation' which traded
limited political freedoms, censorship and lack of consumer goods for the
provision of education, welfare support and family legislation.[6] The aim, it
has been suggested, was to create a *leistungsorientierte Laufbahngesellschaft*
('achievement-orientated career society'), but it is doubtful whether such a
society was ever attained. Certainly, society in the East was more egalitarian
in an economic sense, but new inequalities were created by the system. The
political elite enjoyed numerous privileges that were not available to ordinary
citizens, and political conformists benefited from educational opportunities
and career advancement denied to non-conformists.

Equality between men and women, on the other hand, was a principle
enshrined in the constitutions of both the FRG and the GDR. Although
steps were taken in the East and the West to improve girls' educational opportunities, in the GDR there was arguably a more serious and partially
successful attempt to restructure traditional gender roles. The level of East

German women's participation in the labour force was consistently higher than in the Federal Republic, to some extent as a result of the severe labour shortage in the GDR, but also as a consequence of extensive maternity and childcare provision. By contrast, West German women were encouraged to return to the home and the family after the disruption of war, and many regarded marriage, child-rearing and a good home life as symbols of comfort and stability after the hardship of the 1940s. By 1983 86 per cent of women of working age were in paid work in the GDR compared with around 50 per cent in the Federal Republic.

Notwithstanding the fundamentally different political and economic systems established in the two states, it is undeniable that both were essentially stable systems in that both survived for longer – forty years – than any previous German political regime. Mary Fulbrook has suggested this might be explained by the success of both states in incorporating and diffusing opposition and dissent.[7] In the West, of course, writers, artists and intellectuals were permitted freedom of expression, with the exception of those who stood in hostile opposition to the democratic principles of the constitution. The 1960s and 1970s witnessed a considerable flowering of alternative viewpoints, most notably in respect of environmental issues and opposition to the Vietnam War, but also from the left who mounted sustained intellectual critiques of West German society. While the Federal German government could afford to be tolerant of this form of opposition, when faced with the terrorism of the Baader–Meinhof gang in the 1970s it instituted severe repressive measures which were in turn criticised for being anti-democratic. In the GDR overt opposition was dealt with much more harshly by what was an authoritarian police state. But non-conformity and what was called 'principled dissent', together with widespread popular disaffection with the regime through the 1980s, were potentially more dangerous for the stability of this state. In particular, the Protestant Church came to represent perhaps the single organisation independent of the state, that provided a space for dissenting thought and discussion. Whilst the church can be regarded a safety-valve in its role as mediator between the people and the state, by 1989 it is clear the church was being used to shelter a number of dissident groups. The importance of this was finally revealed during the weeks of the so-called 'gentle revolution' – August to November 1989 – when Protestant churches in Leipzig and Berlin emerged as centres of protest against the regime.

The events of 1989 suggested that East German society was riven by deep tensions, and bore witness to an underlying and widespread dissatisfaction with the regime. In October 1989, Mikhail Gorbachev visited Berlin for the celebration of the fortieth anniversary of the GDR. Two days later around 70,000 participated in peaceful demonstrations, the culmination of two months of such opposition. The legitimacy of the East German regime had already been called into question as thousands of its citizens fled across the borders of Hungary to the West following the Soviet Union's renunciation of its support of Communist governments in Eastern Europe. After a series of concessions to the people by the GDR government, the Berlin Wall – the ultimate symbol of division – was breached on 9 November.

It has been argued that the identity of ordinary Germans in the GDR and Federal Republic was less affected by official government views than by generation and by political and social experience. Those who had experienced an undivided Germany regarded division as unnatural, whereas the younger generation, particularly in the West, found it easier to accept the existence of two separate states. The (re-)unification of Germany on 3 October 1990 has not resolved this identity problem. In many respects, what had become by 1990 two quite different states remain so.

In German-speaking Europe only federal Switzerland has experienced relative stability throughout more than a century of profound economic, political and social transformation. The peoples of Austria and Germany, on the other hand, have seen their fortunes swing wildly as political structures failed to compromise with socio-economic conditions. Whilst the Swiss, it has been argued, defined nationhood in terms of a common consent to a democratic-republican order, Austrians and Germans have continually struggled to define their identity and the appropriate political constellations. From the mid nineteenth century to the present day, German cultural production, and in particular German writing, has both reflected and contested the conception of the German nation envisaged and constructed by the state.

NOTES

1. Karl Renner, Social Democrat chancellor of the Austrian Republic, cited in Barbara Jelavich, *Modern Austria* (Cambridge, 1987), p. 154.
2. Mary Fulbrook, *Germany 1918–1990: the Divided Nation* (London, 1991), p. 74.
3. Dick Geary, *Hitler and Nazism* (London, 1993), p. 53.
4. Detlev Peukert, *Inside Nazi Germany* (London, 1987), p. 239.
5. Henry Ashby Turner, *Germany from Partition to Reunification* (New Haven and London, 1992), p. 7.
6. Volker Berghahn, *Modern Germany: Society, Economy and Politics in the 20th Century* (Cambridge, 1982), p. 233.
7. Fulbrook, *Divided Nation*, p. 266.

FURTHER READING

The following suggestions are for accessible and readable texts in the English language.

Germany: general nineteenth and twentieth century

Berghahn, Volker, *Modern Germany: Society, Economy and Politics in the Twentieth Century* (Cambridge, 1982)
Carr, William, *A History of Germany, 1815–1990*, 4th edition (London, 1991)
Evans, Richard J., *Rethinking German History* (London, 1987)
Martel, Gordon (ed.), *Modern Germany Reconsidered, 1870–1945* (London, 1992)

Imperial Germany and the First World War

Berghahn, Volker, *Imperial Germany, 1871–1914: Economy, Society, Culture and Politics* (Oxford, 1994)
Bessel, Richard, *Germany after the First World War* (Oxford, 1994)
Blackbourn, David, and Geoff Eley, *The Peculiarities of German History: Bourgeois Society and Politics in Nineteenth-Century Germany* (Oxford, 1984)
Eksteins, Modris, *Rites of Spring: the Great War and the Birth of the Modern Age* (London, 1989)
Wehler, Hans-Ulrich, *The German Empire* (Leamington Spa, 1985)

Weimar Republic

Gay, Peter, *Weimar Culture: the Outsider as Insider* (London and New York, 1968)
Kolb, Eberhard, *The Weimar Republic* (London, 1992)
Peukert, Detlev, *The Weimar Republic: the Crisis of Classical Modernity* (London, 1993)

Social and cultural issues

Women

Frevert, Ute, *Women in German History* (Leamington Spa, 1989)
Kolinsky, Eva, *Women in West Germany: Life, Work and Politics* (Oxford, 1989)
Koonz, Claudia, *Mothers in the Fatherland: Women, the Family and Nazi Politics* (New York, 1987)
Stephenson, Jill, *Women in Nazi Germany* (London, 2002)

Working-class culture

Abrams, Lynn, *Workers' Culture in Imperial Germany: Leisure and Recreation in the Rhineland and Westphalia* (London, 1992)
Guttsman, W. L., *Workers' Culture in Weimar Germany: Between Tradition and Commitment* (Oxford, 1990)

Third Reich

Bessel, Richard (ed.), *Life in the Third Reich* (Oxford, 1987)

Geary, Dick, *Hitler and Nazism* (London, 1993)

Kershaw, Ian, *Popular Opinion and Political Dissent in the Third Reich* (Oxford, 1983)

Kershaw, Ian, *The Nazi Dictatorship* (London, 1985)

Kershaw, Ian, *Hitler,* vol. I *1889–1936: Hubris* (London, 1998), vol. II *1936–1945: Nemesis* (London, 2000)

Peukert, Detlev, *Inside Nazi Germany: Conformity and Opposition in Everyday Life* (London, 1987)

1945 to the present

Balfour, Michael, *Germany: the Tides of Power* (London, 1992)

Fulbrook, Mary, *The Fontana History of Germany, 1918–1990: the Divided Nation* (London, 1991)

Fulbrook, Mary, *The Two Germanies, 1945–1990: Problems of Interpretation* (London, 1992)

Fulbrook, Mary, *Anatomy of a Dictatorship. Inside the GDR, 1949–1989* (Oxford, 1995)

Turner, Henry Ashby Jr, *Germany from Partition to Reunification* (New Haven and London, 1992)

Austria

Anderson, Harriet, *Utopian Feminism: Women's Movements in fin-de-siècle Vienna* (New Haven and London, 1992)

Jelavich, Barbara, *Modern Austria: Empire and Republic, 1815–1986* (Cambridge, 1987)

Sked, Alan, *The Decline and Fall of the Habsburg Empire, 1815–1918* (London, 1989)

Sully, Melanie A., *A Contemporary History of Austria* (London, 1990)

Switzerland

Bonjour, E., H. S. Offler and G. R. Potter, *A Short History of Switzerland* (Oxford, 1952)

3

ALAN BANCE

The novel in Wilhelmine Germany: from realism to satire

There are advantages to coming late to an outlook and a set of conventions like realism, and arriving there via a different national tradition. It is sometimes claimed that all the realist writers of note subvert the realism they represent. If this is so, then perhaps those who come last are likely to be more subversive than their predecessors.

For at least three of the novels I am taking as paradigms in this chapter the claim has been made that they bring the German novel at long last into the European realist tradition; and also that each of them is in some way the culmination of that tradition. *Effi Briest*, *Buddenbrooks* and *Der Untertan* have all been ranked among major social novels in the European canon of realism; they embrace 'society' not as a backcloth to individual human experience (as in the *Bildungsroman* tradition described in chapter 6 of this book), but as its constituent element. (It is however worth noting that none of them deals with the conditions of lower-class life.)

Theodor Fontane's *Effi Briest* (1895) is the highly refined product of a writer who came late to the novel, and whose achievement in a German context was to steer a course between, on the one hand, the heavy-handed attempts of Freytag, Gutzkow, or Spielhagen to emulate the teeming abundance of social life found in a Dickens or a Balzac, and on the other hand, the intensely inward German novel of subjectivity.

Thomas Mann's first great novel, *Buddenbrooks* (1901),[1] produced when he was only twenty-six, is the first successful epic Naturalistic novel in Germany; and yet, according to some critics, it transcends Naturalism, which by then was already passé in other European literatures. *Buddenbrooks*, like *Effi Briest*, establishes a balance between retreat into introspection and stress on social reality.

Balance of any kind is hard to claim for Heinrich Mann's novel *Der Untertan* (The Loyal Subject),[2] but it too helps establish German literature within a specific area of the nineteenth-century European realist tradition. Not properly published until 1918, the project was conceived in 1906, and is unique in German literature up to that point, in its incisive social satire, bringing it into line with the socio-political vein of Hugo's *Les Misérables* and Thackeray's *Vanity Fair*.

Buddenbrooks, produced exactly at the pivotal moment of the turn of the century, is a highly conscious reflection of the *fin-de-siècle* or *Spätzeit* mood. The novel studies contemporary life and manners by observing dispassionately, impersonally and objectively. The origins of Mann's reasons for doing so lie in his initial interest in one character, Hanno Buddenbrook, the decadent young artist manqué, the last of his line, who is spared the pain of growing up. Through him, the German tradition of subjectivity is preserved at the height of realism and the tradition of inwardness is complemented in *Buddenbrooks* by a seismographic sensitivity to what is to come.

At the turn of the century, the western tradition turned inwards and the modernist artistic consciousness was created. German writers were well placed to develop this seismographic quality; for their literary tradition had paved the way for that modern exploration of the sensations and emotions of individuals, and for the subjectivity which – as in Proust, Joyce, or Virginia Woolf – created its own time and its own idiosyncratic relation to place.

This early work by Thomas Mann, with its roots in the formal nineteenth-century qualities of Zola's *Les Rougon-Macquart* and *Thérèse Raquin*, or the Goncourts' *Renée Mauperin*, as well as in the novels of Fontane, masks the radicalism of his twentieth-century awareness. But in the decline of the Buddenbrook family we see the movement of consciousness itself – and especially consciousness as awareness of essential solitude – into centre-stage. In the terminology of the time, realism meant a kind of regulative norm; it asserted a moral order which balanced the subject and society and aimed for an uplifting and educative effect. In none of the German realists we are looking at here is this kind of didactic moral design present, except as an implied absence. In this respect, they reflect their German literary origins; they point forward to European modernism; and they can at the same time be seen as products of the special historical conditions of Wilhelmine Germany.

This historical context is reflected in certain themes which these novels share with other, less successful, products of their time. For example, the situation of women in late nineteenth-century Germany, in Gabriele Reuter's powerful but monochrome feminist novel of 1895, *Aus guter Familie* (*From a Good Family*, 1999), provides a foil to *Effi Briest*. Like *Aus guter Familie*, both *Effi Briest* and *Buddenbrooks* reflect the social climate which prevailed after the foundation of the Second Reich, and which moves into central focus in *Der Untertan*. In Fontane's and Thomas Mann's novels, the reflection is more diffuse, the influence of social and political conditions more oblique, but in all three novels a new and confident sense of critical purpose is one discernible effect of Wilhemine conditions. Increasing technical mastery over the modern novel form is the corollary.

The two most significant tributaries of German realism are, first, its antecedents in Poetic Realism and the concentration of the *Novelle* form; and second, the incipient developments of twentieth-century modernism. These now merge in a single stream, a refinement of narrative technique combined with a new confidence in handling the genre of the novel. Fontane's control of dialogue to establish character and atmosphere, and to highlight the role of the spoken word in creating the reality of action, is natural and unforced. His stylistic restraint, symbolic patterning, allusiveness and preference for silence at critical moments in the narrative owe as much to his beginnings in the ballad and *Novelle* genres as to the highly developed sensitivity of the late bourgeois era.

Thomas Mann's bold employment of a 'chronicle' form in *Buddenbrooks* and his virtuoso command of transitions from third-person narrative to free indirect speech and then to interior monologue show a technical confidence previously lacking in the novel tradition in Germany, as do Heinrich Mann's adroit moves from narratorial comment to the perspective of his 'hero' Diederich Hessling in *Der Untertan* and in his bold distortions of reality to provoke in the reader the shock of social-political recognition. The incidental irony of *Effi Briest* progresses to the more pervasive ironic viewpoint of *Buddenbrooks* and the biting satire of *Der Untertan*.

There is a distinct paradigm shift here from a loose to an increasingly close engagement with actual social conditions, which the German novel has never entirely relinquished since, and for which the publication of *Der Untertan* is a very significant moment. Both *Effi Briest* and *Buddenbrooks* modify Naturalism for thematic gain (or in other words, subvert the realism they present). There is no doubt that, for example, the Scandinavian Naturalist Alexander Kielland (e.g. *Garman and Worse*, 1880), much admired by Fontane for his Zola-esque use of precise reportage, constructs a more reliable account than Fontane of the experience of contemporary women, as does Gabriele Reuter in *Aus guter Familie*. But unlike Kielland's or, especially, Reuter's novels, *Effi Briest* does not describe the typical lives of nineteenth-century women. Historically speaking, the pattern of the extended family destroyed in *Buddenbrooks* was smoothly replaced at the end of the nineteenth century by the stable nuclear bourgeois family, a transition faithfully reflected in *Der Untertan*. The Buddenbrooks are hardly the typical merchant family of their day, such as is depicted in another novel of business life in Lübeck, Ida Boy-Ed's *Ein königlicher Kaufmann* (A Royal Merchant) of 1910, which is far closer to the actual historical situation.[3] Culture is elevated over conditions in Thomas Mann's novel, as he plays down the economic and historical determinants which affected Lübeck in the period he is dealing with, in order to privilege the theme of *Verfall* (decline), which pervades every page of his novel.

Thomas Mann is concerned with a decline or decadence which in political or economic terms is not historically grounded; but the author's negative vision is linked to the *Gründerzeit*, the aggressive commercial explosion that led to a fever of speculative investment and the rapid founding of banks and other companies, before the inevitable overheating of the German economy produced the recession that began in 1873. In *Effi Briest*, the link with contemporary conditions is even more oblique but equally substantial; the novel's ultimate theme, I suggest, is the more metaphysical and less chronologically grounded one of 'longing' or 'yearning'.

This story of a young girl of good society who at seventeen colludes in her own mismatch with a man old enough to have married her mother (some twenty years earlier he nearly did so) is not primarily concerned with upholding the prevailing moral order, despite the apparently fitting outcome of her adultery, the death of her seducer in a duel with the husband, Innstetten, and Effi's own ostracising by society. There is a poetic patterning, a 'rounding off' of the novel which is typical of Fontane, the absence of which in the work of Naturalists such as Kielland he found a source of irritation, despite his admiration for the Norwegian. The *Verklärung* or transfiguration Effi undergoes by the end of the book, when her 'ruined' life ends serenely in a return to her beloved childhood home, is in marked contrast to the society scandal on which Fontane modelled his story, and which saw the historical model for Effi, Elisabeth von Ardenne, living on into her nineties, to die only in 1952.

Not that one cannot find unmistakable features in *Effi Briest* of the 'typical' condition of nineteenth-century German women. For example, both Reuter's and Fontane's heroines suffer a fate inseparable from the class they belong to, a point underlined ironically in the title of Gabriele Reuter's novel, 'Aus *guter* Familie', and in the simple inscription, 'Effi Briest', on Effi's gravestone, omitting the aristocratic particle *von*, to which she is 'entitled' but which has by extension been the cause of her downfall. Furthermore, Effi belongs to a recognisable nineteenth-century genre of spirited young women, whose very spiritedness invariably spells trouble for them in the world of bourgeois convention; Agathe in *Aus guter Familie* is just one example, or, to take another almost at random, Kristine in Helene Böhlau's novel of 1896, *Das Recht der Mutter*[4] – in which, however, Böhlau contrives a happy ending after all the tribulations suffered by *her* spirited heroine.

Effi's unquenchable spirit is what makes her such an irresistible heroine (one of those characters in literature with whom readers tend to fall in love, to the detriment of critical distance), but the situation of the woman in this period is realistically reflected in the fact that her vivacity is her enemy. The double bind imposed upon her consists in the 'weightlessness' (the theme of 'flying' is associated with her) and unseriousness expected from the young female, set alongside the remorselessly unforgiving attitude of 'good' society when she commits the faux pas for which her upbringing seems to have predestined her. Her irrepressible liveliness proves fatal in late nineteenth-century Prussia, a country halfway between a feudal, militarised state and a complex, fragmented modern society. This is a time and a place where duelling over a woman's unfaithfulness is still (just) possible, although Fontane underlines its tragi-comic aspect by putting off the discovery of the adultery for nearly seven years, by which time insistence on a duel to the death is uncomfortably close to play-acting.

Part of the fascination of the book is the mixture of modernity – an effect largely created by Effi's perennial quality of impudent freshness, and by the tolerant narrative perspective – with the surviving Prussian military culture of 'honour', a paradigm for the treatment of transitional moments in general which is Fontane's forte. This writer knows also how to exploit the erotic charge of the story through hints, understatement and symbolic allusion, and excels at metonymically expanding his reader's grasp of situation by description of landscapes and living-spaces.

So far, so realist (or so Poetic Realist). But the description of the Kessin house in *Effi Briest* (and of Kessin in general) is instructive, and makes an interesting comparison with a passage in *Aus guter Familie*. In Reuter's novel, Agathe as a child sits dreaming of wider horizons and freedom; the bench she sits on in a quiet corner of a country parsonage forbids movement; it is unsteady and rotten. And the pond she sits by is stagnant: 'the water that on the surface was so clear and seemed bejewelled with cheerful, tiny points of golden sunlight was filled in its depths with the rotting remains of vegetation from past years'. Similarly, the house in Kessin to which Fontane's Innstetten brings his young bride contains the lifeless detritus of the past. The lonely setting for Effi's first fifteen months of married life, the spooky house with its quaint but menacing stuffed shark and crocodile, embodies her stagnant situation perfectly.

Both descriptions convey the weight of the past dragging down and limiting the prospects of young women, before their adult lives have really begun. The Kessin description, however, evokes that tantalising but faintly ironised sense of mystery characteristic of the former ballad writer for whom the poetic ultimately holds sway over the study of 'social conditioning' or 'the woman question'. Effi's social conditioning is indirectly conveyed none the less by her response to the Kessin setting – objectively a cage for her youthful spirit – whose exotic and poetic aspects she both fears and romantically but wrongly associates with the freedom and the wider horizons both she and Gabriele Reuter's heroine yearn for. Her imagination is her enemy as it conspires with her own repression.

Effi, like Agathe, is a sacrifice to the values of a male-dominated society. But though both heroines are betrayed by society, Fontane avoids polemical absolutes. He succeeds in vindicating female values against male ones,[5] but at the same time he elicits a purely human response to his novel by creating a sustained sense of *longing*, detached from any specific object; he evokes to perfection the endless deferring of plenitude that is the modern equivalent of the Fall and expulsion from paradise (Hohen-Cremmen, her childhood home, epitomising Effi's original innocence), the foundation myth of our culture.

Loss as plenitude, plenitude as loss; Fontane's predilection for creating a rounded whole, for composing his novel around poetic as much as 'social' themes, links him with a traditionally German stream of realism influenced by certain aesthetic rules, such as those put forward by Spielhagen and others, which hold, for example, that it is wrong for the author to make his or her presence felt in the novel. Authorial viewpoint should be conveyed by the characters' speech and actions and by symbolic implication. Artistic tenets such as these stem from the desire to create an aesthetic *Ganzheit*, an organic whole in the work of art, which can be seen as a response to the German experience of social division and fragmentation after 1871 in an era of confusingly rapid change and industrialisation.

The aestheticising drive of German realism is backward-looking in that it attempts to create a new harmony to replace the idealist project of Kant and Hegel in the early part of the century, a new wholeness ('heile Welt') not argued discursively but presented directly through fiction, especially that inspired by the 'village tale' or *Dorfgeschichte*.[6] European realism is often described as the product of the assured victory of the bourgeoisie, establishing a confident rapport between the nineteenth-century writer and his/her society. Notoriously, the bourgeoisie never enjoyed quite this confidence in Germany, often referred to as 'die verspätete Nation' (the belated nation) because it came relatively late to industrialisation and to unification. Though earlier claims that in the late nineteenth century the German middle class had assimilated feudal and militaristic values have been subject to revision by recent work on cultural history,[7] few will dispute that the failed liberal revolution of 1848 left a permanent trauma (to which Heinrich Mann's *Der Untertan* can be seen as the ultimate and extreme response).

It was not only in Germany that writers complained of a disjunction between mankind and the world, between idea and reality. But in Germany, as *mal du siècle* turned into *fin de siècle*, what is called *Kulturpessimismus* (cultural pessimism) was especially strong, though a powerful new empire and a booming economy seemed to offer no objective economic or political reason for despair. The result was a dual one: on the one hand, a sense of resignation for which Schopenhauer's newly popular writings offered a philosophical underpinning, and a decadent mood in literature and the arts; on the other, a powerful stimulus to movements of regeneration, often under the banner of Nietzsche's 'Dionysian' vitalism and the impact of primitivism – the search for sources and origins whose progress gains great momentum around the year 1890 (with the beginnings of Freud's psychoanalytical research, and the writing of Frank Wedekind's seminal drama *Frühlings Erwachen* (*Spring Awakening*) – the archetypal 'regenerative' title).

The right-wing version of regeneration, resulting from the radicalising of conservatism after 1890, gave rise to some of the most popular literature of the Wilhelmine period, known as *Heimatkunst* or 'home-town literature', and related to the village-tale genre of the mid nineteenth century which had appealed so strongly to the German realists.[8] The programme of the *Heimatkunst* movement stemmed from books like Julius Langbehn's *Rembrandt als Erzieher* (1890; Rembrandt as Educator), which enjoyed an enormous readership, and formed a part of the ideological baggage the Nazis were later to take up. It is only a short step from the racism and crude Social Darwinism of *Heimatkunst* to the 'blood and soil' literature of the Third Reich, and in general the movement precisely prefigures the Nazi combination of pseudo-science and vulgar romanticism. Social Darwinism was all-pervasive in late nineteenth-century Germany.[9] The conviction that the weakest must go to the wall is expressed time and again in literature, whether approvingly, critically, or simply in a spirit of resignation.

Resignation stands at the opposite pole of response to cultural pessimism. The cult of *Dekadenz* and decline is likewise fuelled by contemporary political reality; not only by a reaction to capitalism at the height of its power, but by the frustrating awareness of a literary sensitivity ahead of its time (and subject to the domination, illustrated in *Effi Briest*, of a military code very much *behind* its time). *Buddenbrooks* is – paradoxically – the exhaustive treatment of *fin-de-siècle* exhaustion. From their sturdy origins in an age of rude mental health and robust religious faith, the Buddenbrooks decline over a few generations into a parody of their former selves. All the strenuous efforts of Thomas Buddenbrook, last head of the family firm, to hold the family and the business together, only turn him into a hollow man acting an increasingly exhausting role. But Agathe in Reuter's *Aus guter Familie*, not overtly a novel of decadence, also experiences the essential *fin-de-siècle Ermattung* or weariness: 'How strange – Agathe found herself already practically at the end of her strength, just as life was about to begin properly.'

The commercial boom and bustle and the military swagger of Wilhelmine Germany appears to non-participants to be an exhausting spectacle, *Entsagung* (renunciation) the only possible response. Women, as non-participants by definition, are often exhorted by this culture to selfless renunciation. 'A tale of renunciation is never bad', remarks the childish Effi Briest at the beginnning of a story which will see her renouncing *everything*, including life itself; and for Reuter's Agathe at the end of her story 'nothing ever changed as far as women were concerned – renunciation on all sides'. The consolations of religion, or religiosity, are ready to hand, often as a sublimation of their sexuality, for women whose fate is subject to men and, through them, to the vagaries of commerce (for in many cases their chance of 'happiness' depended on the patriarchal father's ability to raise a dowry; this is the case with Agathe, as with Diederich Hessling's daughter in *Der Untertan*). Agathe's disappointments lead to an intense religious phase where Christ or God becomes an ideal male imago in a male-dominated society. *In extremis*, Effi rejects religion, the 'natural' consolation after her ejection from good society, but in a sense can be said to retain its support vicariously through the simple faith of her loyal confidante, the Catholic maid Roswitha, herself a victim of the patriarchal order.

In *Buddenbrooks*, the tale of decadence and renunciation par excellence, religion is not available to offer Thomas compensation in the death-agony that is his attempt to preserve intact the world of his forefathers. The loss of their unthinkingly confident Lutheranism is a part of the problem; reclaiming their faith is not a solution. Instead, in a famous episode wedged between his realisation that his son Hanno will never be his true heir, and the drawing up of his last will and testament, Thomas turns for an hour or so to the heady secular religion constructed from his casual reading of Schopenhauer's *The World as Will and Representation* and the vitalism of Nietzsche, which (harnessing Social Darwinism to the resignation of decadence!) tells him he will live on in the survival of the fittest. He attempts to 'tear aside the veil of Maya' (in Schopenhauer's orientalising language) and convince himself of an oceanic sense of oneness with the world in a doomed response to the modern perception of the fatal rise of individualism. At the heart of this individualism is a neurotic divorce between 'representation' and 'being', the face one presents to the world and what one actually *is*, a typical late nineteenth-century awareness of an inauthentic basis to life, often reflected in the central imagery of acting and the stage in all of the novels discussed here. (For the most self-indulgent expression of this 'neurasthenic' 1890s obsession with inauthenticity and painful analysis of nuances of feeling, there is no need to look further than Heinrich Mann's youthful effusion, his novel *In einer Familie* (1894; In a Family), from which he later distanced himself, and which is often ignored in standard histories of literature. At the end of the novel, the effete hero asks his young wife whether she believes that 'after us there will come a generation of men who will once again be simpler, more fitted for life, more rooted in a belief than ours today?' The extreme robustness of a work like *Der Untertan* is more understandable in the light of this early aberration.)

The defensive position of the Buddenbrooks, barricaded against the dominant Wilhelmine ideology, is not strong enough to ensure their survival. All penetration of the closed family from outside hastens their decline. The disasters in *Buddenbrooks* are brought about, as in a parody of classical tragedy, by family attempts to avert catastrophe, such as Thomas's sister Tony's efforts to preserve the Buddenbrooks 'type'. Christian, Thomas's brother, who is a neurotic clown, undergoes a complete *Entartung*, the apt German word for degeneration deriving from the prefix *ent-* indicating 'dis-', a 'breaking away from' or reversal, and *Art*, meaning 'type' or 'kind'. Yet the fate of the heroic Thomas is ultimately similar, for in his efforts to avoid being like Christian he turns into a caricature of the Buddenbrook archetype – outwardly fastidious and controlled, but inwardly decayed.

Through Thomas, the Buddenbrooks disastrously develop a comprehension of the world they live in. This outward movement and its results are depicted metaphorically in the brutal description (part 10, chapter 7) of the fish-market in Lübeck. Life as viewed by Social Darwinism is concentrated in the image of the buckets of fish, all destined to meet the same fate, but meanwhile differing in their acceptance of the transitional stage of captivity that precedes it. Now and again, we are told, a stronger fish leaps off the fishmonger's slab onto the dirty pavement, 'so that its owner was obliged to run after it and with strong expressions of disapproval return it to its duty'. The irony and detachment of the passage is a paradigm for Thomas Mann's style in the novel. It arises out of his ambivalent position: his attraction to the decadence of the *fin de siècle* is clear, and yet he is prevented by his solid, north German burgher inheritance from sustaining a mood of disgust with reality or retreat into decadence. The same detachment is applied to Thomas Buddenbrook's attempt on reading Schopenhauer to escape (like the fish on the slab) and to 'leave his skin' altogether by sinking into a dream of death, timelessness and anonymity. He cannot sustain the vision once 'real' life intervenes once more. For sure, Thomas possesses the artist's compensating 'negative capability', a strange and unnerving capacity to think and feel himself into the minds of others. But in the hands of a non-artist this is no compensation; rather it is a disability which ruins his business sense.

The artist by implication is the true hero of the age, both priest and sacrifice, turning his exhaustion to good account, suffering on behalf of others and giving expression to their *fin-de-siècle* anxieties. Thomas Mann's debt to Naturalism in *Buddenbrooks* is offset by his affinity with the self-appointed role of turn-of-the-century writers as 'mystics without mysticism' (in Hofmannsthal's phrase) who replace the transcendentalism of religion with a conviction of their privileged access to a heightened sense of the wholeness of life; among them Nietzsche, Hauptmann, Rilke and Musil. But finding the answer in oneself is a poetic solution not easily sustained in real-life situations; its equivalent in such contexts is a kind of decisionism. With the loss of the transcendental, Protestant ethic of his ancestors, Thomas Buddenbrook is confronted with the need to construct the meaning of existence from within his own resources, in which task he deploys a self-imposed, almost military discipline not grounded in any ultimate justification.

Thomas Mann has reservations about the subjective and impressionistic art of the post-Naturalist era, for all his affinity with it. These reservations are implicit in his description of young Hanno's musical improvisation, an account based on Richard Wagner's introduction to the prelude of his own opera *Tristan and Isolde*. Hanno, condemned to die of typhus very soon afterwards, extemporises a self-indulgent fantasy whose culmination bears – like the *Liebestod* of Wagner's *Tristan* – strong suggestions both of death and of sexual climax. The individual in Mann's early works is seen as incomplete, a fragment broken away from the whole, and necessarily both tragic and comic. To seek salvation in himself is a pathetic delusion. *Buddenbrooks* as a whole drives home the point by increasingly foregrounding the theme of death, built up overwhelmingly as in a musical score by repetitive motifs, developing from a referential to an ever more symbolic function and establishing the sense of an indifferent universe which we must simply accept as it is. In the end nothing signifies except that the earth continues to turn and be peopled – and that is far from guaranteeing any eschatological significance.

Diederich Hessling, narrative focaliser of Heinrich Mann's *Der Untertan*, is a fictional creation who seems designed to stand at the opposite pole from Hanno Buddenbrook; they are apparently two opposing responses to the same situation. Diederich, too, is a weakling as a child, but instead of following his mother's artistic cult of feelings (as Hanno follows the musical instincts of *his* mother, Gerda), he admires his bullying father, masochistically enjoys being beaten by him, duly despises his mother, as his father does ('No wonder she read novels!'), and decides to become a man of power like his father and that super-patriarch, Kaiser Wilhelm II. Inheriting the family paper-mill, after university in Berlin, Hessling conquers and dominates his home town of Netzig, revealing in microcosm the intrigue that ties together politics and commerce to produce the defeat of liberalism by the new nationalism of the 1890s. The novel was conceived in 1906, as Heinrich Mann, from the vantage point of a café on Berlin's Unter den Linden, observed the pompous and overbearing deportment of his fellow countrymen and very astutely identified the 'secret cowardice' for which their behaviour was a cover.

In relation to *Kulturpessimismus*, Hessling's cult of the 'strong man' as an answer to the *horror vacui* of modern life is the obverse of decadence and resignation. This path was to lead culturally to Futurism and the aesthetic of violence ('what matter the victim, provided the gesture is beautiful') and politically to the First World War, welcomed by a whole generation of young Europeans who pronounced themselves culturally suffocated by peacetime.

The theme of the justified violence of the 'strong man' had already been popularised in the *Heimatromane* (home-town novels), such as, for example, Hermann Löns's *Der Wehrwolf* (1910; The Werewolf), or Lulu von Strauss und Torney's *Der Hof am Brink* (1906; The Farm by the Brink). *Der Untertan* can be read, in some senses, as a satire on *Heimatkunst* values, especially in some of Diederich Hessling's favourite items of vocabulary such as 'smash' and 'wipe out' (*zerschmettern* and *ausrotten*). The values projected by *Heimatkunst* very largely coincide with those adopted by Hessling, as he cultivates in himself the characteristics of the authoritarian personality, including turning back to the past (*Germanismus*) to valorise present action, deference to superiors and aggression against inferiors and non-conformists, as well as worship of power and 'toughness' for their own sake, expressed in *Der Untertan* in a typical sado-masochistic, ruler–subject complex. The notorious 'inverted morality'of the Nazis is prefigured in Hessling's determination that one has to be strong enough to be able to bear causing pain to others.

One influence on Heinrich Mann was the affair of the Captain of Köpenick (later the subject of a famous play by Carl Zuckmayer) which was a press sensation in October 1906, and featured the exploit of an unemployed ex-convict, Wilhelm Voigt, in donning a second-hand captain's uniform to commandeer an army platoon, march them to the town of Köpenick, and make off with the municipal cash-box. Not only are there echoes of the theme of the insanely inflated power of the uniform in Wilhelmine Germany (at one point in *Der Untertan*, Diederich Hessling reflects that 'without a uniform you went through life with a bad conscience'), but Hessling can be seen as a precise inversion of Wilhelm Voigt. Where the latter reclaims his individuality and ceases momentarily to be a mere 'subject', Diederich does his utmost to bring his personality into line with the *Zeitgeist* and offer himself up for external direction by the representatives of power – whoever they may happen to be at a given moment.

Heinrich Mann's satire is extreme, often to the point of wild caricature. The author is careful to indicate the decent human being that his hero might have become, but Hessling, who worships personality (his beloved Kaiser is 'the most personal personality'), ultimately ceases to be an individual at all, and becomes a construct to act as a vehicle for Heinrich Mann's wicked attack on the mores of the Second Reich. An explanation for Mann's extremeness – if one were needed aside from his obvious and justified fear of the megalomaniac tendencies of the Kaiser and the whole Reich – is incorporated into the novel in the words of Wolfgang Buck, the actor-cum-lawyer son of the old 1848-generation liberal who ran Netzig before the victory of nationalism in the town. Wolfgang has resolved to quit the theatre because the power of his art once brought tears to the eyes of a chief of police. He pre-empts Brecht in his dismissal of a kind of 'culinary theatre' which produces a catharsis for the onlooker but has no impact on his behaviour ('afterwards they hand over revolutionaries and shoot at strikers'). He does not suggest the Brechtian solution, the alienating of his audience to parallel the alienated conditions under which they live, but in practice Heinrich Mann adopts this shock-tactic approach. His extreme style is the result of his disappointment at the contemporary failure of liberalism when he reflects upon the capitulation of the SPD after 1891 and its assimilation to the bourgeois parties, which was to culminate in the Social Democrats' support for Germany's declaration of war in August 1914. The traitorous behaviour of the SPD is embodied in the novel by Napoleon Fischer, the workers' leader who strikes a satanic deal with Hessling and the nationalists in order to defeat the liberals and secure his seat in the Reichstag.[10] Mann's bitterness about the eclipse of progressive tendencies is concentrated especially in the centre-piece of the novel, Wolfgang Buck's summing-up for the defence in the court case for lese-majesty that Diederich Hessling brings against the liberal factory-owner, Lauer. It is liberalism itself that is on trial, and Wolfgang is its tired and decadent representative. The truth is overwhelmingly on the side of progress, but the verdict (like the verdict of history in the short term) perversely goes the wrong way. The road ahead is clear for the Hesslings of this world, and once again Diederich's firmest conviction is reinforced: 'nothing human could withstand power'.

A novel which is a study of the deformation of the German character can hardly be anything but bitter. 'Deformation' is the process Diederich himself, the representative of Germany's 'public soul', undergoes in his formative years, so that *Der Untertan* can be seen as a kind of inverted novel of education. Here Mann is closer to Gabriele Reuter than to any of the other novelists who have been considered in this chapter. Reuter too shows us what her heroine *might* have become; Agathe at one point stumbles upon an unsuspected talent in herself for academic research, a career she has as much hope of pursuing as she does of becoming Pope.

To the deformation of her life resulting from the effects of a repressive and lying society is added the tragedy of Agathe's sex and sexuality. In a very effective pun, Bismarck's 'iron and blood' culture has rendered women anaemic. At the end of *Aus guter Familie* they gather in their scores at a spa resort for the treatment of this ailment, their blood necessarily lacking the appropriate (masculine?) admixture of iron. But the mendacious and ideological function of the prevailing sexual repression and 'sexual morality' is even more blatant in *Der Untertan* than it is in the feminist novels. The dehumanising process Hessling undergoes becomes especially clear in his relationship with Agnes, the woman he abandons for careerist reasons. When Diederich brutally decides to break off the relationship with her, for the very reason that (apart from her lack of a dowry) he has become genuinely emotionally involved with her, he deploys the vicious argument that she is a morally unsuitable match, having slept with him before marriage.

Heinrich Mann's love for the exposure of conspiracy is notorious; sex, profit motives and politics are inextricably mixed. The mishmash of self-deceptive motives and politically convenient 'convictions' is exemplified by Diederich's reaction to the worker who is dismissed from his job for bedding his fiancée among the sacks of rags in the Hessling paper works – the very site of a subsequent coupling between Diederich and Guste (later his wife). The 'immoral' worker is automatically assumed to be a shirker, too, offending against the profit-motive as well as 'morality', and ipso facto politically suspect. It is only right and proper in Diederich's eyes when the same worker is later shot by the trigger-happy military guard in front of the town hall; he has condemned himself three times over.

Der Untertan is a diagnosis of the pre-fascist mentality. Heinrich Mann's glimpse of the totalitarian state is 'reality deformed to the point of recognition', but most recognisable with the benefit of hindsight. If we seek positive aspects in the novel, they are to be found in its vitality and in a Nietzschean love of the truth, but also in the passion for democracy incorporated above all in the figure of the 1848 revolutionary, old Buck. In *Buddenbrooks*, Thomas Mann's narrative takes a positive and unironical turn through the figure of Hanno's young friend Kai, a writer in the making, whose imagination is firmly anchored in life and who turns the artist's outsider status – he is rootless, and has a home outside the town – to good account, as did Thomas Mann himself. In *Der Untertan*, there is a minor parallel in an unobtrusive moment where, after his fall from eminence in Netzig, old Buck encounters some young people as they emerge from school. They stop to greet the old man respectfully: 'Their foreheads were not so smooth as most; their eyes were expressive . . . as they doffed their caps to old Buck . . . He saw in these faces full of the future once more the fullness of hope with which he had throughout his life gazed into the faces of human beings.' History was to resurrect that hope; but after what terrible betrayals.

NOTES

1. A recent translation of *Buddenbrooks* is that of John E. Woods, available in an Everyman's Library edition with an introduction by T. J. Reed (London, 1994).
2. *Der Untertan*, in a 1949 translation by Ernest Boyd under the title *Man of Straw*, is available from Penguin Books (1992).
3. See Hugh Ridley, *Thomas Mann: Buddenbrooks* (Cambridge, 1987), p. 89.
4. *Das Recht der Mutter* (The Right of the Mother), appearing just a year after *Effi Briest*, was published by Fontane's son's publishing house.
5. See *Effi Briest*, translated by Hugh Rorrison and Helen Chambers (London, 1995), 'Afterword', p. 244.
6. On the later influence of e.g. Berthold Auerbach's *Schwarzwälder Dorfgeschichten* (1842), see Edward McInnes, *'Eine untergeordnete Meisterschaft?' The Critical Reception of Dickens in Germany 1837–1870* (Frankfurt am Main, 1991), p. 81.
7. See for example Matthew Jefferies, *Politics and Culture in Wilhelmine Germany: the Case of Industrial Architecture* (Oxford, 1995).
8. The most famous novel of this type is Gustav Frenssen's *Jörn Uhl* (1901), the first twentieth-century German bestseller.
9. Social Darwinism was promoted especially by the fashionable philosopher of the 1870s, Eduard von Hartmann, for example in his *Philosophie des Unbewußten* (1869; Philosophy of the Unconscious) (11th edition 1904).
10. Napoleon I is the archetypal betrayer of the people's revolution, and Heinrich Mann's character shares his name with Napoleon, the dictatorial Berkshire boar in George Orwell's *Animal Farm* (1945).

FURTHER READING

Arnold, Heinz Ludwig (ed.), *Text + Kritik: Heinrich Mann* (Munich, 1986)

Aust, Hugo, *Theodor Fontane. Ein Studienbuch* (Tübingen, 1998)

Bance, Alan, Helen Chambers and Charlotte Jolles (eds.), *Theodor Fontane: the London Symposium* (Stuttgart, 1995)

Betz, Frederick, *Erläuterungen und Dokumente: Heinrich Mann, 'Der Untertan'* (Stuttgart, 1993)

Bücher, Max, et al. (eds.), *Realismus und Gründerzeit I* (Stuttgart, 1981)

Craig, Gordon A., *Über Fontane* (Munich, 1998)

Hammelt-Wittke, Monika, *Heinrich Mann, 'Der Untertan'* (Munich, 1988)

Howe, Pat, and Helen Chambers (eds.), *Theodor Fontane and the European Context: Literature, Culture and Society in Prussia and Europe* (Amsterdam, 2001)

Jasper, Willi, *Der Bruder Heinrich Mann: Eine Biographie* (Frankfurt am Main, 1994)

Minden, Michael, 'Realism versus poetry: Theodor Fontane, Effi Briest', in David Midgley (ed.), *The German Novel in the Twentieth Century: Beyond Realism* (Edinburgh, 1993), pp. 18–29

Minden, Michael (ed.), *Thomas Mann* (London, 1995)

Roberts, David, *Artistic Consciousness and Political Conscience: the Novels of Heinrich Mann 1900–1938* (Bern and Frankfurt am Main, 1971)

Robertson, Ritchie (ed.), *The Cambridge Companion to Thomas Mann* (Cambridge, 2002), especially Judith Ryan, '*Buddenbrooks*: between realism and aestheticism' (pp. 119–36)

Rossbacher, Karlheinz, *Heimatkunstbewegung and Heimatroman: zu einer Literatursoziologie der Jahrhundertwende* (Stuttgart, 1975)

Ruprecht, Erich, and Dieter Bänsch (eds.), *Jahrhundertwende* (Stuttgart, 1981)

Sprengel, Peter, *Geschichte der deutschsprachigen Literatur 1870–1900, von der Reichsgründung bis zur Jahrhundertwende* (Munich, 1998)

Stern, J. P., 'The theme of consciousness: Thomas Mann', in Malcolm Bradbury and James McFarlane (eds.), *Modernism 1890–1930* (Harmondsworth, 1976), pp. 416–29

Swales, Martin, '*Buddenbrooks*': *Family Life as the Mirror of Social Change* (Boston, MA, 1991)

Swales, Martin, *Studies of German Prose Fiction in the Age of European Realism* (Lampeter, 1995)

Vogt, Jochen, *Thomas Mann, 'Buddenbrooks'* (Munich, 1983)

Ward, Mark G., *Perspectives on German Realist Writing* (Lampeter, 1995)

Weber, Lilo, *Hysterie in Texten von Theodor Fontane, Hedwig Dohm, Gabriele Reuter und Minna Kautsky* (Bielefeld, 1996)

4

RITCHIE ROBERTSON

Gender anxiety and the shaping of the self in some modernist writers: Musil, Hesse, Hofmannsthal, Jahnn

To begin understanding how the modernist novel explored new conceptions of the self, we may briefly consider two works published in 1895: Fontane's *Effi Briest* and the *Studien über Hysterie* by Freud and Breuer. In Fontane's novel, accurate knowledge about the characters is in principle readily accessible, both to the narrator and to the characters themselves. Not only does the narrator give us authoritative accounts of Effi's personality and motives (chapters 3 and 20), but the major characters, whether in conversation or private reflection, are articulate and self-analytical to an extraordinary degree. They lack that layer of unconscious mental activity which finds expression in all the purposive mistakes that Freud called 'Fehlleistungen' or parapraxes. Despite her wildness and spontaneity, Effi seems preternaturally self-controlled by comparison with the disturbed young women in the Freud–Breuer case histories: Anna O., for example, who at one time was unable to drink any water because she had seen a dog drinking out of a water-glass, and at another time lost her command of German and communicated solely in English. In Fontane's presentation of character, the articulate, controlled social self dominates the private self that is rooted in the body with its unruly, non-verbal drives. But by the end of the century, the fictional conventions of the social novel were wearing thin; they were readily compatible with irony, as in Thomas Mann's *Buddenbrooks* (1901), or with downright comedy, as in Heinrich Mann's *Im Schlaraffenland* (1900; In the Land of Milk and Honey). A fictional exploration of the self, running parallel with the new psychologies, needed a different range of narrative devices and expressive techniques.

Innovation can mean moving backwards as well as forwards. Some of the major modern German novelists carry out their explorations of sexuality, identity and the unconscious within narrative frameworks inherited or selected from classical German culture. In particular, they look back to the *Bildungsroman* (novel of education/maturation), which was canonised by conservative critics as *the* German novel genre and is best represented by

Goethe's *Wilhelm Meisters Lehrjahre* (1795–6; *Wilhelm Meister's Apprenticeship*, 1824) and the Romantic rejoinder to it, *Heinrich von Ofterdingen* (1802), by 'Novalis' (Friedrich von Hardenberg). (A fuller discussion of this tradition is given by Russell Berman in chapter 6 below.) Despite the genre's ostensible commitment to social integration, the *Bildungsroman* of the Romantics and their modernist successors tends to concentrate on the inner life of the protagonist. While Goethe took his hero out into the social world, in a realistic mode tempered with allegory, Novalis undertook to exalt the claims of art by leaving the outer setting of *Ofterdingen* thinly imagined and giving priority to the hero's inner world of dreams and fantasies. Female characters, above all, lose any sense of independent reality, being all too clearly projections of the hero's psyche. We do not sense the recalcitrant otherness of other people. Concentrating on a subjective, egocentric experience, *Ofterdingen* recounts a process of development and education (*Bildung*) in which external encounters serve to educe the hero's innate poetic potential. It conveys little about development through interaction: about how the self is shaped by responding to others and by affecting them in return. The inwardness of the *Bildungsroman* offers a fictional space to be charted with the help of the new psychologies; but it also challenges its modern exponents to find convincing ways of connecting inward experience with social and political realities.

At the turn of the century two antithetical conceptions of the self were available, each with a long ancestry. One located the self in consciousness; the other saw the self as rooted in the body and accessible to consciousness only with great effort.

Philosophical psychology returned to the empiricist scepticism about the self expressed in 1739 by David Hume, who called it 'nothing but a bundle or collection of different perceptions, which succeed each other with an inconceivable rapidity, and are in perpetual flux and movement'.[1] In a book whose findings were widely popularised, Ernst Mach described the self as 'der an einen bestimmten Körper (den Leib) gebundene Complex von Erinnerungen, Stimmungen, Gefühlen, welcher als *Ich* bezeichnet wird' ('the complex of memories, moods, feelings, which is termed *I* and attached to a particular body (the physical body)').[2] By changing only gradually, this complex gives the illusion of permanence; but in fact there is no permanent, substantial self underlying the flux of sensations. 'Das *Ich* ist unrettbar' ('The self is beyond saving'), proclaimed Mach (p. 17). This scepticism fitted well with the anti-metaphysical tirades of Nietzsche, who dismissed the self as a mere projection of the grammatical notion of the subject. It encouraged the deep doubts about the continuity of the self that we find in the early poetry of Hugo von Hofmannsthal, but also focused attention on memory as the thread holding consciousness together. And while seeming to confine the novelist's attention to the contents of consciousness, it invited equal interest in *all* those contents, including the sensory or mystical experiences previously dismissed as undignified or irrational, and licensed the inventive use of imagery – especially by Robert Musil – to capture the most evanescent nuances of experience.

If Machian empiricism returns to the Enlightenment, then psychoanalysis is rooted in Romanticism. For the Romantics, the human mind is ultimately at one with nature, embedded in a cosmic unity, which is unknown to our normal consciousness: we become aware of our cosmic affinities only in altered states such as dreams or hypnosis. Freud found that by hypnotising his patients he enabled them to recover memories concealed beyond the reach of the introspection practised by empiricist psychology. He developed a conception of the self as deeply layered. If for Mach the unity of the self depended on the slender thread of memory, for Freud it was based on those experiences which had been consciously forgotten but survived in the unconscious, sometimes emerging in disguised form as dreams, parapraxes or neurotic symptoms. And that was only the personal unconscious. Freud surmised that dreams 'will lead us to a knowledge of man's archaic heritage, of what is psychically innate in him'.[3] From the Oedipus complex, which supposedly marks the male subject's guilt-laden entry into adulthood, Freud thought he could reconstruct 'the beginnings of religion, morals, society and art' (*SE*, XIII, 156). His rebellious disciple Jung went further, claiming to discover in the unconscious a range of universal symbols or archetypes which also find expression in myth and religion. He also worked out a conception of the psyche as autonomous and self-regulating: an unbalanced personality can be corrected by forces emerging from its depths, so that psychic development is a series of often painful metamorphoses involving confrontations with the unconscious (symbolised in the ancient poetic motif of the journey to the land of the dead) and leading towards a state of psychic balance or 'individuation'. Hermann Hesse, who experienced Jungian analysis, was in many respects a conservative writer who shared Jung's attachment to Romanticism. And the model of the self-regulating psyche corresponds neatly to the Romantic *Bildungsroman* like *Ofterdingen*, whose subjective focus reappears, with some disturbing implications, in Hesse's narratives of psychic metamorphosis, *Demian* and *Steppenwolf*.

All the novels to be discussed here were written by and about men, at a time when, thanks in part to the increased visibility of women in public life, models of masculinity were diverse and often defensive. A long-established conception of the soldier as the masculine ideal was underwritten by Nietzsche, who complained that modern civilisation was feminised and saw in Napoleon the hope for its 're-masculinisation' ('Vermännlichung').[4] This conception finds expression in the 'embattled style' of Ernst Jünger and in the imagery of steel and armour-plating favoured in novels and memoirs by Freikorps soldiers.[5] But we also find a different model of masculinity, one in which the spirit (*Geist*) is gendered as male and credited with powers of intellectual creativity far superior to women's capacity for mere childbirth. The classic exponent of this model is Otto Weininger, whose widely read *Geschlecht und Charakter* (1903; *Sex and Character*, 1906) denies women any ethical or intellectual standing; but it may also be detected in Freud's assumption that women lack the capacity for sublimation which produces cultural achievements (*SE*, XXI, 103). Moreover, Weininger and Freud both assumed that humanity's constitution was bisexual, with various sexualities being constructed by elaborate developmental processes. And this made possible a new understanding of male homosexuality. If masculinity and femininity were the two ends of a spectrum, then homosexuality could be understood as an intermediate stage, as it was by the pioneer sexologist Magnus Hirschfeld, or as an orientation predominant in what the psychoanalyst Hans Blüher called the 'Typus inversus' but latent in all social formations based on male bonding.[6] The drastic representation of homosexuality in Musil's *Törleß* can be read as analysing the sado-masochistic structure of 'embattled masculinity', while Hans Henny Jahnn, the greatest gay novelist in German, explores in *Perrudja* the construction of a homosexual identity and frankly voices male fear of women.

Musil's first novel, *Die Verwirrungen des Zöglings Törleß* (1906; *Young Törless*, 1964), reflects the diversity of its author's experiences. The son of an Austrian engineer and nephew of an army officer, Musil attended military academies before going to university. He studied first engineering at Stuttgart, then philosophy, physics and mathematics at Berlin, where he wrote a thesis on Mach. In his novel, which centres on a sensitive adolescent amid uncomprehending adults, he tries to capture the nuances of consciousness, including quasi-mystical experiences which defy the limitations of language. The setting, however, is an all-male boarding-school with military overtones: the boys wear swords, though the teachers are civilians and the term 'Konvikt' suggests rather a monastery school; and Törless's experiences include not only a deep ambivalence towards women but encounters with sadistic homosexuality. The novel recounts his attainment of heterosexual masculinity, understood as involving detachment and self-control. The novel's epistemological themes have received more critical attention than its disturbing treatment of sexuality.

The official, adult world is presented as conventional, mechanised and soulless. The school educates its pupils according to rigid norms and cannot cope with anyone who breaks conventions as Törless does. His parents, though affectionate, are no better at understanding the peculiar feelings he is trying to articulate. The 'outer' world is one of rigid technical structures and social norms, while the 'inner' world consists of all those sensations and experiences which are unique, new and alarming because they cannot be defined in the limited terms of the 'outer' world.

In revealing the inadequacy of language, Musil is developing Nietzsche's claim that language is not a neutral means of representing reality but an instrument which falsifies reality by generalisation. Törless's ineffable, unique experiences include those in which physical objects take on an uncanny life of their own. He recalls how, in his early childhood, his nurse took him to play out of doors, in a wood, and left him alone for a few minutes; when he realised that he was on his own, he felt as though the trees were standing round looking at him. Another strange experience befalls him in the course of the book: one afternoon, while lying on his back gazing upwards, he notices how unspeakably distant the sky is. This perception makes real to him the concept of infinity. Though familiar with this concept from mathematics lessons, he now thinks about its meaning and feels it to be deeply disquieting. He begins to realise the limits of reason.

Irrationality haunts even mathematics. Törless is perplexed by 'imaginary numbers' such as the square root of minus one. He does not see how one can perform a sum using an entirely imaginary quantity and arrive at an answer; it is like crossing a bridge of which only the first and last supports are intact. His mathematics teacher explains that imaginary numbers are among the necessary but ungrounded assumptions on which mathematics, and indeed philosophy, are based. Törless concludes that the values and assumptions of his society are likewise not necessary but conventional. They are a set of fictions which have to be accepted if one is to go on living.

Another set of experiences which the adult world does not acknowledge is sexual. Some of the schoolboys often visit a prostitute called Božena, though they apparently do no more than talk with her. After seeing his parents off on the train, Törless accompanies Božena to her room, and is offended by the thought that she and his mother have anything in common: 'Dieses Weib ist für mich ein Knäuel aller geschlechtlichen Begehrlichkeiten; und meine Mutter ein Geschöpf, das bisher in wolkenloser Entfernung, klar und ohne Tiefen, wie ein Gestirn jenseits alles Begehrens durch mein Leben wandelte.'[7] ('For me this woman is a tangle of all sexual desires; and my mother a creature who has hitherto walked through my life in the cloudless distance, clear and without depth, like a star beyond all desire.') His awareness is polarised between the completely sexualised woman, the prostitute, and the sexless woman, the mother-figure.

Masculinity and femininity are relational concepts, existing within a system of gender relations.[8] To attain secure heterosexual masculinity, Törless needs to overcome his ambivalence towards women, and for this he needs an intermediate object, supplied by the sexually ambiguous figure of his fellow pupil Basini. Although Basini plays the man by bragging unconvincingly of sexual exploits, he has 'weiche, träge Bewegungen und weibische Gesichtszüge' and 'eine angenehme Art koketter Liebenswürdigkeit' (p. 50: 'soft, indolent movements and womanish features', 'a pleasing kind of coquettish attractiveness') which make him seem effeminate. The narrator, in an apparent echo of Weininger's anti-feminism, compares him to women who are devoid of moral sense. Törless not only feels strangely attracted by Basini, but senses an obscure connection between Basini and his quasi-mystical experiences.

Basini also interests Törless's closest associates, Reiting, a repulsive representative of soldierly masculinity, and Beineberg, who holds forth vacuously about eastern mysticism. Erotic relationships between older and younger boys were common at military schools, the younger boy being called a 'Schuß' (allegedly from 'in ihn verschossen', 'in love with him').[9] Musil exposes the sado-masochism in such relationships. Having discovered that Basini has stolen money, Reiting and Beineberg resolve to punish him. The punishment takes place in a little room under the roof which the boys have discovered and fitted out as a den. This secret room recalls the conception of the psyche as layered and pitted with archaic survivals: Törless thinks it 'wie ein vergessenes Mittelalter' (p. 105: 'like something forgotten from the Middle Ages'), lingering on in the supposedly rational modern world. When Reiting and Beineberg strike, flog, and sodomise Basini in Törless's presence, Törless feels sexual excitement and observes his own sensations at the same time, in keeping with the chillingly analytical and dispassionate tone of the novel. He himself torments Basini by moral humiliation, compelling him to say 'I am a thief'. Eventually Basini gives himself up to the headmaster, and is expelled from school for theft. The activities of Reiting and Beineberg are never revealed.

For Törless, it seems, Basini has been an object both of contempt and of identification. He practises on Basini a refined, intellectual sadism, unlike the brutal sadism of his fellow pupils. But he shows his identification when, feeling unable to explain his obscure sensations to the teachers, he runs away from school. Brought back and taken to the headmaster's study, he finds his explanations translated by the kindly teachers into platitudes. Deciding that he is in a dangerous state of nervous tension and potential hysteria, they recommend that Törless's parents should take him away from the school, and the novel ends with a relaxed, mature Törless setting off home with his mother.

The threshold Törless has crossed may be described in two ways. Musil tells us (pp. 111–12) that he grows into a refined and sensitive young man, one of those who conform to social conventions in a slightly bored, ironic manner while reserving their real interest for those moments that seems to suggest another, spiritual reality apart from everyday routine. He has aesthetic rather than moral standards. He does not regret his participation in the torture of Basini: it leaves behind the drop of poison which removes the banal health of his soul and makes it more refined and sensitive.

Not only does Törless become an amoral aesthete; he also establishes his gender identity. As he and his mother pass Božena's house, it now looks ordinary and unthreatening, while he no longer imagines his mother as a being of disembodied purity: 'Und er prüfte den leise parfümierten Geruch, der aus der Taille seiner Mutter aufstieg' (p. 140). He now responds to his mother as to a woman, a sexual being, 'examining' (with implied detachment) her physical odour, slightly masked by perfume. By temporarily identifying with Basini as feminised male and victim, Törless has overcome the internal obstacles to his attainment of heterosexual masculinity.

Any doubts we may have about the instrumental use of another person are not shared by the narrator, who colludes with Törless's stance as observer and indeed speaks of Basini's 'moralische Minderwertigkeit' (p. 51: 'moral inferiority'). Near the end of his life, in the late 1930s, Musil noted in his diary: 'Reiting, Beineberg: Die heutigen Diktatoren in nucleo' ('the present-day dictators in the making').[10] This is true enough, given Reiting's skill in psychological manipulation and Beineberg's experimental interest in torture; what then is prefigured by Törless's amoral detachment?

In Hesse's novels *Demian* and *Steppenwolf*, psychoanalysis regains contact with the Romanticism from which it originated. Not only did Hesse feel an intense affinity with Novalis and his fictional exploration of the depths of the self; but when he wrote *Demian*, in 1916–17, Hesse was in analysis with Dr Josef Bernhard Lang, a pupil of Jung's, and in 1921 he had analysis with Jung himself. In 1916 he read Jung's *Symbols of Transformation*, an interpretation of myths as archetypal narratives of rebirth, and he shared Lang's interest in oriental and Gnostic religion. His personal life was turbulent. The son of a Swiss Protestant pastor, he rebelled early against his strict upbringing, then had to cope emotionally with his father's death in 1916; after the collapse of his first marriage, he married again in 1924, but this also ended in divorce.

Moreover, his outspoken pacifism during the First World War made him a reviled outsider. His novels may be seen as self-therapy.

Demian (1919; trans. 1923) is a first-person narrative by 'Emil Sinclair', recounting his stumbling attempts to integrate two sides of his personality and to outgrow the cosy but confining bourgeois order in which he is brought up. Hesse focuses on inner experience, showing how Sinclair, as a child, projects his own internal divisions outwards as the parental world of order, security and light, and the outside world of darkness, violence and menace. The quiet authority of his fellow pupil Max Demian guides him through a development whose goal is his own independence – of parents, teachers, pastors and ultimately of Demian. Along the way, he externalises his inner 'shadow' as the schoolboy bully Franz Kromer, while his feminine 'anima' is projected in his later cult of a girl to whom he never speaks but to whom he gives the Dantean name of Beatrice.

This polarity of darkness and light is set within an ultimately Romantic vision of the cosmos as a dynamic, amoral unity. Sinclair is cured of bourgeois moralism by absorbing his mentor's Nietzschean reinterpretations of familiar stories: Cain is understood as someone ostracised for being bolder and cleverer than others, and preferable to the pious coward Abel; the unrepentant thief seems preferable to the penitent one; morality is described as relative; and when Sinclair enters on puberty, Demian tells him that the sexuality which Christianity demonises must be accepted as part of reality, which ought to be held sacred as a whole. In a school lesson he hears mention of 'Abraxas', the Gnostic god who represented both good and evil, and the name recurs in conversation with the ex-theology student Pistorius who teaches Sinclair about ancient mystery religions. Sinclair is stirred by a recurrent dream about the ambivalent, bisexual Abraxas, who recalls both his mother and Demian.

After rejecting his mentor Pistorius, whose concern with ancient religions he finds antiquarian, Sinclair, now a student, resumes contact with Demian and meets the latter's youthful and beautiful mother, Frau Eva, who seems to realise his fantasies and point the way forward on his own journey of self-discovery. The Demian household is part of a community of spiritual seekers, devoted to new cults and ancient religions, but all individualists in contrast to what Demian, in Nietzschean imagery, identifies as the false community of the herd. Sinclair's solitary journey now seems to be opening up into society. Demian predicts that the world will be renewed through death, and that renewal will be led by outstanding individuals who respond to the call of fate as Moses, Caesar, or Napoleon once did. His prediction seems to approach fulfilment when the First World War breaks out. Demian dies of wounds, but survives as an image deep in the mind of Sinclair, whose closing words refer to 'Ihm, meinem Freund und Führer' ('him, my friend and leader').[11]

This narrative of spiritual struggles, told with attractive simplicity, was welcomed by readers weary of the sham heroics of the First World War. Sinclair may be seen as growing away from the patriarchal rigidity of his *Vaterhaus* through identification with older male mentors towards a new form of masculinity – one based on awareness of his own feelings, and on an affinity with the maternal figure corresponding to the union with the mother-bride that Jung finds symbolised at the close both of the Bible and of Goethe's *Faust*.[12] Such an interpretation, though, is qualified by the strangely incorporeal character of Sinclair's experience: sexuality, instead of providing an avenue towards encountering another person, is sublimated into fantasy. Sinclair's relationships with Demian and Pistorius are conceived on a vertical master–pupil model, not as mutuality; individuation apparently consists in discarding outworn mentors and moving on. To the German Romantic dislike of the bourgeois philistine Hesse adds Nietzsche's contempt for the herd. Relationships with other people are seen only as projections of internal conflicts; the role of projection in enabling us to know other people is not addressed. The self-centred fictional model derived from Novalis shelters Sinclair from any arresting confrontation with other people's irreducible otherness or with a wholly unfamiliar aspect of himself.

The more complex and challenging *Der Steppenwolf* (1927; trans. 1929) starts from the distinction between the elect few and the philistine herd, only to undermine and overcome it. Its reclusive protagonist, Harry Haller, is first presented through the eyes of his landlady's nephew – a tidy-minded but not uncongenial bourgeois. When Haller begins his own narrative, he describes himself as an exile from bourgeois order who despises its mediocrity, hates the vulgar modern world, and tries to live among old books and classical music. Yet part of him feels oppressed by the dead weight of German culture, typified by the smug-looking picture of Goethe he sees in the house of a conservative professor, and he feels secretly attracted to the raw, fresh energies of jazz.

The beginnings of self-knowledge are forced on Haller by a pamphlet mysteriously handed to him, the 'Tractat vom Steppenwolf'. In analysing his self-image as a wolfish outcast, the pamphlet hints at his self-pity and maintains that he still clings to his bourgeois childhood. In Nietzschean language, it asserts that the unity of the self is an illusion concealing a multiplicity of selves; humanity is not a firm construction but a bridge between Nature and God, an unfinished project whose completion is infinitely deferred. There can be no return to childhood innocence: life leads 'immer weiter in die Schuld, immer tiefer in die Menschwerdung hinein' ('further into guilt, further into humanisation').[13] The best response is the sovereign detachment described as 'Humor' (p. 237).

Haller's escape from his self-imposed misery is assisted by a sympathetic call-girl, Hermine, who initiates him into the pleasures of jazz, dancing and shopping, but not sex. The taboo surrounding her is implied by the boyish appearance which reminds Haller of his boyhood friend Hermann, and by her insistence that their similar experiences of solitude and suffering enable them to be siblings, not lovers. Instead, Haller sleeps with the purely sensual Maria, while developing an attraction to the saxophonist Pablo, who is described by Maria as 'härter, männlicher und fordernder als irgendein Boxer oder Herrenreiter' (p. 334: 'harder, more manly and more demanding than any boxer or professional horseman'). Within a setting of increasingly polymorphous sexuality, Haller's gender identity is being rearranged as masculine towards Maria but feminine towards Pablo.

The climax of the novel occurs at Carnival time. Haller at last enters the elusive Magic Theatre which permits the imaginary realisation of his many selves. In one booth he releases his inner violence by shooting at motor-cars; in another he re-experiences his early love-life; in another, he finds Hermine and Pablo asleep after love-making, and stabs Hermine, thereby fulfilling her earlier prophecy that he would obey her last command by killing her. This may only symbolise his release from dependence on his therapist; but it is disturbingly reminiscent of the theme of sexual murder that haunts Weimar culture, notably in Döblin's *Berlin Alexanderplatz* (1929; trans. 1929).[14] And the text implies that Haller has to kill Hermine in order to be united with Pablo: as in Döblin, the woman is an instrument in the homosocial relationship between two men. Moreover, this imaginary murder seems to typify life's guilt and horror which, according to the Mozart figure, must not be treated with heavy-handed moralism but accepted with humour: 'das Leben ist immer furchtbar. Wir können nichts dafür und sind doch verantwortlich' (p. 401: 'Life is always frightful. We can do nothing about it and yet we are responsible'). This language of guilt and responsibility is oddly incongruous with the merely imaginary murder – 'murder in jest, no offence in the world' – and suggests that despite his sympathy with modern mass culture, Hesse remains limited by the egocentric fictional model derived from Romanticism. Haller's self-exploration includes the subjective feeling of guilt, but the independent existence of other people, only in relation to whom the concepts of guilt and responsibility can make sense, remains outside the limits of this novel.

Hofmannsthal's early poems, playlets and essays explore diverse conceptions of the self: as fragile and discontinuous ('Terzinen über Vergänglichkeit') yet also responsive to 'the weariness of long-forgotten peoples' ('Manche freilich'); as sedimented with ancestral influences (expressed by the Romantic image of the mine in 'Vorspiel für ein Puppentheater'); as imprisoned in subjectivity ('Über Charaktere im Roman und im Drama'); and yet as bound to the past through moral responsibility towards other people (*Der Tor und der Tod*). Most radically, the fictive author of the Chandos Letter (*Ein Brief*, 1902) explains that judgements like 'Sheriff N. is a bad man, Pastor T. is a good man' have lost their socially accredited meaning for him: unable to exercise 'the simplifying gaze of habit', he finds himself unable to express in language 'the deepest, most personal aspect of my thinking', and now leads an empty life illuminated only by sudden epiphanic flashes of mystical identification with commonplace objects. This is the fate of the merely private self, dissociated from language and the network of shared assumptions that language embodies.

To articulate how the private self may rejoin society, Hofmannsthal turned to drama and the novel. His most successful plays are social comedies representing what he called 'the allomatic solution': the reciprocal process by which the self is both secured and transformed by commitment to a relationship of lifelong fidelity to another person. His unfinished novel *Andreas oder die Vereinigten* (Andreas: or, the United; begun in 1907, written mainly in 1912 and 1913, published posthumously in 1932) conveys the torment and the ecstasy available to the private self; only the title gestures towards the social solution which Hofmannsthal intended.

Andreas falls into two portions. It begins with the arrival of the 22-year-old Andreas, a member of the minor Viennese nobility whose parents have sent him on an educational tour, in Venice in 1778. Soon, however, we have a lengthy flashback to Andreas's experiences on his journey, and within this retrospect there are remoter recollections of traumatic childhood experiences. On the journey, Andreas's servant Gotthelf began initiating him into a sadistic version of masculinity in which women serve as objects of men's violence and material for anecdotes that strengthen solidarity among men. Gotthelf's corrupting influence is countered by Romana, the daughter of the well-to-do farming family with whom they lodge; love for her lets Andreas glimpse a possible relationship based on unembarrassed sensuality and mutuality. The farmstead, Castell Finazzer, is the setting for a pastoral idyll, where domestic and social harmony is presented in vividly circumstantial detail. Evil invades this idyll, personified by Gotthelf, who, after sleeping with a maidservant, ties her to the bed and sets fire to it before escaping; he also poisons the watch-dog. But his sadism externalises an aspect of Andreas. In his dreams, Andreas recalls how as a child he wantonly killed an affectionate puppy and broke the back of a cat, and even fantasises about torturing

Romana. Feeling partly responsible for Gotthelf's evil deeds, he enters on a series of quasi-mystical experiences: a sombre sense of identification with the poisoned dog, and hence with all suffering creatures; a dream in which he meets Romana in a paradisal setting, modelled on Dante's meeting with Beatrice in *Purgatorio* 30, and with appropriate overtones of penitence and punishment; and finally an exultant intuition of the hidden unity of all things.

Andreas is a divided character, a 'sick soul' as described in William James's *Varieties of Religious Experience*, which Hofmannsthal read attentively. In James's account, such a character often finds unity through religious conversion. In Hofmannsthal's novel, the integration of Andreas's personality was to occur through memory – by working through his traumatic and blissful recollections, as he does in the flashback, he shapes and consolidates his self – and, above all, through love. In Venice he encounters two women, one devout, another brisk and playful, who seem to be one and the same. From Hofmannsthal's notes, however, we learn that these women are two aspects of one person who is more radically divided than Andreas. Under the impact of a premature and painful marriage, she has split into two distinct personalities. As Maria she is devout and orderly, afraid of her body and of sensuous experience. As Mariquita she is hot-blooded, sensual and irreligious; she seems to lack a soul. Mariquita knows of Maria's existence, hates her, and plays tricks on her, such as getting drunk so that Maria will have a hangover. Maria only vaguely suspects Mariquita's existence in the form of something chaotic within herself. The two are connected by a lapdog called Fidèle that Maria carries. Throughout this novel, animals, especially dogs, represent the physical being in which our conscious life is necessarily embodied: hence the harmonious relations with animals displayed by Romana, and the peculiar atrocity of Gotthelf's poisoning the dog.

Maria/Mariquita illustrates the phenomenon of 'multiple personality'.[15] In the 1880s, Pierre Janet had found that hypnotised patients sometimes disclosed new and unexpected sub-personalities. Hofmannsthal read *The Dissociation of a Personality* (1905) in which the Boston nerve specialist Morton Prince described Miss Beauchamp, whose normally delicate, timid personality alternated with a boisterous and mischievous self called Sally. Similarly, Andreas would gradually have discovered that Maria and Mariquita were the same person. One note envisages Andreas going to bed with Mariquita and waking up in time to find the bed empty and see Maria rushing away in distress. It seems that Andreas would through love have united the two and become a unified being himself.

Though the novel's incompleteness makes all conjecture risky, it seems likely that Hofmannsthal would have used Morton Prince's case history, not to present a case of female split personality, but rather to objectify Andreas's own divided attitude to women which makes him envisage them as either spiritual or sensual. As in Novalis, the women are primarily projections of the hero's sexual ambivalence. In uniting Maria with Mariquita, he would have resolved his own divided attitude to women. Hofmannsthal then envisaged him returning to Castell Finazzer and marrying Romana. The notes, however, reveal other fascinating possibilities, notably the role as Andreas's mentor assigned to the mysterious Knight of Malta, Sacromozo, whom the notes associate with the homosexual Stefan George and with Proust's Baron Charlus; he recalls also Schiller's unfinished drama *Die Malteser*, with its frank depiction of homoerotic love between two young knights.[16]

Hofmannsthal's novel perhaps had to remain unfinished. A narrative of psychological integration moves towards an implausibly neat closure and risks robbing experiences of their vividness by making them mere stages in a process. Andreas's memories, however, are too vivid and complex to be interpreted smoothly away. Their stubborn and often torturing immediacy resists recuperation as episodes in a psychoanalytic narrative. While the Venetian passages follow the Romantic model of egocentric fiction, the Castell Finazzer section breaks out of it and conveys the vertiginous sense of another person existing independently of one's fantasies. And the antithesis of Romana and Gotthelf points beyond psychology towards the extremes of good and evil as spiritual realities.

Hans Henny Jahnn (1894–1959) undertook path-breaking and taboo-breaking explorations of sexuality within a resolutely secular, vitalistic portrayal of the cosmos. Yet while celebrating sexual 'perversion' in such semi-Expressionist plays as the tortured *Pastor Ephraim Magnus* (1919) and the ecstatic *Medea* (1926), he also founded a kind of religious community, called Ugrino, which met in a Hamburg suburb. Although a comparison suggests itself with the vitalism of D. H. Lawrence and his imagined community of Rananim, Jahnn was (at a later date) inspired by the sprawling rural epics of John Cowper Powys. Like Powys, he projects a challenging and individual imaginative universe in vast novels that make heavy demands on their readers but offer corresponding rewards.

The narrative core of Jahnn's extraordinary *Perrudja* (1929) reworks its author's experience. To avoid military service, Jahnn and his male lover Gottlieb Friedrich Harms spent the years 1915–18 in great poverty and discomfort in rural Norway. The novel presents the Norwegian landscape as the setting for an amazingly frank and richly sensuous portrayal of life under the sway of biological imperatives. With unfussy naturalness, Jahnn ignores literary taboos in presenting Perrudja's difficult, unsteady progress towards a sexual identity. An orphan, lacking parental role-models, but enabled by unexplained wealth to live alone in the mountains, Perrudja suffers from self-doubt and self-dislike and displays a polymorphous eroticism which finds an early focus in his attachment to his horse Shabdez. A flashback tells how, at fourteen, he was infatuated with a somewhat older boy, Haakon, an assistant butcher, and learnt from him to slaughter animals: the account of cutting up a pregnant sow is unforgettable, but also an expression of hostility towards the maternal body. The adult Perrudja formally woos Signe, a strong-willed, enigmatic woman with a sado-masochistic temperament, who is already engaged to the brutish womaniser Thorstein Hoyer. This rivalry leads to a Western-style shoot-out in a remote valley in which Perrudja and Hein together narrowly fail to kill Hoyer; later, however, they succeed, for his corpse is found, but Perrudja lacks the courage to confess this deed to Signe (who would have approved of it), and in fury she rejects him on their wedding night and leaves him, their marriage unconsummated. A close homoerotic friendship develops between Perrudja and Hein. Together they undertake a semi-fantastic boat-trip along the Norwegian coast with a party of schoolchildren, among whom Hein displays a relaxed, bisexual promiscuity, while Perrudja, as usual, remains a prey to shyness and self-doubt. The confident Hein is the *alter ego* of the vulnerable, tearful, insecure Perrudja.

After reading Joyce's *Ulysses* in German translation, Jahnn revised his manuscript, varying the narrative viewpoint, inserting parallel episodes, and thickening the texture with leitmotivs. Late in the novel, Perrudja is revealed as heir to vast riches and owner of countless companies. However absurd, this contrivance initiates a polemic against capitalism, industrialism and colonialism, which are represented as threatening the future of humanity. The destructiveness of capitalism comes home to Perrudja when he learns that an explosion in one of his coal-mines has killed hundreds of people. He fantasises about a cleansing, sacrificial war which would extirpate humanity apart from a small band of survivors trained to be aware of their fleshly nature ('Fleischlichkeit').[17] As this indicates, Jahnn's polemics against capitalism depend on the contrast between inhuman abstraction and the overwhelmingly direct presentation of immediate physical reality, manifest in landscape descriptions, in evocations of sexuality, and above all in the constant emphasis on animals, especially horses, which mediate between humanity and non-human nature. The major leitmotivs are natural, such as the yellow, stinking flower with which Perrudja defines his own difference from others and his inability to feel loved; and the tigress, which defines Perrudja's view of Signe.

Perrudja is hardly a gay manifesto. Its protagonist makes stumbling, painful progress towards a sexual identity. Though physical closeness is finely evoked, his only experience of actual sex is in the brief episode with the boy Alexander. The homoerotic relationships are all unequal, like the vertical relationships in *Demian*: the young Perrudja becomes subordinate to Haakon (reversing the class relationship between them); Hein explicitly offers himself as Perrudja's slave, and Perrudja seals their one-sided blood-brotherhood by incising a sign on Hein's thigh with his knife. If no viable, lasting sexual relationship is depicted, that hardly matters: Jahnn's achievement is to have explored with unembarrassed honesty the vast realm of inarticulate emotions and sensations that were unsuspected, or only obliquely suggested, in the premodernist novel.

NOTES

1. David Hume, *A Treatise of Human Nature*, ed. L. A. Selby-Bigge (Oxford, 1964), p. 252.
2. Ernst Mach, *Die Analyse der Empfindungen und das Verhältniss des Physischen zum Psychischen*, 2nd expanded edition (Jena, 1900), p. 2.
3. *The Standard Edition of the Complete Psychological Works of Sigmund Freud*, ed. James Strachey, 24 vols. (London, 1953–74), V, 548–9; hereafter references given in the text as *SE*.
4. *Die fröhliche Wissenschaft*, no. 362, in Friedrich Nietzsche, *Werke*, ed. Karl Schlechta, 3 vols. (Munich, 1966), II, 236.
5. See J. P. Stern, *Ernst Jünger: a Writer of our Time* (Cambridge, 1953); Klaus Theweleit, *Männerphantasien*, 2 vols. (Frankfurt, 1977–8).
6. Hans Blüher, *Die Rolle der Erotik in der männlichen Gesellschaft. Eine Theorie der menschlichen Staatsbildung nach Wesen und Wert*, ed. Hans Joachim Schoeps ((1917); Stuttgart, 1962).
7. Robert Musil, *Gesammelte Werke*, ed. Adolf Frisé, 9 vols. (Reinbek, 1978), VI, 33.
8. See R. W. Connell, *Masculinities* (Cambridge, 1995), esp. p. 68.
9. Blüher, *Die Rolle der Erotik in der männlichen Gesellschaft*, p. 272.
10. Musil, *Tagebücher*, ed. Adolf Frisé, 2 vols. (Reinbek, 1976), I, 914.
11. Hesse, *Gesammelte Werke*, 12 vols. (Frankfurt am Main, 1970), V, 163.
12. C. G. Jung, *Symbols of Transformation*, trans. R. F. C. Hull (London and Henley, 1956), pp. 222–3.
13. Hesse, *Gesammelte Werke*, VII, 247.
14. See Maria Tatar, *Lustmord: Sexual Murder in Weimar Germany* (Princeton, 1995).
15. See Ian Hacking, *Rewriting the Soul: Multiple Personality and the Sciences of Memory* (Princeton, 1995).
16. Hugo von Hofmannsthal, *Sämtliche Werke: Kritische Ausgabe*, vol. XXX, ed. Manfred Pape (Frankfurt am Main, 1982), pp. 160, 161, 201.
17. Hans Henny Jahnn, *Jubiläumsausgabe*, 8 vols. (Hamburg, 1994), I, 503.

FURTHER READING

Alewyn, Richard, *Über Hugo von Hofmannsthal*, 4th edition (Göttingen, 1967)
Böhme, Hartmut, and Uwe Schweikert (eds.), *Archaische Moderne. Der Dichter, Architekt und Orgelbauer Hans Henny Jahnn* (Stuttgart, 1996)

Boulby, Mark, *Hermann Hesse: his Mind and his Art* (Ithaca, NY, 1967)

Corino, Karl, 'Ödipus oder Orest? Robert Musil und die Psychoanalyse', in Uwe Baur and Dietmar Goltschnigg (eds.), *Vom 'Törleß' zum 'Mann ohne Eigenschaften'* (Munich and Salzburg, 1973), pp. 123–235

Ellenberger, Henri F., *The Discovery of the Unconscious: the History and Evolution of Dynamic Psychiatry* (London, 1970)

Freeman, Thomas, *Hans Henny Jahnn. Eine Biographie* (Hamburg, 1986)

Kingerlee, Roger, *Psychological Models of Masculinity in Döblin, Musil, and Jahnn: Männliches, Allzumännliches* (Lewiston, Queenston and Lampeter, 2001)

Luft, David, *Robert Musil and the Crisis of European Culture, 1880–1942* (Berkeley and Los Angeles, 1980)

Miles, David H., *Hofmannsthal's Novel 'Andreas': Memory and Self* (Princeton, 1972)

Mitchell, Breon, *James Joyce and the German Novel 1922–1933* (Athens, OH, 1976)

Payne, Philip, *Robert Musil's Works, 1906–1924: a Critical Introduction* (Frankfurt am Main, Bern and New York, 1987)

Ryan, Judith, *The Vanishing Subject: Early Psychology and Literary Modernism* (Chicago, 1991)

Sebald, W. G., 'Venezianisches Kryptogramm: Hofmannsthals *Andreas*', in Sebald, *Die Beschreibung des Unglücks. Zur österreichischen Literatur von Stifter bis Handke* (Salzburg, 1985), pp. 61–77

Serrano, Miguel, *C. G. Jung and Hermann Hesse: a Record of Two Friendships*, trans. Frank MacShane (London, 1966)

Stopp, Elisabeth, 'Musil's *Törleß*: content and form', *Modern Language Review*, 58 (1968), 94–118

Timms, Edward, 'Hesse's therapeutic fiction', in Peter Collier and Judy Davies (eds.), *Modernism and the European Unconscious* (Cambridge, 1990), pp. 165–81

Wohlleben, Joachim, *Versuch über 'Perrudja'. Literarhistorische Betrachtungen über Hans Henny Jahnns Beitrag zum modernen Roman* (Tübingen, 1985)

Ziolkowski, Theodore, *The Novels of Hermann Hesse* (Princeton, 1965)

5

STANLEY CORNGOLD

Franz Kafka: the radical modernist

Franz Kafka (1883–1924) was born to a German-speaking Jewish family in Prague, a Czech city under Austro-Hungarian rule. This piling-up of ethnic particulars right at the outset should suggest some of the complexity of Kafka's predicament, one reflected in his very rich confessional writings – his correspondence and journals – his stories and parables, and his three great unfinished novels *America* (*Amerika*, written 1912–14; published in 1927), *The Trial* (*Der Process*, written 1914; published as *Der Prozeß* in 1925; trans. Willa and Edwin Muir 1935) and *The Castle* (*Das Schloß*, written 1922; published 1926; trans. Willa and Edwin Muir 1930).

Kafka's situation, like his city, is mazy, disjunct, overly detailed by history; it held exceptional danger and promise: the danger of becoming lost in a lawless complexity that finally flattens out into anxiety, apathy and nothingness, but the promise, too, of a sudden breaking open under great tension into a blinding prospect of truth. At various moments one can see Kafka laying weight on one or the other of his identity elements in an effort to find his way: he studied law at university, then practised it at the partly state-run Workers' Accident Insurance Institute, where he rose to a position of considerable authority (*Obersekretär*), though he experienced his 'work at the office' mainly as a hindrance to his writing. He learnt Hebrew, understood Yiddish, and toyed with Zionism; expressed socialist sympathies that aligned him with the aspirations of the Czech-speaking working class; and briefly considered literature as a profession that would bring him, like his great contemporary Robert Musil (1880–1942), into the 'world' of writers living and working in a capital city.[1] But though Kafka competed subliminally with his contemporaries for literary fame, the path he took – and to judge from his posthumous glory, found – was, with few interruptions, the path of writing, a discipline that would consume him utterly and produce next to nothing of use to him in his practical life. The deeply private character of his writing enmeshed him in feelings of guilt, since the erotic character of this not-so-innocent game put him at odds with the expectation that he marry and found a family; but he certainly did not fail to take steps in this direction, which meant his raising and disappointing the hopes of more than one woman.

Kafka began writing in the 1890s, and many of the traits associated with literature of that decade colour his earliest literary efforts. The intellectual character of the *fin-de-siècle* cultural ferment is suggested by a listing of the dominant 'isms': aestheticism, empiricism, symbolism, together with decadence, *l'art pour l'art, Jugendstil*. Their main feature is a profiling of surface over depth, and of the broken and fleeting sensation, informed by an acute consciousness of discontinuity, so that all the strands of what mattered in reality appear as a collection of shards and fragments. This view encouraged moods of recklessness and also tense concentration on occasional moments of luminosity – instants of immediate beauty and transparency. In and out of these moments Kafka forged a work that gradually included more and more information about later modernity (commerce, technology and the sway of the simulacrum) and intuitions as to what the missing law might resemble.

Judging from Kafka's manuscripts, the title of the first of his novels should be translated 'The Boy who was Missing' or 'The Boy who was Never Heard of Again' or, perhaps best, 'The Boy who Sank out of Sight' (all are versions of the German *Der Verschollene*, Kafka's preferred title for his 'American novel').[2]

Der Verschollene proved frustrating to Kafka, who once referred to it as 'the lowlands of writing'.[3] This was partly because of its derivative character. The novel is indebted to Benjamin Franklin's *Autobiography*, to various travel journals, and mostly to Dickens: like *David Copperfield* or *Great Expectations*, it recounts the often grim adventures of an outcast boy. The first sentence of Kafka's novel declares that the hero, Karl Rossmann, has been packed off to America by his parents for having been seduced by a housemaid who gave birth to his child. Kafka acknowledged Dickens as a source; but compared with the first-person narrator of Dickens's novels, the third-person narrator of *Der Verschollene* is far less intrusive and imperial, and Kafka's novel is much more episodic, independent in its parts. Indeed they are less chapters than a succession of short novels having a single hero. It is this margin of forgetfulness between the parts that produces effects of uncanniness and beauty.

Kafka thought 'The Stoker', the first chapter of *Der Verschollene*, especially alive and spiritedly written, but this is also true of much of the rest, which is full of surprises, wild humour and audacious sexuality. Its themes are – regrettably – all of current interest: random criminality and violence, homelessness in America, American speed, impersonality, technical know-how, information processing, melancholy, self-help and utopianism. Within its frame of dislocation, technology, arbitrary authority and apocalyptic rumour, its cogency continues to emerge, even more forcefully than that, say, of *The Trial*, which was, for a great many readers, the representative literary work of art during the period of fifty years following its publication. The difference in the reception of the two works runs along the axis dividing audiences responsive to the modernist from those more responsive to the postmodern in literature. The modernist mood of *The Trial* is paranoid, its legal bureaucracy held together by acts of interpretation and writing, its violence mostly concealed until the final page; and that concluding scene – a night of long knives, swung by the arms of killers in frock coats, like 'tenors' – is ostentatiously operatic. The mood of *Der Verschollene* is exterior: it is public, mechanical and touched by a human quality only to the extent that it is anxious. In its world, authority is maintained by brute force; its violence is out in the open, suggesting a bare reminiscence of consciousness as a quality of jerky distractedness: 'the din roared, over pavement and roadway, changing its direction every minute, as if in a whirlwind, not like something produced by human beings but like a foreign element'.[4] The key-word for the public life of the America in which Karl Rossmann is trapped is 'Verkehr' – a word meaning traffic but also the circulation of commodities, socialising and sexual intercourse.[5]

Der Verschollene contains explicit junction-points between the early and the later work of Kafka. Moments of the aestheticism that absorbed Kafka in the years before 1912 figure alongside his growing preoccupation with the power constellations of public life (family, business, law court, government, 'castle') – constellations that point to the conditions of later modernity, in which individuals sense that they are ruled by clusters of laws without a centre. In the middle of Karl Rossmann's reactions – mostly hectic, unfocused, powerless – surface peculiar moments of sensory absorption, of passionless concentration on random particulars, that suggest not so much a doctrine of epiphanies as the 'indifferentism' cultivated by modern painters like Francis Bacon and Dan Ching. The rapture of distraction is heightened by the condition of exile. Even as Karl was reporting the din of traffic (described above), he 'was inattentive . . . to everything except Mr Pollunder's dark waistcoat, across which at an angle a golden chain hung calmly'.[6] At the end of chapter 4, Karl Rossmann addresses the two rough adventurers he has picked up on his travels:

> 'Listen to me! If either of you still has the photograph and is willing to bring it to me at the hotel, he can still have the trunk, and he won't – I swear – be reported to the police.' No actual answer came down, only a broken-off

word could be heard, the beginning of a shout from Robinson, whose mouth
evidently Delamarche immediately stopped. Karl went on waiting for a long
time, in case the men above might still change their minds. Twice, at intervals,
he shouted: 'I'm still waiting!' But no sound came in reply, except that once
a stone rolled down the slope, perhaps by accident, perhaps a badly-aimed
throw. (V, p. 132)

The scene fades, tinged by Karl's exhaustion, into the prolonged, faintly
harried perception of the single sensation of a rolling stone. The next chapter
ends:

> After four o'clock in the morning a bit of calm set in, something that Karl badly
> needed. He leant heavily against the banister beside his lift, slowly eating the
> apple, from which, after the very first bite, a powerful fragrance streamed out,
> and looked down into a lighted shaft, surrounded by the great windows of the
> storerooms, behind which hanging masses of bananas were faintly gleaming.
> (V, p. 162)

The passage ends on a note of weariness and sensory rapture.

In *Der Verschollene* the modern aesthetic moment, unlike the classical one,
is modulated by a mood of exhaustion and anxiety. As a moment of aesthetic
indifference, following on a shock, it can read like a variant carryover from
Kafka's early empiricist, atomistic, aestheticist concerns. But in a fragment
at the close of *Der Verschollene*, there is a forward-looking connection to
the guilty thematics of *The Trial*. Karl, having been abused,

> hardly paid attention any more to speeches of this kind: everybody used his
> power to abuse his inferiors. Once you got used to it, it sounded no different
> from the steady striking of the clock. What horrified him, however, as he
> now pushed the carriage into the entranceway, was the dirt predominating
> here, which surpassed all his expectations. On closer inspection, it was not
> the kind of dirt you could actually touch with your hands. The pavement of
> the passageway was nearly swept clean, the paintwork on the walls was fairly
> new, the artificial palms were not all that dusty, and yet everything was greasy
> and repulsive, as if everything had been misused and no amount of cleanliness
> could ever make it good again. Whenever Karl came to a new place, he liked
> to imagine the improvements that could be made and the pleasure it would be
> to get to work immediately, without paying attention to the perhaps infinite
> labour involved. Here, however, he did not know what could be done.
> (V, pp. 293–4)

The passage ends on a note of resignation, which seems contrived (it belongs
to the history of Kafka's forced conciliatory endings); but what continues to
stand out is 'the dirt predominating here, which surpassed all expectations'.

It is real dirt, perceived at first as real dirt, and, for Karl, in the presence of the threatening Manager, a typical object of distracted perception. But, in this instance, of course, it is more – and worse: for 'it was not the kind of dirt you could actually touch with your hands' – rather 'as if everything had been misused, and no amount of cleanliness could ever make it good again'.

The dirt-object opens up an abyss of unspecifiable abuse (which returns the reader to the entire commodified world of *Der Verschollene*). But this object, coming at the end of the novel, is distinctive for its exemplary, dialectically enriched character. In the preceding examples, a particular object provoked Karl's distracted gaze, while all around him a current of turbulent dangerous life threatened to sweep him away. Here both dimensions are present in a single object: its surface captures Karl's gaze, while at bottom it discloses an abyss. This dirt that is not ordinary dirt breaks through the mystified facade of the other, seemingly natural objects of Karl's fascination, into which he has strained to escape. The pathos of the scene picks up again a moment at the outset when Karl, absorbed in Klara's piano playing, feels 'rising within him a sorrow that reaching past the end of the song, sought another end that it could not find' (*V*, p. 94).

This mood of sad searching, in objects without aura, to redeem a loss impossible to make good, connects *Der Verschollene* with the later novels, as a basic tonality which, in the later work, is modified by higher tonalities: Joseph K., the central protagonist, is older, hardened and more logical, without Rossmann's sweetness and availability; in *The Castle*, K., another central character, is tougher and shrewder than the other K.s, more determined to get what he takes to be his due. In his journal entry for 30 September 1915, Kafka compared Karl Rossmann, the hero of *Der Verschollene*, with Joseph K., the hero of *The Trial*, noting: 'Rossmann and K., the innocent and the guilty, in the end both killed punitively without distinction, the innocent one with a gentler hand, more shoved aside than struck down.'[7] He did not compare this boy with 'the bitter herb' – with K., the hero of *The Castle*, who, although exhausted from his effort, has been neither pushed aside nor struck down at the time the novel breaks off.

Der Verschollene anticipates formal features of the later work: here Kafka tries out his *style indirect libre* (free indirect discourse) in passages where it is impossible to decide whether what is being said are the facts of the case proffered by an authoritative narrator or a reproduction of what Karl takes to be the case – hence, a flawed perception of some indeterminable state of affairs. Another narrative device, dominant in *The Castle*, also figures in *Der Verschollene*: Kafka's tactic of linking together stories told by characters within the novel. *Der Verschollene* foreshadows this technique in Therese's extended description of her mother's death. This narrative strategy also has the effect of dispersing the authority of the narrator and making the novel, to a radical degree, an affair of co-constitution between author and reader.

Kafka was at a low level in mood and fortune when, in late July 1914, he began writing *The Trial*. The onset of composition was dictated by catastrophes: Kafka's engagement to his fiancée Felice Bauer had just been broken off at a family gathering in the hotel Askanischer Hof in Berlin, which Kafka called 'the court of justice in the hotel' (*D* II, 65; translation modified). The event provoked a crisis, which he described in a diary entry of 28 July in rare italic: '*My inability to think, to observe, to determine things, to remember, to speak, to share the life of others: I am turning to stone – that is something I must register* . . . If I don't take refuge in some sort of work, I am lost' (*D* II, 68; translation modified).

Kafka's situation was complicated by no less an event than the outbreak of the First World War. As a result of the general mobilisation, he was obliged to move out of his parents' apartment and 'receive the reward for living alone. But it is hardly a reward; living alone results only in punishment' (*D* II, 75; translation modified). His judgment on this point, while from the ordinary standpoint tactless, even audacious, is, from the writer's standpoint, quite rigorous: 'Nevertheless', he notes, 'I am hardly moved by all the misery and more determined than ever . . . I will write in spite of everything, absolutely; it is my fight for self-preservation' (ibid.; translation modified).

The situation recorded in this second diary entry is remarkable. Craving safety on 28 July, Kafka had, three days later, intuited enough of *The Trial* for him, evidently, once again to be able 'to think, to observe, to determine things' with a vengeance. One might revise the conclusion to the earlier entry of 28 July to read: 'I am turning [not to stone but] to script – that is something I must write down, . . . and I can.'

Kafka continued to work on *The Trial* – and to work well on it – for several months. On 15 August, he noted: 'I have been writing for a few days, may it continue. Today I am not so completely protected by and absorbed by my work as I was two years ago [that is, during the period of the main composition of *Der Verschollene*, 'Das Urteil', and *Die Verwandlung*]; nevertheless I have a direction, my regular, empty, insane bachelor's life has a justification' (*D* II, 79). It is the last such enthusiastic entry during the process of his writing *The Trial*; by the beginning of the next year, the project would have run into the sands. But what is at stake for Kafka in writing *The Trial* goes beyond alleviation of his empirical miseries. He craves justification – redemption 'into the [greater] freedom that perhaps awaits me' (*D* II, 92) – a result that depends on his continuing to write *The Trial*, to go on condemning Joseph K. Indeed, the novel is unusual in Kafka's oeuvre for the marked lack of sympathy it has for his hero, witnessed by the fact that right at the outset Kafka composed the scene of his hero's ghastly execution, as if to make sure that he would not escape punishment. This cruelty could be understood as a reflex of the intensity of his desire to get clear of his own empirical ego in a life-situation he detested. But nothing is simple in Kafka. His condemnation in advance is arranged along ingenious rhetorical lines that cast doubt on its sincerity.

In its first manuscript appearance, the opening sentence of *The Trial* reads: 'Someone must have slandered Josef K., for one morning, without having done anything truly wrong, he was *captured*' [emphasis added].[8] Thereafter Kafka crossed out the word 'captured' and replaced it with the word 'arrested', introducing the more obviously legal term. The shift into legal language supplies Kafka with his inner design for the novel, which he kept elaborating as he wrote it. The design may be grasped as the attempt of Joseph K. to come to terms with his sense of guilt by insufficient – indeed, by childish – means.

Joseph K. supposes that he will be brought to trial by a court constituted like a civil court, which, even in the absence of specific charges, will exonerate him. In this way, Joseph K. repeats Kafka's authorial leap into a seeming legality and takes the lure that will lead to his death, for it becomes more and more evident that there are no ordinary legal means available to redeem him. But it is Kafka as author who has made the leap ahead of him: the manuscript inscribes the impulse to flee an existential drama for a legal one as the very move that K. will be punished for making. Joseph K. acts at odds with the truth of his situation, in opposition to his author who hints at the kind of truth it has, in the sense of being something beyond K.'s grasp.

Joseph K.'s interpretation of his arrest is coerced by the rhetoric of the opening sentence. It comes in the form of a syllogism from which the major premise is omitted, leaving a minor premise – 'Joseph K. was captured/arrested' – and a conclusion – 'Joseph K. must have been accused'. The omitted premise is: 'If someone is [or feels] captured/arrested, then someone must have accused him.' But this is a proposition whose truth is not universal. And because it is not enunciated as a definite feature of Joseph K.'s arrest (it is at most 'someone's' opinion), K.'s harking back to this idea, worrying at it, and assuming its efficacy has no objective justification. The idea of applying 'someone's' logic to his arrest is his own. In fact the Inspector says explicitly to him: 'I can't report that you've been accused of anything, or more accurately, I don't know if you have. You've been arrested, that's true, but that's all I know' (*T*, p. 14). K.'s assumption of having been accused immerses him in his ordeal.

The Trial, whose German title also means 'The Process', is very much about the process by which interpretations of K.'s ordeal become the facts of the case; and Kafka spares no pains to embed this metaphor, on the model of the parable of 'Before the Law', in various details of the action. Events are shaped in advance by a conventional interpretation of them: here is another example from chapter 1. Joseph K. first hears about his arrest from one of the warders, who enters his room. Mitchell's translation reads: 'You can't leave, you're being held' (*T*, p. 5), but this misses a crucial nuance in the German: 'Sie dürfen nicht weggehen, Sie sind ja gefangen.'[9] What is crucial, now, is the little word 'ja', which means, approximately, 'as things are' or 'as anyone can see' or 'right?' This, it should be stressed, is the first time that K.'s arrest has been mentioned by any person in the novel. But as a way of announcing an arrest for the first time, it is indeed very odd, since it appeals to a prior unspoken understanding between the players. What basis is there for such an agreement? None whatsoever, except for the claim mysteriously thrust into the world of the novel, but not in the mind of any particular character, by the narrator's opening statement. One would expect from K. at this point the vigorous – and logical – response: 'How so? I haven't been arrested.' But K. does not say anything of the sort; in fact he says, 'So it seems' – a remark that has its own complexities but which *prima facie* confirms the arrest in the absence of any ground for doing so.

K. is an unreliable and, certainly, less than vigilant interpreter of his own situation. This has disastrous consequences for the reader as well, since in *The Trial* Kafka more or less consistently identifies his narrative perspective with that of Joseph K. With minor exceptions, nothing is reported that Joseph K. would himself be unable to report. This encourages the reader to search the text for other accounts of events – one internal and one external to the protocols of what the speakers literally say. The first is found by systematically resisting K.'s characteristic slant on things, coloured by fearfulness and haughty dismissiveness and also, possibly, class snobbery. The other is external and can be found in the field of bodily gesture. There is no other German novel written before *The Trial* in which the narrator says so little in addition to the protagonist, yet where the body of the protagonist speaks so graphically. Throughout the novel Joseph K. busily denies his guilt – but his body, through the spasmodic violence of its gestures, its bouts of asphyxiation, its increasing lethargy, suggests a different story.

The field of bodily gesture escapes K.'s own notice, of course; he cannot either speak or be silent in the language of his body as part of a conscious decision. No amount of experience can protect him against this shocking display of concerns, desires, intentions. In *The Trial* Kafka explicitly dramatises gesture as a form of language, revelation and (unruly) communication that revolts against the sovereignty of lived experience, which otherwise functions as a will to mastery on the basis of predictable behaviour. K. is a devotee of what can be achieved by experience; he does not treat his arrest, for example, as a senseless practical joke. He will learn from experience, and what prompts him to decide this is the impression he takes from the warder named Franz (!): 'From the moment he'd first seen the guard named Franz, he had decided firmly that this time he wouldn't let even the slightest advantage he might have over these people slip through his fingers' (*T*, p. 7). K.'s confident reading of Franz in a way that is supposed to redound to the authority of experience will lead K. to play a role, with mind and body: 'If this was a farce, he was going to play along' (ibid.). But it quickly emerges that there are at least a couple of things wrong with this decision. One is K.'s confident assumption that he has been able to read the look on Franz's face: indeed, on the next page Franz answers K.'s demand for a warrant for his arrest with 'a long and no doubt meaningful, but incomprehensible, look' (*T*, p. 8). This opacity underscores the pertinence of the gestural order at the same time that it undermines the certainty of such evidence, on which K. has based his decision to play a comedy, a decision not to be taken lightly. For K. never steps out of his role, and his comedic vision persists until the moment before his death. Observing the warders of the court who have come to stab him, he asks: '"So you are meant for me?" . . . The gentlemen nodded, each pointing with the top hat in his hand toward the other . . . "They've sent old supporting actors for me", K. said to himself' (*T*, pp. 225–6). But the death he accedes to does not release him for a curtain call.

In the crucial Cathedral chapter, too, K. will suffer a reproof at the hands of the prison chaplain after giving an account of the court on the basis of '"my own personal experience"' (*T*, p. 214). For the chaplain it is the case that (to quote the words of Oscar Wilde) 'personal experience is a most vicious and limited circle',[10] despite the fact that it is exactly what all men – or, as the chaplain points out, '"all guilty men"' – invoke. K.'s decision to confront his apparent arrest with subterfuges learnt from experience and read his ordeal as a comedy and not as a practical joke – and also not as the most rigorous of interpellations – evidently proves his undoing.

The environment of *The Trial* is different from that of *Der Verschollene*: aside from the shabby law court offices, it is prosperous, urbane, and marked by an intricate cerebrality. The terror of the protagonist runs in a different direction: an anxiety less about death by exposure, crippling and starvation than social and metaphysical disgrace. *Der Verschollene* is shot through with scenes of animality; in *The Trial* these scenes are isolated, and when they occur in a bourgeois setting they seem comic or surreal. In *The Castle*, Kafka's last novel, the environment is practically empty of discrete characteristics. The world is neither that of the road nor of the city but of the country village, into which the outlines of Count Westwest's Castle have sunk – a strange village without contour, blanketed in shadow and snow.

Kafka composed *The Castle* in 1922, two years before his death. It is an epic masterpiece: within the narrow locale of a mountain village and its bureaucracy and the restricted time-frame of its action (it covers a mere six days, only four completely), it encompasses a wealth and depth of human purpose, aspiration and need. The opening paragraph is also rhetorically dazzling:

> It was late evening when K. arrived. The village lay deep in snow. There was nothing of the Castle mount to be seen; it was surrounded by fog and darkness; not even the faintest glimmer of light indicated the great Castle. For a long time K. stood on the wooden bridge that leads from the highway to the village and looked up into the apparent emptiness.[11]

Like the opening of *The Trial* this passage interprets the action by dis-locating its scene to an uncanny place between nature and the linguistic constructions of a human interpreter – indeed of more than one human in-terpreter. For the narrator seems to hold the view that there is a castle, at least as a real thing that may from time to time appear to be hidden. When he (or it) speaks of 'apparent emptiness', he (or it) means a merely illusory emptiness that is in fact the epiphenomenon of something real. But from K.'s point of view, in a strict sense it is only a nothingness that has illuso-rily manifested itself; he sees an emptiness made illusorily visible, and not a castle.

The difference between Joseph K. and K. the hero of *The Castle* lies mainly in K.'s boldness. One can hear this in the German word for his vocation: he is a 'Landvermesser', a word which means at once 'country surveyor', 'materialist "mis-measurer"',[12] and also – by suggestion – 'hubristic lout'. A whole set of narrative intrusions reveals that so little is K. a hapless victim of bureaucracy, he himself aggressively schemes to enter into its toils. In *The Castle* the narrative perspective is less uniformly confined to that of the protagonist than in *The Trial*, although it is significant that Kafka does not use his narrative advantage to assert orientating truths to suddenly illuminate these mysterious events.

This Castle-world without qualities is rife with the danger of endless re-semblances. It is the world prefigured at one point in *The Trial* with the paintings offered for sale by the painter Titorelli; they are identical 'land-scapes' portraying a couple of 'frail trees, standing at a great distance from one another in the dark grass' (*T*, p. 163). After Titorelli offers a simulacrum as the 'companion piece' to the first painting, the narrator remarks: 'It may have been intended as a companion piece, but not the slightest difference could be seen between it and the first one'; the third, too, 'was not merely similar . . . , it was exactly the same landscape' (*T*, p. 163). In the Castle-world we encounter this barren heath in wintertime, covered in a snow eternally blanketing difference. Persons in this world are frequently indistinguishable from one another. When K. says that his place lies somewhere between the peasants and the Castle, the teacher objects, saying, '"There is no difference between the peasantry and the Castle"' (*C*, p. 190). At first sight the men who work for Klamm, the main figure of Castle authority, cannot be told apart. Confronting Arthur and Jeremiah, the assistants furnished by the Castle, K. is puzzled: '"It's a problem with you", he said, comparing their faces, something he'd already done often. "How am I to know one of you from the other? The only difference between you is your names, otherwise you're as like one another . . . as snakes"' (*C*, p. 196; translation modified). The village housing the Castle is a maze of ramshackle buildings. Even as a putative surveyor, K. cannot distinguish the village from the Castle, which is itself 'only a wretched-looking town' (*C*, p. 188); the snowed-in world allows for no distinctions of rank.

Everywhere in the Castle-world lours the presence of something not so much animal as subhuman, prehistorical, in the faces of the peasants, their heads as if beaten flat under the weight of unintelligible authority. The danger for the hero, the surveyor K., who appears to have wandered into the village at the same time that he claims his right to live there, is to be lost in a primitive world of indistinction. Immersed in sexual sensation that might be seen to represent a concentration of what is his own, K. registers instead 'the feeling he was going astray or was so deep in a foreign place as no man before him, a foreign place in which even the air had no ingredient of the air of home, in which one would have to suffocate on foreignness and in whose absurd allurements one could do nothing but go further, go further astray' (*C*, p. 215; translation modified).

K.'s vulnerability to moods of self-loss is the obverse of his strong ego. Not trivially, he appears to be the first human being in this environment ever to have introduced a distinct claim to rights: '"I don't want any act of favour from the Castle, but my rights"' (*C*, p. 241). His counterpart revolutionary, Amalia, separates herself from the Castle by silence and proud reserve, a course that holds no appeal for K. In his own way he will be a great, though chiefly latent producer of differences, of a spirit of factionalism that begins to swirl around him like wind-driven snow around a trunk that has planted itself there.

I said that K. is more daring than Kafka's other novelistic heroes. The thrust of K.'s daring might be put as follows. His relation to the Castle, as he envisions it, suggests a form of truth-seeking. This conception is conveyed to the reader, so that K.'s entry into the Castle appears to be an entry into the truth of things. The Castle being humanly inhabited, the relation of knower and known is necessarily cast in the imagery of interpersonal relations. Where the act of knowing is successful, the knower is acknowledged by the known. Truth is a matter of reciprocal recognition.

An early passage in *The Castle* tells of K.'s serious acceptance of the quest and struggle for admission to the Castle: 'So the Castle had named him Land Surveyor. On the one hand that was not favourable to him, for it showed that the Castle knew everything about him that was necessary to know, had gauged the power relations, and was taking up the struggle with a smile' (*C*, pp. 185–6; translation modified). Here the metaphor restates the failure of knowledge in approximately these Faustian terms: all you know of the spiritual object is what you take it to mean, it is not me. The truth condescends to be known not as it is in itself but in a manner limited by the capacities of the human subject, a manner that does not allow it to be penetrated or exposed. Truth can be known by the human subject only as what it is not.

But this point, for Kafka's Castle, requires adjustment. The condescension of truth figures as only one side of K.'s Castle-vision. 'On the other hand', continues the narrator, of the readiness of the Castle to take up the struggle, 'it was also favourable, for in his view it proved that they had underestimated him, and he would have more freedom than he might have initially hoped for. And if they believed that by this – certainly intellectually superior – recognition of his capacity as Land Surveyor they could keep him permanently terrified, they were mistaken; he felt a slight shudder but that was all' (*C*, p. 186; translation modified). There is a Promethean, an altogether usurpatory, feeling to this parable of selfhood in its independence of legal constraints. K. will prove a match for the Castle authorities: he comes closer than any other one of Kafka's protagonists to entering the gates of the law – at the same time that the institution of the law itself, to the extent that it can be grasped independently of K.'s perspective, seems crazed, hopelessly entangled – and worst, phantasmal.

K.'s daring, a measure of the intensity of felt purpose, can verge on a ruthless abuse of others, and hence stands exhibited in its brutality, a point that does not escape the notice of the other characters. The problematic of *The Trial*, which turned on the reproof of Joseph K. for seeking the kind of help that experience readily suggests, recurs in *The Castle*, where K. makes love to, and peremptorily takes as his wife, a woman he does not know, except as a sign of her intimacy with a Castle official. 'The closeness of Klamm had made her so absurdly alluring, with this allure she had drawn K. to her, and now she was withering in his arms' (C, pp. 289–90; translation modified). Love-making, then marriage, becomes a means to advance him along his way: the woman is the pawn in this struggle.

It is impossible to avoid seeing in this a moment of Kafka's auto-critique: he knew that he had bound himself to women at least in part to secure an effective sign of the nourishment he needed in order to stay sane enough to write. But part of his admirable coolness is to complicate this relation so that there comes to light a law that he intuits and codes often in his writing: the writer, the anguished ascetic, like the accused man in *The Trial*, is attractive to women, who in making love to these martyrs, make love to the suffering quester in them.

In coming to a conclusion about Kafka's novels, one should not fail to note the wildly comic strain that runs throughout them. Kafka reported that when he read his work aloud to his friends, '[I] read myself into a frenzy [...]; Then] we let ourselves go and laughed a lot.'[13] In *The Castle* K. is distracted by his twin assistants Arthur and Jeremiah. This legacy of the madcap helpers survives in the vernacular: a German journal gave this account of a Monty Python gig:

> Equally sad and dotty, for example, is the scene with the African explorer who sees everything in twos. Departing from the two Nairobis, this ocular defective proposes to climb both Kilimanjaros. Alerted to his infirmity, it now dawns on him why the expedition, consisting entirely of twins, whom he sent ahead of him a year ago, still hasn't returned: they were given the job of building a bridge from the first to the second Kilimanjaro.[14]

Every detail in this squib, upon substituting the Castle for Kilimanjaro, holds true of Kafka's novel. This is one sort of marker – there are graver ones – of its compelling modernity. The impossibility of stipulating and finding the right degree of difference between human aspirations and the clumsy machinery of life will issue into bizarre accidents of congruity, of unsuspected resemblances between high and low: here is a genuine source of Kafka's fiction. At the same time the factor of specious identity, being a kind of wit, must come forth, from time to time, as exhilaration, humour and play.

NOTES

1. Kafka did, however, imaginatively centre his literary hopes entirely on Berlin and not at all on Vienna.

2. Another possibility is 'The Man Who Disappeared', the title given to the new translation by Michael Hofmann (1996). This edition includes fragments not previously published in English.

3. Kafka began writing a version of his 'America novel' in late 1911 and then broke it off in August 1912; this version has not survived. The text we have arose in autumn 1912; Kafka worked on it off and on until October 1914.

4. Franz Kafka, *America*, trans. Edwin Muir and Willa Muir (London, 1938), p. 52. Translation modified.

5. Mark Anderson has developed this point in 'Kafka in America: notes on a travelling narrative', in his *Kafka's Clothes: Ornament and Aestheticism in the Habsburg Fin de Siècle* (Oxford, 1992), pp. 98–122.

6. Franz Kafka, *Der Verschollene*, in Franz Kafka, *Gesammelte Werke in zwölf Bänden. Nach der Kritischen Ausgabe (KKA)*, ed. Hans-Gerd Koch (Frankfurt am Main, 1994), II, 60. Subsequent references to this edition will use the abbreviation '*V*'.

7. *The Diaries of Franz Kafka 1914–1923*, ed. Max Brod, trans. Martin Greenberg (New York, 1949), II, 132. Translation modified. Subsequent references to this second volume of the translated *Diaries* will use the abbreviation '*D* II'.

8. Franz Kafka, *The Trial*, trans. Breon Mitchell (New York, 1998), p. 3. Translation modified. Subsequent references will use the abbreviation '*T*'.

9. The analysis that follows was first advanced by Clayton Koelb in *Kafka's Rhetoric: the Passion of Reading* (Ithaca, NY, 1989), pp. 43–6, before scholars had access to the manuscript of *The Trial*. In fact, at this juncture in the original manuscript, Kafka repeats the earlier rejected word-choice 'gefangen' ('captured'). This complicates but does not spoil the force of Koelb's argument.

10. Oscar Wilde, 'The decay of lying', in Oscar Wilde, *Selected Writings* (Oxford, 1961), p. 26.

11. Franz Kafka, *The Castle*, in *The Penguin Complete Novels of Franz Kafka* (Harmondsworth, 1983), p. 183 (translation modified). Future references to this edition will use the abbreviation '*C*'.

12. I owe this expression to Geoffrey Waite.

13. Franz Kafka, *Letters to Felice*, ed. Erich Heller and Jürgen Born, trans. James Stern and Elizabeth Duckworth (Harmondsworth, 1978), p. 322.

14. *Der Spiegel*, 1991, no. 30, p. 167.

FURTHER READING

Boa, Elizabeth, *Franz Kafka: Gender, Class and Race in the Letters and Fictions* (Oxford, 1996)

Corngold, Stanley, *Franz Kafka: the Necessity of Form* (Ithaca, NY, 1988)

Miller, Eric, 'Without a key: the narrative structure of *Das Schloß*', *German Quarterly*, 66, 3 (1991), 132–40

Neumeyer, Peter (ed.), *Twentieth-Century Interpretations of 'The Castle': a Collection of Critical Essays* (Englewood Cliffs, NJ, 1969)

Pascal, Roy, *The German Novel* (London, 1965)

Politzer, Heinz, *Parable and Paradox* (Ithaca, NY, 1962)

Preece, Julian (ed.), *The Cambridge Companion to Kafka* (Cambridge, 2002)

Robertson, Ritchie, *Kafka: Judaism, Politics, and Literature* (Oxford, 1985)

Rolleston, James (ed.), *Twentieth-Century Interpretations of 'The Trial': a Collection of Critical Essays* (Englewood Cliffs, NJ, 1976)

Sheppard, Richard, *On Kafka's Castle* (New York, 1977)

Sokel, Walter, 'The three endings of Josef K. and the role of art in *The Trial*', in Angel Flores (ed.), *The Kafka Debate: New Perspectives for our Time* (New York, 1977)

Spilka, Mark, *Dickens and Kafka: a Mutual Interpretation* (Bloomington, 1963)

Sussman, Henry, *Franz Kafka: Geometrician of Metaphor* (Madison, 1979)

6

RUSSELL A. BERMAN

Modernism and the *Bildungsroman*: Thomas Mann's *Magic Mountain*

Thomas Mann's *Der Zauberberg*, published in 1924 (the translation *The Magic Mountain* appeared in 1927) describes how a talented if somewhat simple young bourgeois of Hamburg, Hans Castorp, postpones his internship in a shipbuilding firm in order to visit his cousin Joachim Ziemssen, a patient with tuberculosis in the Berghof sanatorium in Davos. Castorp has planned on a comfortable three-week visit; he ends up staying for seven years, and with him the reader of this *magnum opus* is confined within the institution and the nearby countryside for hundreds of pages. Yet the copious attention that Mann devotes to life among the moribund and the convalescent – including Castorp who, soon after his arrival, is diagnosed with a not inconsequential problem in his lungs – does not produce a novel which one could accurately describe as being 'about' a sanatorium. On the contrary, *The Magic Mountain* is about Castorp's growth and transformation, his 'heightening' or 'transsubstantiation', to use the novel's own categorical terms, in a context, the sanatorium, populated by an array of characters constituting an allegory of European culture on the eve of the First World War. It is, in other words, about Castorp's education and can therefore be usefully discussed within the tradition of the novel of education, the German *Bildungsroman*.

That genre designation derives from lectures by the early nineteenth-century critic Karl Morgenstern who pronounced that 'a work will be called a *Bildungsroman* first and primarily on account of its content, because it depicts the hero's *Bildung* as it begins and proceeds to a certain level of perfection, but also secondarily because, precisely by means of this depiction, it promotes the *Bildung* of the reader to a greater extent than any other type of novel'.[1] The implied dialectic between thematic representation (the story of the hero's growth) and aesthetic reception (the reader's experience) stages fundamental assumptions of a German bourgeois credo in which personal subjectivity, social integration and aesthetic education (to use Schiller's term) constantly reinforce each other. Through the genuine encounter with authentic art, internal life is deepened and enriched which, paradoxically, also allows the individual to share in the objective life of community; aesthetic education, in other words, is the vehicle with which social tensions, conflicts among individuals with inimical private interests, may be overcome.

The *Bildungsroman* participates in this set of cultural assumptions on several levels. It is surely foremost a representation of *Bildung* as change and process, a novel of development, within which initial structures and values are transformed and refashioned. Moreover such change takes place with regard to an overriding assumption of the possibility of improvement or progress towards a goal, i.e. it is not arbitrary or chaotic change but rather a teleological development. This change, however, in external circumstances proceeds through the hero's reflection and the internalisation of experience, suggesting an understanding of education as an activity of an autonomous subjectivity and not as the inculcation of the precepts of some dogma. The novel of *Bildung* as education is therefore an exploration of how the hero – and perhaps the reader – might learn to think independently, gradually rendering the fictional mentors obsolete. Of course, the hero's education, undogmatic as it may appear to be, takes place with reference to a particularly privileged curriculum, works of art or, collectively, culture as canon, and this reveals a further sense of *Bildung*, for it is after all a matter of a specifically aesthetic education. Schiller proposed this trajectory as an alternative to politics, as he recoiled from the Jacobin turn in the French Revolution. The German literary tradition consequently faces the problem of describing a hero's integration into society through education, while simultaneously trying to avoid any specifically political discourse. *The Magic Mountain* casts an ironic glance at much of this: that Castorp is an aspiring engineer collides with the aesthetic predilections of the genre and draws the reader's attention to the question of the fate of traditional culture in the technological twentieth century; and for all of the cultural profundity of the sophisticated conversations in the novel, it moves, inexorably, towards the crudely political catastrophe of August 1914.

The reader of *The Magic Mountain* therefore does well to give some thought to this three-fold meaning of *Bildung* as development, internal growth and culture. At the same time, it is worth considering why narratives of personal growth seem to be a preferred subject of the novel, at least in Germany. The literary critic Georg Lukács offered a particular sort of answer in his *Theory of the Novel*, in which he argues that the novel or 'epic' as genre attempts to provide a representation of an extensive totality, by which he means that its material ought to be wide ranging, in contrast to the single moments of conflict he associates with drama or the inward orientation of lyric poetry. Yet to transform the plenitude of worldly experience into the cohesive form required by art, i.e. to structure a totality, is an extraordinary challenge, which Lukács places in a historico-philosophical frame. Homer, so he argues, was able to present a unified world in his epics of antiquity because the world was still whole, and meaning was immanent in the things themselves. In contrast, the experience of modernity entails disruption, confusion and alienation: the freedom we have gained is paid for with metaphysical homelessness. For a novel to encompass, as a coherent form, a world that is innately chaotic, Lukács notes that the genre may choose to focus on a single biography simply as an organisational device: the individual searches for meaning in a world which, however, is ultimately meaningless. The appropriate stance of the narrator of the novel reporting on this always hopeless search is therefore one of irony.

The Theory of the Novel, with its neo-Hegelian history of aesthetic form, dates from 1916. Within a few years, however, Lukács would propose answers to alienation very different from narrational irony and fictive biography. As war and revolution swept through Europe, this son of a prominent Hungarian banker moved quickly to the political left, discovering Marxism, and publishing, in 1923, *History and Class Consciousness*, a classic of Marxist philosophy (even though its Hegelian abstraction made it of little use for the communist orthodoxy that had already begun to harden its own thinking and which quickly suppressed the work). This background is especially interesting for readers of *The Magic Mountain*, and not only because of the light it sheds on the status of the biographical hero, Castorp, in the midst of his rarefied world in Davos. One of his mentors, the Jesuit Naphta, is modelled on the communist Lukács: his contempt for capitalist society is bolstered both by a nostalgia for the premodern world and a messianic hope in a radical revolution. Naphta's mixture of reaction and radicalism is countered by the voice of reason, Castorp's first teacher, Settembrini, who preaches progress, civilisation and humanity. Much of this novel of ideas involves debates between these two figures who, eventually, rent rooms in the same boarding house run – here a small joke of Mann's – by a tailor named Lukaçek.

Approaching the *Bildungsroman* as the individual hero's search for meaning, one can place *The Magic Mountain* in a literary tradition that reaches back into the Middle Ages with Wolfram von Eschenbach's *Parzival* from the first decade of the thirteenth century. While some may quibble over whether this medieval verse epic is properly treated as a novel, its narrative structure clearly anticipates structural aspects which became characteristic of the genre. For the central search to become credible, the hero Parzival, like his latter-day successor Castorp, loses his father early, leading to a situation of greater disorientation as well as, perhaps, greater spiritual freedom. A plethora of mentors then appears in Wolfram's courtly and mythical world, just as the trajectory of the hero is highlighted through contrasts with the vicissitudes of various companions: Parzival's Gawan anticipates Castorp's Ziemssen. Yet it is in the very substance of Parzival's search, his quest for the Holy Grail, the sublime knowledge of divinity, that the terms of the genre are most clearly established. Of course not every *Bildungsroman* has that same emphatically religious or philosophical scope; nevertheless the search for meaning is always, ultimately, a search for God – even if for the moderns it takes place in a godless world – and it is precisely this proximity of *The Magic Mountain* to *Parzival* which Mann himself conceded: the hero, he writes, 'is forever searching for the Grail – that is to say, the Highest: knowledge, wisdom, consecration, the philosopher's stone, *aurum potabile*, the elixir of life'.[2] At its source, then, the *Bildungsroman* derives from the Christian narrative of the journey of the soul towards salvation, and this heritage is resonant even when Mann traces Castorp's *via dolorosa* in his own characteristically post-Nietzschean and mythological landscape.

Yet the construction and refinement of the individual is certainly more properly a modern rather than a medieval topic, and it can be traced through various works of the early modern era. In Jörg Wickram's *Der Knabenspiegel* (1554; A Lesson for Boys), the poor son of a peasant succeeds through hard work and perseverance, while his counterpart, a profligate aristocrat, squanders his gifts and patrimony. In an atmosphere of Reformation-era didacticism and moralising, the narrative of personal progress unfolds as a lesson for emulation by the reader. In contrast, Hans Jakob Christoffel von Grimmelshausen's *Der abenteuerliche Simplicissimus Teutsch* (1669; The Adventurous Simplicissimus, 1912) is fraught with questions and doubts about the possible success of the quest. The presumed orphan Simplizius begins without knowledge or social graces, and while he soon acquires schooling in prayer as well as in war, the novel concludes with a baroque despair about the possibility of individual happiness, far from the teleological resolution which an overly simplistic understanding of the *Bildungsroman* as genre might expect. The bourgeois harmony of education and subjectivity and the prospects of a secure and stable existence are out of place in this picaresque frame. Simplizius curses the world, chooses the life of a hermit, and looks forward to death. Interestingly, a polarity of life and death – this time in the post-Christian guise of optimistic progressivism versus a Romantic fascination with death – also structures Mann's novel, uncovering a pessimistic undertone with deep roots in the history of a genre otherwise associated with a confident sense of progress.

Christoph Martin Wieland's *Agathon* (1767) sets the standard for the modern *Bildungsroman* in that it is now the internal spiritual growth of the hero which is the clear concern of the novel, and not the sort of external adventures which occupied Parzival and Simplizius (no matter how allegorical their significance). Taking place in Greek antiquity, the narrative traces Agathon's development, especially his passage from youthful enthusiasm to a wisdom of mature resignation. The 'things of this world' are not so much impediments, as for Grimmelshausen, as objects which are internalised, appropriated, and comprehended by the hero's psychology. Henceforth in the genre the external plot is genuinely secondary to the transformation of inner life, which is the processual understanding of *Bildung*. This structure of internalised biography found its fullest expression in one of the grand works of German literature, Johann Wolfgang von Goethe's *Wilhelm Meisters Lehrjahre* (1795/6; *Wilhelm Meister's Apprenticeship*, 1858).

Wilhelm is a merchant's son, destined for a pedestrian merchant's life but endowed with a powerful imagination and filled with yearnings for spiritual growth. His prosaic brother-in-law Werner remains bourgeois through and through, while Wilhelm, infatuated with an actress, moves inexorably towards a life in the theatre. If he cannot acquire the perfection of refinement reserved for the aristocracy, he can at least attempt to achieve its illusion on the stage. Yet life with a travelling troupe has its own disappointments, while at the same time Wilhelm comes into contact with different aristocratic groups, most importantly the secret Society of the Tower (Turmgesellschaft), replete with Masonic trappings and a programme of enlightened progress. By the end of the novel, it becomes clear that the Society of the Tower has been guiding Wilhelm from the start, educating him towards a role as a productive and influential member of society.

The novel appears to follow a Hegelian path of progress in the hero's search for an identity: from the narrow confines of mercantile parochialism through the illusions and delusions of art to the objectivity of maturity, power and social station. More than its predecessors, *Wilhelm Meister's Apprenticeship* is able to intertwine external circumstance and internal development in a single trajectory, a unity of subject and object, form and content. For example, the hero's sojourn in the world of theatre revolves around his seminal interpretation of *Hamlet*, the performance of which depends in an important way on a mysterious appearance of the ghost of the father, just as Wilhelm endeavours to clarify his relationship both to his own family background and his son Felix: the question of identity is phrased in terms of paternity. Given the extensive discussion of pietist theology, the novel could lend itself to a teleological reading as a description of *Bildung* as a pilgrim's progress, a rebirth and passage from a natural family, in the middle class, to the spiritual fathers of the Society of the Tower, and much of the reception history has indeed assumed that Wilhelm successfully completes this straight and narrow path of education. Nevertheless there are many signs in the text warning the reader to reserve a healthy scepticism towards a model of educational progress that is too peremptory or linear.

Much as Wilhelm wants to escape his bourgeois background, he is barred from entry into the inherited nobility, despite his adventures on its margins. The world of the Society of the Tower, which accepts him, includes aristocratic members, but its class character remains ambivalent. This solution might be taken as an indication of the particular social history of Germany where – as an alternative to the radicalism of the French Revolution – Goethe in Weimar proposes a moderate compromise between the classes. Yet the very moderation and pedagogic reasonableness of the Society turns quickly into a self-parodying sententiousness (not unlike the oratorical excesses of the incorrigibly rationalist Settembrini in *The Magic Mountain*), suggesting that the initiation into the Society is hardly an unproblematic or utopian conclusion. On the contrary, the progress towards the Society has required considerable sacrifices, renunciations of youthful illusion and the demise of the figures of pleasure and imagination, notably Philine and the Harpist. In other words, if the novel, on one level, appears to celebrate education and identity formation, it simultaneously exposes the costs of maturity, a striking anticipation of Freudian notions that civilisation and discontent go hand in hand. It is no wonder that the Romantic critic Friedrich Schlegel welcomed *Wilhelm Meister's Apprenticeship* as one of the fundamental events of the age (alongside the French Revolution and Fichte's philosophy), and that it also elicited a series of Romantic novels of education which were prepared to lend even greater credence to the temptations of passion and imagination, which Wilhelm, for better or for worse, was able to renounce: Tieck's *Franz Sternbalds Wanderungen* (1798), Hölderlin's *Hyperion* (1799), Novalis's *Heinrich von Ofterdingen* (1802) and Jean Paul's *Titan* (1802). Where Goethe's representation of the educational programme balanced pedagogical optimism with underlying doubts, the Romantic novelists raised even greater questions about the possibility of reconciling individual aspirations with the presumed imperatives of social rationality.[3]

In the context of changing social and economic conditions, nineteenth-century fascination with the prospects of individualism led to various novelistic redefinitions of the programme of *Bildung*. Gustav Freytag's *Soll und Haben* (1855; *Debit and Credit*, 1857), a bestseller of the era, describes the growth and success of Anton Wohlfahrt within the commercial bourgeoisie, i.e. precisely the class which Wilhelm Meister tried to escape. This inversion is characteristic of the contemporary rejection of the Classic–Romantic era, which mid-century writers regarded as lacking the sort of realism that became current after the defeat of the 1848 revolution. Anton grows through

capitalism, rather than against it, and Freytag contrasts him with the incompetence of aristocrats and the unlimited venality he ascribes to the Jewish
figures. The duality of the positive hero and his counterpart, Veitel Itzig,
a paradigm for subsequent anti-Semitic caricature, represents a particular
variant of the *Bildungsroman*'s predilection for setting off its hero through
a foil.

Gottfried Keller's *Der grüne Heinrich* (1854–5 and 1879–80; *Green Henry*,
1960) seems considerably closer to Goethe's model, because the hero,
Heinrich Lee, like Wilhelm, struggles with initial artistic aspirations: not
as an actor, however, but as a painter. *Bildung* is therefore still part of an
emphatically aesthetic education, and as with Wilhelm, the artistic phase is
eventually surpassed, although the tone and Heinrich's entrance into the civil
service are marked by a considerable degree of resignation. Still the novel also
entails a celebration of sensualism and worldliness, associated with the philosophy of Ludwig Feuerbach, which underscores its particular modernity.

In Adalbert Stifter's *Der Nachsommer* (1857; Indian Summer), young
Heinrich Drendorf, hiking through the Austrian countryside, chances on
the estate of Baron von Risach who, in lengthy disquisitions, becomes the
mentor in Heinrich's education. Yet the dynamic development of growth inherent in the genre gives way to a fascination with stability and permanence
more characteristic of a utopian novel. Indeed even if it is Heinrich who is
the student in the narrative, he changes little, while we eventually do learn
about Risach's background; *Der Nachsommer* gives expression to a desire
for permanence as a response to the painful memories of the Romanticism
of the first half of the century. Whether it is a matter of artistic appreciation or the economy of agriculture, Risach imposes an unyielding order of
form, as if endeavouring to put off decay and halt the passage of time. While
twentieth-century criticism has appreciated *Der Nachsommer* as a formally
innovative novel and an anticipation of later aestheticism, it found little
interest let alone acclaim among Stifter's contemporaries.

The novels of Freytag, Keller and Stifter represent the high-points of the
German *Bildungsroman* in the era of realism, and, different as their particular
solutions may be – the celebration of capitalism in Germay, the mature resignation in Swiss democracy, and the conservative aestheticism in Austria –
all focus on the progressive development of the individual and the integration of individuality into social obligation. This ultimately optimistic stance
became problematic in the era of modernism. The term 'modernity' generally refers to social structures and values oriented towards norms of reason,
rather than unquestioned dogma or tradition; with reference to European
history, 'modernity' is taken to describe the period since the end of the Middle Ages, with the rise of humanism and scientific expectations. In contrast,

'modernism' usually refers to the innovative artistic and literary movements in the decades around 1900, as well as some of the intellectual precursors, which intended to shock the contemporary public, call conventional taste into question and thereby question other wider-reaching assumptions. The simultaneity of artistic modernism and major political upheavals, notably the revolutions in the wake of the First World War, led to some implied linkages between aspirations for a new world and programmes for a new art. Modernism has therefore always been susceptible to political readings: the end of nineteenth-century bourgeois conventionalism was greeted by various intellectuals, in often contradictory political registers – from the right and from the left – in terms that assumed a deep-seated crisis in the prevailing social order. Early on Marx announced the demise of bourgeois social forms, Nietzsche dissected the untenability of Christianity, and Ibsen held bourgeois hypocrisy up to public view. The aestheticists, Oscar Wilde and Stéphane Mallarmé, Stefan George and Gustav Klimt, turned their back on bourgeois objectivity and, *mutatis mutandis*, on aspirations of progress. Freud and Einstein revolutionised the interior and exterior worlds, while communism and fascism appeared to render individuality a relic of a bygone era. Yet if modernism ignites a crisis of individuality, is the *Bildungsroman* still possible? The answer is *The Magic Mountain*.

A narrative of individual development depends centrally on a concept of time in which progress can freely unfold, yet it is precisely this notion of 'empty, homogeneous time', as Walter Benjamin put it, that is questioned by modernism: by Nietzsche's notion of an eternal return, by Freud's insights into the longevity of infantile experiences, and by Einstein's theory of relativity.[4] Even more importantly, perhaps, the optimism inherent in the developmental structure of time could hardly survive the carnage of the First World War. It is therefore noteworthy that the war appears at the beginning and the end of the novel: at the end, as already noted, Castorp has descended from Davos to the fields of Flanders, and we find him on the battlefield with an uncertain future; at the beginning, in the foreword, the narrator underscores the fact that the novel takes place 'before the epoch when a certain crisis shattered its way through life and consciousness and left a deep chasm behind' (p. ix). The novel therefore is examining the prewar project of *Bildung* retrospectively and asking whether it can be rescued, in whatever transformed character, into the postwar world. *The Magic Mountain*, consequently, might also be classified as a *Zeitroman* in a two-fold sense: it is a novel that – with reference to the immediate past – poses fundamental questions about its own time, and it is a novel thematically and structurally concerned with time and its duplicities. While the *Bildungsroman* typically took time for granted in order to describe the difficulties of growth, *The*

Magic Mountain explores the character of time itself: it is a *Bildungsroman* concerned with the very possibility of the *Bildungsroman* after the shock of the Great War and given the new sense of time associated with modernism.

The reader's attention is drawn repeatedly to the question of time. The new arrival at Berghof plans to stay for only three weeks, but he soon discovers that the residents count in units of time no smaller than a month, as Settembrini puts it. Eventually Castorp himself grows accustomed to using the term 'just the other day' ('neulich') to refer to events in the distant past. The narrator plays with the differences between narrated and real time, and between subjective and objective experiences of time. Indeed the overarching structure of the novel flaunts an accelerating compression: as progress slows, time flies. The third chapter describes Castorp's first day in the sanatorium; the fourth chapter his first three weeks; the fifth concludes the seventh month, while the sixth and seventh complete the seven years.[5] The theme is further enriched by the unpredictabilities of the seasons, with snow in the summer and bright sun in the winter, as well as Castorp's own meditations on astrology, astronomy and the course of the earth around the sun.

The complexity of time in *The Magic Mountain* depends on a further component, Mann's deployment of the leitmotiv as a device to characterise individual figures as well as complexes of ideas. Particular terms, linked initially to a character, may recur later, sometimes in new contexts, in order to revive the association with the original context. It has been frequently noted that this compositional technique has much in common with Wagner's music, which Mann so appreciated; in any case, the leitmotivic repetition establishes a certain temporal permanence which undercuts any superficial notion of historical progress. For the past is not at all past and forgotten but recurs, on the contrary, in the present, reasserting itself, albeit in new and unexpected ways. The most salient examples have to do with Clavdia Chauchat, the mysterious and enchanting woman who so fascinates Castorp. She is described, repeatedly, as letting doors slam behind her: a habit that annoys the certainly too fastidious and well-behaved Castorp (the novel shows how this dislike is transformed into love) and which simultaneously characterises Clavdia as slovenly and undisciplined, terms which quickly undergo a dialectic inversion and take on the meaning of freedom.

While the slamming door echoes through the novel in order to point again to this complex of issues, Clavdia is linked to a particularly dramatic repetition of leitmotivic permanence. She is a Russian, with a Central Asian physiognomy and 'Kirgiz' eyes which seem to have a particular allure for Castorp. In a visionary scene, he comes to understand that those eyes remind him of an acquaintance from his young years at school, Pribislav Hippe, whom he admired and from whom he once borrowed a pencil. Hippe's admonition to the young Castorp to return his pencil is repeated, verbatim, two hundred pages later, by Clavdia in the Walpurgis-Night section, where Castorp casts conventionality aside and declares his love. The repetition of the sentence breaks through the empty continuum of time, rendering the past and present congruent, if only for a single mystical moment. The device certainly highlights the intellectual integration of the novel, but, more importantly, it shows Mann exploring a construction of time in which permanence and change, myth and progress, intertwine, rather than representing incompatible alternatives. Progress is never unambiguous, since archaic material may always reappear; conversely the return of the past is not necessarily reactionary, since it may be associated with the most advanced stages of progress. Clearly the simple time-lines of nineteenth-century thinking have become much more complex. Intellectual historical comparisons might be drawn to modernist authors, such as Joyce, fascinated with myth, or to modern painters and their primitivist borrowings.

Castorp's own temporal coding is ambivalent from the start. At the end of the second chapter, which reviews Castorp's family background and youth, the narrator reports how the citizens of Hamburg might have wondered if Castorp would become a conservative or a progressive in the city's Senate. On the one hand, his legacy and his resemblance to his grandfather seemed to predict a backward-looking orientation and a loyalty to tradition; on the other hand, as an engineer, he seemed to be linked to the forces of science, change and reason. If Castorp was, at the age of twenty-three, a 'still unwritten page' (p. 36), this indeterminacy is of course exactly the precondition of the novel of education: it is in the magic mountain – the reference is to the myth of Tannhäuser's sojourn in the Venusberg – that the opposing forces would battle over the young soul in the form of two teachers competing for the student.

The case for reason and progress is argued by Castorp's first mentor, Settembrini. With the conservatism and propriety of his Hamburg background, Castorp is at first put off by the voluble liberalism of the Italian intellectual. Yet even as he comes to appreciate Settembrini's attention and rhetorical elegance, he retains a certain sceptical distance, developing his own intellectuality, while delighting in his discovery of faults in Settembrini's glib logic. As a description of the intellectual world before 1914, the novel's portrayal of Settembrini is an incisive account of the nineteenth-century faith in progress, with its unbounded optimism and its curious contradictions: for all of Settembrini's humanism and internationalism, there is no doubt in his mind that Italy should be willing to go to war for the Brenner border.

Settembrini is the incarnation of enlightenment; when Castorp, bedridden, is musing about Clavdia, his mentor enters the room unexpectedly and switches on the electric light. The leitmotivic echo of this scene takes place in a seance in the section entitled 'Highly questionable', when it is Castorp, for once truly Settembrini's student, who reaches to the light in order to dispel the appearance of a ghost. Science should triumph over superstition, progress should triumph over oppression, and life will triumph over death: this is the credo of Settembrini's liberalism, and his pedagogical mission therefore involves rescuing Castorp for life. For he recognises Castorp to be 'life's delicate child' (p. 308), threatened by death and its seductiveness.

As a child, Castorp encountered several deaths in his family, hence his nearly congenital fascination with death, the expression of which is disease. The trope underlying the fiction is that disease and death provide access to a higher knowledge; deriving from religious assumptions about the nobility of suffering, the Romantic tradition regarded enlightenment progressivism as superficial, and searched instead for connections between faith, beauty and death, culminating in the decadence of the late nineteenth century. The case for a reactionary Romanticism is argued by Settembrini's opponent, Naphta, through whom Mann is able to expose the limits of conventional liberalism. Yet Naphta, for all his brilliance, cannot present a fully credible position: his paeans to suffering are ultimately as unconvincing as Settembrini's projects to end all suffering. The novel, playing the two positions out against each other, exposes the inadequacy of each. Mann's irony is directed at both, since no single answer is adequate. Naphta's communism is belied by the luxury of his dwellings; Settembrini's humanism is undercut by his own name, recalling the Jacobin September of 1793.

If the *Bildungsroman* since *Agathon*, if not earlier, tended to lead the hero through distinct stages, a large section of *The Magic Mountain* entails a dialectical oscillation between Settembrini and Naphta, with Castorp, the unwritten page, learning from both, while deciding for neither. The modernist novel of education relies less on a linear teleology than on a representation of a problematic constellation. The hero's acquisition of knowledge, i.e. the process of education, is consequently less a matter of growth than of analytic perspicacity within a static field of contradictions. The constellation towards which *The Magic Mountain* points finds an initial expression in the heated conversation between Castorp and Clavdia during the costume party in the Walpurgis-Night chapter (replete with references to Goethe's *Faust*), but it becomes clearest perhaps in the section entitled 'Snow'.

Castorp has gone off on a skiing tour one afternoon and is caught in a sudden blizzard. Finding shelter under the roof of a mountain hut, he is lost in a daydream. At first he is delighted by a vision of a Mediterranean scene of brilliant nature and beautiful humanity, but behind this classical civilisation, hidden in a temple, he discovers a horrible secret of ugliness and human sacrifice. In this spiritual climax of the novel, the dialectic of two competing principles comes to the fore in a manner that illuminates the whole pedagogical enterprise. He has taken Settembrini at his word, ventured out into nature and away from the moribund decadence of the sanatorium, but he has also ventured into the unknown, tempting death, in a way the rationalist would surely not countenance. Yet it is through this foolhardy adventure, in which he has risked all, that he gains the insight of the dream: the point is not that culture is a mere veneer beneath which a genuine truth of horror lurks – that would lend an ultimate superiority to the force of death. Instead there is a balance; civilisation and culture are celebrated as achievements, despite death, but their glory certainly does not banish destruction from existence. The metaphysics is akin to Nietzsche's *Birth of Tragedy* and the interplay between Apollonian and Dionysian forces (before commencing *The Magic Mountain*, Mann had explored that Nietzschean problematic in *Der Tod in Venedig* (1912; *Death in Venice*, 1932), to which *Magic Mountain* was initially conceived as a small companion novella). The dialectic vision describes Settembrini and Naphta as opposites dependent on each other; progress and reaction, life and death are inseparable from one another, rather than alternatives between which one must choose.

Nevertheless, the vision in the snow marks a subtle turning point in Castorp's development. From the start, he had been moving, sometimes slowly, sometimes accidentally, away from the propriety of life in Hamburg towards disease and irrationality; fundamental assumptions regarding individuality were being called into question, not least through the experience of psychoanalysis – a crucial component of the intellectual history of modernism – which he encountered in the sanatorium. With the insight from 'Snow', however, a reversal commences, and Castorp begins to move towards life and a new sort of responsibility. The friendship with Mynheer Peeperkorn, the dominant figure of the second part of the book, represents an allegory of an initiation into the mysterious rites of a celebration of life. Castorp's progress can be measured through a comparison between Peeperkorn and the earlier mentors. For Mynheer mixes attributes of Bacchus and Christ, the suffering God of life, who gives Castorp a maturity and magnanimity he surely lacked when he first arrived in Davos. In contrast, Settembrini's Freemasonry and Naphta's Jesuitism seem sectarian and crudely conspiratorial, lacking the overwhelming and profound humanity Castorp now inherits. It is also through Peeperkorn that Castorp's passion for Clavdia is sublimated and transformed into a life-affirming friendship, based on his knowledge of death, no longer a debilitating fascination. Instead of either celebrating irrationality, as Naphta suggested, or, following

Settembrini, repressing it, which would only guarantee its underlying power, Castorp has matured by harnessing it in the wisdom of a humane knowledge.

It is useful to know that Peeperkorn's physiognomy is a portrait of the German author Gerhart Hauptmann, whom Mann had recently celebrated as the 'King of the [Weimar] Republic'.[6] Mann's own support for the young republic, after the fall of the Kaiser, had disappointed conservatives, for during the war years Mann himself pleaded the case for a conservative, Romantic Germany as a superior alternative to the rationalist civilisation of the western democracies. Yet the experience of the war itself, with its mobilisation of the nation, and the collapse of imperial Germany, forced Mann to come round to supporting the new democratic state. During the 1920s, he spoke out repeatedly in its defence and against the opponents on the right with their nostalgic dreams of a return to the Kaiser and an older era. *The Magic Mountain* gives expression to these concerns, representing a novel of education of Germany, and not only of one young man.

Castorp is torn between Settembrini and Naphta, progress and reaction, but before Naphta's arrival at the beginning of the second volume, the opposition is played out between Settembrini and Clavdia. Again and again, we see the mentor convey his disapproval of Castorp's attraction to her, and the hostility is clearly mutual, as we learn in the conversation in the Walpurgis-Night chapter. On one level, this tension is an allegory of reason and desire. On another, however, Settembrini makes it clear that a geographical and cultural divide is at stake. He claims for himself the principles of occidental civilisation – reason, order and clarity – while he attributes to Clavdia and, through her, to the Orient a barbarism of irrationality, dissolution and confusion. The choice between them is not only a function of Castorp's educational process; it is also the German question, i.e. the extent to which Germany is part of the rationalist West or, alternatively, an outpost of an East impervious to enlightenment.

Both versions of German identity are plausible against the background of national history in the nineteenth century, and the choice appears uncannily predictive of the division of Germany after 1945. Is Germany part of the East or the West? The question has even been posed after the unification of 1989–90, with regard to the character of the new Germany and its possible role in world affairs. *The Magic Mountain*, touching on a fundamental issue in German national identity, treats Germany as the *Land der Mitte*, in between East and West and therefore, conservatively perhaps, as the land which eschews extremes. It is this vision which Mann presented in 'Von deutscher Republik' (On the German Republic), the speech in which he praised Hauptmann. For his conservative public, the very notion of a 'German Republic' was anathema and an oxymoron, for they assumed a

German character inimical to republicanism and essentially monarchistic. Mann countered through a demonstration of republican strains in the most Romantic of German writers, Novalis, whom he attempted to link to Walt Whitman, the poet of American democracy. If Novalis could be shown to have harboured republican sympathies, then surely Mann ought to be able to do so as well. Yet the notion of a republic undergoes a subtle transformation in the speech, for a 'German Republic' is contrasted implicitly with western and eastern variants of republicanism: the West is regarded as the site of excessive individualism, and the East as the home of an exaggerated collectivism, while Germany, in the middle, has the potential to balance the principles of freedom and obligation, individualism and community, in the name of an authentic humanism.

The Magic Mountain is the novel of education of Germany towards the democracy of the Weimar Republic. While it certainly encapsulates the intellectual debates of the prewar world, it is written with the postwar resolution in mind, posing the question as to how to integrate the specific German Romantic tradition, the cultivation of interiority, and the fascination with death, with the modern exigencies of freedom and progress. *Bildung* is challenged by new forces of technology; marvellous chapters in the novel describe the experience of the cinema and the phonograph and their consequences for aesthetic experience. The final fantastic scene of Castorp on the battlefield with a Romantic *Lied* on his lips stages the cultural–political questions: is it Romantic Germany that goes to war? can Romanticism survive the war? Hence the novel's own concluding question: 'Out of this universal feast of death, out of this extremity of fever, kindling the rain-washed evening sky to a fiery glow, may it be that Love one day shall mount?' (p. 716). In 1924, the answer is hardly certain, but the project of *The Magic Mountain* is clear: to inquire into the possibility of culture and *Bildung*, despite the carnage of the war, in the same sense that beauty and death could coexist, however tenuously, in the dream in the snow.

Traditional notions of *Bildung* were challenged by the modernist restructuring of time, by the changing character of the 'work of art in the age of mechanical reproduction', and by the experience of the war.[7] *Bildung*, understood as the development of an educated subjectivity, was also threatened by democracy: would the egalitarian societies that appeared to be emerging after the war leave room for cultivated individuals? It is true that Mann would try to redefine democracy in a manner to make it compatible with German cultural traditions, but this was a problem to which he would return so often, one is forced to wonder if he was ever convinced of the success of his efforts. In fact, the novel of aesthetic education was particularly developed in Germany of the eighteenth and nineteenth centuries, while the broader *Gesellschaftsroman*, or novel of society, had less currency there than in other countries. Neither modernist orientations nor the collapse of the German Empire could end the *Bildungsroman*, but it is fair to say that a particular sort of *Bildung*, based on predemocratic political structures and on the economic basis of the German middle class, entered a crisis after the First World War. It is equally fair to say that while the *Bildungsroman* continued – one thinks of Mann's own *Doktor Faustus* (1947) or Günter Grass's *Die Blechtrommel* (1959; *The Tin Drum*, 1963) – the genre has not been as central to German literature in the twentieth century as it was in the nineteenth. *The Magic Mountain* can be taken as an effort to bridge the gap between the individualism of cultivation and the levelling forces of democracy. A last effort? Castorp can still return from the mountain top, rejoin the nation, and attempt to participate in a collective identity that would not require renouncing his own individuality. In contrast, in *Doktor Faustus* the proximity of culture and masses nearly snaps, after the experience of the Third Reich. If in the course of the century, the tension between *Bildung* and democracy has grown greater than *The Magic Mountain* implied, different sorts of explanations are possible.

Perhaps the specific German tradition of *Bildung*, and its expression in the *Bildungsroman*, has dwindled as Germany has grown closer to other western European societies. In this case, one would be treating the genre as an aspect of a diminishing national particularity. Alternatively, *Bildung* itself, with its emphatic insistence on privatistic and non-political constructions of individuality, could be found to be fundamentally premodern, a relic of old Germany, incongruous in a twentieth-century democracy. In either of these two cases, the judgment on the *Bildungsroman* would depend on assumptions implying a deep-seated anachronism, as if *Bildung* had not kept pace with progress.

Another sort of answer is possible however. One might ask if the tensions between education and democracy, culture and country, might be due less to the allegedly dated aspirations of *Bildung* than to the character of modern societies themselves, in which individuals are restricted by the 'iron cage' of professionalism and pressures towards one-dimensionality and conformism.[8] The greater the attraction of mass cultural identities, the more difficult it becomes to speak of individual development. Does Castorp's extraordinary sojourn – seven years in Davos – indicate how unlikely *Bildung* had become and how much it was reserved for a privileged few? The tenuousness of the *Bildungsroman* demonstrates the refusal of society to realise the utopian aspirations it might have inherited through the project of *Bildung*. Can social equality and quality of education be combined? *The Magic Mountain* preserves education as a universal human potential, not merely a bourgeois privilege. For Castorp, like Wilhelm Meister before him, sets out to escape the constrictions of social class, and by proceeding from this foundational moment, the *Bildungsroman* suggests that the education necessary to fulfil the potential of individuality ought to be accessible to all.

NOTES

1. Cited in Hildegard Emmel, *History of the German Novel*, trans. Ellen Summerfield (Detroit, 1984), p. 78.
2. Thomas Mann, 'The making of *The Magic Mountain*', in *The Magic Mountain*, trans. H. T. Lowe-Porter (New York, 1955), p. 725. Subsequent quotations from this edition are included in the text.
3. Cf. Rolf-Peter Janz, 'Bildungsroman', in *Deutsche Literatur: eine Sozialgeschichte*, vol. v, ed. Horst Albert Glaser (Reinbek, 1980), pp. 144–63.
4. Walter Benjamin, 'Theses on the philosophy of history', in *Illuminations*, ed. Hannah Arendt (New York, 1969), p. 262.
5. Hermann J. Weigand, *The Magic Mountain: a Study of Thomas Mann's Novel 'Der Zauberberg'* (Chapel Hill, 1964), pp. 14–15.
6. Thomas Mann, 'Von deutscher Republik', in *Politische Schriften und Reden in Deutschland*, in *Gesammelte Werke* (Frankfurt am Main, 1984), xv, 119.
7. Cf. Walter Benjamin, 'The work of art in the age of mechanical reproduction', in *Illuminations*, pp. 217–51.
8. Max Weber, *The Protestant Ethic and the Spirit of Capitalism*, trans. Talcott Parsons (New York, 1958), p. 181. Cf. Herbert Marcuse, *One-Dimensional Man: Studies in the Ideology of Advanced Industrial Society* (Boston, 1964).

FURTHER READING

Beddow, Michael, *The Fiction of Humanity. Studies in the Bildungsroman from Wieland to Thomas Mann* (Cambridge, 1982)

Berman, Russell, *The Rise of the Modern German Novel: Crisis and Charisma* (Cambridge, MA, and London, 1986)

Dowden, Stephen P., *A Companion to Thomas Mann's 'The Magic Mountain'* (Columbia, SC, 1999)

Foster, John Burt, *Heirs to Dionysus: a Nietzschean Current in European Modernism* (Princeton, NJ, 1981)

Goldman, Harvey, *Max Weber and Thomas Mann: Calling and the Shaping of the Self* (Berkeley, CA, 1988)

Kontje, Todd, *The German Bildungsroman: History of a National Genre* (Columbia, SC, 1993)

Lukács, Georg, *The Theory of the Novel*, trans. A. Bostock (London, 1971)

Minden, Michael, *The German Bildungsroman: Incest and Inheritance* (Cambridge, 1997)

Moretti, Franco, *The Way of the World: the 'Bildungsroman' in European Culture* (London, 1987)

7

GRAHAM BARTRAM AND PHILIP PAYNE

Apocalypse and utopia in the Austrian novel of the 1930s: Hermann Broch and Robert Musil

In 1930, six years after the publication of *The Magic Mountain*, there appeared the first parts of two novels by Austrian writers that were destined to take their place alongside Mann's work as summative achievements of European modernist fiction. Hermann Broch's *1888. Pasenow oder die Romantik (Pasenow the Romantic (1888))* was the first volume of the trilogy *Die Schlafwandler (The Sleepwalkers*, 1932), whose second and third parts were published in 1931 and 1932;[1] Book 1 of Robert Musil's *Der Mann ohne Eigenschaften (The Man Without Qualities*, 1953–60) was followed by a portion of Book 2 in 1933, but the work remained incomplete, a massive fragment, on its author's death in 1942.[2]

Like *The Magic Mountain*, both *The Man Without Qualities* and *The Sleepwalkers* take the First World War as the chronological end-point of their fictional worlds. In Musil's novel, set in Vienna on the eve of its outbreak, the war hovers as a huge irony, a knowledge, shared by author and readers, of the destruction that is about to engulf the traditional social world that its unwitting characters inhabit. Broch's trilogy, whose first two parts *1888. Pasenow oder die Romantik* and *1903. Esch oder die Anarchie (Esch the Anarchist (1903))* are set in 1888 Berlin and 1903 Cologne/Mannheim respectively, locates its third novel *1918. Huguenau oder die Sachlichkeit (Huguenau the Realist (1918))* amidst the débâcle of Germany's defeat. In Musil's and Broch's works the chronological gap of the 1920s separating the fictional world from the time of writing and publication exists as a kind of dead space, obliquely referred to by both of them, but not evoked in its social, let alone political, reality. While, as Russell Berman points out in chapter 6 of this book, Mann's *Magic Mountain* can be seen to contain an implicit hope for the fledgling democracy of the Weimar Republic, such socially grounded optimism is absent from both these Austrian novels. Their historical vantage-point is one suspended between a 'nicht mehr' (no longer) and a 'noch nicht' (not yet), between the end of one era and its values and the beginning of the next, whose contours can be but dimly perceived.

By 1930, Musil was already fifty years old, Broch forty-four. Awkward colleagues and rivals on Vienna's literary scene, they were both driven by an immense intellectual ambition. Confronted by a world in which rapid modernisation had brought with it a profusion of conflicting belief-systems and ideologies, in which the positivistic 'rationality' of mathematics and the physical sciences was increasingly divorced from the 'irrationality' not only of the human emotions but of any kind of metaphysical thought, they each set themselves the goal of achieving an understanding of their fragmented culture that would point a way beyond such sterile dichotomies. They both saw the social and political upheavals of war, revolution and economic crisis as secondary factors;[3] what Broch and Musil experienced as intellectuals was essentially a *cultural* crisis.[4] And at its centre lay Nietzsche's epistemological assertion – liberating for Musil, a source of anguish for Broch – that the notion of 'objective' truth is an illusion, a theological relic: our 'truths' are fictions, self-produced 'systems of happiness and equilibrium' as Musil called them, created by individuals to help them on a tightrope walk over the abyss of nihilism and unmeaning.

Musil and Broch came to fiction by unusual routes – Broch was originally a mathematician and technologist, Musil had first graduated as an engineer, then went on to carry out original research at the very first institute of experimental psychology in the world (in Berlin in the first decade of the twentieth century). Their training in science shaped their approach to creative work (and in fact Musil's novel contains an odd reference to a 'utopia of exactitude', which appears to have been the hero's earlier attempt to shape his life as if he were a scientist conducting an experiment). But to both Broch and Musil the novel, rather than any kind of non-fictional writing, seemed ultimately to offer the best means of grappling with the cultural crisis of modernity. Massive, multidimensional and stylistically heterogeneous (in stark contrast to Kafka's mythical/parabolic visions of modernity), their works combined a detailed fictional representation of modern society and its competing ideologies and worldviews – a kind of Domesday Book of modern culture – with an attempt to capture and comprehend the workings, both 'rational' and 'irrational', of the individual psyche. In their defiance or subversion of many of the conventions of traditional narrative Broch and Musil shocked their readers into an awareness that modern life – in contrast to the nineteenth-century world depicted by Dickens or Balzac – had itself become incoherent and (to quote Musil's hero Ulrich) 'un-narrateable' ('unerzählbar'); but in their conscious structuring of a multiplicity of styles and a multiplicity of 'realities' into an *aesthetic* whole (or at least, in Musil's case, the promise of an aesthetic whole that can be partly reconstructed from his literary papers), they both expressed that longing for 'totality' and 'wholeness' that is a feature of the German novel tradition,[5] and which, at this late 1920s turning-point in that tradition, most clearly distinguishes the novel of classical modernism from its late twentieth-century postmodern counterpart.[6]

Unlike Musil, for whom *The Man Without Qualities* became the project that consumed the rest of his life, Broch went on after *The Sleepwalkers* to produce several other major works of fiction and cultural criticism, including the lyrical, in parts incantatory novel *Der Tod des Vergil* (1945; *The Death of Virgil*, 1945); in this work Broch, using the fictional time-framework of the last eighteen hours in the life of the Roman poet, meditates on the experience of dying, and on the situation of the writer in the last stages of a decaying civilisation. It is, however, in *The Sleepwalkers* rather than in the historical *Death of Virgil* that Broch engages directly with the cultural crisis of his own time, presenting readers with a diagnosis that invites direct comparisons with Musil's work.

Anyone approaching the first novel of Broch's trilogy – *Pasenow the Romantic* – with expectations shaped by *The Man Without Qualities* will immediately be struck by a radical difference of tone and perspective between the two. While, as we shall see, Musil's hero Ulrich shares with his creator a probing, open-minded rationality, one that challenges accepted understandings of 'reality' and invites us to share in this adventure, with Broch's novel we are plunged from the first page into the obsessive and often illogical mindset of a character, Joachim von Pasenow, who is made perpetually anxious by the uncertainty and fluidity of the outside world and of his own body and emotions. In this novel (as in the trilogy's second part, *Esch the Anarchist*) the confused thought-processes of the main character are central, while the role of 'rational' observer is allocated to Joachim's friend, ex-army officer turned businessman Eduard von Bertrand. Vital (as critical thinker) to the trilogy's intellectual schema but not to its action (in *Esch* he looms as a shadowy, larger-than-life presence, and finally commits suicide), Bertrand enacts a resignation of the critical mind in the face of historical reality.

Pasenow narrates a turning-point in the life of its 'hero', an unremarkable young army officer from a minor Prussian Junker family. Joachim, as the younger son, had been predestined for a military career, but following the death of his older brother Helmuth in a duel, he is urged by his father to take over Helmuth's role as *Landwirt* in charge of the family estate. He reluctantly does so, simultaneously giving up a love-affair (only just begun) with Ruzena, a Bohemian woman, for a conventional and financially advantageous marriage to the fair-haired Elisabeth, daughter of the Pasenows' neighbours, Baron and Baroness von Baddensen. Within the framework of this conventional story, however, Broch's third-person narrative draws the reader in provocatively modernist fashion into the struggles of the protagonist's psyche to make sense of what is happening to him. While the external plot is schematic, the inner one traces the interaction in Pasenow's mental world between ill-defined but powerful emotional–existential states – love, fear, longing, obsessive anxiety, feelings of exile and loss – on the one hand and, on the other, the cultural values and symbols with which family and society surround him and from which he constructs his precarious self-image.

Central to Joachim's adult identity at the outset of the novel is his belief in the uniform and the code of honour (*Ehre*) that it symbolises. In a passage of theoretical discourse loosely attributed to Eduard von Bertrand, Broch identifies the 'cult of the uniform' as the pseudo-religion of the age, and highlights – in a way peculiarly relevant to the anxiety-ridden Joachim – the sense of security the uniform offers its wearer as a tangible symbol of order amidst life's chaos (*KW* I, 23–4; *S*, pp. 20–1). But this 'security' is purchased at the price of the demonisation of large areas of reality – not only the body and its unruly urges but also the whole of civilian life. Implicit in Bertrand's discourse here is the Nietzschean recognition that our self-protective 'truths' are but partial (and in Joachim's case rather fragile) fictions. Furthermore, we have just learned – from the disconcerting memories of childhood that surface whenever Joachim goes to meet his father – that as a ten-year-old boy he had in fact found his predestination to a military career nonsensical and unappealing (*KW* I, 13–18; *S*, pp. 11–15). His departure for cadet school, ordained by his father, meant expulsion from his family home and deracination from his childhood world and its warmth, represented above all by the Polish servant girls and Joachim's confidant, the estate's steward Jan. However, with the passage of time, the sense of loss and banishment has been repressed and the uniform imposed by the patriarch has changed its allegiance, becoming for Joachim a means of defining his identity over *against* his father and the now 'treacherous' civilian world the father inhabits.

All that is about to change. Helmuth's pointless death 'for honour', and the obligation laid upon Joachim to take his brother's place in civilian life 'on the land', combine coincidentally with Joachim's experience of erotic self-surrender in his love for Ruzena (*KW* I, 42–5; *S*, pp. 36–40) to destabilise the military self-image he has constructed over the years. In the ensuing inner turmoil, the dominant Prussian Protestant identity that Joachim has grown into is besieged by disturbingly seductive memories of the servant culture of Polish Catholicism that formed such a comforting part of his childhood. The linked 'exotic' notions of Polishness and Catholicism are in turn associated with ideas of the dark and the maternal, all embodied in Joachim's suddenly resurfacing memory of the black-haired Polish cook, and the entrancing Catholic picture of the Holy Family she had shown him as a boy (*KW* I, 129; *S*, p. 115). Reawakened by his love for the dusky Bohemian Ruzena, these subversive memories seem now to threaten not only his already crumbling 'uniform identity' but his psychological fitness for any kind of future role in the Prussian Junker caste. At this moment of crisis, however, Joachim's psychic landscape undergoes a seismic shift: the 'heterodox' Catholic picture, that has risen unbidden to his mind's eye while he is taking part in a military church service, is dissolved by his concentrated inner gaze into its conformist Protestant counterpart (*KW* I, 130; *S*, p. 116). With this, the disruptive memories of childhood are partly annihilated, partly incorporated into a new sense of self in which Protestant religiosity and the institution of marriage assume a new importance alongside the remnants of military 'honour'. This is the belief system with which, in part III, Pasenow will confront the obscene horrors of the World War; for the time being, we are left to contemplate the ironic fact that he has expended so much mental/emotional energy, not in influencing his own fate, but in simply adapting himself to its vicissitudes.

By placing the narrative of *Esch* in 1903, fifteen years after that of *Pasenow*, Broch implies a historical development: a process of social disintegration that was to continue and culminate after a further fifteen years in the chaos depicted in *Huguenau the Realist*. But *Pasenow* and *Esch* are separated not only in time but also in milieu; the social background (and corresponding obsessions) of the thirty-year-old August Esch, a book-keeper on the margins of lower-middle-class life, are far removed from those of the aristocratic young lieutenant. The novel's cast of characters, some living in Cologne, others in Mannheim, includes a 36-year-old widow, 'Mother Hentjen', who runs a bar in Cologne patronised by a clientele (including Esch) that largely disgusts her; the vegetarian and teetotal owner of a cigarette shop, Lohberg, who regards his own merchandise as 'poison' and preaches the physical and moral purification of the German nation; a trade union official, Martin Geyring, whose game leg and crutches earn him the sobriquet of 'the cripple'; a pair of Hungarian variety-performers, Teltscher the knife-thrower and his wordless partner Ilona; and the organiser of the show they are part of, the seedy theatrical impresario Gernerth, with whom Esch and Teltscher go into a short-lived partnership to organise women's wrestling contests, featuring costumes that 'burst' under stress. Esch – crude, sexually promiscuous and endowed with an impetuous temperament – is by no means out of place in this company. Yet the opening incidents of the novel – Esch's unfair dismissal from his job, and his resulting sense of injustice – set in motion a series of inner upheavals that take him and the reader into realms of religious experience, sexual ecstasy and utopian longing that seem markedly at odds with his outward existence.

This apparent disjuncture is however fully intended by Broch. As he made clear in a letter to his publisher's wife, Daisy Brody (5 March 1931; *KW* XIII/I, 130–1), his ambition in *Esch* was to show that religious feeling and utopian hope were not the exclusive preserve of the philosophically literate. Esch's spiritual longings are in fact shaped by their social and historical context: early twentieth-century Wilhelmine Germany, with its growing SPD-led working-class movement, but also its many petit-bourgeois 'reform' sects and groups, each wedded to an exclusive recipe for social and spiritual 'salvation'. While Esch's visions of the cross (and himself as crucified 'sacrifice') are (bizarrely) triggered by the image of the variety-performer Ilona 'crucified' on a blackboard by her knife-throwing partner, his preoccupation with 'Erlösung' (redemption, salvation) is derived from Lohberg's belief that the 'salvation' of the German nation lies in vegetarianism and teetotalism, and from proclamations of 'redeeming love' heard at a street-gathering of the Salvation Army. But in addition to these influences from the sectarian groups around him, Esch's quixotic quest to put the world to rights is shaped by his own impetuous personality, and above all by his book-keeper's mentality and its demand for 'Ordnung' (order). Despite the English translation of the title of Broch's novel, Esch is not so much an anarchist, as someone who increasingly sees anarchy everywhere around him.

In his new quest for salvation, Esch embarks on a sexual relationship with 'Mutter' Hentjen. This is quite unlike his previous, casual, affairs. The challenge presented by Gertrud Hentjen's lack of physical attraction, her locked-away feelings and her attitude of rejection towards all men, including him, fuses in Esch's inner world with his religious obsession with sacrifice and salvation. The moment of Gertrud Hentjen's first sexual climax with him – signalled by her 'hoarse grunting noise' (*KW* I, 286; *S*, p. 255 (translation modified)) – brings Esch a transient but intense experience of 'redemption' – a sense of release from his orphan-like isolation, and a transcendence of the limits of his ego and of time itself. As this unlikely liaison begins to settle into routine and respectability (by the end of *Esch* the pair have got married), and as Esch's utopian dreams of emigrating to America come to nothing, he has to recognise and accept the disjuncture between ideal and mundane reality. But this outcome, as banal as that of *Pasenow*, does nothing to negate the force of what has gone before: the descent into the irrational depths of an ordinary man's psyche and into the 'anarchy' of belief-systems, symbols and half-formed ideologies that in early twentieth-century Germany compete to articulate his existential wants, questions and desires.

In *Esch* (as previously in *Pasenow*) the narrative perspective is overwhelmingly and obsessively that of the main character. *Huguenau*, the final and longest part of the trilogy, abandons this mono-perspectivism in a radical fashion. Set mainly in the year of Germany's defeat, 1918, the third novel does indeed have an eponymous main character, the Alsace-born Huguenau, who arrives in a small town in a tributary valley of the Mosel after deserting from the German army. But his story is only one of a series of interwoven narrative strands, each focused on a different character or group of characters living in the same town. (They include Joachim, now Major von Pasenow, living apart from his wife and surviving son as the town's military commander; and Esch, who has recently inherited the local newspaper.) Two further sequences of chapters, identified by their running titles ('Story of the Salvation Army Girl in Berlin'; 'Disintegration of Values') are interspersed among the others; these are not part of the Mosel narrative at all, but originate with a first-person narrator living in post-First World War Berlin, who is inserted at this late stage into the trilogy's hitherto third-person narrative. At first the connection between these two strands is not clear: 'Disintegration of Values' is a series of 'anonymous' historical/philosophical essays, while the 'Story of the Salvation Army Girl', told in the first person by a Dr Bertrand Müller, looks back at his encounter after the war with the Salvation Army girl Marie and his attempt to foster a relationship between her and Nuchem, one of the Eastern European Jews lodging in the same Berlin apartment block as Müller. Later, however, Müller refers to his philosophical work, in a way that identifies him as the author of the essays as well (*KW* I, 488; *S*, p. 439); and further clues suggest that his structural role in the trilogy is even more far-reaching than this. As well as the name 'Bertrand', Müller shares significant biographical details (revealed in his musings on his past (*KW* I, 617; *S*, p. 558)) with the Eduard von Bertrand who links parts I and II and who committed suicide at the end of *Esch*. It seems at least plausible that Bertrand Müller is constructed by Broch as not only a philosopher but also a novelist, the fictional author of the whole trilogy; and that in Eduard von Bertrand, Müller has in turn created a character whose life and values have much in common with his own.

Müller the philosopher is however also the means whereby Broch introduces himself *in propria persona* into his trilogy. In his essays on the 'Disintegration of Values' (based on theoretical writings that Broch had embarked on in the 1920s, before commencing his novel), and also in the several short 'self-commentaries' he wrote to accompany the publication of *Die Schlafwandler* (reprinted in *KW* I, 719–35), he makes explicit the philosophy that frames his depiction of Pasenow, Esch and Huguenau and their attempts (intense and obsessive in the case of Pasenow and Esch, almost non-existent in the case of Huguenau) to make sense of their lives. Man is in Broch's view a 'value-creating' animal, whose life is an unending struggle to impose meaning upon the flux of external events and inner feelings and drives; but this individual struggle takes place in interaction with society's evolving belief-systems. The title 'Disintegration of Values' refers to the long-term historical trend that Broch – along with many other German thinkers from the Romantics on-wards – saw as governing the evolution of (western) beliefs from the Middle Ages to the twentieth-century present: one of a progressive fragmentation of the medieval Catholic worldview, which had encompassed many different areas of human experience and religious belief within a unified theological whole, into modernity's plethora of 'autonomous' (and often warring) value-systems that makes it impossible for an individual to form a coherent picture of the world (*KW* I, 495–9; *S*, pp. 445–8). What for the postmodern world-view is a value-free or even welcome 'fact' – the loss of totality – is depicted by the modernist Broch in tones of anguish, culminating in an apocalyptic view of the present as a 'zero hour' of total disintegration, in which the God of medieval Catholicism, unifying the sensuous and the metaphysical realms, has been replaced (at the end of a process set in train by the 'rebellion' of Protestantism) by a cold, infinitely distant abstraction: an 'Absolute' drained of all content, and thus powerless to offer hope to the disorientated human being (*KW* I, 578–83; *S*, pp. 523–7). Against this bleak background, Broch, in a bravura 'Epilog', draws hope from a variety of disparate sources, among them a belief in an irreducible 'core' of humanity in each and every individual, and an essentially cyclical view of history that sees the 'zero-point' of the present value-chaos as a necessary stage on the way to a new, as yet indecipherable 'Totalsystem'.

At times, Broch's discourse in the 'Disintegration of Values' essays seems provocatively to identify with the totalising claims of medieval Catholicism – as in the reference to 'that criminal and rebellious age known as the Renaissance' (*KW* I, 533; *S*, p. 480). His own worldview, however, rejects nostalgia for a lost totality as 'Romanticism': a flight from unbearable reality into comforting illusion (*KW* I, 596, 597; *S*, p. 540). In a related sense, not only the 'Romantic' Pasenow but also Esch are 'guilty' of Romanticism – not in a longing for the past, but in seeking an ultimate or 'absolute' meaning in one or other of the increasingly fragmented 'partial' value-systems of the present. As characters caught up willy-nilly in the last stages of the collapse of the old value-system, they are 'sleepwalking' through life, lacking the conceptual tools to make sense of it, and thus condemned to inadequacy. In parts I and II of the trilogy, it is the marginal character Eduard von Bertrand who possesses the rational insight into the historical situation that Pasenow and Esch both lack; but his response is the equally inadequate one of the 'aesthete' who retreats from involvement with others and finally commits suicide. Only Huguenau is described by Broch, with more than a hint of irony, as the 'adequate child of his time' ('Ethische Konstruktion in den *Schlafwandlern*', *KW* I, 726–7 (p. 726)); his 'adequacy' consists in an utter freedom from moral 'baggage' that, together with the survival instinct of a somnambulist, allows him in part III to outwit Major von Pasenow and the town's dignitaries, to murder Esch and rape his wife amidst the social breakdown of November 1918, and to adapt with a ruthless opportunism to the rapidly changing political situation. In his lack of self-understanding he is in Broch's eyes as much of a 'sleepwalker' as Pasenow and Esch; but his inner monologues are not tortuous rationalisations as theirs are, but have the realist's seemingly 'normal' matter-of-factness, whose clipped phrases only occasionally hint at the murderous and lustful impulses lying just below the surface of consciousness.

Within the historical scheme expounded in the 'Disintegration of Values' Huguenau represents a state of 'value-freedom' marking the final bankruptcy of the Catholic-Christian 'Totalsystem'; the 'zero point' that Broch posits as a necessary transition to the gradual emergence of a new worldview. The other Mosel-centred narrative strands of *Huguenau* also depict this historic 'zero point', but in a different way: focused partly on the doctors, nurses and patients in a local military hospital (in particular the poison-gas victim Lieutenant Jaretzki and the reservist Gödicke, who has been buried alive in a collapsed trench), partly on the bourgeois housewife Hanna Wendling, they portray a society in which the still intact forms of communication (snatches of banal conversation between doctors and nurses, for example) mask individuals' largely unspoken inner feelings of meaninglessness, futility and isolation. Hanna Wendling, whose lonely, relatively pampered existence is only briefly interrupted by the home-leave of her soldier husband, experiences a progressive atrophy of the psyche that cuts her off from those around her. Only Gödicke is used by Broch to symbolise the possibility of a new beginning based on that very same reduction to the atomised self: lying in a coma for several days following his rescue, he (a bricklayer in civilian life) embarks on the painful process of reconstructing his identity, visualising himself perched on his mental 'scaffolding' and fixing the haphazardly returning building blocks of personal memory into their proper places (*KW* I, 428; *S*, p. 382).

Broch, far more than Musil, wrote with a sense of the limitations imposed upon his vision by the historical moment – the end of a cultural era – that he was living through. To the present-day reader, who has largely lost sight of the urgent epistemological questions Broch posed, the pathos of the trilogy's closing pages may seem curiously dated. But taken as a whole, *The*

Sleepwalkers, a novel of contradictions rather than monolithic certainties, remains a powerful and eloquent document of the ideological conflicts of the late modernist age, and of one modernist writer's attempt to transcend them.

The plot, or rather plots of *Der Mann ohne Eigenschaften* (*The Man Without Qualities*) – Musil used the work as a vehicle for at least two novels which he had planned in the early 1920s – are hard to follow through the interruptions of narrative commentaries and reflections that reach far wider than the action. Musil uses these commentaries to convey the inadequacy of 'straight-line' narrative. Contemporaries, Musil argued, saw themselves as being at the centre of a story: 'die meisten Menschen sind im Grundverhältnis zu sich selbst Erzähler' ('most people relate to themselves as storytellers') (*MoE*, p. 650; *MWQ*, p. 709). Reality, as we have seen, is fiction. Further, the very stuff of contemporary 'reality' ('Wirklichkeit') is the product of many such narratives merged into one. In one sense *The Man Without Qualities* indicates that Musil, too, wanted to be the narrator of his own life – certainly the core of the novel is built around Musil's experiences. But what marks Musil out from others is the kind of narrative he made. Many contemporary authors wrote novels from a perspective similar to earlier ones. But in so doing they failed to register changes: physicists were opening up the microcosm to human inspection, psychologists were investigating the subconscious, philosophers were charting the limits of the knowable. What had seemed substantial to earlier novelists (and to the majority of novelists in the early twentieth century as well) – the natural order, the social world, the consensus on what constituted acceptable behaviour, together with the language that took such phenomena for granted – all of these were now in doubt. Language and the processes of understanding had moved on, and Musil as a modernist was determined to show how things had changed. To succeed as a novelist one needed a keen mind and wide learning; to portray social life the author had to get behind the surface and work with the principles that experts in many fields had identified – the methodologies of scientists, economists, statisticians and a whole team of different specialists. (Musil was consumed by anger when fellow authors suggested that he was too intelligent to be a novelist. In Musil's view, the task that confronted contemporary novelists presented, very specifically, a challenge to their intelligence.)

Of course, the very intensity of sustained mental effort could indeed (this was a partial explanation for the judgment of Musil's peers) put at risk the acceptability of the work he produced. Could a novel be successful when it was in fact designed to subvert the collective urge to narrate? But this subverter of stories had some good stories to tell! First, the tale of a year in the life of a rich young man, Ulrich von –, in pre-First World War Vienna and his intellectual and sexual adventures; second, Ulrich's involvement with the aristocracy, with entrepreneurs, top civil servants, bankers, military officers, artists, in short with representatives of the social and intellectual elite of Austria, in the 'Parallelaktion' ('Parallel Campaign') – a plan for a whole year of celebrations to mark the occasion (in 1918) of seventy years of peace under the Austro-Hungarian Emperor Franz Joseph (this is supposed to put in the shade Germany's celebrations of a mere thirty years of rule by Kaiser Wilhelm – the irony that the celebrations in each country will coincide with the military defeat which will bring both empires to an end is, of course, to be fully exploited!); third, there is the account of how a simple carpenter, Moosbrugger, comes to murder a prostitute (extensively reported in the press, this incident and the trial of the murderer fascinate the Austrian public and obsess Ulrich and Clarisse, the eccentric and emotionally unstable wife of his friend Walter); fourth, the hero meets his sister, Agathe, whom he has not known since childhood, and powerful emotions are released as the relationship deepens. Good stories, but set in an enterprise that alienated readers from the narrative. The title advertises this feature of the novel.

The label 'man without qualities' has become a literary commonplace. In the narrative of Musil's novel it is first used as a term of abuse by Ulrich's oldest friend, Walter, but Ulrich sees it as a mark of being in touch with the times. He is surrounded by men and women who make a show of knowing who they are, where they are going and where they stand; Ulrich, by contrast, finds within himself no consistent inward responses to external stimuli, no bedrock of selfhood, no moral tablets of stone to provide absolute guidance. There is, in this modern world, no consensus of what it means to be human, no common code to govern behaviour, no single substratum of belief. But to recognise this, to know (where others fail to recognise this shared condition) that we are 'without qualities', is to be a full citizen of the modern world, and to take upon oneself the task of attempting to find a way forward into a new era. Ulrich's task in the narrative, and Musil's goal in the novel, is to find this way.

One feature of Musil's work presents a particular challenge to the reader. Because it was never finished, the architecture of the whole enterprise is difficult to perceive. Broadly, *The Man Without Qualities* falls into two parts corresponding to the two books of the original design. The first of these is a narrative, based in Viennese 'reality' ('Wirklichkeit'), that contains within it two themes designed to expose the fiction of 'reality': first, the intellectual enterprise of the central protagonist, which he calls his 'year's leave of absence from life', second, excursions by the narrator (as it were, by courtesy of the hero's imagination) into the mind of a victim of contemporary Austrian 'reality', the social misfit and man-child Moosbrugger. To this are added moments of mystical intensity, including an account of Ulrich's first passionate love-affair, that are germs of later developments in the novel. The second part is, in the main, a private exploration of the world of spiritual experience beyond 'reality' (the world of the 'Parallelaktion' occasionally intervenes as a satirical background to the main narrative) or, to use the image chosen by the author, a 'journey to Paradise' by lovers, brother and sister, who try to break not only the incest taboo but also the drive towards worldly success, the nexus of personal ambition, envy, lust for power and influence that drives contemporary society and leads it to destruction in the First World War.

Since most readers are unaware of the author's plans for the whole novel, they may be left with an impression of the work as backward-looking and predominantly ironic, even satirical, in tone. In a key chapter towards the end of Book 1, Musil presents, in the shape of an elaborate image, two primal forces that shape all human life; these are 'Gewalt' ('brute force' or 'violence') and 'Liebe' ('love'). Book 1 is under the aegis of 'Gewalt' – it presents the hero on his own, racking his brain to make sense of his life, embroiled in unsatisfactory liaisons, his mind wandering compulsively to contemplate a sex murderer, and watching the constant struggle for influence and control within the 'Parallelaktion' (the literary vehicle through which Musil presents his verdict on the bankruptcy of culture on the brink of war); the predominant mood of Book 1 is indeed retrospective, reviewing the processes that had led mankind to this dreadful pass. Book 2 was designed to provide a counterweight, by looking forward into a future in which the other principle, 'Liebe', came into its own as a guide to the potential for a more harmonious future; however, its unfinished state diminished the impact and left the novel unbalanced.

The novel's long drawn-out creation went hand in hand with an unusually complex process of character construction. Each major figure lived for many years in some corner of the author's mind; Musil would withdraw into himself and, in protracted spells of mental exploration of the individual mindset (inspired by his work before the First World War as a research student with the leading experimental psychologist, Carl Stumpf of Berlin University, who encouraged his students to experiment in this way), remake the figure for the novel. Most of these figures were taken from life. (Arnheim, for example, was based on Walter Rathenau; Musil remoulded this Prussian Jew, entrepreneur, author and polymath, who was later to become Germany's Foreign Minister and was assassinated in 1922, into Ulrich's rival for pre-eminence as leading intellectual at the 'Parallelaktion' gatherings.) But, having inhabited their second creator's mind for such extended periods, it is not surprising that they share attributes and concerns.

Arnheim and Ulrich, for all their rivalry, draw from the same reservoir of feeling. Each vies for influence at the salon of Ermelinda Tuzzi ('Diotima' as Ulrich calls her) where the 'Parallelaktion' participants gather. Ulrich, Arnheim and Diotima all pursue different goals. For Diotima the redemption of society will come about through intensity of feeling alone; and this, the power behind all those moments of aesthetic ecstasy she has ever experienced, she calls 'Seele' ('soul'). For Arnheim, it can only come through exertion of the will, through the domination of the weak by the strong in business, politics and society at large; his watchword is 'Gewalt' ('violence' or 'force'). For Ulrich, inspiration and enlightenment for the future of civilisation comes through exercising the faculty of 'Geist' ('spirit' or 'intellect') that he hopes will control and shape 'Seele', as it will moderate and channel the destructive energies of 'Gewalt'. But when the author probes beneath the surface of the two men and the woman they desire, he discovers that they share a sense of the void at the heart of civilisation. In each, the emotional core of humanity is identical.

The drives of 'Seele', 'Geist' and 'Gewalt' are Musil's shorthand for experiences that his characters have in common. In the making of the novel, Musil works and reworks a given experience and attributes it to characters almost at random. In his youth he had been overwhelmed by empathy with the vision of 'Seele' transmitted by the Danish intellectual and essayist, Ellen Key. But after the first rush of enthusiasm, Musil's innate scepticism returned. While not denying that the emotions which Ellen Key had reawakened for him were powerful and vital, he could not give his whole-hearted support to the conclusions she had drawn. So Musil transferred this experience from his narrative persona, Ulrich, to Ulrich's sensitive but intellectually inexperienced 'alter ego', his sister, Agathe. This, however, was in an early draft stage of the novel. By the time that Book 1 was published some years later, the Ellen Key vision of 'Seele' had been handed on to Diotima and, in the process, injected with teasing irony. Arnheim, for all his external toughness, is transfixed with the experience of faith as transmitted through the medieval sculptures in his private gallery; 'Seele' touches him, too, in the sense that his life is rich in esoteric pleasures but at base void. And Ulrich himself gives 'Seele' some space in his reflective life without allowing the grip of 'Geist' to weaken. Thus, for all the diversity of their personalities and ways of life, Arnheim, Diotima and Ulrich are, at a deeper level, related.

Musil's drafting of the characters in his novel, as we saw earlier, was informed by a process whereby he entered their minds and bodies by extrapolating from emotions that he first experienced in himself. (He felt that this process was more than mere imagining; he was very pleased to discover evidence that some of the thoughts and feelings which he attributed to his fictional figure, Arnheim, were vindicated by revelations of Rathenau's emotional experiences.) The most striking example of his method of creative extrapolation is Musil's construction of Moosbrugger's inner world. The process itself is made manifest in the narrative of Book 1; the reader is able to watch the interaction between Ulrich as obsessive experimenter and Moosbrugger, as Ulrich reads the accounts of the murder, attends the trial to observe the murderer at first hand, then finds himself caught up in involuntary musings on the murderer and pulled along by powerful impulses right through to the point of murder and beyond – the only thing which stops him from sharing the fate of the other man is that the whole sequence takes place entirely in Ulrich's imagination. Ulrich's observations and the intense feelings which accompany them are derived directly from Musil's researches into a Viennese murderer in the period before the First World War that took the author, albeit vicariously, much closer to insanity than might be considered necessary for such a purpose. The account of the murder in the novel is a masterly synthesis of objective knowledge about psychosis, derived from the most up-to-date research of the day, and the exploration of a phobia that Musil dredges up from his own mind and expresses in a language that is precise yet rich in metaphor, complex yet taut, and of a beauty that has rarely been surpassed.

Where did Musil expect this vast undertaking to lead? In a scene towards the end of Book 1 when the 'Parallelaktion' has lost its initial impetus and the leading members are wondering what to do, Ulrich is asked for his advice. What he says, though he has no doubt that it will lead nowhere, has a millennial weight to it – it is no less than the proposal to set up what he calls a 'world secretariat of precision and soul'. It is Ulrich's view that the renewal of civilisation as a whole can only come about through a collective change of heart. His proposal would throw the energies of the 'Parallelaktion' behind an attempt to galvanise concern about the loss of humanity in contemporary society. The interest groups at the 'Parallelaktion' are tokens of this loss since so many promote 'Gewalt' in different forms: business, represented by Arnheim, exploits the baser human qualities; the bureaucracy seeks to perpetuate its self-interest via the repression of centrifugal nationalism in the Empire; the Army moves to subvert pacifism within the 'Parallelaktion' by promoting the development of new improved artillery as its 'big idea'. What lies behind Ulrich's call for such a 'world secretariat'? First, it implies a break with the past, and the replacement of imperial Austrian 'Durchwursteln' ('muddling through') with an exact social-engineering approach to modern culture; second, it proposes to merge approaches which are commonly considered to be mutually exclusive – the application of serious thought to matters of human emotions which businessman, bureaucrat and soldier habitually leave out of account. The proposal has, of course, not the slightest hope of being adopted and is received with diplomatic scorn by Arnheim. However, this absurdly ambitious plan is kept alive, if not in the counsels of the 'Parallelaktion', then at least in the literary undertaking that is the *Man Without Qualities* itself, in which Musil spares no effort to reach a synthesis of the major intellectual activities of the times.

Poised at the start of Book 2, Ulrich, surrounded by the elite of the old dispensation, is Musil's 'New Man', physically strong and attractive to women, hyper-intelligent but highly-strung and lacking direction, sexually promiscuous but looking for the right relationship, 'without qualities' but passionately committed to the search for 'the right way to live', Austrian in origin, adoptive German by cultural and intellectual affinities. Compared to the sister, Agathe, who will be his 'Siamese twin' and better half, he is the more restless, the more knowledgeable, more sure of himself, more critical, but also the more reluctant to take decisions and act; Agathe, a vision of beauty and grace, lacks self-confidence, is less forceful but more intuitive, has a far more retentive memory, and possesses a capacity for spontaneous action that Ulrich admires and cannot match. Each brings to their relationship a sequence of failures with others: Agathe has decided to terminate her present (and second) marriage to a pedantic teacher and writer on education, Professor Hagauer; Ulrich has tried without complete success to detach himself from Bonadea, outwardly a conformist, secretly a nymphomaniac. Both brother and sister, as they enter their new relationship in Book 2, turn away from partners who embody tradition and convention.

Book 2 is at heart the record of this relationship that may seem an unusual vehicle for such a weight of meaning. But it meant much to Musil. He had grown up an only child because his parents' first-born, Elsa, had died in infancy before his birth. He was obsessed with his dead sister and her image was taken up into the figure of Agathe. But the powerful sexual chemistry between the fictional brother and sister (in the published version of the novel they avoid sexual relations) was drawn directly from Musil's own marriage. This provided the 'scientific data', as it were, for the exploration of the relationship of man and woman. (Though their marriage was not without tensions or quarrels, Martha and Robert Musil were virtually inseparable from the time of their first meeting in 1906 until Musil's death in 1942.) Musil seems to attempt to transcend, in this investigation of 'Liebe', the barriers that cut civilised humanity off from emotional reservoirs of feeling whose energies would be needed if mankind were to recover its potential in the mid twentieth century. The love of brother and sister stands for a willingness to challenge received wisdom or, as Musil's teacher, Friedrich Nietzsche, saw this, to break idols.

In exploring this relationship, Musil has his fictional persona, the 'man without qualities', ask the question that has constantly pursued him: 'Who/what am I?' Sometimes Ulrich can identify in himself that 'male' self that strives to dominate, that seeks worldly success. But he also perceives his 'female' side. If the lonely and tormented hero of Book 1 is to achieve inner equilibrium he needs the gentle companionship, the corrective of a sister who, as his 'Selbstliebe' ('self-love'), his 'philautia', helps to reconcile him with himself.

In *The Man Without Qualities*, the quest of an individual for inner harmony is linked with the health of a whole culture. Musil as author exploring the elements of his own self and happiness is also the student of European society making a contribution to criticism and renewal. Art is not a passive process; it is not a mirror which the author holds up to his own life and to the world around him. *The Man Without Qualities* is, in Musil's phrase, a 'moral laboratory' where the best kinds of human being are subjected to test.[7] What was it that had precipitated the social and political discords that led to the cataclysm of war in the twentieth century? Ultimately it was a crisis that lay beneath society and politics, a breakdown in culture that in turn had its roots in imbalances in the lives of individuals, in typical traumas which his novel laid bare.

NOTES

1. The trilogy, together with Broch's own short commentaries on it, has been republished as volume 1 of Hermann Broch, *Kommentierte Werkausgabe*, ed. Paul Michael Lützeler, 13 (17) vols. (Frankfurt am Main, 1974–81). Future references to the complete works will be abbreviated to *KW*. Willa and Edwin Muir's translation *The Sleepwalkers* (1932) has been reprinted with an introduction by Michael Tanner (London, Melbourne and New York, 1986). All references to this edition will use the abbreviation *S*.
2. The novel, together with a considerable quantity of unfinished chapters, sketches and notes from his posthumous papers, is published as the first of the two volumes of Musil's *Gesammelte Werke*, ed. Adolf Frisé (Reinbek, 1978). References abbreviated to *MoE* are to this edition. References to *MWQ* are to the 2-volume translation by Sophie Wilkins and Burton Pike, *The Man Without Qualities* (New York and London, 1995).
3. Broch was upset by a reviewer who saw *The Sleepwalkers* as being 'about' the First World War, which he regarded as a 'secondary symptom' (letter to his publisher Daniel Brody, 29 January 1931, *KW* XIII/1, 127).
4. In this, they were perpetuating that elevation of 'culture' over 'conditions' that Alan Bance has identified in some of the major novels of the Wilhelmine era (see chapter 3).

5. See Alan Bance in chapter 3, p. 36.
6. See the discussion by Paul Michael Lützeler in the final chapter of this volume.
7. Musil, *Gesammelte Werke*, II, 1351.

FURTHER READING

Musil, Robert, *Tagebücher*, ed. Adolf Frisé, 2 vols. (Reinbek, 1976) (The second volume contains extensive information on Robert Musil's life and intellectual interests, and the genesis of his creative work.)

Cohn, Dorrit C., *The Sleepwalkers: Elucidations of Hermann Broch's Trilogy* (The Hague, 1966)

Corino, Karl, *Robert Musil. Leben und Werk in Bildern und Texten* (Reinbek, 1988)

Corino, Karl, *Robert Musil* (Reinbek, 2003)

Dowden, Stephen D., *Sympathy for the Abyss: a Study in the Novel of German Modernism* (Tübingen, 1986)

Durzak, Manfred, *Hermann Broch. Dichtung und Erkenntnis* (Stuttgart, 1978)

Hickman, Hannah, *Robert Musil and the Culture of Vienna* (London, 1984)

Horrocks, David, 'The novel as history: Hermann Broch's trilogy *Die Schlafwandler*', in A. F. Bance (ed.), *Weimar Germany: Writers and Politics* (Edinburgh, 1982), pp. 38–52

Kessler, Michael, and Paul Michael Lützeler (eds.), *Hermann Broch. Das dichterische Werk* (Tübingen, 1987)

Kundera, Milan, *The Art of the Novel* (London, 1988) (includes a discussion of *Die Schlafwandler*)

Luft, David S., *Robert Musil and the Crisis of European Culture, 1880–1942* (Berkeley and London, 1980)

Luserke, Matthias, *Robert Musil* (Stuttgart, 1995)

Lützeler, Paul Michael, 'Hermann Broch: *Die Schlafwandler* (1930–32)', in P. M. Lützeler (ed.), *Deutsche Romane des 20. Jahrhunderts. Neue Interpretationen* (Königstein, 1983), pp. 200–17

Lützeler, Paul Michael, *Hermann Broch. Eine Biographie* (Frankfurt am Main, 1985)

Lützeler, Paul Michael (ed.), *Hermann Broch* (Frankfurt am Main, 1986)

Payne, Philip, *Robert Musil's 'The Man without Qualities': a Critical Study* (Cambridge, 1988)

Pike, Burton, *Robert Musil: an Introduction to his Work* (Port Washington and London, 1972)

Ritzer, Monika, *Hermann Broch und die Kulturkrise des frühen 20. Jahrhunderts* (Stuttgart, 1988)

Roth, Marie-Louise, *Robert Musil, l'homme au double regard* (Paris, 1987)

Schlant, Ernestine, *Hermann Broch* (Boston and New York, 1978)

Steinecke, Hartmut, and Joseph P. Strelka (eds.), *Romanstruktur und Menschenrecht bei Hermann Broch* (Bern, 1990)

Stevens, Adrian, Fred Wagner and Sigurd Paul Scheichl (eds.), *Hermann Broch. Modernismus, Kulturkrise und Hitlerzeit* (Londoner Symposion 1991) (Innsbruck, 1994)

Strutz, Josef, and Endre Kiss (eds.), *Genauigkeit und Seele. Zur österreichischen Literatur seit dem Fin de siècle* (Munich, 1990)

8

BURTON PIKE

Images of the city

French, English, Russian and American novels have been able to call upon grand, semi-mythical metropolises – Paris, London, St Petersburg, New York – as metaphors, but the German novel has never had a centrally symbolic city that it could call its metaphoric home. To a much greater extent than in these other literatures, cities in German literature have been for the most part either regional or foreign. This reflects in part the tri-national character of literature written in German. Austria and Switzerland, as well as Germany, have produced major German novels. It also reflects the quite different historical, political and social development of all three countries. In addition, within each country there have been, over the centuries, marked regional differences.

This situation has posed a particular problem for the novel written in German in the twentieth century. In the heyday of realism, in the later nineteenth century, what we might call regional urbanism (to the extent that novels in German were urban) was the norm in prose; Gottfried Keller's Swiss towns and cities, Fontane's Berlin, and even the Lübeck of Thomas Mann's *Buddenbrooks* all revel in detailing specifics of geography, language and customs in representing the particular culture of particular cities. But if one jumps ahead only ten years from *Buddenbrooks* (1901) to Rilke's novel *Die Aufzeichnungen des Malte Laurids Brigge* (1910; *The Notebooks of Malte Laurids Brigge*, 1930), in which the cities, Paris, St Petersburg and Venice, are not German at all, one has entered an entirely different urban world. Gone are the fixed hierarchies of class, speech and local customs that mark the life of a particular city; instead, in Rilke's Paris we are inside the fragmented consciousness of a would-be poet who is trying desperately, and without much success, to create art out of his fugitive sense-perceptions and impressions of a hostile and unyielding urban reality. Baffled by the Paris of poverty and estrangement he has come to as the novel opens, and unable to make his impressions of it coherent, Malte takes refuge in memories of his aristocratic childhood among the Danish landed gentry, in memories of his experiences in two other cities, St Petersburg and Venice, and in retelling chronicles and legends of the distant past. Kafka's New York, in his *Amerika* (1927), the unnamed Prague in *Der Prozeß* (1925; *The Trial*, 1935), and even the setting of *Das Schloß* (1926; *The Castle*, 1930), which might be regarded as a skeletonised city, as well as Musil's 'crossed-out' Vienna in *Der Mann ohne Eigenschaften* (1930–43; *The Man Without Qualities*, 1953–60), visible but abstract, show the image of the city losing its thematic specificity and dissolving into what it has generally become in prose fiction since the 1950s, a kind of cosmic, random, background noise.

In postwar German literature, as in other western literatures, the city as image has more or less totally lost its 'face', its unique identity. Urbanness has become a universal characteristic of western societies; even rural communities share an urban culture these days. As Musil puts it in *The Man Without Qualities*, 'we overestimate the importance of knowing where we are because in nomadic times it was essential to recognise the tribal feeding grounds'. Why should we insist on knowing exactly what city we are in? Musil asks. 'It merely distracts us from more important concerns.'[1]

This discussion will focus on the city in earlier twentieth-century literature, in which the city is in transition from having a strong thematic profile to becoming a ubiquitous and semi-anonymous atmosphere within which characters move.

The city both actualises and symbolises the notion of society and community – the word 'citizen' is derived from 'city'. Its importance as an expressive literary figure is a natural extension of its social, historical and even its mythic aspects. Most fundamentally, cities are collective images, organised societies to which an individual character must relate in some fashion.

The topos of city versus country was formalised by Theocritus (270 BCE) and in Virgil's *Eclogues* (43 BCE), and has had a long history. But it is worth remembering that the *Eclogues* and most subsequent writings that praise the country over the city, including Rousseau's, were written by urban authors for an educated urban audience; the country–city opposition is a literary and cultural convention, not a fact of nature. This convention has faded in the course of the twentieth century, as even small-town life has become increasingly and overwhelmingly urban and suburban in its habits and values, so that to champion rural or village life over urban life is really only possible in fantasy recreations such as Rothenburg-ob-der-Tauber or Western films. Biblical-style imprecations against the city as the place of corruption, which we still find in Nietzsche, Spengler, and even in Döblin, now strike us as quaint.

At various times a few cities have achieved mythic status in literature for a period of time, as well as in film and television. Walter Benjamin called Paris the capital of the nineteenth century, and New York can lay claim to being capital of the twentieth – even in German literature (Frisch's *Homo Faber* (1957) and *Montauk* (1975; trans. 1976), Johnson's *Jahrestage* (1970–83; *Anniversaries*, 1975 and 1987), Bachmann's *Der gute Gott von Manhattan* (1958)).

Aside from cultural, historical, social and archetypal factors, as a purely literary device the city offers the writer an incredibly rich field of operations: dynamic interactions, collisions and games of power among myriad characters, types, occupations and social classes, all colliding in an architecturally imposing place whose functioning is determined by complicated and subtle social and political powers and codes. (Someone once called the corner of an urban street an 'angle of surprise'.) For a writer facing an increasingly complex world, the city in the twentieth century has become more than ever the space in which life itself takes place. In *Civilisation and its Discontents*, Freud compares the structure of the mind to a city and a city's history. The city in the novel acts as a spatialising device for consciousness, providing a grid that orders perceptions and actions.

In the search for an analytic method to categorise how cities are used in literary works, one is confronted with a bewildering variety of approaches. The city can be regarded historically, sociologically, politically, anthropologically, psychoanalytically, phenomenologically, statistically, existentially, archetypically, or mythically; as structuralist, deconstructionist, or postmodernist. The line between the literary critic on the one hand and the social/cultural critic and historian on the other is blurred, and no single approach imposes itself; everything depends on the critic's angle of attack. Earlier attempts by critics to classify literary cities according to fixed types and categories have fallen out of fashion since the 1970s in favour of an ad hoc, often multidisciplinary approach which, while often confusing, at least has the merit of respecting the complexity of the subject.

If classifying generalisations are to be avoided, the question remains how the city can be understood and analysed as an organising metaphor in individual literary works. The basic problem is that the city in literature is an image and not a concept, an 'unreadable rebus' (Paul Ricoeur), and thus not readily accessible to purely analytic approaches. The city can be discussed fairly well in novels that are nominally realistic and that present a coherent image of it, an image that resembles or feigns a social reality. But even here the better the writer, the more difficult it is to isolate the city as a thematic device from its literary context. In conjuring the image of the urban environment, lesser writers tend to rely on stock or stereotypical ideas, attitudes and language, notions that are more historically timebound and more loosely connected to the novel's imaginative structure. This makes it difficult for a later reader to connect the characters and action with the implied values of the urban setting, which would have been clear to the first readers from their own knowledge. The better writer is able to incorporate the values ascribed to the city into the novel's structure in such a way that they will still be accessible to later readers. For instance, it is difficult to follow Heimito von Doderer's characters through the labyrinthine Vienna of his novels if the reader does not already have a good social and geographical knowledge of that city. Yet Musil's much less sharply defined Vienna in *The Man Without Qualities* could not be more vivid, even for the reader who has never been there.

In novels of the 1920s and 1930s, the presence of the city is much harder to separate out, since prose fiction generally came to rely so much less on formal thematic structure, and the urban environment had become so thoroughly diffused throughout western culture. Sociologically, the period of modernism, before and after the First World War, was a response to the widening realisation that the era of the individual was over, and that industrialised society had become collective culturally as well as literally. Reflecting the widespread recognition of this change, the individual character and his problems in the novel were seen in a new context.

In modernist literature the society of the city becomes a fragmented collectivity that crowds out the nomadic individual. Such individuals are portrayed as reactive or mostly passive rather than as confident actors. We find novels in which individuals are typically shown as withdrawn or ineffective in their efforts to grasp the essence of a hopelessly diffused, but overwhelming, urban society. (Josef K. in Kafka's *The Trial* comes to mind, or the failed artist Walter in Musil's *The Man Without Qualities*.) In Musil's novel, Ulrich points out that today there is no longer a whole person standing over against a whole world, but a human something moving around in a general culture medium. The modernist city novel becomes the place of conflict between the devalued, largely helpless individual and a collectivity governed by unknown and uncontrollable forces. In novels written after the Second World War, the city as cultural metaphor has undergone a further attenuation. It is no longer the nexus of a society in crisis. Culture has simply become urban wherever it is found.

Examining the role of the cities in a few major novels and a novella will perhaps best illuminate this complex subject: Rilke's *The Notebooks of Malte Laurids Brigge*, Mann's *Der Tod in Venedig* (1912; *Death in Venice*, 1932), Kafka's three novel fragments, Döblin's *Berlin Alexanderplatz* (1929; trans. 1929), Musil's *The Man Without Qualities* and Johnson's *Anniversaries*. The cities in Rilke's novel are Paris, St Petersburg and Venice (characteristically, but still curiously, Rilke avoids German-speaking cities altogether); Kafka's cities are New York and that 'crossed-out' Prague; Döblin's city is of course Berlin, and Musil's is Vienna, presented subtly but with incredible precision. Johnson's metropolis is New York. Some other literary conjurations of cities in the modern German novel add up to an interesting list: Thomas Mann's Lübeck, Munich and Venice, Broch's Cologne and Berlin, Böll's Cologne, Doderer's Vienna, Grass's Danzig. Even this brief sampling shows that we are dealing in large part with an odd perspective: in American novels the cities are American, in English novels English, in French novels French, and in Russian novels Russian. Only in the German-speaking countries of Europe is there such a large admixture of the cities of other nations in the literature of one's own.

Rainer Maria Rilke, *The Notebooks of Malte Laurids Brigge*

All three cities in Rilke's novel, Paris, St Petersburg and Venice, are famous as aesthetic cities, works of art in themselves and containing great art. But with the partial exception of Venice, these are not the cities we see in Rilke's novel, in which daily life is that of the poor and the outcast. These cities of art present themselves to Malte, who is struggling to 'learn to see' in order to become a poet, as insuperable problems of representation. By implication, the three cities of art are a measure of how far removed from them Malte's own struggles with art are. St Petersburg is the city of anonymous neighbours in rooming houses, the emblem of disconnected urban life, the opposite of Malte's childhood memories of country estates in Denmark. As Malte remembers them, these estates are not seen as rural but as communities of close-knit families and their circle of friends, the opposite of his isolated social situation in St Petersburg. Close-knit societies are also central to the old legends that Malte retells later in the novel. These childhood and legendary worlds are somehow to be combined – this is the task Malte sets himself – in a new poetic vision with the sharp, hyperrealistic observation and depiction of life in the fragmented modern city. Yet this task presents Malte with artistic problems that are beyond his abilities: he sees the life of Paris as consisting only of isolated and isolating snapshots, like the man who has an attack of St Vitus's dance in the street, or the blind newspaper seller, rather than consisting of 'stories' that would tie the isolated perceptions together as the expression of an integrated, storytelling community. (Malte's cry, 'I need a narrator!' sums up his problem neatly.) It is in the three cities, each of which poses a different task, that Malte has to learn how to become a poet. City works of this period in which the hero is a writer (*Malte Laurids Brigge* and *Death in Venice*, among our samples) rest on a basic paradox: art is seen as the collective expression of a community, but the artist is a nomadic individual who is excluded from the community that it is his calling to express.

Rilke's novel is anchored in Paris, the city of the present. 'September 11, rue Touiller', the date and place of a journal entry, are its first words. This Paris is not the glittering social and art capital of the world, the 'capital of the nineteenth century' (Walter Benjamin), but a harsh working- and lower-middle-class city full of that jangling onrush of perceptions and sensations outlined in Georg Simmel's famous essay on 'The metropolis and mental life'. (Rilke attended Simmel's lectures in Berlin.) Malte remains an isolated outsider in the city, a *flâneur* in the line of descent from Baudelaire and Poe. He struggles to see Paris without illusion, trying to somehow capture the flow of his perceptions of city life in the fixed permanence of art. As a neurotic outsider, he is devastatingly open to these random impressions of things and people; if he were an ordinary citizen, his perceptions would be governed by purpose and habit, and he would screen out precisely those impressions that for Malte are the jagged material out of which art has to be made.

Paris is the novel's present. St Petersburg is for Malte a city remembered from a past visit. Its beauty and artistic richness are ignored as Paris's are ignored. Like Raskolnikov's St Petersburg in *Crime and Punishment*, Malte's is a city of isolation, of anonymous rooming-house neighbours and anonymous noises coming from other rooms. The free-floating anxieties induced in Malte by these perceptions and sensations terrify him because they are completely disconnected. His fantasy, unchecked by reality, runs riot. Rilke's point seems to be that the imagination must be yoked to the hard task of 'seeing' realities in order to produce true poetry.

Venice, another city that Malte conjures up from memory, is a city of beauty, but in his eyes it is a beauty testifying to the relentless will of its founders. It is the powerful force of this lurking, historical will that Malte seems to connect with the will to art. In a memorable scene in the novel, a song is sung at a party, specifically as an act of will, by a Danish singer. The worlds of childhood, woman, and the urban past and present join in the singer's artistic performance, providing Malte, who is listening, with at least an intimation of the possibility of creating a genuine art of his own.

Art in *Malte Laurids Brigge* can only be created in the city of the present, Paris. For Rilke's poet, cities set the implacable task of making poetry out of a combination of material from one's own memories, perceptions and sensations, and the hard, scientific observation of the post-Nietzschean, post-idealist, empirical world. It has to be a new kind of poetry, a new way of seeing; the traditional conventions of beauty and artistic expression derived from Idealism and Romanticism are no longer adequate to our understanding of the world. Rilke seems to be following Nietzsche's dictum in *The Birth of Tragedy* that the world can only be grasped as an *aesthetic* phenomenon. Malte is attempting to assimilate his experience of the modern city into a new artistic form, an urban form, and the Paris he experiences is not the nostalgic old 'city of dreams'. The result is an unplotted, open novel whose cities represent something startlingly new compared to the panoramic urban canvases of Fontane or Mann's *Buddenbrooks*.

Thomas Mann, *Death in Venice*

Death in Venice is a tale of two cities, Munich and Venice. Munich is the site of the aging Aschenbach's exhausting struggles with art; the city is presented from a peculiar perspective of borrowed classical, Byzantine and death-longing aspects. Munich as the pulsating, glittering German city of art is as oddly absent in this story as glittering Paris is absent from *The Notebooks of Malte Laurids Brigge*. (How deliberate Mann's choice of perspective is can be seen from his near-contemporaneous story about a shining Munich, 'Gladius Dei'.) In *Death in Venice*, Munich serves metaphorically to establish the themes of entropy and death in Aschenbach's unconscious, which Venice then bodies forth.

To ask the question: 'why Venice?' is to evoke a whole tangled web of cultural associations that Venice conjured up in nineteenth-century European culture and that would have been alive for Mann's readers in 1912. Venice had long been the arch-symbol of romantic passion, will, death, decay and disease, figured principally in its physical beauty and in the contrast between its glorious Renaissance past and its crumbling, decadent present. Mann's readers in 1912 would have recalled Goethe's *Venetian Epigrams* of 1790; the sonneteer August Graf Platen (1796–1835), two of whose *Sonnets from Venice*, 'Tristan' and 'Venice', Mann echoes in his story. Platen, a priest of pure, classical literary form, was known for his preference for young boys, and he died from a mysterious infection contracted in Venice. Venice was Nietzsche's favourite among cities, and he wrote several atmospheric poems about it. Richard Wagner, like Nietzsche another god in Mann's private pantheon, not only wrote the third act of *Tristan and Isolde*, that paean to illicit love, in Venice in 1859, but he also died there in 1883. The common thread seems to be illicit passion in an exotic, ruined and diseased city, as opposed to Aschenbach's previous puritanical sense of duty in his northern mode of life. Venice in *Death in Venice* represents a seduction of the will, the life force, by a growing death force, the slackening of physical and creative powers. It is the opposite of Venice as the image of indomitable will that Rilke saw.

Kafka's cities

The city is a major thematic element in Kafka's writing, a place of communities – of families and bureaucracies – from which an individual is outcast. We can see in his cities a further blurring of sharp thematic outline; in Kafka the literary image of the metropolis is well on its way to becoming an atmosphere rather than a place. This can be seen most clearly, perhaps, in the attenuated way the unnamed city is presented in *The Trial* compared to the mappable St Petersburg in Dostoevsky's *Crime and Punishment*, on which Kafka's novel is a gloss.

Upon close examination it is astonishing how many aspects of modern, anonymous urban life are present in *The Trial*, and how seamlessly they form the matrix in which Josef K.'s guilt or innocence is embedded. The city is not thematised as such, but is simply the transparent atmosphere that the characters live and breathe. The bank and its employees, the lodgings, the court officials, the lawyers, the women, Joseph K. himself, are all creatures of the city. The realistic details of modern urban life in *The Trial* are superbly rendered. To recognise how thoroughly the notion of the city permeates *The Trial* is to realise that the question of Joseph K.'s guilt is not his alone, but a failed relation between himself and the beehives of urban collectivity that make up his world. The city is a similarly inescapable enclosing presence in *Die Verwandlung* (1915; *Metamorphosis*, 1946).

The New York of Kafka's *Amerika* with its welcoming Statue of Liberty holding aloft a sword instead of a torch, is a fantastic setting. Kafka gives us a cinematic space–time warp of the modern Metropolis and its unimaginable suburbs, with Karl Rossmann moving inside it as if it were an iridescent bubble. *The Castle* might be regarded as a skeletonised city, whose overwhelming bureaucratic apparatus, the castle, is totally out of proportion to the 'village' that it governs and over which it looms – like the castle that looms over Prague. Although the community of the castle seems to be feudal, its organisation is legalistic and impenetrably bureaucratic, as is only possible in the modern city or nation-state. (Foucault has argued that the nation-state was established on the model of the city.)

Alfred Döblin, *Berlin Alexanderplatz*

In this novel, Döblin wants to do for Berlin what Joyce had done for Dublin in *Ulysses* (1922): present an outsider drifting through the daily life of the modern fractured city, but with a moralising rather than an aesthetic aim. *Berlin Alexanderplatz* is a morality play, a twentieth-century *Pilgrim's*

Progress using the technical devices of literary modernism and Expression-ism. Döblin's kaleidoscopic city is contained within an imposed religious allegory rather than the much more lightly used classical frame of Homer's *Odyssey* that Joyce employed. Döblin does not write in Joyce's impression-istic, aesthetic style but in a realistic and idiolectic style that mimics the actual sounds of various levels of Berlin dialect. As in *Ulysses*, and more explicitly than in Kafka, Döblin's Berlin is an enveloping culture medium. It is presented as a montage, a collation of fragmented elements. Each of Joyce's pseudo-archetypal figures carries his archetypal function (Wandering Jew, quester, father, son) around with him while still remaining a citizen of Dublin. Döblin's characters, on the other hand, lack this archetypal dimension; as allegorical figures they are counters, exemplars in the author's moral tale. Their larger significance derives not from their situation but from the mean-ing imposed on them by the allegorising author. But allegory and realism are warring categories: the city in *Berlin Alexanderplatz* is supposed to be, at the same time, a literal, realistic Berlin and the iniquitous setting of the struggle for a man's soul. By contrast, Joyce rather neatly avoids making *Ulysses* into an allegory as he weaves the sights, sounds and significances of Dublin into a unified fabric.

Franz Biberkopf is a proletarian Everyman whose potential good qualities are crushed by the cynical amoralism of the modern urban world. As a common labourer he does not have the intellectual resources to master his environment; for him, finding the right path through life is a long, painful and arduous process. Various guides help him when he is down and out, and at the end of the novel, after facing and overcoming death in an insane asylum (that ultimate institution of the modern city), he emerges from his trials a better person.

In trying to combine the literal and the allegorical in his novel, written in 1929, Döblin was relying on Berlin's reputation in the Weimar Republic years for extravagance and licentiousness, although the novel deals with the proletariat rather than with the bohemians. Berlin in Döblin's novel stands for the sinfulness of modern life on the basis of a specific city; it does not stand for a national culture. As Germany has never had a single cultural metropolis, its cities have always been attenuated as cultural magnets in fiction, in contrast to the roles played by Paris and London in French and English novels. But Berlin gained mythic status of a sort for a time by being a national and cultural capital in the Weimar Republic, although the political aspect is ignored in *Berlin Alexanderplatz*. Because of his overriding allegorical purpose, Döblin, in spite of the vividness of his presentation of Berlin, sees it as an archetypal 'city', a Sodom. There is a connection to the strong anti-urban German tradition, as found for instance in Nietzsche and Spengler. Still, if the novel were set in Stuttgart or Frankfurt, much of whatever mythic aura it has would evaporate, just as one can hardly imagine *Ulysses* set in Cork or Belfast. Both Joyce's and Döblin's novels trace the fortunes of individuals within urban social systems to which they do not belong, and from which they are actively excluded – the one by his religion, the other by his status as an ex-convict – but on which they still depend for their self- and social identity and their livelihood.

Newly released from prison as the novel opens, Biberkopf drifts randomly through different circles on the fringes of urban society, such as the Jews who, themselves a collectivity of outcasts, befriend him for a time as a fellow outcast. The author's moralising, sermonising framework seems at cross-purposes with both his novelistic technique and the fragmented urban world he is presenting. Imposing stern moral strictures on his city and its inhabitants, rather like an Old Testament prophet, Döblin calls Sodom to account. This heavy allegorical picture frame surrounding a chaotic modernist canvas makes *Berlin Alexanderplatz* an odd city novel. Döblin's Berlin is the constricted opposite of the infinitely expanding diffusion of unanchored city life that was Rilke's view in *Malte Laurids Brigge*.

Robert Musil, *The Man Without Qualities*

Vienna in Musil's novel is a discreetly ubiquitous and informing presence. In a note in the posthumous section of *The Man Without Qualities*, Musil wrote 'Why Vienna instead of an invented metropolis. Because it would have been more effort to invent one than a "crossed-out" Vienna' (p. 1724).

A '"crossed-out" Vienna': together with the statement in the first chapter of the novel about overemphasising where one is, referred to above, this typifies the changed attitude toward the city in the modernist city novel. What Musil has done, rather like Kafka but with far more social and political depth and skill, and on a far broader canvas, is to create a palimpsest in which his 'crossed-out' city is both the specific Vienna of 1913 and the modern metropolis in general. The city is doubled, functioning both as a real and as an abstract place. This is the modernist equivalent of the real Jerusalem–Heavenly Jerusalem axis in the Bible, or the real Paris–mythic Paris pairing that we find in Balzac, Baudelaire and Proust (a doubling that Rilke consciously elides in *Malte Laurids Brigge*).

In Musil's novel there is a much greater emphasis on abstraction from the real setting. The 'realness' of city life has lost much of its thematic value for the novelist, who looks for the essence of the city elsewhere. (The character in *The Man Without Qualities* who speaks the line: '"Ah, Vienna, city of dreams! A beautiful place!"' is a madman in an insane asylum.) Geographical reference is sharply attenuated: there are no landmarks, nor do we know, for instance, the specific locations of Ulrich's house or Clarisse and Walter's suburb. The narrative emphasis, insofar as it concerns the city, has shifted from geography to atmosphere, and the emphasis in presenting the characters is confined to their momentary perceptions of whatever part of the city they happen to be in at a particular moment.

There are many marvellous descriptions of acutely observed details of streets, suburbs, archways and interior decoration that give the city an unmistakably Viennese imprint, but each detail is isolated from any geographical context. The city cannot be separated out thematically, the way Venice can in *Death in Venice*, or Paris and Venice in *Malte Laurids Brigge*. While remaining Vienna, the capital city in *The Man Without Qualities* is presented as a ubiquitous atmosphere (hence 'crossed-out'), not a mythic or thematised place. The cacophony of Viennese society comes closest to being thematised as a paradigm for pre-First World War (and later) Europe in the splendid comic device of the 'Parallel Campaign', which shows the city as the place where clashing cultures, nationalistic, political and social, are thrown together to shout at each other mutually incomprehensible notions in mutually incomprehensible words. The mass of citizens in this novel go about their lives busy and unthinking, each on an individual trajectory instead of elements of a whole community. They are, the author says, living on an arc without being able to close the circle.

By treating Vienna in this fashion, Musil gains a great deal of freedom in counterpoising the inner and outer lives of his characters with the complex social, political and cultural worlds of the capital of the doomed Austrian Empire. And not only the capital: in *The Man Without Qualities*, as in *Death in Venice*, the characters move from one city to a second city, and from there to 'another world'. In Musil's case this other world is one of temporary mystic suspension. This device of a second city is curious: Aschenbach's journey from Munich to Venice is interrupted by an aborted stay in the 'wrong' city of Pola; Ulrich and Agathe's journey from Vienna to Italy is mediated by their return to the 'crossed-out' provincial city of Brünn (Brno) that was their childhood home and the home of their just deceased father. For Musil's brother and sister pair, this journey from one city to another has the feeling of a regression to childhood.

The city in *The Man Without Qualities* embodies both the fragmentation of modern daily life and the inability of a fragmented social structure to form a community. As the art that Malte is searching for will have to be a new kind of poetry, so the community that is Musil's goal will have to be a new kind of society.

Uwe Johnson, *Anniversaries*

One cannot conclude a discussion of the city in the twentieth-century German novel without mention of Manhattan, and Uwe Johnson's tetralogy may be considered representative of postwar visions of the city. In Johnson's novel, Manhattan, the capital of the twentieth century, is Metropolis, but for the transplanted German Gesine Cresspahl it is a place of displacement. She lives in New York as an alien, as the Dane Malte Laurids Brigge lives in Paris. As in Rilke's novel, the metropolis represents a dominant culture profoundly different from that of the provincial resident visitor, who is left hanging between two urban worlds that are worlds apart, in time as well as in space. Gesine is displaced between New York and her German home town of Jerichow, in the then East German state of Mecklenburg-Schwerin.

Johnson's long novel takes place between 1967 and 1983. Gesine Cresspahl had come to New York in 1961 with her small daughter, Marie. The novel interweaves their present humdrum life in New York, detailed accounts of current political and social events such as the Vietnam War (Gesine buys the *New York Times* every day), and scenes from her German family and small-town past in and visits to Jerichow. For all its richness of factual detail and complexity of technique, *Anniversaries* shows a striking absence of emotion; the narrative is flat, almost documentary reportage. The characters are ordinary, life-size people who lead ordinary lives; they are not heroes charged with larger significance, such as the Poet or the Criminal. While the juxtaposition of Gesine's life in the metropolis with scenes from Jerichow recalls the counterpoint of Paris and Danish estates in *Malte Laurids Brigge*, Gesine is no poet, and the juxtaposition is not so clearly one between a real present and a past that exists only in memory; it is rather a simple back-and-forth time/place shift, like a sequence of projected photographic slides. Life in the metropolis flows past Gesine, not through her as it does through Malte; we are not privy to her feelings and impressions. The same is true of her past life in Germany. Her perspective is dislocated and detached.

Berlin Alexanderplatz looms larger in the background of *Anniversaries* than does *Malte Laurids Brigge*; indeed, Johnson's novel might be taken as a critique of Döblin's. Here there is no heroising or demonising of the central figure or the metropolis, no sermon, no allegory, almost no affect; *Anniversaries* makes *Berlin Alexanderplatz* look like a tendentious, overblown melodrama. Johnson's metropolis is not Babylon or Sodom, but simply a place; a great place, maybe, but its greatness does not impinge on Gesine Cresspahl or the novel. Not much is made thematically or culturally of the contrasts in size, scale and life between New York and Jerichow. (It is odd that the town rather than the metropolis gets the biblical name.) Johnson's point would seem to be that the polyphony of western culture's long and rich associations connected with the city has simply been lost. In *Anniversaries*, the big city, the metropolis, a major thematic element in the German novel since the later nineteenth century, has been cut down to size.

NOTES

1. Musil, *The Man Without Qualities*, trans. Sophie Wilkins and Burton Pike (New York and London, 1995), pp. 3–4.

FURTHER READING

Donahue, Neil H., *Forms of Disruption* (Ann Arbor, 1993)

Klotz, Volker, *Die erzählte Stadt: ein Sujet als Herausforderung des Romans von Lesage bis Döblin* (Munich, 1969)

Lefebvre, Henri, *Everyday Life in the Modern World*, trans. S. Rabinowitch (London, 1971)

Pike, Burton, *The Image of the City in Modern Literature* (Princeton, 1981)

Ryan, Judith, *The Vanishing Subject: Early Psychology and Literary Modernism* (Chicago, 1991)

Schorske, Carl, *Fin de Siècle Vienna* (London, 1980)

Simmel, Georg, 'The metropolis and mental life', trans. H. H. Gerth and C. Wright Mills, in Kurt H. Wolff (ed.), *The Sociology of Georg Simmel* (Englewood Cliffs, NJ, 1950), pp. 409–74

Timms, Edward, 'Musil's Vienna and Kafka's Prague: the quest for a spiritual city', in E. Timms and D. Kelley (eds.), *Unreal City: Urban Experience in Modern European Literature and Art* (Manchester, 1985), pp. 247–63

Timms, Edward, and P. Collier (eds.), *Visions and Blueprints: Avant-Garde Culture and Radical Politics in Early Twentieth-Century Europe* (Manchester, 1988)

9

ELIZABETH BOA

Women writers in the 'Golden' Twenties

Throughout the western world, the bob-haired, short-skirted, athletic young woman was an icon of the 1920s. The new constitution of the Weimar Republic brought women the vote and most formal educational bars were removed. The feminisation of clerical employment, the fastest growing sector of the economy, continued apace. Young women earning a wage packet were in less of a hurry to marry and men, it seemed, no longer expected to marry a virgin. As Lynn Abrams points out in chapter 2, however, the perception of a gender revolution was not entirely borne out in practice: the figures for female employment scarcely changed between the turn of the century and the mid-1920s although the distribution across different sectors did; only 8 per cent of girls took higher school grades compared with 25 per cent of boys; and the new sexual culture was accompanied by a massive abortion rate, estimated at one million in 1931.[1] In practice sexual liberation often meant sexual exploitation, intensified demographically by the surplus of women following the war and by gender hierarchy in employment. German abortion law, the most liberal in Europe following reform in 1926, still prescribed criminal sanctions and remained the focus of large-scale protest.[2] The first generation of women graduates entered the work-force just as a first devaluation of the academic professions was setting in, worsened by the great inflation and the crisis of 1929. Psychologically, an acute generation gap between young working women and their mothers fuelled the tensions between emancipation and femininity.

The perceived advent of a new kind of sexually liberated, economically independent woman provoked bitter debates in which woman served as a metaphor for the archaic and the new, for tradition and modernity, for nature and nation and for the repressed other self within the male psyche. Yet the voices of actual women continued to be muted. The crushing of emancipation during the Third Reich continued to affect the postwar canon which elevated the male masters of modernism but relegated women to the biographical footnote – Marieluise Fleißer in Brecht's life, for example, or

Irmgard Keun in Joseph Roth's.[3] While the lives are of interest, I shall concentrate here on a selection of works and leave biography for further reading. The novels dating from the late 1920s and early 1930s by Vicki Baum (1888, Vienna – 1960, Hollywood), Gabriele Tergit (1894, Berlin – 1982, London), Irmgard Keun (1905, Berlin – 1982, Cologne) and Marieluise Fleißer (1901, Ingolstadt – 1974, Ingolstadt), offer a kaleidoscope of perspectives on that interval between the First World War and the Third Reich that has been called the 'Golden' Twenties. My theme will be how realist techniques, modernist montage and the semiotics of bodies, clothes and locations in these novels convey women's changing self-image under the impact of modernity.

Vicki Baum: modernity, romance and modernism

Serialised in the popular magazine, the *Berliner Illustrirte*, Vicki Baum's novel, *stud. chem. Helene Willfüer* (1928) confirmed her in a career as best-selling author which continued after her emigration to America in 1931. It opens as the eponymous heroine, a doctoral student in chemistry, meets her professor, Valentin Ambrosius, on a night-time train journey, during which Helene's intellectual awe of her *Doktorvater*, the massively built man with the phallic cigar and giant shadow, is transmuted into a mix of daughterly and erotic feeling. Thereafter Helene tests the Oedipal bond almost to breaking point, becoming a scientist, a businesswoman and an unmarried mother – her young lover commits suicide before the birth of his child – only to be finally united to a now almost blind Ambrosius who, betrayed by his unfaithful wife, had tried to kill himself. As in Brontë's *Jane Eyre*, a union of equals requires not only the Daughter's emancipation but the Father's castration. For a reader of today, the sexual melodrama, which appealed at the time to a popular market, vividly illuminates the interplay of gender, class and racial discourses in the constructs of modernity circulating in the 1920s, while overlying the romantic clichés shaping Baum's novel is a wealth of realist detail which offers a fascinating insight into women's encounter with modernity in the 1920s.

At first *willfährig* or compliant as her name suggests, Helene becomes a heroine in liberal feminist mode as Baum exposes the poverty and misogynistic discrimination which the female apprentice must face to become *Meisterin* (master) within the hitherto male domains of the university, science and business. Besides educational and economic emancipation, modernity Weimar style created 'a new norm of rationalised and perfectly planned sexuality which was anything but simple to execute'.[4] Major obstacles to sexual fulfilment were inadequate birth control and a punitive abortion law. Baum exposes the horrors of back-street abortions, but goes on to offer her readership the triple pleasure of righteous indignation against an oppressive law, identification with a successful unmarried mother *and* a happy return to the harbour of marriage. If Helene is the New Woman, Ambrosius's wife, Yvonne, is the equally modern type of the vamp. At once primitive in following the urges of her body (p. 124), she is a degenerate creature of her nerves, just as her lover, a black American painter, is at once sophisticated yet primitive, as signalled in the tango which he and Yvonne dance in the jungle fresco in his atelier.⁵ Yet it is Yvonne, the castrating phallic woman, who breaks Ambrosius's dominance and so transforms him into a suitable partner for Helene. Helene and Yvonne exemplify the divides pervading Weimar culture between maternalism and sexuality, and between social emancipation and erotic liberation. Antithetical types – Helene's sexuality, initially sacrificed to her career, is maternally protective; sexy Yvonne is denied motherhood and professional success – they signal the limits of emancipation in the 'Golden' Twenties.⁶

In this novel's positive portrayal of cosmopolitanism (Helene's helpers include a Russian painter, a Japanese scientist and the Jewish student, Morgenthau), Baum anticipates her most famous work, *Menschen im Hotel* (1929; *Grand Hotel,* 1930). In the 1920s cosmopolitanism came under right-wing attack just as the metropolis of Berlin was assuming mythical lure. With the shift of scene to Berlin, Baum moves from the novel of development focusing on a central character to a modernist montage of narrative lines and a generic mixing of New Objectivity, romance and the thriller. Like Döblin's Alexanderplatz, Baum's hotel is a microcosm of Berlin; as cosmopolitan as the sanatorium in Thomas Mann's *Der Zauberberg*, it also stands in for Europe; and it points across the Atlantic through the motif of jazz to America where Kafka's Hotel Occidental was located. The characters range through *déclassé* aristocrats, entrepreneurs and financiers, professionals and office workers, artists and entertainers, an army of porters, lift boys, and chambermaids, even a couple of electricians: modernity is the mixing of people in the melting pot of the city. Tempo was the sign of the times. Physical speed becomes a metonym for social change and psychic transformation. Rhythmic syntax rivalling the moving camera evokes travel in an open motor car, rapid acceleration, whirling, blurring images and rushing air, then deceleration as the speedometer needle falls when Baron Gaigern takes the little man, Kringelein, for a spin round the Avus speedway which, completed in 1921, is still today sometimes given over to car racing (pp. 262–3). Then they loop the loop in the skies over Berlin, turning the new world upside down, as the new world was turning the social order upside down (Vicki Baum worked for the Ullstein publishing house which sponsored a Prize of the Skies). Filmic too is catburglar Gaigern's climb across the hotel façade criss-crossed by bars of inky black and brilliant floodlight (p. 179). Or there is the semiotics of light in a hotel bedroom as Grusinskaja, instead of taking an overdose of veronal, makes love with Gaigern: 'The teacup on the table trembled slightly whenever a car passed by below. At first the white light from the chandelier was reflected in the poisoned liquid, then the red of the bedside-lamp, then only the fleeting light of flashing advertisements coming through the curtains' (p. 179). That flashing light would play through myriad movies as the sign of love in the city, whether as a sordid commercial exchange, or a moment of humanity, or both at once.

The exhilarating pace and freedom of city life go along, however, with double images of illusion created by decor, clothes, make-up and the consumer luxuries which the rich buy but the poor can only dream of. The revolving hotel doors suggest that through all the frenzied activity nothing changes, but Dr Otternschlag's double profile, one half of his face destroyed by shrapnel and gangrene, suggests that the 'Golden' Twenties, born out of the First World War, could with drastic suddenness turn black again. The hotel is a scene of encounters which mix classes and change lives as strangers make love in bedrooms and businessmen drive bargains. The cloth which Director Preysing's company manufactures will make the clothes in Berlin's shop windows which transform the typist, Flämmchen, into the elegant image in a fashion photograph after whom businessmen lust. A material economy of production and consumption and a psychic economy of desire interfuse: each drives the other as the circulation of lust passes through bodies and commodities, turning commodities into dreams and bodies into commodities. One escape from this market might seem to lie in the classicist ideal. Grusinskaja contrasts her classical ballet with the new grotesque style (an allusion to the expressive dance of Valeska Gert or Mary Wigman). But even Grusinskaja, played unforgettably by Garbo in the film of *Grand Hotel*, must go to market, her public is deserting her, and her narcissistic self-absorption conveys the isolation which her art entails. Performance art is a common modernist motif, here intensifying doubts as to whether there is any authentic identity behind the greasepaint in this world of gentlemen-thieves, businessmen-frauds and typist-prostitutes. Romance breaks through the cynicism, however. In an intensely filmic scene Gaigern, hidden behind a curtain, watches Grusinskaja watching herself in a mirror: even off-stage and alone Grusinskaja's body remains an image to be looked at. But then Gaigern performs a declaration of love which gradually becomes authentic, just as the tears falling down Grusinskaja's face wash away powder and mascara. Yet the intended reader wants both faces: the real face under kisses (assuaging the anxiety which the cult of beauty induces) but also the glamorous mask (promising escape from the typing pool).

The figure closest to Baum's intended readership of young working women is Flämmchen (Joan Crawford in the Hollywood film), who belongs squarely in the ambit of New Objectivity. Clutching her typewriter, she rushes from job to job to earn money for clothes and make-up to attract a man who might liberate her from her treadmill. She agrees to spend her days typing for Preysing and her nights in bed with him. This was the kind of cynical portrayal of German womanhood which, along with Baum's Jewish provenance, provoked the National Socialists. To a reader of today, however, the sobriety uncovers the exploitation of cheap female labour without making a victim of street-wise Flämmchen. But sentimentality takes over when Flämmchen learns for the first time, so the narrator asserts, to value herself not for the little pleasure which she can give men, but for the overwhelming fulfilment which she can bestow on one man, the clerk Kringelein. (And no wonder, for he is a 47-year-old consumptive and she is a nineteen-year-old model.) The closing imagery evoking Flämmchen's gift of herself to Kringelein is maternal (p. 417). Thus the New Woman is valued by the old measure of what she means to a man and her sexuality legitimised through a grotesque metaphorical maternalism. Fortunately, sobriety, cynicism and saccharine fail to blend and the tension between celebration and critique of city life retains an astringency which makes *Menschen im Hotel* a fascinating document of the 1920s.

Gabriele Tergit: a dance of death

Like *Menschen im Hotel*, Gabriele Tergit's *Käsebier erobert den Kurfürstendamm* (1931; Käsebier Conquers the Kurfürstendamm) radiates out through Berlin from one central location, the offices of a newspaper, the *Berliner Tageszeitung* (based on the *Berliner Tageblatt* for which Tergit worked). In a radical montage, kaleidoscopic cutting drives the reader along the criss-crossing itineraries of the journalists as they traverse the overlapping circles of the media, the arts, architecture and finance. Rather than emotional identification, Tergit provides the intellectual pleasures of satire laced with cynicism in depicting speculative enterprise, the mass market and the follies of a cast of wordsmiths and money-makers. The novel describes the rise and fall of the music-hall singer Käsebier, discovered by the intelligentsia, fêted by the press, turned into a trademark for cigarettes, beer, shoes and children's toys, who becomes the nominal rationale for a speculative development on the Kurfürstendamm to include a Käsebier theatre. The hero is entirely eponymous: he gives his name to anything and everything, but figures scarcely at all otherwise. Lauded by some for closeness to the people, despised by others for lack of class-consciousness, Käsebier is a mere cypher for the class in whose name socialists and communists claimed to act and liberal journalists to speak. The novel shows an impotent intelligentsia facing a ruthless yet chaotic capitalism which will enter an unholy alliance with the National Socialists to restore profits following the crisis of 1929.

Till near the end the characters are portrayed without inwardness, but an Oedipal constellation does gradually emerge in the woman journalist, Charlotte Kohler, her paternal editor, and the writer she falls in love with. Yet the reader cannot so easily identify with Tergit's Fräulein Dr as with Baum's *stud. chem*. The coincidence within the character of pain and cool distance is paralleled in the text, which conveys the self-division of an intellectual woman with a discretion which prevents masochistic wallowing. Towards the end the reader is offered more direct identification with the editor Miermann, who falls victim to capitalism's mix of rationalism and chaos: following management changes precipitated by the collapse of the Käsebier project he is dismissed after eighteen years' service and collapses after wandering the night-time streets, horrified by a phantasmagoric vision of the old fabric of the city torn down to make way not for modernist experiment or inhabitable homes but speculative rubbish. Miermann represents the liberal spirit of Germany. That he comes (as did Tergit) of a Jewish family and murmurs a Jewish prayer in the moment of death as uniformed youths roam the streets preaching German renewal, lends this novel in retrospect a terrible prophetic force. Beginning with its blackly ironic title, *Käsebier erobert den Kurfürstendamm* signals the end of the 'Golden' Twenties and the advent of death-dealing reaction. That this striking novel remains so unknown exemplifies the muting of prewar women writers other than those who could be integrated into the socialist canon of the GDR. The new Gabriele Tergit Promenade is a belated but welcome recognition, though whether the author would have wished to conquer Berlin's Potsdamer Platz complex is another question.

Irmgard Keun: girls in the city

Whereas Tergit's Charlotte Kohler remains bound by an umbilical cord of pity for her impoverished, widowed mother, Irmgard Keun's first novel, *Gilgi – eine von uns* (1931; Gilgi – One of Us), begins with the heroine's emancipation from traditional maternal ties when she discovers that she was adopted, an emancipation confirmed at the end when a now pregnant Gilgi, fearing engulfment by her feelings for her lover, Martin, leaves Cologne for Berlin to become a mother unbound in marriage. The key signifiers of epochal change here are bodies and clothes. Like Baum's Flämmchen, Gilgi begins as that alluring goddess of modernity, the young office worker. Her emblems, her Erica typewriter and her gramophone, signify work and plea-sure: work means money, which means buying-power, which means pleasure. If Helene Willfüer escaped from a father figure (only to be finally recuper-ated), Gilgi escapes an embarrassment of mothers: her adoptive mother, Frau Kron; Fräulein Täschler who acted as go between at the time of her birth; and her birth-mother, Frau Greif.[7] Gilgi embodies modernity rather literally. Her muscular, boyish body, her little breasts, her long legs, her dark curly hair, her sun-browned skin contrast with Frau Kron's ageing body, sagging breasts, fat shoulders, grey skin. Even Frau Kron's thumbs are fat and fleshy as she brushes crumbs from the table, whereas Gilgi has firm, lean fingers, though her index and second fingers are slightly roughened by typing: when she dresses up for her lover, these seem to her more truly hers than the mani-cured perfection of her other fingers. Gilgi's energy and attractive body make her doubly employable. Employers choose pretty girls over plain ones; girls in the dole queue are uglier than those in work, for they cannot buy clothes and make-up, because they did not get the job in the first place. Despite a greater physical likeness to her rich birth-mother's groomed body, Gilgi feels a threatening affinity with Fräulein Täschler, whose skeletal body signifies the lower depths of poverty and alcoholism. Unemployed Hans and his wife present a similar threat. Their bodies too – his waxy skin and hollow features, her roughened hands and heavy breasts, their children's scabby mouths – signal their difference from Gilgi, but empathy threatens to expunge the boundary and destroy her sense of separate identity as a modern woman in control of her fate. And even her own body which made her employable leads to unemployment when, in a brilliantly comic scene, she finally rejects her boss's advances. Thus Gilgi, the goddess of modernity, threatens to top-ple into the abyss of poverty which swallowed so many at the end of the 'Golden' Twenties.

Gilgi's rights as a New Woman to work and to the pursuit of happiness are threatened externally by the economic crisis. Initially she evinces the new objective spirit: those with the will to work have the right to get on; women have the same rights as men to act on their desires. Like Helene Willfüer, Gilgi will be an unashamed, unmarried mother: that at least survives as a new ideal. New Objectivity could, however, shade into old Social Darwinism, but Gilgi lacks that final ruthlessness. Along with social empathy signalled in a merging of the self in the pronoun 'we', sexual desire drives the self to merge in the pronoun 'du'. These modes of identification beyond the self, altruistically with others or erotically with another, are shown as antithetical. Yet both tend to overwhelm the subject. In a discourse echoing Freud, Nietzsche and Schopenhauer, Keun evokes a bodily self of impersonal desire underlying the social subject or ego (p. 129). Gilgi's body is thus a site of conflicting meanings, signifying visually her difference as a modern woman from woman enclosed in the patriarchal family, yet through the ache of desire expunging her autonomy. Her lover Martin, an aesthete of independent means and a *flâneur* who wanders the city streets, would turn Gilgi's body into an artwork draped in exotic silks and jewels.[8] Gilgi has broken free socially and economically from her mother(s), but femininity as psychic subjection and loss of defining boundaries (p. 113) threatens to overwhelm her and so she takes flight to Berlin. Such feminine subjection will remain a major theme in women's writing nearer our time.

Some left-wing reviewers were hostile.[9] Gilgi has a hard little face which only occasionally softens (p. 16). She does not follow her friend Pitt's commitment to socialism. Righteously indignant about Paragraph 218, the anti-abortion law, Pitt fails to heed pregnant Gilgi's plea for help, his masculinity wounded by her rejection of him as a lover. Thus Keun anticipates that anger against the sexism of left-wing protest politics that fuelled second-wave feminism. Keun's novel expresses a humanist feminism, of liberal hue but marked by high awareness of class difference, which would be swept away in the deluge. But *Gilgi – eine von uns* still justifies its title in conveying dilemmas which continue to engage women: Gilgi remains still nowadays one of us.

Keun's second novel, *Das kunstseidene Mädchen* (1932; The Artificial Silk Girl), takes the form of a journal written by Doris, a picaresque heroine who travels from her provincial home town to Berlin where, a twentieth-century Simplicissima, she wanders the streets, witness to the pleasures of the city but also to economic struggle, petty criminality, and political violence. Doris dreams of becoming 'ein Glanz', of achieving the sophisticated polish of true cultivation: she wants not artificial silk but the real thing. Purified through suffering and love, however, she comes to realise that caring for one another matters more than glamour. Compared with *Gilgi – eine von uns,* the emphasis moves from the threat to autonomy posed by feminine desire to the more socialist themes of poverty and alienation. Whereas Gilgi opts for independence, Doris feels more threatened by isolation and penury, and comes to want love or at least companionship. Willing to work out of love or solidarity, she explicitly rejects wage labour as a path to individual independence.

The opening section signals the interlocking themes of gender and class. With comic bravura, Doris turns down her boss's advances, but at the cost of her job. Then comes her moment of glory in the local theatre when she steals the right to say a sentence and so rise from the ruck of walk-on parts by locking her snobbish, upper-class rival in the lavatory. But disaster strikes and in a last access of defiance Doris steals a fur coat and runs off to Berlin. Henceforth Doris turns her back on wage labour, aiming instead to market herself. If petit-bourgeois Gilgi's emblems were her typewriter and gramo-phone, Doris's emblem is her stolen fur coat. Like real silk, so too the coat has incalculable, imaginary value for Doris, who has suffered all the petty humiliations of the poor, notably her lover Hubert's claim to want a virgin as wife, when he really wanted to marry 'well' to further his career. Yet their love-making remains in her memory along with the feel of real silk as two modes of the authentic which her life lacks (p. 70).

In the second part, in passages reminiscent of Döblin's *Berlin Alexander-platz*, a flow of impressions conveys the excitement of city life as a succession of nights out, of cafés and adventures. Eager to learn, Doris wants to discuss politics, but the men only talk of sex. Right-wing violence and anti-Semitism create a grim background as Doris's initial euphoria gradually fades. Woman in the city is ambiguous. Doris is a free agent. True, she has little or no money, supplementing petty gifts with petty pilfering from the men who take her home for a night, but the streets of Berlin are full of penniless unemployed men. Yet cutting across such identity in poverty is the difference of roles in the exchange of pleasure which even in the lower depths makes woman the object and man the agent who buys or sells. As a new city girl Doris seems to elude this law, for instead of a father or pimp she does her own marketing. But her body remains the commodity. A symbolic reflex of the difference is the metaphorical femininity of the city as object of aesthetic contemplation and sensual pleasure for the male *flâneur*. When Doris takes the blind man Brenner out for a night she oscillates between being the camera-eye which registers the city for Brenner and herself being the city for him: she will bring him Berlin which lies in her lap. Doris uses the word 'Schoß' (p. 65), which can mean lap, womb or female sexual organ. Doris has hitherto merged euphorically with Berlin and wants to give herself as the city to Brenner, but as one critic notes, she describes herself to him in the same objectifying terms in which she would appear to the male gaze.[10] Yet paradoxically, it is through the eyes of the blind man who cannot see her that she comes to per-ceive the truth beneath the glittering surface and to recognise the alienation of her own sex in the pleasure market. Thus in identifying with the empty gaze of a blind man Doris comes closest to being a distanced, female *flâneur*. Following this grim vision, the roller-coaster brings Doris one glorious in-terlude when a dubious businessman installs her in a luxury flat where she prances about like a film star, in pink slippers and a négligé, so proud she could say 'Sie' to herself. But the roller-coaster begins its downwards plunge again.

Unlike Lorelei in Anita Loos's *Gentlemen Prefer Blondes*, Doris fails to market herself successfully and reaches the edge of the abyss.[11] But she is saved by Ernst, an older educated man whose wife has left him and who takes Doris in as one might a stray dog. Initially disconcerted by his lack of sexual demands, Doris gradually falls in love and starts wife-like to cook, and clean, and darn socks. Such a relationship, which in *Gilgi* threatened the heroine's autonomy, here has positive value compared with commodified sex. Doris has briefly come inside, like her mother who married because it was so hard outside (p. 137). How cold the world outside is also comes out in the story of Ernst's wife, a dancer who felt stifled in marriage yet who chooses to come back in, so driving Doris out. Cultural differences too divide Ernst and Doris; she feels socially inferior, a theme which Karin Struck would take up in her novel *Klassenliebe* (1973; Class Love). Forty years on, Struck is much more critical than Keun of middle-class intellectuals who take up with lower-class women. But both authors stress women's self-construction through writing. As much as her fur coat, Doris is attached to her journal and finally, as she sets off to look for socialist Karl whose offer of companionship in a garden commune she had once spurned, she will give up the coat, but will go on writing. Doris writes a language for today. A montage of snippets from advertising slogans, songs and films such as *Der Kongress tanzt*, *Die Drei von der Tankstelle* or *Mädchen in Uniform*, such language is performative as Doris imitates a variety of styles, mixing slang and malapropistic philosophising, self-revelation and shrewd observation, vivid evocations of sights and sounds and snatches of dialogue. Like artificial silk, her language is neither organic nor authentic, but manufactured from bits and pieces circulating in the marketplace of popular entertainment and intellectual exchange. Doris's hybrid borrowings often reflect her negative self-image as not the real thing. But her incongruous juxtapositions also act as a devastating critique of dominant class and gender discourses and the ramshackle construct of fragments transmits a palpable personality. *Das kunstseidene Mädchen* might seem to retreat from the feminism of *Gilgi – eine von uns* in reinstating that old antithesis of pleasure versus love. Doris's mentors in her purification through suffering are blind Brenner and kind Ernst, with proletarian Karl waiting to save her from the desert of the city. But the reader is left feeling that as long as she goes on writing, Doris will not quite knuckle under.

Marieluise Fleißer: country girls and the modern world

Doris and her creator deploy an urban language to write of city life. But one of Doris's men friends writes bestsellers with titles like *The Meadow in May* whose heroines feed hens and run through vineyards, their plaits coming loose (p. 54). In favour of (double) morality and against decadent art and Jewish subversion, he writes in the tradition of *Heimat* literature.

German unification under Prussian dominance was marked by tensions between regional and national identity, intensified by rapid industrialisation and urbanisation. The discourse of *Heimat* (homeland) set province against metropolis, tradition against modernity, organic culture against artificial civilisation, local roots against cosmopolitanism and the faceless mass. In part reactionary rhetoric, in part concern for the environment and the cultural heritage, the *Heimat* movement was multi-faceted, but by the late 1920s had polarised between quietist retreat before impending catastrophe and an activist *völkisch* ideology of *Blut und Boden* (Blood and Soil).[12] There was, however, also a tradition of critical writing about country life by writers such as Oskar Maria Graf or Ödön von Horváth. In exploring the impact of modernity on the provincial *Heimat*, Marieluise Fleißer's novel *Eine Zierde für den Verein. Roman vom Rauchen, Sporteln, Lieben und Verkaufen* (revised edition 1975; A Credit to the Club: A Novel about Smoking, Sport, Loving and Selling) offers if anything more of a provocation to conservative sentiment than the urban novels so far considered. The change from the original 1931 title, *Mehlreisende Frieda Geier* (Frieda Geier, Travelling Saleswoman), emphasises retrospectively the political implications of the cult of sporting manhood, Frieda's loss of eponymous status silently indicating how aspirations such as hers would be crushed.[13] The unnamed setting is easily identifiable as Ingolstadt, a garrison town on the Danube in Lower Bavaria, which, demilitarised under the Treaty of Versailles, suffered loss of trade, as witness Gustl's difficulties in starting up as a tobacconist. The great inflation too has left its traces on townsfolk who are all descended from peasants: the harsh life of the small peasant can turn fingers into claws (p. 75). Economic struggle and narrow mental horizons produce a mood of smouldering resentment in stark contrast to the idealising sentimentality of *Heimat* literature.

Yet the novel opens optimistically. Frieda's bobbed hair and the masculine style of her black leather jacket signify her modernity. As a commercial traveller she transgresses the traditional bounds set on women's freedom of movement. She has no surviving parents, herself replacing the paternal provider for her schoolgirl sister, Linchen. Gustl's choice of Frieda as lover poses a question: can Gustl carry forward a new mode of human relations beyond the patriarchal structures of the past? That Gustl is a representative citizen, socially through his family, economically as a shopkeeper, and culturally as a leading member of his sports club, extends the challenge from one man to the whole milieu. The goods he sells, tobacco and alcohol, signify the pleasures of the male community. But times are changing: the smoke mingles companionably and sexily when Gustl and Frieda enjoy cigarettes together. A provincial culture-hero, Gustl must choose between the new, embodied in Frieda Geier, and the old, embodied in his dragon of a mother, Filomena, who upholds the double morality and family values (p. 83). (The names ironically revalue femininity: Geier means vulture, Filomena nightingale.) But when Frieda refuses to solve his cash-flow problems with money set aside for Linchen or to give up her job to work unpaid in his shop as womenfolk are supposed to, Gustl reverts to type, even appealing to the law which prescribed that wives might only work with their husband's permission (p. 127).[14] When displays of his magnificent physique, seductive massage, attempted impregnation by force, and threatened suicide all prove of no avail, Gustl hatches the diabolical plan to seduce virginal Linchen. As the narrator's repeated exhortations to Frieda to beware signal, Linchen stands as Frieda's younger alter ego, her vulnerable core-self. Gustl's seduction and Linchen's masochistic compliance, intensified by the tales of martyrdom purveyed in her convent school, thus convey a still living psychic threat to women's autonomy from male phallic power sanctioned by a patriarchal symbolic order.

If Gustl reverts to type in seeking a hard-working wife as one might a good milking cow, as a sportsman he is a quintessentially modern figure. Organised sport is a central feature of modern society. In Germany sport, especially gymnastics, was loaded with ideological significance stretching back to the rise of German nationalism during the Napoleonic wars. The 1936 Olympic Games, designed to display German might, stand in a long tradition, and all the major political groupings encouraged sports. Fleißer's subtitle signals a tension, which ideally should be creative, between business, sport, love and other pleasures. Sport draws energy away from money-making, but sporting friendships foster trade; Gustl gets his first big order from a cyclist friend. Sporting achievement demands, so Gustl claims, an ascetic life; energy spent in love-making cannot be spent in winning the crawl. Before falling for Frieda, Gustl had enjoyed sex casually during the winter but kept the summer for sport. Socially too Gustl's swimming club is a male institution; sportsmen are merely embarrassed by women trailing along. Yet Gustl's muscular body and his will to sporting self-transcendence draw Frieda. She can love Gustl the swimmer as she cannot Gustl the household tyrant and moneybags. Comic verve mixes with a bleak, even sinister mood in Fleißer's subtle analysis of the institution of sport. The swimming club models the external relations and internal workings of the community. Competition between clubs and sponsorship to attend provincial or international meetings both widen horizons. The club sustains local pride over against big cities such as Munich. Internal competition is bitter, but enemies come together again as when Gustl's rival, having humiliatingly defeated him, recognises his skills as a life-saver. Gustl's paternal qualities are benevolent when put in the service of saving drowning citizens or stopping bullying and cruelty: in this guise he embodies the best spirit of his community.

But the sporting spirit can turn into mass fanaticism focused on an enemy and on excluding aliens. And it demands subjection, however benevolently, of females. Any woman who does not accede can at best stand on the margins of this community and will eventually be excluded. Women often embody the *Heimat* which men desire or possess: men are the travellers who long for the maternal *Heimat* or as the alienated agents of history seek solace in the embrace of unchanging feminine nature. Fleißer subtly changes this symbolism. If the shop interiors, winding streets and onion-domed churches of Ingolstadt are the scene of getting and spending and of petit-bourgeois patriarchy underwritten by a patriarchal religion, the mouthpiece of the law is Mother Filomena. Conversely, the Danube and the green wildernesses along its banks figure the lure of the imaginary *Heimat* which is here personified not, as so often, in a nymph but in a male spirit, the swimmer who is at home in the watery element. Through the gaze of a feminine focaliser Gustl's body is erotically charged, although the charge is often comically defused. Gustl's will to transcendence is rooted, as Nietzsche demanded, in a natural bodily energy, whereas the woman is alienated. But Gustl has a dark alter ego. Whilst Linchen embodies a still vulnerable femininity inhering in modern woman, there is latent in Gustl, innocent spirit of sport and the *Heimat*, the vengeful rage shown forth in sadistic Raimund Scharrer. Scharrer is Gustl's double rather as Reinhold is Biberkopf's in Döblin's *Berlin Alexanderplatz*. Gustl's direct, open will to self-transcendence can turn into the creeping indirectness of Scharrer's *ressentiment*. Like the woodland where Reinhold murders Mietze in *Berlin Alexanderplatz*, the wooded banks of the Danube are the scene of Scharrer's sadistic exploits as of Gustl's regression to misogynistic manhood. That Scharrer turns from sexual sadism to blowing up railway lines, a favoured tactic of the paramilitary right, draws the connection between misogyny and militarism.

Economic crisis and the murderous destruction wrought by the Third Reich sprang as much from the small-town *Heimat* as from the cities and ended the era of the New Woman. As one commentator noted in 1933: 'Bobbed hairdos and short skirts have beaten a retreat; economic conditions have done away with the office chair and the teacher's desk and closed the door in women's faces.'[15] It must be hoped that the closing of doors to a generation of women writers, exiled or silenced during the Third Reich, may in some part be redressed by long overdue recognition of their work.

NOTES

1. See Ute Frevert, *Women in German History: from Bourgeois Emancipation to Sexual Liberation* (Oxford, 1989), pp. 168–204.
2. See Cornelie Usborne, *The Politics of the Body in Weimar Germany: Women's Reproductive Rights and Duties* (Basingstoke, 1992), esp. p. 174 on the 1926 reform.
3. See J. M. Ritchie, 'Irmgard Keun's Weimar girls', *Publications of the English Goethe Society*, 60 (1988), 63–79 on Keun's exclusion from the canon for reasons which might equally apply to the other writers considered here.
4. Frevert, *Women in German History*, p. 192; also Hanna Vollmer-Heitmann, *Wir sind von Kopf bis Fuß auf Liebe eingestellt. Die Zwanziger Jahre* (Hamburg, 1993), pp. 61–87.
5. On Americanism and primitivism in Weimar culture see Thomas Kniesche and Stephan Brockmann (eds.), *Dancing on the Volcano: Essays on the Culture of the Weimar Republic* (Columbia, 1994).
6. The judgment on lesbian love as 'abwegig' (p. 89) signals another limit. But see Vicki Baum, 'Leute von heute' (1927), cited in Anton Kaes, Martin Jay and Edward Dimendberg (eds.), *The Weimar Republic Sourcebook* (Berkeley, 1994), pp. 664–6, on the radical chic of lesbianism with a hint of S-M.
7. See Barbara Kosta, 'Unruly daughters and modernity: Irmgard Keun's *Gilgi – eine von uns*', *The German Quarterly*, 68 (1995), 271–86, on modernity and motherhood.
8. On the *flâneur* see Eckhardt Köhn, *Strassenrausch. Flâneries und kleine Form* (Berlin, 1989) and Keith Tester (ed.), *The Flâneur* (London, 1994); also Elizabeth Wilson, *The Sphinx in the City: Urban Life, the Control of Disorder, and Women* (Berkeley, 1991), on the female *flâneur*, if she exists.
9. On critical reception see Joey Horsley, 'Irmgard Keun 1905–1982: "Auf dem Trittbrett eines rasenden Zuges". Irmgard Keun zwischen Wahn und Wirklichkeit', in Sibylle Duda and Luise F. Pusch (eds.), *WahnsinnsFrauen* (Frankfurt am Main, 1992), pp. 280–308, and Gabriel Kreis, *Irmgard Keun. 'Was man glaubt, gibt es'* (Munich, 1991), pp. 63–72. Kurt Tucholsky welcomed a woman writer with humour, but most condescendingly, while one left-wing reviewer concluded that Gilgi was 'keine von uns' (not one of us) (Kreis, pp. 64–5).
10. Katharina von Ankum, 'Gendered urban spaces in Irmgard Keun's *Das kunstseidene Mädchen*', in Katharina von Ankum (ed.), *Women in the Metropolis: Gender and Modernity in Weimar Germany* (Berkeley, 1997), pp. 162–84 (p. 177).
11. See Katharina von Ankum, 'Material girls: consumer culture and the "New Woman" in Anita Loos's *Gentlemen Prefer Blondes* and Irmgard Keun's *Das kunstseidene Mädchen*', *Colloquia Germanica*, 27 (1994), 159–72.
12. On *Heimat* see Elizabeth Boa and Rachel Palfreyman, *Heimat – a German Dream: Regional Loyalties and National Identity in German Culture 1890–1990* (Oxford, 2000).
13. The edition cited here also notes added material concerning anti-Semitism. Fleißer later married Joseph Haindl, on whom Gustl is based; thus Günther Lutz, *Marieluise Fleißer. Verdichtetes Leben* (Weiden, 1989), pp. 124–5, takes independent Frieda as Fleißer's ideal alter ego.

14. On German patriarchal marriage law, only finally repealed in 1977, see Eva Kolinsky, *Women in West Germany* (Oxford, 1989), pp. 41–54.
15. Alice Rühle-Gerstel, 'Zurück zur guten alten Zeit', cited in Kaes et al., *The Weimar Republic Sourcebook*, p. 219.

PRIMARY TEXTS

Baum, Vicki, *stud. chem. Helene Willführer* (Munich, 1983)
Baum, Vicki, *Menschen im Hotel* (Frankfurt am Main, 1986)
Fleißer, Marieluise, *Eine Zierde für den Verein. Roman vom Rauchen, Sporteln, Lieben und Verkaufen* (Frankfurt am Main, 1975); original version, *Mehlreisende Frieda Geier. Roman vom Rauchen, Sporteln, Lieben und Verkaufen* (Berlin, 1931)
Keun, Irmgard, *Das kunstseidene Mädchen* (Munich, 1989)
Keun, Irmgard, *Gilgi – eine von uns* (Munich, 1989)
Tergit, Gabriele, *Käsebier erobert den Kurfürstendamm* (Frankfurt am Main, 1977)

FURTHER READING

Baum, Vicki, *Es war alles ganz anders. Erinnerungen* (Cologne, 1987)
Beutel, Heike, and Anna Barbara Hagin, *Irmgard Keun. Zeitzeugen, Bilder und Dokumente erzählen* (Cologne, 1995)
Gill, Anton, *A Dance between the Flames. Berlin between the Wars* (London, 1993)
Keun, Irmgard, *Ich lebe in einem wilden Wirbel. Briefe an Arnold Strauss 1933 bis 1947* (Munich, 1990)
Larsen, Egon, *Die Welt der Gabriele Tergit* (Munich, 1987)
McGowan, Moray, *Marieluise Fleißer* (Munich, 1987)
Meskimmon, Marsha, and Shearer West, *Visions of the 'Neue Frau': Women and the Visual Arts in Weimar Germany* (Aldershot, 1995)
Peukert, Detlev J. K., *The Weimar Republic* (Harmondsworth, 1991)
Schrader, Bärbel, and Jürgen Schebera (eds.), *The 'Golden Twenties': Art and Literature in the Weimar Republic* (New Haven, 1990)
Schütz, Erhard, *Romane der Weimarer Republik* (Munich, 1986)
Soden, Kristine von, and Maruta Schmidt (eds.), *Neue Frauen. Die zwanziger Jahre BilderLeseBuch* (Berlin, 1988)
Tergit, Gabriele, *Etwas Seltenes überhaupt* (Berlin,1983)
Tergit, Gabriele, *Atem einer Welt. Berliner Reportagen* (Frankfurt am Main, 1994)

IO

MICHAEL MINDEN

The First World War and its aftermath in the German novel

Erleben tun es viele, gestalten kann es niemand (Many experience it, no one can describe it)

Paul Feldkeller, 1915

Given the political circumstances in Germany between the end of the First World War and the Nazis' assumption of power, any treatment of the experience of serving at the Front – literary or otherwise – was automatically political. There were vested interests on both the left and the right, but especially the latter, in making the war experience work to the advantage of ideology. Hence, in the first years of the Weimar Republic, and then again towards the end of the 1920s, the war as a literary topic was predominantly the domain of nationalist elements, all the more so because of the historical role of militarism in the Prussian ethos. For these elements, who clung to the view that the German army had remained 'undefeated in the field', the experience of the war was to be esteemed as a forcing ground for *völkisch* values, which would come into their own once the compromise of Weimar had been overcome. So politically charged was this topic, that when Remarque's apparently unpolitical novel *Im Westen nichts Neues* came out in 1929 (the translation *All Quiet on the Western Front* appeared in the same year), its effect was the most political of all. There were two main reasons for this. First, it tapped a need for a discussion of the horrors repressed by many millions of survivors, and second, it provoked a backlash from the right, whose 'holy' war experience, and the mass appeal it involved, seemed threatened from an undesirable quarter. The response was a wave of bestselling prowar books such as Beumelburg's *Sperrfeuer um Deutschland* (1929; Germany under Barrage) and *Gruppe Bosemüller* (1930) or Schauwecker's *Aufbruch der Nation* (1930; *The Furnace*, 1930), anticipating the institutionalisation of this view of the war under the Nazis.[1]

Bearing in mind the always political nature of the topic, we need to ask here how the historical event of the First World War impacted upon the discourses of the novel in Germany. The Great War happened when the literary discourses of the previous century were still more or less firmly in place (troubled at the cultural edges by various forms of modernism), and its effects upon modes of representation were complex. We will explore them with reference to four representative texts, beginning with an example of a nationalistic, *völkisch* war text, which, although forgotten now, once enjoyed singular popularity, eventually selling over a million copies.

In Walter Flex's memoir *Der Wanderer zwischen beiden Welten. Ein Kriegserlebnis* (1916; The Wanderer between Two Worlds. A War Experience)[2] the experience of the war is dealt with in almost entirely conventional literary ways. It is an account of the author's friendship with another young officer, who is killed in action on the Eastern Front. This young man, Ernst Wurche, is physically and morally a paradigm of the virtues of the 'Wandervogel' (a patriotic, neo-Romantic youth movement, devoted to outdoor activities and influential in Germany at the beginning of the twentieth century). As the 'wanderer between two worlds' he unites the empirical world of conflict ('it was all so senseless, senseless . . .' (p. 74)) with the enduring world of these values and virtues ('Above the noise and glory of the strife and conquests the image of this hour lives gloriously in my heart – the most intense impression my soul and my senses have ever received' (p. 46)). The narrator's role is to interpret and embody the empirical death of his exemplary friend as not inconsistent with the higher world of *völkisch* values: the fallen Wurche speaks from beyond the grave: 'God has struck a chord in your heart: Sing, poet!' (p. 95).

Flex's book meets the war with the aesthetic of the nineteenth-century *Novelle* (Flex was the author of a cycle of 'Bismarck-Novellen'). According to Tieck, '[the *Novelle* genre] can solve and reconcile the contradictions, the irrationalities, even the tragic occurrences of life', by effecting a change in the readers' perceptions of what is represented, a 'turning-point'.[3] This is certainly the effect for which Flex is striving when he evokes the 'radiant' image of Wurche's glistening body after swimming: 'the eternal beauty of the Almighty shone upon this expansive garden of God, illuminating, at once sun and shield, the radiant image of the youth . . .' (p. 46).

One question faces all the literature of the First World War: how to deal with the mutilated human body. No doubt bodies have always been mutilated in wars, but the First World War was both larger in scale than other wars, and the first war to be exhaustively photographed.[4] Moreover, technological warfare is particularly impersonal and shocking in its effects upon the human body. It is instructive to see how Flex's work is absolutely clear on this issue. The death of Wurche is by a single bullet, not in any way disfiguring. If the glistening body of the youth can be the aesthetic turning-point between one world and another, mutilation is not a matter for literary discourse at all: 'Once a man has received the fatal shot that tears out his entrails, we should avert our gaze. For what now follows is ugly and no longer part of him. The grandeur, the beauty, the heroism of life have all passed . . .' (p. 36). The 'Bauchschuß' (abdominal wound), the emblem of the horrific experience of technological warfare (as in Joseph Heller's *Catch 22*, for instance), is explicitly censored.

Yet for all its anachronistic aesthetic in the service of distasteful nationalism, in one way Flex's work is typical of the impact of the First World War upon German prose literature. It is not just a literary construction, but claims at the same time to be true. The war increased the status of truth in relation to that of art, and the early years after the war saw a wave of diaries and memoirs.[5] This effect was not, however, limited to these militaristic self-justifications. Not only Flex, but also Jünger, Remarque, Renn, Köppen and Plievier challenge inherited genre definitions by deliberately mixing up authentic testimony with literary representation. Whilst obviously stylised in diction, imagery and sentiment, Flex's work insists upon its autobiographical status. Indeed, it was this very generic hesitation between autobiography and hagiography that accounted for the little book's singular and enduring popularity.[6] Both the author's name from the title page, and that of the dedicatee, Wurche, also occur as the names of the principal figures in the narrative, and the book was published with an afterword by the poet's brother recording Flex's own death in 1916, as well as his unfulfilled hope of returning to the Western Front, 'inwardly as keen to volunteer as on the first day' (p. 100). The text thus disavows its obvious literariness in order to stress its immediate involvement in the great historical event. Although this blurring of categories is achieved in many different ways by different novels, the colonisation of literature by autobiographical–documentary authenticity is a characteristic effect of the Front experience upon previous conventions of writing.

We find a strongly contrasting approach to the representation of the war in Ernst Jünger's work *In Stahlgewittern* (1920; *The Storm of Steel,* 1929). Not for him the Novellistic aversion to the 'Bauchschuß'. On the contrary, the extreme carnage of the war is the ideal test of a new kind of man, able to withstand the collapse of the old aesthetic rules and the world which went with them. While Jünger's work belongs broadly to the same part of the ideological spectrum as does that of Flex, is likewise dedicated to a fallen friend,[7] and suspends discourse, as does Flex, between literature and autobiographical testimony, it is far more complex and sophisticated in its attempt to find the appropriate aesthetic.

If Nietzsche figured in Flex as a fashionable accessory (*Zarathustra* accompanies Goethe's lyric poetry and the New Testament in the knapsack – all strong, honest and perfectly compatible 'Kameraden' of the mind

(*Der Wanderer*, p. 8)), Jünger's work is pervaded with Nietzschean diction: 'No matter the cause for which he fought, the fight was superhuman ('übermenschlich').'[8] The aesthetic Jünger has in mind is an existential rather than just a literary-artistic matter.

To an extent, Jünger's work belongs to the mass of ideologically right wing writing about the war which was also 'existential' in the sense that it (a) took the diary form adopted by Jünger and claimed the authenticity of experience or claimed documentary authority in other ways; (b) strove to represent (in the sense of justify) the experience of the war to those who had not been there, and in the light of the fact that the war had ended in Germany's capitulation. Yet throughout the text Jünger is clearly preoccupied with the way the mind makes and uses representations. One example illustrates strikingly how intertwined the extreme existential situation and Jünger's reflections about representation are. During the actions around Regiéville in July 1917 Jünger leads a platoon into enemy trenches. He records: 'In situations like this the mind registers unconsciously even the most unimportant detail. Thus at the point where the trenches crossed, the image of a cooking pot with a spoon in it impressed itself upon my memory. Twenty minutes later this observation saved my life' (p. 112). In the extreme situation (*within* the trenches of the enemy, where definitions – boundaries – are no longer given, but bitterly contested), it is the capacity of the mind to make images – of a mundane sort more at home in a naturalist or impressionist still-life than within the Novellistic world of a Flex – that saves the warrior's life. And it does this because, as a mental event and the creation and recording of an image, it provides the crucial aid to orientation in the otherwise chaotic world of combat. Furthermore, not only are we told about this as an existential event, we are also presented with it in the text, so that one can argue that it functions as an aesthetic one too: mind – image – survival; they are bound together in an immediacy which eschews the redundant constructions of the nineteenth century – an immediacy of which Nietzsche had always dreamed.

The generalisation ('in situations like this . . .') which precedes the observation is typical of the discourse of *In Stahlgewittern*. It is as if Jünger is always trying to think things through afresh and without prejudice on the basis of the experience of the war. He is radically discontented with the old order, but unlike some strains of modernism,[9] his desire for a new order, a new discipline is equally radical (again, a Nietzschean predicament). His commitment to a fresh formalisation of experience is shown in his development and formulation of new combat techniques more suited to the circumstances of trench-warfare than the received practices of Prussian militarism ('since these were new forms, I drew up the regulations myself').[10] His idea for a new formation in which to approach a position possibly defended by hostile troops was later included in a military training manual.

As far as *writing* is concerned, the 'new order' is an ideal of impassivity which does not so much fall short of subjective, humane feelings, and certainly does not smother them in kitsch anachronistic jingoism, but rather comes out on the other side of them and represents them in an undifferentiated series alongside registrations of carnage. The method is perhaps best encapsulated in the extraordinary phrase 'the mind ['das Bewußtsein', consciousness] was constantly expecting a direct hit'.[11] Consciousness – one's own consciousness – is simply another entity among all the others, and the *fear of mutilation and death* is expressed in the most impersonal way possible, yet not thereby dismissed, or so Jünger intends it. It is the very enormity of this demotion of subjectivity, of this historical and empirical revocation of Romanticism, that for Jünger provides the impetus for future development: 'With horror you realise that your whole intelligence, your abilities, your spiritual and physical strengths have become something insignificant, laughable' (p. 101). Yet the meticulous and unafraid registration of the unthinkable, so the logic of this discourse goes, makes it thinkable.

Since the morally and politically problematic nature of Jünger's position is evident, it is perhaps not inappropriate to stress how this impassive gaze is unsparing with regard to Jünger's own subjective involvement as well as the destruction of others. Indeed, the reduction of his own subjectivity is the whole novelty and strength of this writing: 'I openly admit that my nerves let me down completely. Go on! go on! get out of here! Without a further thought I just made a run for it. I am no friend of euphemism: nervous collapse. I was simply afraid; cold, senseless fear' (p. 15). The heroism, the lack of which is here being admitted, returns on the level of style in the reckless defiance of euphemism.

Structurally the book culminates in an event of such horror that it exceeds and encapsulates the apocalyptic nature of the Front experience. At the beginning of the great German spring offensive of 1918, Jünger's company receives a direct hit and is literally reduced to a crater full of flesh and ignited machine-gun ammunition. Whilst it is true that Jünger explains that the way he took shelter meant that he had a balcony seat, from which to witness 'the utmost abyss of terror',[12] this can hardly be represented as the derivation of any kind of pleasure. Rather, I would read it as pointing to the reduction of subjectivity to a condition of pure seeing, empty of any content other than the horror of existence (here too one is reminded of Nietzsche, who attributes this sort of annihilating vision to the uncorrected Dionysian insight into the true nature of the world). The human level of this experience is conveyed by Jünger in many unforgettable details – 'such moments engrave themselves ['graben sich ein'] upon the memory'[13] – given heightened significance by the fact that at this point again he collapses and weeps.

Jünger thus meets the representation of mutilation head on, making it a touchstone of a highly charged detachment which one might well feel is adequate to representing the personal, cultural and historical dislocation of the First World War. However, this impersonality is undermined by the elaboration of a myth of heroism which it is not so easy to accept. It is sometimes said that the text does not involve any characters (presumably since characterisation belongs to the humanistic style Jünger wishes to supersede).[14] However, this is not quite correct. There *is* one character implied by the discourse of the novel as a whole, and that is the kind of person implied by this kind of style. Who can speak like this?

The answer is clear from the original subtitle 'Aus dem Tagebuch eines Stoßtruppführers'. The word 'Stoßtruppführer' (literally an assault group leader) has an historically specific meaning. Like Jünger's new rules for engagement, the 'Stoßtruppführer' was a product of the unprecedented conditions of the Western Front – a new breed of frontline officer with the berserker-like nature required to lead the sort of attack which might succeed where the frontal mass attack had failed. The kind of vision and the kind of voice which would correspond to this kind of man is described thus in the text: 'Nothing remained in this voice but serene indifference. It was a voice toughened like steel in a furnace. You can fight alongside men like that.'[15] Those who speak (and write) in such a voice are those who have replaced the redundant concept of the 'two worlds' by a new unity, in which the war is both seen for what it is, and transcended: 'Here, at the point where the spiritual leaders and pioneers of the front assembled, the will to victory ['Wille zum Sieg'] was concentrated and became form in the features of weather-hardened faces. An element was alive here that at once underlined the desolation of the war, and spiritualised it . . .' (p. 79). The Nietzschean virtue, 'Wille zum Sieg', moreover, has made them into aesthetic entities, *formed* them into the statuesque, more-than-human instruments of a new future: 'At moments like these, the human spirit triumphs over the overwhelming effects of technology, the fragile human body, steeled by the will, defies the most fearsome storm' (p. 55). The Nietzschean will, again, enables the weak human subject to overcome the depersonalisation brought about by the *Materialschlacht* (the battle of machines) by trumping it and becoming machine-like itself.

This attempt at a new mythology is not persuasive. There is evidence that Jünger himself was not persuaded by it. He rewrote the text from edition to edition, and as we have seen in some instances above, the changes were not insignificant.

The most significant hesitation concerns the ending. Jünger did not in fact hesitate about the very last moment of the book – this was always the award of the German army's highest award for valour – *Pour le Mérite*. The award legitimates the writing. Yet this ending is ambiguous. On the one hand it imbues the conventional 'sign' of meaning in battle *par excellence* – the decoration – with the *new* significance which the formulation of the text as a whole has grasped in its super-impassivity; but on the other hand, it seems to validate the very system of meanings, perfectly represented by the medal, which the rest of the text is undermining.

The difficulty of conveying a meaning that separated itself sufficiently from prevailing ones, yet retained the edge of reality, is expressed also in the changes Jünger *did* make to the end. In the first version, the deadpan account of the author's last wounding of the war remains unelaborated. Later, Jünger does try to manipulate its significance. He inserts an 'epiphany' just before the end, which once again threatens to lead him into conventional meanings – this time in the style of Flex. He also muses on the meaning of his mutilated body – wounded fourteen times not counting exit wounds – proud that the majority of these mutilations are the result of fire aimed at him rather than at a topographical area in which he happened to be.[16] The grotesque nature of this attempt to clinch a point about new individualism as against the threat of the impersonality of the technological age is symptomatic of the insurmountable difficulties Jünger encounters in his attempt to draw meaning from the *Fronterlebnis*.

The way Arnold Zweig's novel *Der Streit um den Sergeanten Grischa* (1927; *The Case of Sergeant Grischa*, 1928) represents the war can be put very simply: it sets it in its historical, moral and philosophical context. In other words, it puts it into a proper novel, and this is what Zweig claimed for his book.[17]

What of the threat to traditional representations, however, posed by what we might call, in a sort of brutal shorthand, the mutilations of the war, epitomised by the trench-warfare of the Western Front? In a sense, Zweig avoids the issue by siting his action in the east. Here, at least, he does not have to struggle to find a means of representing the monotony of life in the trenches. On the contrary, the circumstances on the Russian Front favour the novelistic: what nineteenth-century capitalism was to Balzac, the upheavals of the Great War of imperialist capitalism are to Zweig: 'Movement everywhere: people, livestock, vehicles, objects',[18] an opportunity to bring all different kinds of people together in a turbulent and – in some senses, productively volatile – time.

Yet it would not be the whole truth to say that Zweig evaded this issue. What we have in *Grischa* is the nineteenth-century novel's – intelligent, civilised, ironic – answer to the mutilations of the First World War. This thematically rich and satisfying novel concerns the *cause célèbre* of an escaped Russian POW, who, despite the efforts of a range of characters, is finally executed unjustly as a deserter, dying at peace with himself, but a victim of the ideology of Prussian militarism. Zweig pitches maturation against mutilation. Grischa starts as a figure from a novel ('it's as exciting as a novel' (p. 143)), but transcends this to become, in a modest way, a representative human being; one who would rather die in one piece (albeit the victim of an injustice), than in pieces anonymously in a mass grave. The difference is that to die the victim of an injustice is to die a legible death (as in: 'this is an injustice'), rather than an illegible – anonymous – one (the fate of millions) (pp. 365–7; 403).

While Grischa develops from a novel character into a symbol, the other characters become all the more human. There is a sort of relay: Grischa resigns from the world in which there is any hope of effective action ('Gradually he was crossing from the active to the contemplative side of life; without leaving the first, he was also becoming accustomed to inhabiting the second' (p. 182)), while his cause is taken up by a group of people who, as novel characters *par excellence*, resemble a Stendhalian 'Happy Few' (p. 444). While Grischa (in the chapter 'A Lieutenant and a Corporal') declines, after more vicissitudes than he can humanly cope with, to refuse the injustice threatening him and to take flight (declines, in other words, to become an abstraction), the other characters are left with the burden of making sense of this injustice – the injustice that is to blame for the whole war ('the most tyrannical of all social orders, that militarism which with the technology of the twentieth century and the bloodlust of human cruelty subjugates men's souls . . .' (p. 195)). This they do, in the chapter 'The Meaning of It All', in which Zweig can present sense-making as a polyphonic process, since he has already implanted in the reader's mind his conviction (a convincing one!) that 'Man was so constructed as to be unable to do without making some sense of things' (p. 114).

This is a skilfully executed double development, making Grischa into a symbol, whose non-abstract and existentially vital significance is passed on to those to whom a symbolic (and *significantly* non-mutilated) death is not guaranteed, and who must therefore *live out* what 'humanity' means, representing it in that way rather than in the symbolic one to which Grischa is condemned. Of course this means challenging injustice, including the injustice of the war, as far as the Happy Few may, in the knowledge that they may fail, but in the hope that humanity as a whole will not (p. 444).

Zweig thought his novel the paradigm of what a war novel should be because it provided a context for the war, and gave serious intellectual and artistic encouragement to the construction of the sort of society that would be able to prevent a recurrence of this masculine barbarism.[19] Although Zweig's novel was by no means unsuccessful, readers in their millions throughout the world settled upon another novel as the paradigm of what a war novel should be. It was, in some ways, the exact inverse of Zweig's novel. 'Novel' has important etymological associations with novelty, newness, movement and progress. The book in question contains a negation of this in its very title: *Im Westen nichts Neues* (*All Quiet on the Western Front*; but literally: 'nothing new in the west'); and in its celebrated and controversial motto, it explicitly puts mutilation before maturation: 'This book is to be neither an accusation nor a confession. It is simply the attempt to tell of a generation that was destroyed by the war – even if it escaped its shells.' In contrast to *Grischa*'s rich cast of developing, complex characters (even Zweig's Ludendorff figure – Schieffenzahn – was bullied at school), we have the assertion that the development of a whole generation of young men has been destroyed by the war.

Remarque's book was the subject of great controversy for many reasons, but the motto we have just quoted and the end of the book, the death of the first-person narrator/diarist, Paul Bäumer, caused at least one contemporary reviewer special perplexity.[20] There is something curious about this, because it is probable, in my view, that precisely these two elements made the text 'legible' to the millions who bought and read it.

The opening motto makes explicit something which millions knew, but which had been disavowed by the prevalent discourse about the war until then: namely that not only had the experience of the war been wounding at the time, but the wounds had not healed after ten years, and that to many in 1928 it did seem as if their lives had been blighted. Whatever the objective truth of the matter, Remarque's motto *made sense* to many people (to judge by the sales figures, to an overwhelming number). And what the common reader likes, genuinely traumatised or not, is that what they are about to read should make (some kind of) sense.

The end of the novel, Bäumer's death, on the other hand, made a more familiar sort of sense than the harsh but compelling generalisation with which the book begins. As we have seen, what infuriated the right about the novel, apart from the non-heroic representation of German soldiers, was that it stole 'their' war experience from them, and made it into *belles lettres*. The *Vossische Zeitung* in its pre-publicity to the first publication stressed the 'Gestaltungskraft', 'formal power'[21] of Remarque's work, a feat of composition which threatened the discursive monopoly upon the memory of the Front and its political meaning hitherto jealously protected by the right. The poetic ending vouchsafed Bäumer was, I suspect, a decisive component of that sense of satisfying form felt not only by the newspaper publicists, but by many reviewers, even when they also registered the right's unease at this misappropriation of 'authenticity'. But what, one supposes, was reassuring about the ending, and the formal properties of the text in general – for instance Kemmerich's boots as a leitmotiv for the uselessness of sentiment and the proximity of death – to the millions of readers not preoccupied with ideology, was precisely their literary character, that satisfying sense of closure associated with non-modernist fiction.

It is worth considering this ending for a moment longer, since it is in significant tension with other elements elsewhere in the novel. At one point, Paul Bäumer takes home leave, and fulfils the difficult duty of reporting the death of a friend and comrade, Kemmerich, to Kemmerich's mother. He tells her a lie about her son's death – 'I tell her that he received a shot to the heart and died immediately . . . "He died straight away. He didn't feel a thing. His expression was quite peaceful"'[22] – because the truth about his mutilation and suffering would be too difficult for her to bear. The reader, on the other hand, has not been spared the suffering and death of Kemmerich. He has had a leg amputated at the thigh (a pointless further mutilation, since he will not survive), knows that he will not recover despite the well-intentioned but only half-hearted attempts of his comrades to cheer him up, and is shocked at his own skeletal emaciation, which is evoked for the reader in some detail (p. 31). In Remarque not only mutilation, but worse, an individual subject's awareness of his own mutilation, is characteristic. The cruel motif consists of consciousness registering, often without the benefit of physical aid and always without metaphysical consolation, that brute materiality of the body that (until now) had been its tacit condition. Indeed, this topos is a key element of the nightlong encounter Bäumer has with a French soldier who is dying of the wounds Bäumer has inflicted upon him, the major compositional 'set-piece' of the novel. This topos is a guarantee of 'authenticity' in the Front novel: the gaze into the broken subjectivity of another. Yet of course, in the last words of the novel, the death of *Bäumer* is represented to the reader with exactly the same forbearance as that with which Bäumer reports Kemmerich's to his mother – 'Turning him over one saw that he could not have suffered long; his face had an expression of calm, as though almost glad the end had come' (p. 263). In the end, we are not told the truth about death in the war, we are given what we want and need, a literary lie: a death without the hideous unconsoled consciousness of the dying man.

And here, I think, we have one secret of the unique commercial success of Remarque's novel.[23] In its narrative of Front experience, its numerous deadpan reports of mutilation, its episodic development, its alternation of picaresque and horrific, its effective mimicry of the language of the Front soldier, it gives the reader the truth, or at least the sensation of it. But at the same time, it contrives to take what threatens to be an unbearable truth – namely a depiction of a world devoid of human meaning – and make it bearable, palatable, even, by lying to the reader in the socially sanctioned lie of fiction.

As Remarque owned up in a *New York Times Book Review* interview: 'It was really, simply a collection of the best stories that I told and that my friends told as we sat over drinks and relived the war.'[24] What Remarque had arranged into a novel seemed new in terms of literary genre, but was actually preformed in the minds of millions, corresponding 'quite closely to the surviving European folk-memory of trench-warfare'.[25] Yet it seems to me that this does not undermine the claim I have just made for the perfect mixture Remarque happened to achieve in his novel. No representation can ever give the truth of something – that is a contradiction in terms. But what we have in Remarque is a mixture of modes of representation, and that mixture, as well as its extraordinary reception, has intimately to do with the Front experience in the First World War.

The memory, the construction, of millions of people was about a subjective insight into meaninglessness familiar (if that is the right word) before 1914 only to the lunatic and the modernist. At one point we read: 'I am young, I am twenty years old; yet I know nothing of life but despair, death, fear and a completely meaningless surface of things linked to an abyss of suffering' ('die Verkettung sinnlosester Oberflächlichkeit mit einem Abgrund des Leidens') (p. 236; cf. also p. 245). This describes the Front experience, but describes also a crisis for representation. Feelings must assume appearance, suffering must assume surfaces, if aesthetically conventional representation is to come about. Where the two are discrete, you have a disjunction, an aesthetic space which is very different from that of Walter Flex, who can describe 'moments' at which, and indeed revere a character in whom, 'two worlds' meet. Where Jünger, recognising the disjunction of which Remarque writes, sought to hammer all experiences, regardless of the subjective stake, into a single steely discourse, Remarque struck a much more universal chord by diagnosing the disjunction, and proposing a plotless, episodic, empty ('nichts Neues') writing and the jargon of the Front to convey it.

Remarque does it both ways, and in doing so he achieves something that only high art had done before: finds form for formlessness. He gives the authentic feel of a historical actuality in which authenticity must have seemed a patent anachronism, yet suffuses it (on the penultimate page!) with a redemptive lyricism: 'It cannot really be lost: the tender promise that troubled our blood, that uncertain, perplexing, sense of what is yet to come, the thousand faces of the future, the melody of dreams and books, the whispers and anticipations of women, it cannot be true that it has all perished in the barrages, the despair and the company brothels' (p. 262). The whole sweetness of being a Western Individual is at stake.

In this he is closer to Kafka than he is to Zweig. In Zweig the depiction of the toils of bureaucracy – will the appropriate message ever reach the person with whom it can make some difference? – is prominent, but in the service of clear humanist thematisation. Everybody and everything has its name. In Remarque, experience appears largely stripped of dates and places, because he is on the threshold of the modernist aesthetic territory where to be disoriented is alright, where authority has lost its bearings, and where there is little more than this to show. Only the date of Bäumer's death is given. With that, we return to familiar territory.

It is Jünger and Remarque who suggest new forms for the representation of modern warfare, not Flex or Zweig, who adapt old ones. For all their difference in approach, Remarque appreciated Jünger's work ('it has a salutary detachment; precise, serious, powerful and strong')[26] and both display some elements of modernism, for instance the cruel Nietzschean vision in Jünger's prose, or the provision of form for formlessness in Remarque's narrative. *In Stahlgewittern* and *Im Westen nichts Neues* were also two of the most influential German prose works for German writers in the aftermath of the Second World War.[27] They played an important part in providing the literary means developed in the early post-1945 period by writers such as Heinrich Böll, Arno Schmidt and Walter Kolbenhoff who undertook 'experiments' in the search for a writing reduced enough to come to terms with the ravages, both physical and linguistic, suffered by Germans between the years of 1933 and 1945.

NOTES

1. See Richard Bessel, *Germany after the First World War* (Oxford, 1993), p. 268; and the reference there to Bernd Hüppauf's thesis that Remarque's novel helped establish the conditions for a new 'irrational mythologizing of war'.
2. Munich, 1916. All further references are to this edition.

3. See Roger Paulin, *The Brief Compass: the Nineteenth-Century German Novelle* (Oxford, 1985), p. 100.

4. See Bessel, *Germany after the First World War*, p. 262.

5. See Hans-Harald Müller, *Der Krieg und die Schriftsteller. Der Kriegsroman der Weimarer Republik* (Stuttgart, 1986), pp. 12 and 211.

6. See ibid., pp. 18–19.

7. This became generalised in subsequent editions to 'Den Gefallenen' ('the fallen').

8. Ernst Jünger, *In Stahlgewittern. Aus dem Tagebuch eines Stoßtruppführers* (Hannover, 1920), 'Vorwort', p. vii. Since Jünger made significant and frequent changes to his text, reference is made here to the first edition, with references to other editions signalled in notes where relevant.

9. For Jünger's relation to modernism, see Jeffrey Herf, *Reactionary Modernism: Technology, Culture, and Politics in Weimar and the Third Reich* (Cambridge, 1984), pp. 70–108, and David Midgley, 'The ecstasy of battle: some German perspectives on warfare between modernism and reaction', in *The Violent Muse: Violence and the Artistic Imagination in Europe, 1910–1939* (Manchester, 1994), pp. 113–23.

10. These words do not occur in the first edition. They are to be found in the later version collected in Ernst Jünger, *Werke*, 10 vols. (Stuttgart, 1960–5), vol. 1, *Tagebücher* 1 (Der erste Weltkrieg), *In Stahlgewittern*, pp. 9–310 (p. 172).

11. Jünger, *Werke*, 1, 169. Intriguingly, the first edition has 'das Unterbewußtsein' (p. 168).

12. Jünger, *Werke*, 1, 243 – this detail is not in the first edition.

13. Jünger, *Werke*, 1, 243.

14. See, for instance, Martin Travers, *German Novels on the First World War and their Ideological Implications, 1918–1933* (Stuttgart, 1982), p. 35.

15. Jünger, *Werke*, 1, 103; the first edition speaks of 'a great and virile indifference', p. 49.

16. Jünger, *Werke*, 1, 309.

17. See Arnold Zweig, 'Kriegsromane', *Die Weltbühne*, 25, 1 (1929), 597–9 (p. 597).

18. Arnold Zweig, *Der Streit um den Sergeanten Grischa. Roman*, in Arnold Zweig, *Ausgewählte Werke in Einzelausgaben*, 16 vols. (Berlin and Weimar, 1959–70), IV, 109. Future references are to this edition.

19. See Zweig, 'Kriegsromane'.

20. See Müller, *Der Krieg und die Schriftsteller*, p. 78.

21. Cited in Herbert Bornebusch, *Gegen-Erinnerung. Eine formsemantische Analyse des demokratischen Kriegsromans der Weimarer Republik* (Frankfurt am Main, 1985), p. 115.

22. Erich Maria Remarque, *Im Westen nichts Neues. Roman*, mit Materialien und einem Nachwort von Tilman Westphalen (Cologne, 1987), p. 166. Future references are to this edition.

23. For both Müller, *Der Krieg und die Schriftsteller*, pp. 61–4, and Alan Bance, '"Im Westen nichts Neues": a Bestseller in context', *Modern Language Review*, 72 (1977), 359–73, Remarque's novel owes some of its appeal to managing to be 'all things to all men' (Bance, p. 372).

24. Cited in Bornebusch, *Gegen-Erinnerung*, p. 116.

25. Bance, ' "Im Westen nichts Neues" ', p. 362.

26. Cited in Müller, *Der Krieg und die Schriftsteller*, p. 41, from a review written by Remarque in 1928.
27. See Jochen Pfeifer, *Der deutsche Kriegsroman 1945–60. Ein Versuch zur Vermittlung von Literatur und Soziologie* (Königstein/TS, 1981), pp. 18–23.

FURTHER READING

Fussell, Paul, *The Great War and Modern Memory* (New York and London, 1975)
Gollbach, Michael, *Die Wiederkehr des Weltkrieges in der Literatur. Zu den Frontromanen der späten Zwanziger Jahre* (Kronberg/TS, 1978)
Hüppauf, Bernd (ed.), *Ansichten vom Krieg. Vergleichende Studien zum Ersten Weltkrieg in Literatur und Gesellschaft* (Königstein/TS, 1984)
Köppen, Edlef, *Heeresbericht* (1930)
Renn, Ludwig, *Krieg* (1928)
Winter, Jay, *Sites of Memory, Sites of Mourning: the Great War in European Cultural History* (Cambridge, 1996)

11

RONALD SPEIRS

The German novel during the Third Reich

The novels discussed in this chapter all adopt a critical stance, though from widely different points of view, towards the period of National Socialist rule in Germany. Most, of necessity, were written outside the country, but one was written and, surprisingly, published inside the Third Reich. This selection is based not merely on political preference but on the quality of writing, for, as far as I am aware, no pro-Nazi novel of any literary merit exists.

National Socialism mainly had itself to blame for the lack of readable novels sympathetic to the cause, for the anti-critical mind-set of Nazism was inherently hostile to the spirit of free, often irreverent and disturbing inquiry that has inspired novels of any literary ambition from the mid sixteenth-century *Lazarillo de Tormes* onwards. The novel became one of the pre-eminent modes of engaging imaginatively with the modern world precisely because it dealt with things which the ideology of the National Socialists (if not their practice) abhorred as decadent, corrupting and debasing: the city, social conflict, sexuality, the role of the subconscious, or the relation of disease or weakness to creativity. Goebbels's desire to see the diet of historical and 'blood and soil' fiction varied by novels of contemporary, urban reality in the new Germany was bound to be disappointed, not simply because of the discrepancy between Nazi wish-dreams and observable reality, but because the 'cultural–political' practices of the Nazis – the public book-burnings in May 1933 by students at universities up and down the country, the 'black lists' of forbidden and undesirable literature, the control of the means of literary production – had resulted in the immediate and continuing exodus from Germany of the great majority of talented writers from 1933 onwards. Those who stayed had extreme difficulty in expressing themselves freely and critically.

Rather than attempt to list, in the restricted space available, the authors and novels of the period, I have selected examples of different kinds of novel, ranging from purported eye-witness accounts to more generalised or symbolic representations, either of conditions in Germany or of their allegedly historical, moral or natural origins. Such differences of approach were partly the result of difficulties in getting at the 'facts' once the writers were in exile (so that the frequency of novels about current conditions in Germany diminished, the longer the writers were away from home), or in describing them honestly (and having the result published) where they were not. As we shall see, however, other considerations played a part in the transformation of life into fiction.

Didacticism of one kind or another is one of the most striking characteristics of many German novels from this period, as more and more writers became involved in the battle for the hearts and minds of readers. Frequently they would turn to history for parallels or counter-models of development. Thomas Mann, for example, worked doggedly throughout the 1930s on an extended *Bildungsroman*, a cycle of four novels entitled *Joseph und seine Brüder* (*Joseph and His Brothers*), in which he treated the mythical story in a complex, ironic, playful manner calculated to undermine the portentous and dogmatic mythologising which lent support to the National Socialists' claim to understand and voice the primal truths of the German race.[1] Heinrich Mann similarly devoted much of his early period in exile to writing his two-volume[2] fictional life of Henry IV of France, the 'good king', beloved of his people, whom he intended as a corrective to the example of the National Socialist leaders; in this case the author's didactic urge issued in explicit 'moralités' spelling out the lessons to be learned from each stage in Henry's development to political maturity and wisdom.

In other cases didacticism takes the novel in the direction of the parable. Werner Bergengruen's *Der Großtyrann und das Gericht* (1935; *A Matter of Conscience*, 1952), for example, one of the most widely read novels of the period, is an extended parable on the fallibility of human nature and of man's need for repentance and humble submission to the will of God. The generality of the theme and the setting of the events in a distant time and place made it possible for the novel to be published and republished in National Socialist Germany and yet to be generally understood as a criticism of the dictatorial regime. Bergengruen was indignant, however, when he heard that some readers identified his Grand Tyrant with Hitler, since the former actually conducts the central moral experiment of the work and draws from it lessons both for his people and for himself;[3] on the other hand, the fact that the novel at least allowed for the possibility of enlightened tyranny may have been one of the reasons why it could be reprinted so often during those years.

A parable which deals more directly with the present, and hence could not appear in Germany, is the Austrian Ödön von Horváth's *Jugend ohne Gott* (1937; *Youth without God*).[4] The plot recalls that of Kleist's comedy,

The Broken Jug, except that in this case it is a broken casket which bears witness to the wrongdoing of a minor figure of authority, a schoolteacher who has broken open the box in order to read a pupil's diary during the class's compulsory stay at a cadet camp. Just as Kleist made Judge Adam try the case in which he was the guilty party, so Horváth has the teacher face the court of his conscience by telling his story and gradually uncovering his own self-deceptions and evasions. He felt prompted to invade the privacy of the pupil 'Z' after seeing him receive a letter secretly one night from an unknown boy from the locality. The teacher justifies the intrusion to himself on the grounds that the letter and the nocturnal meeting might be related to the recent theft of a camera from another pupil at the camp. He discovers, however, that 'Z' is actually having a liaison with a local girl, the leader of a band of juvenile thieves. His first reaction is one of (self-)righteous indignation: 'Not just Eva, Adam too had to answer for what they had done. Z ought to be arrested immediately' (*JG*, p. 70). Underlying the outrage, however, is the teacher's own suppressed sexual interest in the girl ever since he first saw her stand up and stretch her young back. His own muddled feelings of jealous identification with the youngsters lead the teacher to become their accomplice by not denouncing them, and then to compound this guilt by not admitting that it was he who broke open the casket when another pupil, 'N', is accused of doing so. As it happens, the teacher harbours personal resentment of 'N' for having conspired with his father to denounce him for criticising the racist ideology of National Socialism in class. Beyond this, he has a material interest in keeping quiet about what he has done, since it could cost him his position and his pension. To salve his conscience he tells himself that he will tell 'Z' privately about what he knows, and return the two young lovers to the path of virtue: 'I will pardon Z. And the girl too' (*JG*, p. 71). This misguided attempt to 'play God' by judging and pardoning others is thwarted, however, by the discovery that 'N', whom 'Z' had sworn to kill, is dead, and by the subsequent arrest and trial of 'Z' for murder.

By means of this concatenation of events Horváth leads the morally un-reliable narrator, who may at first strike the reader as being on the side of the angels when he challenges racism in the classroom, into many of the very same faults he has criticised in the Nazis: arrogance, self-delusion, self-interested cynicism and, above all, 'lying, the mother of all sins' (*JG*, p. 112). Horváth then allows the protagonist to redeem himself by admitting in open court that it was he, and not 'N', who broke open 'Z's' box and intruded on his privacy. Thereby the teacher is eventually able to prove that it was not in fact 'Z' who killed 'N'. This comes about because a small group of pupils are so impressed by the extraordinary sight of an adult who is prepared to tell the truth, even at considerable cost to himself, that they form a secret society sworn to discover who really killed 'N'. The culprit proves to be another pupil – 'T' – whose cold stare makes him seem the plainest embodiment of the prevailing 'age of the fish' (*JG*, p. 26), and whose motivation for the killing was the sheer cold-blooded desire to observe exactly what happened to another human being at the point of death. Prophetic though this character is of the agents of larger atrocities in the Third Reich, Horváth does not simply divide people into the good and the bad, but shows the fish-eyed boy to have been damaged in his turn by the condition of the age. He is the unloved son of a wealthy manufacturing family responsible for the misery of cheap child labour from which the girl thief and her juvenile accomplices have sought refuge in robbery. The initially sceptical, almost cynical narrator thus comes to recognise God's presence in the world as a principle, terrifyingly severe on first acquaintance, which causes the cruel consequences of human actions to become apparent and thereby prompts the easily corruptible human conscience to pay the price of its failings, to overcome the fear which perpetuates them, and to seek to put right the wrongs committed by individuals and the social order alike. In the end the narrator leaves the country to pursue missionary work amongst the negroes whom he had once defended against the officially inculcated racist prejudices of his pupils. The escape route is too neat, of course, but typical of the feeling amongst writers at the time that it was not enough to show the rise of evil under fascism, but that they should show both its inner weaknesses and the latent strengths which would ultimately defeat it.

There were other strategies of imaginative resistance to the depressing sight of the progressive Nazification of life in Germany. A welcome and unusual lightness of touch is to be found, for example, in Irmgard Keun's unpretentious but revealing little novel from 1937, *Nach Mitternacht* (*After Midnight*, 1938).[5] Sanna, the heroine-narrator of *After Midnight*, is an eighteen-year-old from a village in the Mosel valley who has come to Frankfurt to get away from a vindictive aunt and who, contrary to the National Socialist idealisation of 'community' life, finds life in the city more congenial, initially at any rate, than the constricting life in 'Lappesheim'. Sanna's combination of relative political naiveté with a sharp eye and astute common sense supplies a narrative perspective well suited to the task of unmasking the nastiness of life under National Socialism without the need to resort to heavy-handed didacticism. Within the perspective of an eighteen-year-old who would like to be beautiful, but fears she is not, National Socialism appears like some vast, artificial distraction from what really matters to a person of her age, namely falling in love and making a life for herself. Comic effects result from the contrast between National Socialist pretensions and the banality, vanity and stupidity of the individual SS and SA men Sanna and her friends meet in the pubs. The humour turns black, however, when a child dies having fever-ishly fulfilled her duty to the Fatherland by 'breaking through the cordon' to greet the Führer. In Sanna's experience those who are enthusiastic about the regime are without exception spiteful, bullying and self-interested, and she regrets that adults lose the childhood instinct to take revenge immediately on those who are 'mean', like her Aunt Adelheid, a 'beast' and 'sow', who had reported a chance remark of Sanna's to the local Gestapo simply because she resented feeding her and paying her the small amount of money left to her by Sanna's dead mother. Sanna's observations on individuals are synecdoches of the spirit of a regime which her friend, the despairing journalist Heini, sums up aptly: 'The fact is that we are living in the time of Germany's great denunciation movement. It is the duty of everyone to spy on everyone else. Everyone can have everyone else locked up' (*NM*, p. 87). From numerous snapshots a picture of small-scale fascism is built up which shows how the new regime both depends on, and gives free rein and a spurious justification to, the least admirable impulses in human nature, so that the majority, even including many of those who join the organisations of National Socialism, live in fear of betrayal. Two such denunciations provide the turning-points for the meagre plot of the novel. The first is Aunt Adelheid's reporting of Sanna, the second, more serious one is committed against Franz and his friend Paul by the owner of a tobacco shop (and member of the SA) who does not want competition from another shop in the same street. On his release from prison the otherwise gentle Franz strangles his denouncer, trav-els to Frankfurt to find Sanna, and flees with her on the first train out of Germany 'after midnight'.

Keun's aims and achievement in this novel are clearly limited. It offers no overall explanation of fascism (other than the self-aggrandisement and self-interest on which it feeds), and Sanna's comments are sometimes a little too perceptive for someone who, as she keeps saying, really does not understand what is going on in Germany. However, this lack of a grand design is offset by the verisimilitude of Sanna's guileless observations and her perceptiveness about her own shortcomings and those of others. The case against National Socialism is made simply and effectively by showing how much it is at odds with the ordinary decencies on which life depends. Although the novel ends with Sanna's relief at having got out of the country alive, the simple fact that the couple's modest claims on life cannot be realised in the 'new' Germany allows for some faint hope at least that a regime so hostile to love and kind-ness will not be able to survive for long, and certainly not for the thousand years of which it boasts.

Probably the most celebrated German novel about resistance to Nazi per-secution is Anna Seghers's *Das siebte Kreuz* (*The Seventh Cross*).[6] Like Jan

Petersen (pseudonym of Hans Schwalm), whose *Unsere Straße* (1936; *Our Street*, 1938), subtitled 'A chronicle written in the heart of fascist Germany in 1933–34', concentrated on the efforts to resist Nazi tyranny, Seghers tries to give some grounds for hope in the face of the National Socialists' growing suppression of all opposition. Writing just four or five years after Petersen, however, she is compelled to acknowledge just how strongly entrenched the regime has become, now that many of those who were once prepared to resist the takeover of 'our street' by the National Socialist storm-troops are dead, or have fled the country, or are imprisoned in one of the numerous purpose-built concentration camps needed to hold the many detainees. Indeed, so well established is the apparatus of terror, that it has acquired the reputation of being invincible. The task Seghers clearly set herself was to expose the underlying weaknesses of the rule of terror while yet conceding the extent of its power and the vested interest of its agents in defending the system. Her approach was to take a relatively minor incident, the escape of seven men from the concentration camp 'Westhofen', and to show that the regime's reliance on its reputed 'omnipotence' necessarily invests the incident with a significance far greater than the facts might otherwise warrant. If just one of the escapees eludes recapture, it is suggested, both the agents and the opponents of the regime will account it a major tear in the net of terror. Georg Heisler, the sole successful escapee, is able to endure hardships that would have broken men of lesser spirit precisely because he believes that so much depends on the outcome. Thanks to Georg's personal victory, not only does the 'seventh cross' remain empty on the seventh day after the break-out, but the other six crosses are promptly felled by the commandant who replaces the disgraced Fahrenberg. The control exercised by a purportedly totalitarian regime has been demonstrated to be less than total, the efforts and sacrifices of individuals to be crucially important.

The plot – the hunt – is a simple one. Its quality of sheer excitement has ensured the novel's continuing popularity, particularly with generations of the younger readers whom Seghers was determined to reach. At the same time, Seghers's multi-perspectival rendering of the experiences of those who are affected directly or indirectly by the race to save or recapture Heisler embeds the narrative in a much more nuanced picture of the circumstances and motives underpinning the Nazi regime than Petersen had drawn in 1934. Like Georg Heisler's successful escape, the narrative differentiation implicitly challenges the totalitarian claims of the regime by showing life to be complex and resistant to reductive formulae.

Rather than simply denouncing as evil those who support the National Socialist regime, Seghers shows that such support stems from a wide range of motives and varies greatly in depth. To embittered veterans of the First World

War like Commandant Fahrenberg and his henchman Zillich, for example, the SA held out the prospect of revenge and dreams of glory, while the posting to Westhofen offers them the opportunity to direct their aggressions at the camp's inmates. So complete is their attachment to their newly acquired power, however, that its loss will leave them with nothing at all. Thus, during the week-long hunt for Georg Heisler, it is not Georg or his recaptured mentor Wallau who breaks under the strain, but Fahrenberg. Like the collapse of Fahrenberg's and Zillich's world in the course of a single week, the revulsion at violence felt not just by bystanders but even, fleetingly, by those who have to practise it, forms part of an argument (varied in numerous novels of the period) that National Socialism both feeds and feeds on a perversion of human nature, and is therefore unsustainable in the longer term. The point is reinforced by interspersed narrative reflections on the history of the region around Mainz which has seen many barbarously cruel regimes come and go, none of them having endured for the thousand years of which Hitler dreamt.

A camp like Westhofen depends, however, not just on the cruelty of those in charge but also on its social, economic and moral hinterland. The small-holders in the area, for example, are more likely to welcome a new market for their produce than to question the camp's purpose. Those who cycle daily to the factories of the nearby town are happy to have work again after years of unemployment. This is true even of Franz Marnet, an erstwhile close friend of Georg Heisler and no friend of the regime, a man in whom the German work ethic is, however, so deeply ingrained, that he would work to the limit of his ability, 'even if his employer had been the devil himself' (SK, p. 20). Like Petersen, Seghers was a communist who wanted to believe that National Socialism would collapse from economic as well as moral weakness. Yet, as she acknowledges, the capacity of German workers to accept such conditions is very elastic, particularly amongst those who, like Paul Röders (another friend from Heisler's youth), are taken in by the 'bread and circuses' policies of the regime, the subventions for numerous children, the mobile cinemas and subsidised sports events and holidays. The largest bribe of this kind was the tenancy of a home in one of the state's new model villages, such as that enjoyed by Herr and Frau Kreß. In the event, however, all these characters are willing to risk everything in order to help the desperate Heisler. In each case there are obstacles to overcome: Franz resents the fact that Georg deserted him and went off with his girlfriend; Paul's wife does not see why the family's happiness should be put at risk for Georg's sake; Herr and Frau Kreß risk losing a privileged way of life for a stranger. Yet all of this counts as nothing when the life of another helpless human being is at stake. In return for the risks they take, all those who help Georg escape gain a new lease of life. Their experience inverts that of Fahrenberg and Zillich:

whereas a life built on power ultimately proves to be empty, a life capable of caring for another is one which gains even as it puts itself at risk. In their own spheres each of these courageous characters embodies a facet of the central symbolic figure of the novel, St Martin, patron saint of the cathedral in Mainz, in and around which much of the action takes place. The forces mobilised by Seghers into a united front of moral opposition to the regime are drawn not just from the political left but from an older humane tradition, Christian in origin (although often betrayed by the Church), which survives in secularised form in the present.

Technically, *The Seventh Cross* is both a virtuoso piece of writing and a flawed one. The virtuosity lies in the carefully judged changes of pace and perspective, the latter shifting repeatedly from that of a distanced, reflective narratorial voice to the empathetic rendering of the thoughts, feelings and physical sensations of a large cast of characters. The flaw lies in a plot that allows Georg to escape out of moral conviction that this is what 'ought' to happen, since merely to register what is the case would be to neglect what could be the case. This utopian tendency is linked in turn to the narrator's omniscience. The narrator speaks at times as one of the inmates of Westhofen and at others as a hovering presence able to report on matters widely separate in time and space, in the public domain or within the recesses of many different individuals' minds. This omnipresence is rooted in the narrator's belief that (s)he knows what is going on at the heart of the world because (s)he belongs to the worldwide network of the communist movement with its claim to understand the inherent laws of history and to act as their agent. This same conviction sustains Heisler and Wallau in the loneliest moments of their struggle. They, it has been aptly observed, are secular saints; correspondingly the narrator pretends to the kind of certain knowledge that has inspired all books of revelation.

In the years 1933–45 novelists returned again and again to fear as the central feature of life under National Socialism; the chilling leitmotiv 'weistu was, so schweig' ('if you know something, keep quiet'), which echoes and re-echoes through Thomas Mann's *Doktor Faustus* (discussed later in this chapter), could find a place in many other novels of the time. For Anna Seghers the strength to overcome fear springs from a person's bonds with others, and from the associated belief in a future form of human society which will be the antithesis of all that fascism represents. For Horváth, as for Bergengruen, overcoming fear is the first step to recovering self-respect, moral freedom and the decision to resist tyranny. Ernst Jünger's 1939 novel *Auf den Marmorklippen (On the Marble Cliffs, 1947)* too was widely understood, both outside and inside the Third Reich, to offer a model of resistance to tyranny and its fifth column, fear.[7] Its very publication in Germany in that year provoked astonishment and may only have come about because Jünger had friends in high places. True to his recalcitrant, disdainful disposition, Jünger insisted long after the defeat of Hitler, when so many claimed to have belonged to one form of resistance or another, that he was suspicious of the word 'resistance' and critical of 'superficially political' readings of the novel, particularly where these simply identified the images of tyranny in the novel with National Socialism. Certainly, while certain features of the Oberförster's practice of terror, the sporadic, gradually intensifying application of violence, for example, or the skinning-house at Köppelsbleek, can be seen to resemble conditions in Germany before and after Hitler's seizure of power, the ebullient, excessive Oberförster and the petit-bourgeois, vegetarian Hitler are about as dissimilar a pair of figures as one can imagine.

Jünger's method of viewing the base reality of Nazism from a higher perspective was to construct an imaginary, symbolic world that patently deviates from the real events of recent history. The explanation for the destruction of this world comes from the application to human history of 'laws' purportedly derived from myth and nature (as understood by a mind steeped in Goethe's thought). The marble cliffs inhabited by the narrator and his brother lie between the civilised, initially idyllic world of Marina at the foot of the cliffs, and two semi-circles of territory above them, the first a steppe-like area, the Campagna, inhabited by semi-nomadic herdsmen with a primitive sense of justice and intense piety towards their pagan gods, the second a swampy, forested region, the 'horns' of which reach down into the steppes below, a place beyond the reach of any law, where rabble gather who have fled the inner rings of civilised life. This outer fastness is the domain of the green-coated Oberförster whose genealogy reaches back, not just to Hitler or Stalin, but to Nietzsche's Dionysos, from whom he takes his 'fearful joviality', and to such manifestations of the daemonic as 'the Green One' in Gotthelf's *The Black Spider*. He is the Wild Hunter and the embodiment of violent, lustful anarchy in one. The emergence and ultimate triumph of sheer destruction for its own sake, as exemplified by the Oberförster, is for Jünger a symptom of decadence in a civilisation that has lost the ability to contain and discipline instinctual violence. Disturbingly, the grim delight evident in the descriptions of the ferocious fight with the Oberförster and his terrifying dogs of war indicate that such instincts are present even in normally peaceable men like the narrator. Moreover, the collapse of order into blood-lusting anarchy is presented as an inevitable consequence of the cyclical, organic processes governing all forms of life, indeed as a necessary condition of renewal.

Jünger returns to this theme repeatedly, but its clearest expression is to be found in the twentieth of the novel's thirty chapters, where the narrative structure embeds human events within the processes of nature. The main event, on the human level, is the visit to the cliff-top retreat of two senior Mauretanians, Braquemart and Prince Sunmyra. Their bold purpose is to halt the advance of the Oberförster, yet neither seems to have the combination of qualities needed for the task. The fateful separation of spirit and power in these two men is symptomatic of the fissures in the civilised world that have their external counterpart in the Oberförster's assault on it, and it signals clearly to the narrator just how far 'decadence' and 'decline' (MK, p. 92) have progressed already. Framing the meeting of the brothers with their noble visitors, however, is an event in the plant world which points to a larger order transcending society's imminent descent into the abyss. Just before the arrival of the guests Brother Otho takes the narrator into the garden to admire the freshly opened 'gold-banded lily of Zipangu' as it waits to be pollinated by the evening moths. The description of the flower is full of symbolic detail, such as the 'golden flame' in the midst of its white cup, or the six fine pollen heads which 'order themselves in a circle' around the stamen. The fragrant flower exemplifies both the fragility of individual life and its function as the vessel of a mighty, vital and erotic charge: 'It will for ever remain a miracle that the soul of these tender beings is filled with such a great power of love' (MK, p. 88). The flame-red at the heart of the white lily links it with a pattern of fire imagery running through the entire novel, weaving together the forces of destruction (the 'fireworms' who do the bidding of the Oberförster by burning Marina) and the forces of magical preservation at work, for example, in the flame of Nigromontan's lamp. All life, the narrator reflects, is subject to the law of the Phoenix, which renews itself out of destruction: 'Human order resembles the cosmos in that, from time to time, it must plunge into the fire to be born anew' (MK, p. 55). He sees this law enacted in the lily, to which he returns after the guests have departed:

> Insects had already flown onto the fine pollen-vessels and the green-golden depths of the cup were stained with purple dust. It had presumably been scattered by the great moths of the night during their wedding feast. Thus sweetness and bitterness flow from every hour. And as I bent over the dew-covered cups of the blossoms the first call of the cuckoo sounded from the distant edge of the forest.
>
> (MK, p. 97)

The mocking cuckoo signals the advance of the Oberförster, stressing the proximity of creation and destruction. Yet the work of pollination has been done, so that the brief beauty of the lily may return in the next generation. To help his readers confront their fear and to face the horrors of the National Socialist perversion of humanity, Jünger could offer only the belief that there exists a mysterious, objective order in the worlds of nature, spirit and justice, that offences against this order will bring about destruction, that the forces of anarchy will ultimately be contained again within an enduring, balanced whole – but not that they will (or even should) ever be banished entirely from human life. If this seems fatalistic and of little practical value in fighting evil, since its generalising, symbolic equation of historical with biological processes pays scant attention to the specific political conditions that made fascism possible, one must remind oneself of how dark the world seemed in Germany on the eve of the Second World War.

Whether judged by the controversy provoked on its publication in 1947 or by its enduring interest for later generations of readers, Thomas Mann's *Doktor Faustus* (begun in 1943) is arguably the most important and ambitious German novel from the years of the National Socialist dictatorship, and the account it gives of the attractions of fascism one of the most disturbing.[8] The core of the work is the biography of a German composer, Adrian Leverkühn, who, apart from a period in Italy, lives his entire life in Germany until his collapse into syphilis-induced insanity in 1930 and his death ten years later. Mann's treatment of this fictional life yields a complex amalgam of the main types of German novel of this period: the novel of contemporary life in Germany, the novel of German society in the years leading up to the advent of fascism, the historical novel, the artist novel, the intellectual novel, even the novel of exile, to the extent that the inner exile of the narrator, Serenus Zeitblom, allows Mann to express some of his own feelings of loss (and guilt). The novel's unusual range is achieved by a technique of 'montage' whereby materials drawn from many historical, biographical and literary sources are assembled to construct the character and experiences of the protagonist and the other figures with whom he comes into contact. The result is a kind of 'psycho-history' or diagnosis of the 'German problem' as the expression of a personality structure which Mann believed German culture had produced and reproduced across the centuries.

Adrian Leverkühn is clearly intended to represent Germany, but he does so in a contradictory, complicated and indirect way. Although he makes periodic attempts to join in with the social trends of his times, with a pro-German student fraternity, for example, or, after the First World War, with the more radically nationalist Kridwiss circle in Munich, these sallies into society are short-lived, and he soon withdraws again into his accustomed solitude. Yet this very isolation is one of the characteristics which make Adrian, in Mann's view, typical of Germany as a whole for, by accepting reactionary, authoritarian forms of governance and rejecting the general European trend towards parliamentary democracy, the Germans seemed determined always to follow their own path or *Sonderweg*. During the years when Hitler was elaborating his regressive *Führerprinzip* of unconditional obedience, Adrian too is devising his own, idiosyncratic ideal of social organisation – albeit a radically egalitarian one, quite different from that of National Socialism. This is expressed in a new musical language that sets aside traditional key-based tonality. In Adrian's system (partly modelled by Mann on Schoenberg's twelve-tone method) the structure of a piece of music is based on its 'tone row', the composer's arrangement of all twelve notes of the chromatic scale into a particular sequence. (No note in a row may be used again until all the other notes have been played.) All thematic developments are based on structural variations of the original tone row, but within this framework each note is free to combine with all the others in the row (since no key signature dictates what are 'right' and 'wrong' notes).[9] Adrian needs to construct such an abstract theory precisely because, in reality, he finds most social relationships impossibly difficult. The freedom of combination posited by his theory is mocked by the compulsive, neurotically repetitive aspect of his own conduct, particularly from that point in his adult life when he takes lodgings at a farmstead that is virtually an exact replica of the one on which he spent his childhood – but which he now shuns, and with it his brother and mother. The egalitarian theory is similarly undercut by his individualistic ambition to create something entirely new in the history of music and (like those of his countrymen who chose to follow Hitler) to experience a 'große Zeit' at whatever cost the Devil may exact for it.

The central characteristic shared by the (self-destructive and self-martyring) creativity of Adrian Leverkühn and the sheer destructiveness of National Socialism is a tendency to radical extremes of feeling or action. It is a quality Mann detected in the German thinkers and artists from Luther to Nietzsche, from Beethoven to Hugo Wolf, from whose lives he culled details for his biography of Leverkühn (which, translated, means 'one who lives boldly'). The same trait links Adrian's obsessive determination to 'break through' to a new musical language with the attempts of generals to break through the enemy's lines of defence, whatever the cost in soldiers' lives. This national disposition supposedly has the quality of a latent communal neurosis or 'psychic epidemic' (DF, p. 39) which would break out in witch-hunts in late medieval Kaisersaschern and, it is implied, is doing so again in the racist mania unleashed by the Nazis.

If Adrian's life offers an insight into the alleged persistence of this predisposition in the Germans, it appears to lie in the reaction to a particular type of ascetic culture. Adrian's musicality is inherited from his mother. More importantly, as far as his psychic development is concerned, it is inherited along with a reluctance to make music, for although gifted with a naturally melodious speaking voice, Adrian's beautiful mother is never heard to sing. Her restraint in this area is just one expression of the puritanically coloured piety evident in her decorous bearing, dress and neatly parted and tied-up hair. Without being dominating or censorious, Adrian's mother, a model of graceful self-control, becomes for her unusually excitable son a source of desire and repression, making him so uneasy about anything that touches his emotions that he tends to flee such experiences or intellectualise or laugh at them. His seeming intellectual coldness, however, will then give way periodically to utter abandonment to impulse. The predictable antithesis of this Madonna figure in Adrian's experience is the uninhibited cow-maid Hanne, whose bare feet are permanently caked in dung, and whose 'wobbly bosom' attracts the gaze of the young Adrian and Serenus when she introduces them to the pleasure of singing simple rounds. The opposing associations of music, pleasure, sex and dirt on the one hand and, on the other, of decency and the repression of desire, prove fateful for Adrian, pitching him between extremes of heat and cold and from severe self-discipline to masochistic self-indulgence. When he first yields to sexual attraction, the woman, inevitably, is a prostitute from whom he knowingly contracts the syphilis that will progressively destroy his nervous system and thus punish him for his passion. Music becomes the symbolic battleground for the extremes of feeling in Adrian. When these conflicts finally lead to his collapse into insanity, Adrian's mother comes to fetch him home to the family farm at Buchel. Adrian's response is to attack her violently, the clear implication being that he blames her (quite unjustly) for all that has gone wrong in his life. His mental collapse in 1930 coincides with a huge surge in electoral support for the National Socialists. The extremism that produced Adrian's creativity and madness up to this point is followed by the years of destructive extremism orchestrated by the Nazis, of which the now docile Adrian is utterly unaware.

It is easy to accuse *Doktor Faustus* of tendentiousness in its account of National Socialism. The selective line of descent the novel traces through history, for example, simply omits those periods (in the 1840s, say) when Germans fought unsuccessfully for the introduction of democracy. The focus on Adrian's life is too narrow to show the historical possibilities in the Weimar Republic that might have led, not to the victory of the National Socialists, but in quite other directions. Above all, critics have questioned the novel's implication (which recalls Freud's argument in his essay *Civilisation and its Discontents*) that Adrian's development shows how both the creative and the destructive potential in the Germans could spring from the same source, namely a psychological reaction to the repressive effects of German culture. In defence of the novel one could respond firstly that it shows paradigms which are not restricted to Germany (so that fascism could potentially emerge wherever the same cultural conflicts exist) and secondly that socio-economic factors, taken in isolation, are equally incapable of explaining the emergence of fascism. Despite its undoubted success as a psychological and intellectual novel, however, the ambition of *Doktor Faustus* to be more than that does highlight the problems of turning the novel of individual development into a vehicle of historical explanation. On the other hand, the value of the genre during the period of National Socialist rule lay precisely in its insistence on personal complexity and its refusal to let personal singularity become submerged in the homogenised abstraction 'Volk'.

With the possible exception of *Doktor Faustus*, the novels discussed in this chapter are not 'modernist', if this is taken to mean radically experimental in form and technique. Nor, on the other hand, did these authors generally turn to nineteenth-century models of dispassionate realism to record the advent of National Socialism. Mostly they employed a mixed mode of fiction, well established in German literature since the Enlightenment, one which incorporated realistically observed detail into various types of didactic or exemplary narrative. Their common aim was to defend humanity against its despisers, and to offer some vision of hope, however precarious, to set against the fear on which tyranny depends.

NOTES

1. *Die Geschichten Jaakobs* (1933; *The Tale of Jacob*, 1934), *Der junge Joseph* (1934; *Young Joseph*, 1935), *Joseph in Ägypten* (1936; *Joseph in Egypt*, 1938), *Joseph der Ernährer* (1943; *Joseph the Provider*, 1944). *Joseph and His Brothers* was published in one volume in 1948.
2. *Die Jugend des Königs Henri Quatre* (Amsterdam, 1935; *King Wren*, 1937), *Die Vollendung des Königs Henri Quatre* (Amsterdam, 1938; *The Last Days of Henri Quatre, King of France*, 1938). Amsterdam, especially the publishing house Querido, was the most important centre for the publication of anti-fascist novels in the 1930s, a role later taken over by Mexico.
3. See Werner Bergengruen, *Schreibtischerinnerungen* (Zurich, 1961), p. 180.
4. References here (as *JG*) are to the edition published by suhrkamp taschenbuch, Frankfurt am Main, 1994. The English translation, first published in 1938, was reissued as *The Age of the Fish* in 1978.
5. References here (as *NM*) are to the paperback edition published by dtv in Munich, 1989.
6. The novel was written during 1937–9 in exile in Paris. It was published in 1942: in English in Boston, and in German in Mexico. References here (as *SK*) are to the paperback edition published by Aufbau Verlag, Berlin, 1996.
7. References here (as *MK*) are to the paperback edition published by Ullstein in Frankfurt am Main, 1995. The English translation appeared in 1947.
8. The novel's full title is *Doktor Faustus. Das Leben des deutschen Tonsetzers Adrian Leverkühn erzählt von einem Freunde*; references here (as *DF*) are to the Fischer paperback edition (Frankfurt am Main, 1971). The English translation *Doctor*

Faustus: the Life of the German Composer Adrian Leverkühn as Told by a Friend appeared in 1948.
9. Patrick Carnegy has shown that there are in fact major differences between Leverkühn's fictional system and Schoenberg's Method. See *Faust as Musician: a Study of Thomas Mann's Novel 'Doctor Faustus'* (New York, 1973), pp. 37–54.

FURTHER READING

Berman, Russell A., *The Rise of the Modern German Novel: Crisis and Charisma* (Cambridge, MA, 1986)
Denkler, H. and K. Prümm (eds.), *Die deutsche Literatur im Dritten Reich* (Stuttgart, 1976)
Emmel, H., *Geschichte des deutschen Romans*, vol. III (Bern, 1978)
Ketelsen, U.-K., *Literatur und Drittes Reich* (Vierow bei Greifswald, 1994)
Köpke, W., 'Antifaschistische Literatur am Beispiel Deutschlands', in *Propyläen Geschichte der Literatur*, vol. VI (Berlin, 1982), pp. 100–17
Ritchie, J. M., *German Literature under National Socialism* (London, 1983)
Rüther, G. (ed.), *Literatur in der Diktatur* (Paderborn, 1997)
Schäfer, H. D., *Das gespaltene Bewußtsein. Deutsche Kultur und Lebenswirklichkeit 1933–1945* (Munich, 1981)
Schoeps, K.-H., *Deutsche Literatur zwischen den Weltkriegen III. Literatur im Dritten Reich* (Bern, 1992)
Siefken, H., 'National Socialism and German literature', *German Life and Letters*, 38 (1984), 177–93
Stern, J. P., *The Dear Purchase: a Theme in German Modernism* (Cambridge, 1995)
Strothmann, D., *Nationalsozialistische Literaturpolitik* (Bonn, 1960)
Trapp, F., *Deutsche Literatur zwischen den Weltkriegen II. Literatur im Exil* (Bern, 1983)
Wulf, J., *Literatur und Dichtung im Dritten Reich. Eine Dokumentation* (Frankfurt am Main, 1983)

12

DAGMAR BARNOUW

History, memory, fiction after the Second World War

At the end of the most destructive war in historical memory, Germans were confronted with the near-impossible demand that they look at the now visible enormity of material and moral devastation and accept collective responsibility. Collectively they had become 'the German question', as the photo-journal *LIFE* announced on the title page of the issue that published the first images of the opening of the camps. In the pre-television period, these images had enormous power, and they made ordinary Americans ask how the German people could have committed such acts of unspeakable, unbelievable cruelty. The assumption of collective guilt and demand for collective remorse was to endure for over half a century, creating the politically potent notion of a uniquely German 'unmastered' or 'uncompleted' past. At the end of the war German civilians, at that time women, children and old men, were taken to the camps to view the atrocities committed in their name. This was documented in a large number of photos taken by US Army Signal Corps photographers whose task was to show the viewers' criminal culpability and lack of remorse; and their notoriously 'stony' faces do indeed show horror and repulsion rather than sadness.[1] Obviously, they did not know how to react to what they saw and they did not understand what was asked of them. They were ordinary women who had just barely survived a total war of hitherto unknown dimensions, with most of the men either killed or prisoners of war, and when the victors asked the notorious question, 'How could you have done it?' they would answer 'We did not know anything about it', which confirmed the victors' certainty that they 'must all have known'. Whether they did or did not know is politically still a 'live' but ultimately moot question, because from the beginning it failed to address the different ways of knowing and of remembering. Instead it imposed an enduring sameness of guilt – they all knew everything and did not do anything – and of memory: they will now all remember, and in the same way, that they did know and did not act. The resulting conflicts between private and public memory made it difficult to remember spontaneously, though over a period of more than five decades Germans have been abundantly reminded of their responsibility for the atrocities and unfailingly pious in their rituals of collective, public remembrance. The general cultural collapse at the end of the war inhibited the formation of a 'normal' temporally constructed identity sustained by a 'normally' selective and fluid complex of memories. What the evidence forced Germans to believe and thereby accept as their responsibility contradicted in most cases their memories of what they had known at the time when the events occurred. The burden of responsibility seemed overwhelming precisely because it denied them authority over their past, their memories, their historical identity: collectively guilty, they had become collectively *unmündig*, minors without a voice.[2] Moreover, the new German collective memory of having participated in the most brutal acts of victimisation was constructed to endure because of the nature of that victimisation and of the Allies' absolute moral and military victory. This new collective memory which supported German collective guilt, though embraced by many Germans in the immediate postwar period because they wanted to understand what had happened and atone for it, remained alien but inescapable, removed from the 'normal' gradual changes in time.

As the Allies had hoped, the new collective memory producing a collective German bad conscience arguably did contribute to West Germany's democratic development: having learned its lesson, the *Bundesrepublik* has been a remarkably stable political presence in postwar Europe. Yet the nature of the lesson and the way in which it was taught have also been responsible for the often deceptively smooth symbiosis of political and moral arguments in German postwar culture, creating its own considerable problems. Where the history of Germany's 'uncompleted' past is concerned, the inclination to impose taboos has always been stronger than the willingness to invite questions. Whenever history became an issue, it was in the context of an, in somebody's view, (un)desirable politics of history – the most notorious example being the 'historians' dispute' of the late 1980s concerning historiographical approaches to the Holocaust.[3] Fragmented and uncertain, German historiography of the recent past has reflected quite accurately a general cultural and political inability to deal with the historical reality of Nazi aggression, particularly the persecution of Jews. For over half a century it has been difficult to approach these events in relational, historical terms, that is, as phenomena whose current cultural significance would not be exempt from changing, like all things, in time. Soberly critical inquiry into the historical events that were later subsumed into the increasingly ritualised, monumentalised 'Holocaust' has been suspect as sinful 'revisionism' that would diminish their political and cultural 'uniqueness' – curious in view of the fact that all historiography worth its salt draws on new research that would 'revise', at least to some degree, the old orthodoxy. The 'historians' dispute' had little to do with questions of historiographic methodology and everything to do with the political uses of memory and remembrance in postwar Germany. It was ended by political *fiat* rather than professional consensus: namely, by the German President's declaration 'Auschwitz remains unique. It was perpetrated by Germans in the name of Germany. This truth is immutable and will not be forgotten.'[4] The Holocaust commemorations of 1995 were to confirm his verdict; so too, in the late 1990s and in the new millennium, were many other similar disputes: the controversy surrounding the construction of an appropriate *Mahnmal*, a monument to the persecution of Jews in the heart of the new–old capital Berlin; the argument between the writer Martin Walser and the Chair of the Board of Jewish Deputies in Germany, Ignatz Bubis, over the silencing of a multivocal, more differentiating German memory; the debates over German involvement in the Kosovo conflict; and most recently debates about a renewed German anti-Semitism.

All these disputes and controversies have drawn on the intense politicisation of German cultural memory that goes deeper than the usual political affiliations and interests, though 'the left' has seen itself as Germany's conscience in this matter, even more so after reunification and the discrediting of communism. Unless they are rigorously focused on collective guilt and remembrance, discussions of recent German history tend to provoke politically overheated mutual suspicions and accusations. The right is then seen as prettifying German history for political gains, the left as imposing on all Germans a politically opportune singular significance of Auschwitz. Self-appointed *preceptor Germaniae*, the social philosopher Habermas started the historians' dispute but then simply refused to differentiate between different historiographical positions: disagreeing on principle with all historians on the right, he assumed that they would all be the same. All of them would look for the wrong evidence in that 'unredeemed' past, whereas he, speaking for the left, would look for the only true evidence – the signs of collective guilt and lack of remorse. This huge and harmful simplification has contributed to the fact that after more than half a century there is still no psychologically realistic attempt at understanding the very real difficulties of individual memory caused by the never clarified concept of collective guilt and collective atonement through public remembrance. The increasing 'fetishisation' of Auschwitz is the result not so much of questionable historiographical method as of the unquestioned politics of history.

One of the most prolific defenders of the uniqueness of Jewish persecution, Saul Friedlander has consistently argued for retaining a transhistorical remoteness or, the other side of the coin, ahistorical immediacy of Auschwitz. He has rejected 'historicisation' because it would mean 'reinserting the Nazi

phenomenon into normal historical narrative', which to him equals 'minimis-
ing or abolishing what still makes it appear as singular'.[5] In all his writing,
Friedlander has emphasised an unquestioned and enduring centrality, for
cultural modernity, of the collective remembrance of Auschwitz. He sees no
problems with privileging memory and remembrance over historiography,
since in his view 'no amount of factual information' will 'resolve' the issue
of a 'centrality or noncentrality' of Jewish persecution in western culture.[6]
The historian Martin Broszat argued in his 'Plea for a historicization of
National Socialism' (1985) and in an exchange of letters with Friedlander,
that representation of the entangled German-Jewish past required a history
that was not exclusively shaped, as was collective remembrance, by the perspective of extreme victimisation during the final stage of the Nazi regime.[7]
But Friedlander has been adamant that in the case of Auschwitz historicisation would mean an unacceptable 'normalization' of the past: there has
to be an enduring 'total dissonance' between the past apocalypse and the
present normality.[8] And indeed, since the end of the war, narratives of victimisation have commanded complete belief, no matter how consistent or
contradictory, how clear or how confused, how concrete or how formulaic,
how believable or unbelievable they are. They have been accepted on their
own terms of reference, which, certainly for German readers, has made them
different in kind from all other discourses. Born out of experiences beyond
civilised imagination for which all Germans were held accountable, these
accounts of memory were rarely questioned as to the veracity and validity
of the stories they told. Archetypal stories of victimisation, they are complete by virtue of their own authority; by definition they cannot and need
not be corroborated. Acceptance of such complete authority of remembered
persecution has called for the essential primacy of poetic over historical discourse where 'the Holocaust' is concerned. In this scenario, supported by
many Holocaust experts, all historiographical representation of the Nazi period not firmly anchored in the transhistorical uniqueness of Auschwitz is
eo ipso suspect – a position that reflects the collective hyper-subjectivity
regarding mass victimisation which, explosive and exploitable, has also
contributed significantly to the politics of memory and history in postwar
Germany.

Public remembrance of Jewish victimisation has been remarkably static and
exclusive in German postwar culture, despite the fact that the lives of millions
of non-Jews were prematurely ended or painfully disrupted and changed
by the experience of a total war that they had feared above all else. If recalled, their memories, too, would make present normality seem strange. But
these memories have been individual, not group memories and, recalled into

different presents during the past half century of (relative) normality, they have not remained the same. Their authority has been partial and temporary, to be questioned and corroborated. Separating the fully authorised narrative of Judeocide so radically from an only partly authorised 'normal' history of the period has prevented us from looking at the German-Jewish catastrophe as part of a complex, contradictory and insufficiently understood historical experience. 'Normally' the past is recalled under the conditions of the present and since its recalling is provoked and shaped by that present, it is, in each instant of recalling, no longer the same past. Precisely this insight, central to the modern concept of cultural historicity, has been suppressed in German postwar culture with its emphasis on 'honest confrontation', generation after generation, with past Jewish persecution. This emphasis has disregarded the fact that the past is a creation of historical time, fluid, porous and multilayered. Events in the present can be confronted. The past can and must be revisited – but not without critical acknowledgment that these visits, departing for the past from different presents, will not leave it unchanged.

In its open perspectivism and multivocalism, fictional discourse differs from the largely monological discourse of remembrance but also from historical discourse with its critically shared and controlled processes of establishing evidence. There is a different relation between representation and knowledge in each case, and fictional discourse is characterised by the fact that it withholds both affirmation and negation. In principle it could create more space for exploring different positions – different visits to the past, different returns to different presents – including areas where psychologically painful and politically potent aspects of individual and collective memory are concerned. Fictional discourse may clarify, but also obscure issues; it may help understanding, but also create misunderstandings: it is the reader's role and privilege to negotiate them. However, the 'uncompleted', 'unmastered' German past that has been present, at least as a subtext, in all of postwar fiction, seems on the whole to have defeated that privilege: the potential of fictional discourse for non-assertive accommodation of many different voices has here been severely restricted. As in historiography, representation of the Nazi period and its aftermath has met with formidable obstacles, not least because these went largely unexplored. 'Normally' the different status of truth statements in fictional discourse opens up, for both author and reader, a variety of interpretative choices in relation to a shared life-world. But here the cultural context of collective memory and guilt has proved, on the whole, too massive to allow for such flexibility. Many of the novels dealing with the 'German question' are curiously reluctant to ask questions; they inhibit critical dialogue, even where they seem to invite it. George Steiner, speaking here for many professional and non-professional readers, unwittingly confirmed this in his 1964 review of Grass's *Dog Years* (*Hundejahre*, 1963), the third novel in what is now called the 'Danzig Trilogy':[9] he praised especially Grass's 'bawling voice' that had managed 'to drown the siren-song of smooth oblivion, to make the Germans – as no writer did before – face up to their monstrous past'.[10] Grass's 'enormous success' with *The Tin Drum* (*Die Blechtrommel*, 1959) – 300,000 copies sold in Germany, more than 60,000 in France, almost 200,000 in the US – was therefore highly important to Steiner and, he suggested, to every civilised reader in the western world.[11] The issue was not partial illumination of an extraordinarily difficult and painful past, but total confrontation.

But what were the reasons for Grass's success that put 'German literature back on the market'?[12] Steiner seems to overlook the fact that the boom enjoyed by what he calls the Grass 'industry' would seem to undermine his assertion that Germans did not want to remember – unless Grass had been devilishly clever in forcing them. But how? and much more importantly: who were 'they'? Clearly, Steiner did not give Grass's readers a second thought as long as 'they' were made to 'face up to their monstrous past'. His argument here is exuberantly eloquent, conceptually contradictory and instructively cliché-ridden. Thus he acknowledges the problems with Grass's self-consciously tortuous prose but lauds him for throttling 'the falsehood and cant out of the old words, trying to cleanse them with laughter and impropriety so as to make them new'. More, this forceful prose, in his view, managed to counteract the 'arrogant obscurities of German philosophic speech'. Steiner, whose general observations on Grass's style apply both to *Dog Years* and *The Tin Drum*, is clearly referring to Martin Heidegger, notorious for his difficult poetic-philosophical style and his temporary association with the Nazi regime. Yet the mostly Jewish, Hegelian–Marxian intellectuals of the Frankfurt School share this indeed culturally arrogant verbal obscurantism and so, in the thick, sprawling wordiness of his fiction, does Grass. Steiner himself admits Grass's 'uncontrolled prolixity, his leviathan sentences and word inventories', and concedes that 'in the end . . . his obsessed exuberance undermines the shape and reality of the work'. But where the 'monstrous' German past is concerned, such reservations do not seem to matter, and Steiner concludes his review with the familiar judgment that Grass's readers more than deserved what they got: he 'has rubbed the noses of his readers in the great filth, in the vomit of their time. Like no other writer, he has mocked and subverted the bland oblivion, the self-acquittal which underlie Germany's material resurgence. Much of what is active conscience in the Germany of Krupp and the Munich beer halls lies in this man's ribald keeping.'[13] It was a question of separating the sheep from the goats, 'us' from 'them': many German reviews of *The Tin Drum* in 1959 shared Steiner's celebratory appropriation of Grass's position and his righteous distaste for the morally dimwitted.[14]

The Tin Drum is a richly grotesque variation on the arch-German Bildungsroman.[15] Its commercial and critical success in forcing confrontation with the past was predicated on approaching it through the allegorical figure of the little monster Oskar Matzerath with his glass-shattering drum, who literally refuses to grow up by ceasing to grow at the age of three, and whose senses retain the peculiar acuity of the very young. Seeing, feeling, smelling the kleinbürgerlich (petit-bourgeois) environment of Germany during the Nazi era, Oskar's perceptions of the 'Night of Broken Glass' (Kristallnacht) in 1938 are close-focused but illuminate only a small area. This is the case with the ruined shop of one Jew, Sigismund Markus, who supplied Oskar with the original toy drum that has become vital to his sense of identity and capacity to assert himself. The discovery of the lifeless body of Markus in his shop is narrated through a consciousness so overwhelmed with sense impressions that the shock of finding the corpse barely registers as something extraordinary. For Oskar everything is equally unexpected and equally interesting and the opportunity to loot some spare drums is juxtaposed with the evidence of the brutality of Nazi thugs. Among contemporary readers this narrative perspective and the intermingling of images from fairy tales and blasphemous references to Christian traditions gave rise to both fascination and revulsion. The Kristallnacht chapter is entitled, with reference to one of Paul's Letters to the Corinthians, 'Faith, Hope, Love'; but the promise of the birth of Christ leads here not to salvation but to Grass's figure of the Nazi 'Gasman' with its implicit reference to the fate of Jews, the 'final solution'.

A more openly sinister version of Peter Pan, Oskar is a highly unreliable narrator of his picaresque story – as is his author, younger by a few years and sharing with him part of that story. Oskar is an intricately composite, deliberately ambiguous and confusing character, and Grass's proverbial logorrhea and meandering narration further complicate the matter. Is Oskar, in his own grotesque way, a Jesus figure? or is he the anti-Christ?[16] Is he or is he not responsible for the deaths of his mother, his uncle and his father (who suffocated trying to swallow the Nazi Party badge that he thought safely hidden from the Russians but that was found – maliciously? – by nosy Oskar)? Is he or is he not the real father of his father's son by his second wife? He seems to think that he is guilty on all counts. Whose past is represented by him and his exotically petit-bourgeois family, depicted with so much gusto and familiarity by Grass? It seems doubtful that the readers who made The Tin Drum such a success acknowledged that past as theirs; certainly not the (intellectual) critics; they knew (had always known) better. Oskar is the artist son who exorcises his Nazi father by (perhaps) killing him at the age of twenty-one and then giving up his drum (his art), promising to grow up after all and become a responsible member of society – the conclusion of all *Bildungsromane*. However, after a short-lived attempt in the late 1940s at replacing the artist's life with that of the stonemason (Grass, too, was apprenticed to a stone mason about the same time), he returns to art, his drum (Grass enters the academy of art) and thereby, on a higher level, his childhood. This return appears connected to the 1948 currency reform and the beginning of West Germany's return to the 'normality' of a politically stable, democratic, bourgeois technocracy. But, earning good money with his records even while he is in a mental institution, Oskar both has and has not withdrawn from West Germany's economic miracle, achieved mainly by the parents' generation.

With his darkly comical, grotesque aspects, Oskar, the 'anarchist turned collaborator'[17] who refuses to grow up, is the perfect allegory of Adorno's Freudian–Marxian 'theory' of fascism: all Germans were Nazis and the price they all had to pay for their monstrous regression was acceptance of collective guilt in confrontation with their monstrous past. They did as they were told. But what did such obedient acceptance say about *their* memories of that past? Grass, though roughly half a generation older than the student generation of 1968, shared in the early 1960s some aspects of that cohort's definition of itself as utterly different from its parents and, consequently, its forceful insistence that the parents acknowledge their guilt and thereby redeem the past for the children. The parents' greatest failure, largely unavoidable under the circumstances, had been to protect their children from having to become adults. Rebuilding at a frantic pace, creating that seemingly instantaneous 'economic miracle', they created what looks with hindsight like a curious suspension of time. It was as if their 'normal' temporality had been ruptured in the physical and political collapse of their country.

This disruption profoundly affected their children's passage into adulthood. For them the parents could never have been different people: younger, more hopeful, less certain, less lucky as survivors, more vulnerable. Their identity was frozen, defined by their knowing involvement with the criminal acts of the Nazi regime then and their denial of them now. Projecting their parents back into a past largely unacknowledged by them, the children refused to understand both their parents' and their own temporality. But any more or less successful passage into adulthood involves at least a tentative understanding of the temporal instability of identity. Failing in that respect, the children also did not understand that the ambiguities of guilt and atonement had their source in the changing symbiosis of past and present. For the parents the expectation that they accept their identity as monstrously guilty Germans became both more concrete and more impossible, the more unbelievably horrible the victimisation: the victims were so clearly nothing but victims. Born in Danzig in 1927, Grass focused the *Schuldthema* ('guilt-theme') of the 'Danzig Trilogy' on the persecution of Jews and Poles. The two come together in the character of the Jew Fajngold who represents millions of murdered Jews, bringing with him his large invisible family who died in Treblinka. Like many Poles in 1945, he has come to Danzig to take over the homes and businesses of Germans forced to leave the Eastern provinces – places where their families had lived for centuries. Fajngold is happy with the well-run Matzerath food store, explaining its advantages in great detail to his dead family. Without consulting with his dead wife, he proposes to help Matzerath's pretty young widow and her children (perhaps half-brothers, perhaps father and son) to stay in Danzig and give her a share in the business; but she wants to leave the past behind and go west.

Fajngold and the Poles have an inalienable right to their new properties. Germans of their generation will never be able to pay their moral debt to them, especially not to Fajngold and his dead family; nor will their children. How could they even begin to explain to them what they thought had been *their* past, without seeming to deny the past of the victims? Across the generational divide, the children responded precisely to the extraordinary violence of Jewish victimisation, and it made their demands on the parents all the more forcefully absolute: *they* were the true victims of their parents' inevitably wrong memories; speaking about the past, the parents could not but indict themselves. Ironically, given their general anti-Americanism, the children's perspective on their parents was in certain instructive ways similar to that of most young American soldiers in 1945: in their double role as liberators and invaders, they had penetrated Germany, revealed all her horrible secrets and turned the whole country into evidence against itself. Both shared an innocence, seductive for us but terrible for the parents. Like travellers on another planet, in a totally different time and space, they saw certain things overly clearly, and others not at all: they *did* see stony-faced 'monsters' refusing to acknowledge their guilt and show remorse. Much of postwar (West) German fiction shares the righteous obscurities of their innocence, which has arguably hindered rather than helped the process of knowing more about the past, let alone understanding it.

In the early 1950s, Wolfgang Koeppen published three novels which were unusually sensitive to the changing symbiosis of past and present and the temporal, unstable nature of memory: *Tauben im Gras* (1951; *Pigeons on the Grass*, 1988) analyses one day in Munich in the early spring of 1951; *Das*

Treibhaus (1953; *The Hothouse*, 2002) describes two days and two nights in Bonn in the spring of 1953; *Der Tod in Rom* (1954; *Death in Rome*, 1956) takes the reader through two and a half days in May of 1954. Intent on cultural witness and anamnesis, the undoing of forgetting, the three novels employ an explicit interplay between different strata of time and memory. The relation between an immediate postwar past and present is mirrored in the short space between the time in which the novel is set and the time of its contemporary reader. In *Pigeons on the Grass*, Munich is still the setting for pantomimes of power-relations between the German 'have-nots' and the American 'haves', focused on the instant gratification offered by cigarettes, liquor, chocolate, coffee. Need in its most naked black-market form is already a memory, but one that is right underneath the surface of the present, not yet transfigured: a level of memory easily accessible to the characters acting in the now of the fictional world and to (contemporary) readers in the, as it were, adjacent future of their life-world. In the preface to the second edition (1956) of the novel, Koeppen explained that his intention had been to show the anarchy and chaos of the immediate postwar years as symbiotically linked to the restorative, affirmative 1950s. A growing attitude of tolerance towards economic corruption and inequality, towards social–political ruthlessness and forgetfulness is traced back to missed opportunities for German renewal after the fires of war and persecution. In order to argue that 'undoing the forgetting' of these difficult years might have helped to undo the cultural–political shortsightedness of the still young Federal Republic, Koeppen rooted anamnesis at greater temporal depth, in a period more remote from the reader's present and yet more painfully entangled with it, the past reality of war and persecution. His elaborate orchestration of temporal interdependencies supports a sharp critique of postwar developments in West Germany that is predicated on the acknowledgment that Hitler, repressed, demonised or domesticated, has remained with us.

Koeppen's protagonists are not able to use this insight constructively; they are either stunted or destroyed by it. In *Pigeons on the Grass*, Philipp, a writer and observer like his author, is helplessly caught up in the confusions of his present which he cannot really relate to the past. The result is silence and noise: he is unable to find a language in which he could tell others what he sees and clarify his perceptions for himself. The same is true for the protagonists of *Death in Rome*, the sons in their too easily aborted confrontation with their fathers, who either murdered or condoned murder. Terrified by the past, the sons reject it so totally as to do themselves harm, without helping their fathers who still seem untouched by the meanings of their past acts. Committing suicide, the politician Keetenheuve in *The Hothouse* withdraws into the ultimate silence, too desperately intent on escaping from the corruption and complications of the politics of rearmament.

The search for a connecting language, a shared system of reference, is the subtext to *Pigeons on the Grass* and the author's comment on the characters' despair of meaning. Men and women in their social and political relations and actions appear like pigeons on the grass; if there are patterns they cannot be recognised. The young American soldier Richard is struck by the fact that he cannot fathom the people he meets in Munich. They appear to him in some inexplicable way distorted, caught in a sick lack of balance between hustling and inertia. The reader sees the confusion with the eyes of an outsider, but she also sees the inside through Philipp, the author's delegate witness. His perspective is contrasted with that of the 'great' poet Edwin, a combination of Thomas Mann and T. S. Eliot. Celebrating European *Geist* (mind, spirit) as the future of freedom, Edwin is successful, dignified and futile. He dismissively quotes Gertrude Stein – 'Pigeons on the grass alas', rejecting her and other *Zivilisationsgeister* (mere intellectuals) with their emphasis on man's contingency, that is, his lack of connection with the divine origin and meaningful order in which Edwin believes. Every pigeon knows its home in the hands of God, he declares; meanwhile his audience has gone to sleep.

Koeppen is not like Edwin: he is in some important ways close to Philipp, who shares Edwin's futility; he is close to Keetenheuve in *The Hothouse*, who is too imaginatively apprehensive to be a competent politician; and also to the young composer Siegfried Pfaffrath in *Death in Rome*, son of the fellow traveller Friedrich Wilhelm and nephew of the murderous SS general Judejahn. Pfaffrath decides to delight in the beauties of the world rather than go on being hurt by the challenge to remember. In his 1962 acceptance speech for the Büchner Prize, Koeppen spoke of the writer as naturally involved in the struggle against the abuse of power, violence, the coercion of mass culture – a struggle which would naturally make him an outsider. All art is responsible to society, but society can defeat the artist. Born in 1906, Koeppen saw his generation of writers as the truly defeated, the lost generation that had suffered too intensely through too many speechless years. Yet while admitting these doubts and reservations, he insists on the enduring importance of the artist's social–political role and function.[18] 'Who but the writer should play the role of Cassandra in our society?' he had asked in a 1961 interview; and in 1971 he referred to his books as manifestos against war and oppression: 'As a human being I feel powerless; not so as a writer.' But on this occasion he also spoke of the difficulties of communicating the disturbing implications of a West German postwar reality in a period of rapid, 'unheard-of' technological development and mass communication.[19]

In stark contrast to Grass's *Tin Drum*, Koeppen's novels did not reach many readers, though he has always had a substantial number of sympathetic reviewers from across the political spectrum.[20] Almost all these 'professional readers' assumed that his novels would have difficulties with a general educated readership. Krämer-Badoni titled his perceptive 1952 review of *Pigeons on the Grass* 'They will Cry "Crucify Him!"'[21] – mainly on account of the novel's relentless pessimism regarding a German *Wiedergeburt* (rebirth) or meaningful 'restoration'. And Koeppen's consistently modernist though, in contrast to Grass, fully accessible narrative strategies did not help. In reality 'they', the readers of *The Tin Drum*, neglected rather than crucified Koeppen. *Pigeons on the Grass* had two editions and sold 6,500 copies in 1951 – a figure which, given the circumstances of that time and the fact that Koeppen was an unknown author, was not all that low. However, paperback editions of 1956 and 1966 did not do much better. When the novel was included in the highly successful Bibliothek Suhrkamp in 1974, at a time of heightened sensitivity to the danger of forgetting the 'uncompleted past', it sold no more than 5,000 copies, though it was generally acclaimed as one of the most important postwar novels. The 1953 *Hothouse*, thought to be a *roman à clef* about the world of Bonn, did better, selling 12,000 copies; but the 1954 *Death in Rome*, which dealt most explicitly with the problem of cultural memory and generational conflict, sold only 6,000.[22]

The highly subjective but historically reflected, adult perspective that guided Koeppen's conceptual and narrative strategies left no doubt about his scepticism concerning a 'completion' of the German past and the finding of a meaningful order in history. But Koeppen has also made it clear that such order, even if possible, could never be a task for him. All the poet can do is consider history a cultural challenge rather than a given. Here, I think, is the locus of the most formidable obstacle to a fuller acceptance of his novels – even for sympathetic critics impressed by their dark beauty of loss, resignation, elegiac withdrawal, despair, negation, significant silence.[23] When *Death in Rome* came out in English translation in 1961, a lone reviewer wrote in *Library Journal* that 'this modern *Götterdämmerung . . .* should have been published in this country much sooner; however, its appearance during the Eichmann trial does seem timely'.[24] In contrast to Siegfried Lenz's *Deutschstunde* (1968; *The German Lesson*, 1972), a bestseller in the Federal Republic and highly successful with the American public, *Death in Rome* found few readers in Germany and fewer in the United States, precisely because it was and had been so timely. The ghosts from the past which Koeppen visits on his readers are not the picturesque goblins of *The German Lesson*; they clearly pose threats and their claims to be heeded are unambiguous.

The German Lesson was published in the midst of a lively cultural debate on the issues of guilt, memory and remembrance which had begun in the mid 1960s as a political disruption of the status quo by the sons turning against the generation of the economically successful fathers. The political, if not the personal energy of this disruption was soon dissipated. The reason why *The German Lesson* was so successful was that Lenz was much less clear about the significance of the past for the present than Koeppen, and readers, professional and general, were much freer to read into or out of his text positions with which they agreed or disagreed. Like Oskar Matzerath, Lenz's protagonist Siggi Jepsen is not an adult and is a highly 'unreliable' narrator. His search for the unmastered past is intimately connected with his father, the petit-bourgeois policeman Jepsen, with the artist Nansen (based on the Expressionist painter Emil Nolde), and with the complexly antagonistic relation between Nansen's devotion to the demands of his art and Jepsen's devotion to the demands of his duty. Despite the prohibition of his paintings by the Nazis, which Jepsen tries to enforce with obsessive zeal, Nansen's artistic credo shares (as Nolde's did) certain aspects of Nazi ideology, most clearly a significant rootedness in the landscape of *Heimat*. In the view of one critic, the great success of the book depended on its readers' failure to understand Nansen's/Nolde's ambiguity; they simply 'identified as the positive features of *The German Lesson* its story of a family divided under Nazism and its evocative descriptions of familiar North German landscapes and of what they take to be re-creations of the spirit of Nolde's vision of this landscape'. This assumption makes it possible to insist both on Lenz's clear insight into Nansen's/Nolde's 'basic ambiguity' or 'inner dualism', and on the inability of the readers of a bestselling novel to follow him.[25]

But why would all these readers have been unable to follow Lenz's narrative strategies? Many other reviews of the novel attributed its success, rightly, to the fact that Lenz approached the problems of the uncompleted past in ways that made them more accessible – something that Koeppen's novels with their specific temporal complexities and general cultural anxieties had not achieved. On the occasion of the publication of the American edition of *The German Lesson* in the spring of 1972, Michael Hamburger reviewed the book for the broad educated readership of *Saturday Review* (March) under the title 'A Third Reich with no demons', meaning a discussion of the German 'monstrous past' that enabled the readers to see beyond the monsters. Hamburger's reading did much for the reception of the novel in the USA; yet it still seems to me that the effectiveness, the pleasure of the book was predicated precisely on the *presence* of demons, if of the manipulable, domesticated kind. Lenz presented to his readers a very clear construct of Nansen–Nolde's 'inner dualism' and of Jepsen's obsessive belief in duty that made him the perfect petit-bourgeois tool of the criminal regime; it turned out to be highly successful and much too simple. It would have been more difficult, (probably) less successful but more useful to show how important social-psychological needs and desires were shared by the supporters of the Nazi regime as well as its opponents; how Jepsen's inarticulate, abstract concept of duty, dangerous to himself and others, was rooted in the same search for metaphysical order that had entangled the artist Nansen. But the demonically sparkling buttons and clasps of Jepsen's uniform and the demons that live under the artist's old blue cape resist such sober analysis. These demons may be fun, but they do not tell us how Jepsen and Nansen got caught in the dualisms of their author's making; nor how the son Siggi will be able to disentangle himself. The monstrous German past may have become more accessible; the challenge of the uncompleted past has become both more remote and more exploitable.

The monstrous past emerged again in the mid 1980s, this time as an intergenerational conflict about the uniqueness of Auschwitz as the basis for the evil singularity of the German past. The bitterness of that past, unresolved, enduring, surged up powerfully in the bitterness of the confrontations of the historians' dispute, in a way that seemed to bear out the urgency of Koeppen's warning. In *Pigeons on the Grass* and *Death in Rome*, the question of the singularity of the German past was asked and then deferred in a manner which might suggest, more than four decades later, a way to circumvent the permanent stalemate in which many of today's debates on this question are mired. In Koeppen's lucid analyses of memory as the complex temporal shaping of past experience, the notion of a singular past appears in conditional terms: if Hitler 'remains' with the Germans in any significant way, then only because they will finally be able to accept into their present the challenge of his different meanings in the past – Broszat's plea for a historicisation of the Nazi period.

The controversy in the early 1990s about Christa Wolf's involvement with the East German Stasi more than three decades earlier (see also chapter 15 below) reads like a tragi-comical epilogue to the historians' dispute, as does the whole issue of the 'collective' responsibility of GDR intellectuals for the repressive cultural policies of the regime from which they also derived their power.[26] Like those of Grass and Lenz, Wolf's attempts at dealing with the memory of the past have been highly successful with large readerships, because, like them, she kept her distance where Koeppen came too close for comfort. Wolf was helped here by the official GDR position that the victory of communism had made the 'German question' irrelevant; this part of the German past was completed and forgettable. This allowed her to pose her arguments for not forgetting in the different, as it were more innocent, terms of 'moral memory'. The great interest in East German literature outside the Eastern Bloc was partly based on that fact – as well as on the curiosity about life in that (for West Germans) so near yet so radically unfamiliar communist utopia. Unlike West German intellectuals, East German writers did not have to affirm at all times their profound *Betroffenheit* (concern) about the meanings of the Nazi past for the democratic present. They could worry – if in all manner of intriguingly secretive ways – about the meanings of the socialist present for their individual futures; they could write openly about their private memories and be all the more relevant. Wolf's best text remains *In Search of Christa T.*, in which she at least stated the conflicts between the demands of social and individual memory and identity, allowing them to remain unresolved because irrevocably private.

Kindheitsmuster (1976; *A Model Childhood*, 1980) and *Kassandra* (1983) were more problematic in this respect. Wolf had in the meantime become a bestselling author in the West, not least because of feminist interests. Increasingly she presented herself abroad as the conscience of her country, but managed all the same to avoid open dissent and to hold on to her 'travel cadre' status and other 'Eastern' privileges. Intellectuals safely ensconced in the West could not possibly blame her for that; but it *was* a dilemma and it did blur her awareness of the actual limitations of the GDR perspective – a blurring that inevitably extended to her private vision, which became more self-centred the more it claimed larger social and political relevance. The 'moral memory' she advocates in *Kindheitsmuster* is not convincingly realised, because the novel's intricately temporal and geographical search for the Nazi past remains essentially concerned with her own writerly identity. In the spring of 1971 Wolf travelled with her brother, husband and youngest daughter to the places of her childhood in what is now Poland, writing the book in 1972–5. These three time spaces are interwoven: the past of childhood, the past of the journey, and the ongoing present of the writing process. The narration shifts constantly between Nelly, who inhabits the childhood space and whose voice is rendered mainly in narrated monologue, and the adult author in search of her childhood. She alternates between third-, second- and first-person narration, an erratic interior monologue, interspersed with sententious reflections on narration and memory.

In the end, Nelly merges into the identity of the author, who then states that this composite 'I' is now in need of being narrated differently – an intimation of the 'limits of the expressible' ('Grenzen des Sagbaren') or the promise of another novel? Her book is finished and the reader is left, in its last sentences, with a list of questions concerning identity and memory that are self-centred to the point of coyness; but Wolf does seem to say that she will respect those 'limits'. Her neo-Romantic preoccupation with them has little to do with the questions posed by the uncompleted past, but is intimately connected with her sense of the cultural significance of her 'Schreibarbeit', her writerly identity articulated in increasingly stilted, self-conscious language.[27] *Kassandra*, another search for the writer's identity, this time from an anti-war, anti-technology, rigidly feminist position, clearly suffers from this self-indulgent writerly self-reflection. In the five lectures on the 'presuppositions' of *Kassandra* at Frankfurt University in May 1982, Wolf presented the subtext of the short novel, the familiar arguments against the logocentrism, dualism, domineering systemicity, violent objectification of western (Greek) patriarchy in the familiar fuzzy terms.[28] The attractiveness of this troubled text, especially but not only to certain groups of feminists, is arguably based on this summary 'critique', the subtext of Cassandra–Wolf's reflections on her cultural role as seer, vates, poet, to which she attributes her heroic desire to remain a witness beyond the end of human time.[29] Speaking for victims and against victimisation in such totalising, supra-historical terms, she can rely on her absolute writerly authority in the by now hallowed tradition of Holocaust discourses: no questions allowed; no reservations, qualifications, differentiations, no new evidence, no knowledge that changes with time.

The Cassandra of Greek myth was not a victim; she wanted the gift of prophecy but was not willing to pay the price, to sleep with Apollo. Brilliantly, he did not withdraw the gift but punished her by adding to it the condition that she would not be believed. Wolf could have done much with the implications of that 'modern' dilemma: there is no prophecy in modernity because the future, shaped by ever more complex interdependencies of contingencies and choices, is truly unpredictable. If Cassandra's vision is not shared by others, is it really *their* fault that they cannot believe her? Might it not be the quality of her witnessing, of her rigorously monological discourse of victimisation? Whatever repressive properties can be found in Greek culture from late twentieth-century hindsight, that culture has also produced the enormous achievement of conceptually organised discourse which enables the participants to persuade and be persuaded by the power of rational argumentation – not the violence of physical strength. A persuasive argument is dialogical; it has to be constructed in a way that enables the person to whom it is addressed to reconstruct it critically and to her intellectual satisfaction. Wolf's Cassandra is never made to understand that she has to be convincing. Like her author, she speaks with the pre-established authority of prophecy and expects to be listened to, though she knows from experience that, speaking the way she does, she will not be believed. At no point in the narration of her conscientious suffering for womankind, for humanity, does she ever consider intelligibly the implications of her position: does she want to be partially right in her warnings, which others could consider but also question; or does she want to insist self-righteously on the absolute truth of her vision? Assuming too easily the authority to speak for others, Wolf has shown little imagination for the difference of other people. The myth of Cassandra is of course a complex of stories interwoven in many temporal and cultural layers – an interweaving that scholars have traced painstakingly but that is hard to disentangle. The same is true of the stories of the Trojan War. Apollo, god of the light of reason so much disliked by Wolf, does play an important part; but so does Athena, the goddess of wisdom.[30] Wolf – and this is her privilege – took from this complexly composite story what she could use for her own much simpler, predictable narrative; but to claim for it general cultural significance is another matter.

Here is the link to Wolf's panicked reaction to the critical discussion of her Stasi involvement. The existence of her Stasi file was seen by many critics as regrettable but unimportant, since the information obtained from her thirty years earlier was harmless and her involvement due mostly to political naiveté and a young writer's ambition. The real harm was done by Wolf's playing simultaneously to East and West, her success in giving both sides what they wanted, which over the decades dulled her cultural–political sensitivities and allowed her to claim equal victim status with the exiles of the 1930s and 1940s and equal significance for GDR and Weimar literary culture. This 'hubris' predictably caused much consternation among (West) German intellectuals, but it also demonstrated that they shared with Wolf the belief in an, as it were, pre-authorised higher moral status of 'the writer',[31] especially when drawing on it to deny it to others. Such authority soothed their own identity problems as intellectuals in a western mass democracy and technocracy that, involved in its own politics of self-interest, expected them to cope with the uncompleted German past. GDR writers like Wolf seemed to have accepted that task voluntarily, nobly, altruistically; they had given her too much credit and now they asked too much back.[32] Perhaps the most curious aspect of this instructive tempest in a teapot was the reluctance of (West) German intellectuals to accept, along with the banality, also the obscurity of the alleged 'betrayal'. Their 'profound disappointment' at the Stasi revelations echoes their reactions to the 'uncompleted' Nazi past, which they have held up to others whose public (not to mention private) memories of their collective guilt have always seemed unsatisfactory in that they did not, after all, yield enough moral certainty. The political and moral muddle following the fall of the Wall half a century after the end of the Second World War might be a useful occasion to consider more soberly the obscurities, the moral grey zones, the avoidable and unavoidable compromises, conflicts and ambiguities of the 'German question' – its all-too-human mix of closeness and remoteness.

NOTES

1. See the images reproduced in chapter 1, 'To make them see', in Dagmar Barnouw, *Germany 1945: Views of War and Violence* (Bloomington, IN, 1996), pp. 1–41.
2. On this predicament see Barnouw, *Germany 1945*, pp. 6–33.
3. See Charles S. Maier, *The Unmasterable Past: History, Holocaust and German National Identity* (Cambridge, MA, 1988); Peter Baldwin (ed.), *Reworking the Past: Hitler, the Holocaust and the Historians' Controversy* (Boston, MA, 1990).
4. For excerpts from Richard von Weizsaecker's speech, see 'Facing the mirror of German history', *The New York Times*, 22 October 1988, International section, p. 4.
5. Saul Friedlander, ' "A past that refuses to go away": on recent historiographical debates in the Federal Republic of Germany about National Socialism and the Final Solution', in *Wissenschaftskolleg-Jahrbuch* 1985/86, ed. Peter Wapnewski (Berlin, 1986), pp. 105–15.
6. Saul Friedlander, *Memory, History, and the Extermination of the Jews of Europe* (Bloomington, IN, 1993), p. ix.
7. *Merkur*, May 1985, now in Baldwin, *Reworking the Past*, pp. 77–87. Saul Friedlander, 'Reflections on the historicization of National Socialism' (1987) and 'Martin Broszat and the historicization of National Socialism' (1991), both now in *Memory, History*, pp. 64–84 and 85–101.
8. 'The Shoah in present historical consciousness', in *Memory, History*, pp. 42–63 (p. 51).
9. Namely *Die Blechtrommel* (1959; *The Tin Drum*, 1961), *Katz und Maus* (1961; *Cat and Mouse*, 1963), *Hundejahre* (1963; *Dog Years*, 1965). Grass himself has repeatedly emphasised the connections between the three texts, which share the setting and some characters. On the thematic integration of the three novels see J. Reddick, *The 'Danzig Trilogy' of Günter Grass* (London, 1975). For secondary literature on the three novels see Volker Neuhaus, *Günter Grass* (Stuttgart, 1992), pp. 219–32.
10. George Steiner, 'The nerve of Günter Grass', in *Critical Essays on Günter Grass*, ed. Patrick O'Neill (Boston, MA, 1987), pp. 30–6 (pp. 30–1).
11. Heinrich Böll's *Wo warst du, Adam?* (1951; *And Where Were You, Adam?*, 1974), one of the first successful novels after 1945, had sold 800,000 copies by the late 1970s (Manfred Durzak, *Der deutsche Roman der Gegenwart* (Stuttgart, 1979), p. 63). Less interested in forceful 'confrontations with the past', Böll's novels were often close to sentimentality but also psychologically imaginative and shrewd.
12. Steiner, 'The nerve', p. 30.
13. Ibid., pp. 35–6; see also the more coherent, if bemused critique of Grass's hyperactive verbosity in Stanley Edgar Hyman's review of *Cat and Mouse*, 'An inept symbolist' (1963), in *Critical Essays on Günter Grass*, pp. 27–30.
14. See the reviews collected in Gert Loschütz, *Von Buch zu Buch – Günter Grass in der Kritik* (Neuwied, 1968), pp. 8–26.

15. See Judith Ryan, *The Uncompleted Past: Postwar German Novels and the Third Reich* (Detroit, IN, 1983), pp. 56–7; Hans Magnus Enzensberger, 'Wilhelm Meister auf Blech getrommelt', in Loschütz, *Von Buch zu Buch*, pp. 8–12.
16. For a summary of different interpretations of the Oskar figure see Neuhaus, *Günter Grass*, pp. 54–61.
17. Ryan, *Uncompleted Past*, p. 95.
18. Wolfgang Koeppen, 'Rede zur Verleihung des Georg-Büchner-Preises 1962', in *Jahrbuch der deutschen Akademie für Sprache und Dichtung*, 1962, pp. 103–10.
19. See Horst Bienek, *Werkstattgespräche mit Schriftstellern* (Munich, 1965), pp. 55–67 (p. 65); Christian Linder, 'Im Übergang zum Untergang. Über das Schweigen Wolfgang Koeppens', *Akzente*, 19 (1972), 41–63. See bibliography in Eckart Öhlenschläger (ed.), *Wolfgang Koeppen* (Frankfurt am Main, 1987), pp. 440–1.
20. For a good sampling of reviews see *Über Wolfgang Koeppen*, ed. Ulrich Greiner (Frankfurt am Main, 1976). See also Peter Demetz, *Postwar German Literature* (New York, 1970), pp. 168–72 and Marcel Reich-Ranicki, *Literarisches Leben in Deutschland. Kommentare und Pamphlete* (Munich, 1965), pp. 26–35.
21. Now in *Über Wolfgang Koeppen*, pp. 30–2.
22. Ibid., pp. 11–13.
23. See the titles of reviews in the bibliographies in *Über Wolfgang Koeppen*, pp. 283–94, Thomas Richer, *'Der Tod in Rom'. Eine existential-psychologische Analyse von Wolfgang Koeppens Roman* (Zurich, 1982), pp. 149–53, and Öhlenschläger, *Wolfgang Koeppen*, pp. 444–70. Peter Demetz, *After the Fires: Recent Writing in the Germanies, Austria, and Switzerland* (San Diego, 1986), links Koeppen's silence to his being 'exhausted by these explosive novels' (p. 316).
24. J. R. Blanchard, *Library Journal*, 86 (1961), 1620.
25. Ryan, *Uncompleted Past*, pp. 15, 117–27.
26. Hermann Vinke (ed.), *Akteneinsicht Christa Wolf. Zerrspiegel und Dialog* (Hamburg, 1993); see also the essays collected in Michael Geyer (ed.), *The Power of the Intellectuals in Contemporary Germany* (Chicago, 2001).
27. Overly generous, many critics have found here a significant *Sprachskepsis* (scepticism about language). For a summary of critics' reactions see Sonya Hilzinger, *Christa Wolf* (Stuttgart, 1986), pp. 94–105.
28. Christa Wolf, *Voraussetzungen einer Erzählung: Kassandra* (Darmstadt, 1983).
29. Ibid., p. 27.
30. Robert Graves, *The Greek Myths* (Baltimore, MD, 1955), II, 332–3.
31. Fritz Raddatz, 'Von der Beschädigung der Literatur durch ihre Urheber' (1993), now in *Akteneinsicht*, pp. 168–71.
32. Walter Jens, 'Christa Wolf bekümmert mich' (1993), now in *Akteneinsicht*, pp. 233–5.

FURTHER READING

Augstein, Rudolf, et al., *'Historikerstreit'. Die Dokumentation der Kontroverse um die Einzigartigkeit der nationalsozialistischen Judenvernichtung* (Munich, 1987)
Barnouw, Dagmar, *Visible Spaces: Hannah Arendt and the German-Jewish Experience* (Baltimore, MD, 1990)
Baumgart, Reinhard, *Glücksgeist und Jammerseele. Über Leben und Schreiben, Vernunft und Literatur* (Munich, 1986)

Buruma, Jan, *The Wages of Guilt: Memories of War in Germany and Japan* (New York, 1994)

Durzak, Manfred, *Der deutsche Roman der Gegenwart. Entwicklungsvoraussetzungen und Tendenzen* (Stuttgart, 1979)

Krüger, Horst, *A Crack in the Wall: Growing up under Hitler* (New York, 1982 (1966))

Krüger, Horst, *Zeit ohne Wiederkehr. Gesammelte Feuilletons* (Hamburg, 1985)

Mommsen, Hans, *Auf der Suche nach historischer Normalität. Beiträge zum Geschichtsbildstreit in der Bundesrepublik* (Berlin, 1987)

Mommsen, Hans, *The Rise and Fall of Weimar Democracy* (Chapel Hill, 1996 (1989))

Pross, Harry, *Memoiren eines Inländers* (Munich, 1993)

Raddatz, Fritz J., *Die Nachgeborenen. Leseerfahrungen mit zeitgenössischer Literatur* (Frankfurt am Main, 1983)

Reich-Ranicki, Marcel, *Entgegnung. Zur deutschen Literatur der siebziger Jahre* (Stuttgart, 1981)

Reich-Ranicki, Marcel, *Wer schreibt, provoziert. Kommentare und Pamphlete* (Munich, 1966)

13

J. H. REID

Aesthetics and resistance: Böll, Grass, Weiss

At the end of Peter Weiss's play *Hölderlin*, the eponymous poet is visited by the young Karl Marx. It is an entirely apocryphal encounter, but one which is revealing in terms of the relationship between writers and politics in the 1960s and 1970s. Marx describes how the encounter with Hölderlin's poetry has led to his realisation of the need for a materialist, dialectical political philosophy. He concludes that in furthering the aim of societal change the artist's individual vision is of equal status with political analysis.

Hölderlin appeared in 1971. Just a few years previously West Germany had experienced the most radical questioning of this position. The student movement had sought to enlist all aspects of social life in the cause of global revolution. In September 1968 the influential journal *Kursbuch* contained no fewer than three articles which proclaimed that literature was 'dead': in the current world-political situation, *belles lettres* had no discernible function; rather it was the duty of writers to document exploitation and oppression, whether of the South Vietnamese peasants or of the foreign workers in West Germany, and to engage themselves directly in combatting the concentration of the mass media in the hands of a few reactionary figures, such as Axel Springer. Peter Weiss himself had embraced this line. From the experimental prose of *Der Schatten des Körpers des Kutschers* (1960; *The Shadow of the Coachman's Body*, 1972) and the madhouse atmosphere of his play *Marat/Sade* (1964; trans. 1965), he had turned to the increasingly austere documentary mode of the plays *Die Ermittlung* (1965; *The Investigation*, 1972) and *Vietnam-Diskurs* (1968; *Discourse on Vietnam*, 1971). With *Hölderlin* he appeared to be turning back to more traditional positions.

The events of 1968 were the culmination of a development which from 1961 onwards had seen an increasing willingness on the part of writers to engage directly in West German politics. One major issue was the question of attitudes to the Nazi past. A new, self-confident generation began to question the involvement of the previous one in the crimes of the Nazis. 1961 witnessed the trial of Adolf Eichmann in Jerusalem, which focused international attention on the German past. From 1963 to 1965 some of those who had been in charge at Auschwitz were on trial in Frankfurt am Main, the first major trial of Nazi criminals carried out by German courts. *Die Ermittlung* documents the trial. After this it was no longer possible to regard the past as over and done with. Moreover, as Heinrich Böll had pointed out, Eichmann's fault was to have done what he was told; the 'honourable' Germans of the Third Reich had been those who had refused to carry out the orders to take part in the execution of hostages and the razing of villages.[1] Accordingly, the refusal to obey unthinkingly was to be one of the most lasting features of the student movement. Failure to resist had allowed the Nazis to do their worst; the readiness to resist whatever was perceived as injustice pervaded the 1960s and 1970s.

The radical politicisation of literature was short-lived; documentary literature, although it lived on in the texts of the Werkkreis Literatur der Arbeitswelt, was already being parodied in Böll's novel *Gruppenbild mit Dame* (1971; *Group Portrait with Lady*, 1973). Journalists seized on this gleefully and proclaimed a return to traditional literary values, a rediscovery of the importance of the individual with his or her problems, even a revulsion against politics. As always, reality was more complex. By no means all writers had indulged in the depoeticisation of literature; so, too, it was an unwarranted generalisation to claim that literature had now been depoliticised. While for various reasons, not least the insecurity caused by urban terrorism with its kidnappings and assassinations, the revolutionary optimism of the mid to late 1960s had evaporated, literature which was both imaginative and committed continued to be written. This chapter will explore these issues with reference to novels by three representative figures, Heinrich Böll, Günter Grass and Peter Weiss.

The last decade of Weiss's life was dominated by work on his three-volume novel *Die Ästhetik des Widerstands* (1975, 1978, 1981; The Aesthetic of Resistance), the very title of which encapsulates the topics under discussion. Weiss, born near Berlin in 1916, was the son of a Jewish businessman who emigrated to Sweden in 1938. His earliest interests had been in painting and drawing; later he experimented with photography and film. In 1959, however, the breakthrough to literature came when Suhrkamp accepted the manuscript of *Der Schatten des Körpers des Kutschers* for publication. In 1965 he announced his commitment to socialism, and for a time he was courted by the regime in the GDR; the invasion of Czechoslovakia by the Warsaw Pact armies in 1968, however, provoked his protest and relations cooled. Nevertheless, he remained a Marxist. Weiss always felt an outsider in Germany, indeed there was some personal hostility between him and Günter Grass, who rejected his 'Gespräch der zwei Gehenden' (Conversation of Two

Walkers) as 'amoral, antihumanist'; when Weiss later read to the Gruppe 47 from his *Marat/Sade* play with the help of a little drum, Grass took it personally.[2]

Böll and Grass were always more central to the West German literary scene, although it is striking that for them, too, 1959 was a key year, in which Grass became instantly famous with the publication of *Die Blechtrommel* (*The Tin Drum*, 1962), and Böll with *Billard um halb zehn* (*Billiards at half-past Nine*, 1961) was perceived to have moved away from a provincial realism into the realm of international modernism. Unlike Weiss, Böll was never a Marxist, although he once described himself as a communist *manqué*.[3] Born in 1917 into an intensely Catholic, if non-conformist family, which despised the Nazis, he served in the German army from the outbreak of war until its end. Böll remained a non-conformist all his life, and although he publicly supported the Social Democrats in the 1972 election and at the end of his life was associated with the new Green Party, he was too much of an individualist ever to identify wholly with any political grouping.

The contrary was the case with Günter Grass, ten years younger than Böll and spared military service until almost the war's end. Also a Catholic, Grass came from the opposite end of Germany, the city of Danzig (now Polish Gdansk). From the early 1960s and through the 1970s he worked tirelessly on behalf of the Social Democrats, and it was he who persuaded Böll to contribute to the 1972 campaign. *Aus dem Tagebuch einer Schnecke* (1972; *From the Diary of a Snail*, 1974) documents his political activity. Grass was highly critical of those whom he regarded as extremists, whether on the right or on the left, those who, as he put it, 'wish to straighten the banana in the service of mankind'.[4] This applied particularly to the radical students, whose intolerant behaviour he compared to that of the Nazis. There were no simple solutions to mankind's problems: the assumption that there were had led to Auschwitz. Hence his metaphor of the snail, whose pace is laborious and which from time to time is forced to withdraw into its shell: such is historical progress, which Grass identified with social democracy by contrast to revolutionary Marxism. Böll was more conciliatory towards the students, publicly defending them on occasion. When in November 1968 the journalist Beate Klarsfeld slapped Chancellor Kiesinger in the face in protest at his Nazi past, Böll sent her flowers, for which he was in turn publicly scolded by Grass, who regarded both gestures as encouraging violence. The difference between Grass and Böll was largely a matter of temperament. Böll's natural spontaneity led in January 1972 to an article published in *Der Spiegel*, in which he attacked press hysteria over the Baader–Meinhof urban terrorists, defending some of their humanitarian aims while condemning their methods, and appealing to Ulrike Meinhof to give herself up to the police, whereupon he was subjected to an unparalleled storm of criticism, accused of fostering violence and of sympathising with terrorism. His novel *Die verlorene Ehre der Katharina Blum* (1974; *The Lost Honour of Katharina Blum,* 1975) was partly prompted by these events: its subtitle, 'How violence arises and where it can lead to', adumbrated the central topic of political debates in the 1960s and 1970s.

A key document of the *literary* debates of these years is an address given by Grass in Princeton in 1966, in which he took issue with the question of literary, as opposed to direct political commitment. Weiss, as we have seen, had adopted a revolutionary Marxist position; in the term made fashionable by Sartre, Böll had frequently spoken of his own *engagement*.[5] In his address Grass sarcastically imagined Böll and Weiss being 'consulted' by Chancellor Ludwig Erhard in West Germany and by First Secretary Walter Ulbricht in East Germany respectively, whereupon utopia would break out overnight. Life, said Grass, was more complex. In order to influence the course of political events it was necessary to become involved in 'democratic minutiae', and that meant being prepared to compromise; poetry, however, knew no compromises.[6] Grass's position here was akin to the conventional modernist one expressed in Adorno's critique of Sartre: by accepting the discourse of his target, the writer *engagé* was colluding with what he purported to attack.[7] It was a position which Grass himself was subsequently to abandon, as his novels of the 1970s and 1980s increasingly focused on topical issues such as the 'German question' (*Kopfgeburten*) (1980; *Head-births,* 1982) and the threat of nuclear annihilation (*Die Rättin*) (1986; *The Rat,* 1987), but in *örtlich betäubt* (1969; *Local Anaesthetic,* 1970), as we shall see, there is already a tension between modernist structures and didactic contents.

The relationship between artist and society is explored by Böll, not for the first time, in *Ansichten eines Clowns* (1963; *The Clown,* 1965), a novel which, however, marks a watershed in his writing and has a fiery immediacy which is possibly its most enduring quality. It is the story of a struggle: gone is the passive acceptance of injustice to be found in Böll's earlier texts, where, for example, even in *Der Zug war pünktlich* resistance, including that of the Polish partisans, was presented as contributing merely to further misery. The immediate cause of the struggle is Schnier's belief that the Roman Catholic Church has cheated him of his long-standing partner Marie, to whom he regards himself as married, although neither church nor state had pronounced them so. Initially his 'weapon' is the telephone, with which he inflicts himself on his family and on his and Marie's acquaintances, mainly persons prominent in the church. All appeals to him to 'come to terms' with his lot are met with a blank refusal.

Schnier is a *young* man; in his relation to his parents there are elements which point forward only a few years to the student movement's slogan: 'Trust no one over thirty!' Schnier broke off relations with his parents over the death of his sixteen-year-old sister Henriette, who in February 1945 had been encouraged to go off to defend the 'sacred German soil' against the 'Jewish Yankees'. She never returned, nor was her body ever found. Böll's whole oeuvre is dominated by the motif of remembering the dead, and *Ansichten eines Clowns* is no exception. Again and again Schnier returns to the memory of Henriette, whose loss in the past corresponds to the loss of Marie in the present.

This link between past and present permeates the narrative. The novel's time structure alternates between past and present, as Schnier remembers a variety of episodes from his past life. His protest is largely against those he believes have failed to keep the past alive, the opportunist fellow travellers of the Third Reich, who because they had never been Party members were allowed to retain their privileges after the war, or the ex-Nazis who either escaped punishment by having protected the token dissident or who now claim, hypocritically in Schnier's opinion, to have become devoted democrats. The latter include Herbert Kalick, who in the closing weeks of the war was to be found mobilising the local orphanage against the American invaders and demanding the death penalty for 'defeatism', but who has just been publicly honoured for his 'efforts in instilling democratic ideas in the young', and Schnier's own previously anti-Semitic mother, who now chairs an organisation devoted to 'reconciliation between the races'.

Hypocrisy is Schnier's major bugbear. He sees it in the paradox that the 'sacred soil' of Germany, which Henriette was sent out to defend, was the main source of his family's wealth, through coal-mining. But it is at the church, epitomised in the 'Circle of Progressive Catholics', that he directs his fiercest criticism, the church as a bureaucratic institution, more concerned with wealth and influence than with humanity and helping the poor. Prelate Sommerwild, for example, is proud to have fought in two world wars: the church is allied with the military–industrial complex. Dr Kinkel possesses baroque madonnas of dubious origin. Both are linked to the ruling party in Bonn, on whose behalf Fredebeul, a third member of the circle, makes election speeches. Central to Schnier's polemic, however, is the church's attitude to sex and marriage. He recalls the different treatment meted out to Besewitz and Frehlingen, both of whom had been living with a divorcée: the latter, a prominent writer, is granted a dispensation and allowed to marry, the former, being a mere 'working man', is forced to leave his 'concubine' and their children. In this way the church identifies itself and its interests with the class-based structures of West German society.

Schnier's strictures go further, however. His problem with Marie and the church was that he was unable to accept what he saw as the bureaucratisation of personal relationships in the form of the marriage certificate and the insistence that he sign a written undertaking that his children will become Catholics. This is perhaps at the heart of Schnier's character, his belief in spontaneity, his insistence that 'moments cannot be repeated' (p. 231), that one must do things at once, even if they appear 'absurd' (p. 211). Again his sister Henriette, a Dostojevskian character given to mild epileptic fits, is a key figure, for spontaneity was her defining characteristic, emblematised in the singed Seven of Hearts, still in the family's pack of cards, which she had once thrown in the fire. The disruptive nature of these spontaneous acts points forward to the early, non-dogmatic stages of the protest movement, the 'happenings' which Böll later thematised in *Ende einer Dienstfahrt* (1966; *The End of a Mission*, 1968) and *Gruppenbild mit Dame*, the art form which attempts most radically to obscure the divide between art and reality.

Schnier's narrative is entirely subjective, and largely consists, as the novel's title makes clear, of 'views'. When Sommerwild patiently tries to reason with him, keeping things 'as objective as possible', Schnier retorts that Marie's departure is his affair and 'as subjective as it could possibly be' (p. 164). He himself admits to being unjust at one point. He is anything but a 'reliable narrator'.[8] Nor should we be taken in by the impression of spontaneity conveyed by the narrative – Böll wrote at least five versions of the text – any more than we should with Goethe's *Die Leiden des jungen Werthers* (1774; *The Sorrows of the Young Werther*, 1988), with which Böll's text has much in common. Schnier is a clown, an actor, who carefully rehearses his turns. In places there is a certain amount of self-irony, as one might expect in the case of a professional clown: when Schnier speaks of his 'Nibelung complex' (p. 175), for example, we cannot take him altogether seriously.

Schnier is in fact a portrait of the artist in the West German society of the early 1960s. As a satirist he is an example of the 'committed writer' akin to Böll himself. At one stage he suggests that in earlier centuries he would have been a court jester (p. 138). This is a metaphor for the artist which figured prominently at the time and was taken up by Grass in his Princeton address.[9] It implies, however, the artist's ultimate impotence, as the jester who went 'too far' was invariably silenced. The novel's structure is revealing in this connection. The extreme temporal and spatial compression of the text – just over two hours in Schnier's flat – together with the mingling of past and present through flashback and memory contribute to an overwhelming impression of stasis and of artistic inwardness. But firing off salvoes by telephone from the safety of his flat is ultimately an inadequate response to injustice, and accordingly the narrative explodes into action at the end when Schnier leaves the safety of his flat for the railway station to confront Marie and, by implication, her church directly.

Grass's *örtlich betäubt* echoes and develops this position in the figure of Scherbaum, a student who plans to register his protest against the Vietnam War by setting fire to his dog outside the Kempinski café on the Kurfürstendamm in full view of the elderly ladies consuming their coffee and cakes there; indifferent to the burning of humans with napalm, their proverbial love of dogs is more likely to shock them into action. There is something of the 'happening' in this plan, too.

örtlich betäubt was Grass's first novel after the 'trilogy' of *Die Blechtrommel*, *Katz und Maus* (1961; *Cat and Mouse*, 1963) and *Hundejahre* (1963; *Dog Years*, 1963), all of which were largely set in Danzig during the Nazi years and which, making extensive use of traits of the grotesque and the absurd, treated the question of the responsibility of the petty bourgeoisie for the German catastrophe. *örtlich betäubt*, by contrast, is set entirely in the contemporary world, West Berlin in the winter of 1966/7, by which time the protest movement of the young against their elders was well under way. In place of the parent–child conflict of *Ansichten eines Clowns*, Grass foregrounds the teacher–pupil relationship, as Siegfried Lenz and Christa Wolf were doing at the same time in *Deutschstunde* (1968; *The German Lesson*, 1971) and *Nachdenken über Christa T.* (1968; *The Quest for Christa T.*, 1970) respectively. Grass, however, looks at the younger generation from the point of view of their elders. His narrator is the forty-year-old teacher Eberhard Starusch, whose credibility is reinforced by the fact that he is a history teacher and one who came to the profession relatively late. A crucial difference between *Ansichten eines Clowns* and *örtlich betäubt* is that the passion of the former, told by the rebel himself, is replaced by enlightened objectivity, youthful 'views' being refracted through adult insights.

Starusch, who describes himself as 'a liberal Marxist, who cannot make up his mind' (p. 152), does his best to understand the preoccupations of his pupils. Anti-authoritarian teaching methods are on stream; demands for innovations ranging from pupil representation in the school administration to a smokers' corner are being discussed. He appreciates that the younger generation is searching for a 'new myth' (p. 151); as one who remembers the myth which seduced large numbers of his own generation he is concerned that this search may equally lead to disaster. Unlike Schnier, who is alone in the 'labyrinth' of contemporary society,[10] Scherbaum has his supporters. 'Youth' in this text is considerably younger; it has also become a recognisable group. The most radical of his friends is Vero, a Maoist, who believes they are on the threshold of the 'third revolution' – the revolutionary stance of Gudrun

Ensslin is foreshadowed here. Schnier's standpoint was fundamentally non-political. These young people have all read their Marx and their Marcuse.

In the end Scherbaum capitulates and decides to devote himself to politically committed journalism instead – to the relief of his teacher. Hans Schnier would never have seen reason in this way, and one may feel that in this respect Grass has betrayed the principles of his Princeton address: didacticism has taken over, compromises have been made.

Scherbaum's story, however, is only part of the text. His Vietnam protest reflects the protests of other characters against the inadequacy of responses to past German guilt. As with Böll, the Third Reich is a reference point for attitudes in the present. Thus the release from Spandau prison in 1965 of Baldur von Schirach, the leader of the Hitler Youth movement, is in the context of a novel which focuses on the revolt of youth against their elders the reminder of a youth which failed to revolt. One of Starusch's colleagues is Irmgard Seifert, who is filled with self-disgust at the memories of her own conformism as a teenager under Hitler, and is all too uncritically prepared to fall in with the new extremism, constantly preaching 'resistance and the duty to resist' (p. 145). She admires Scherbaum, regarding him as embodying the spontaneity which her generation has lost.

The novel, however, centres on the doubts and conflicts within Starusch himself. Here, too, there are parallels to be drawn with *Ansichten eines Clowns*, for Starusch, like Schnier, is suffering from the loss of his girl friend Linde and indulges in violent fantasies, to the extent of imagining himself as a baths attendant and killing her and his rival with the wave machine. Linde's father is Ferdinand Krings, modelled on General Ferdinand Schörner,[11] famous for his refusal to accept defeat and his readiness to sacrifice countless soldiers, who had returned from captivity in the Soviet Union determined to reinterpret history and 'win' the battles he had in fact lost – intriguingly, as the owner of a cement works, like the Schniers he owes his wealth to the exploitation of the German soil. His daughter is equally determined he must not succeed. In the figures of Linde and Irmgard Seifert we find the neurotic response to the past which Margarete and Alexander Mitscherlich describe in *Die Unfähigkeit zu trauern*. As with Böll there is both a political and a private dimension to the text, but here the private motivation is explicitly used to cast doubt on the genuineness of the political commitment.

This takes place through the other major figure of the text, Starusch's dentist, the only character not to be given a name. A large part of the novel consists of conversations between Starusch and his dentist, as the latter sets about 'correcting' the teacher's teeth. Its title, 'local anaesthetic', not only refers to the physical suppression of pain, but is a metaphor for a social programme diametrically opposed to that of the student revolutionaries.

The dentist believes in 'bridge-building' – in the dental sphere but also in that of human relationships – , in evolutionary progress – the development of more efficient drills, for example – and in a universal health service which will render politics superfluous. Political action he regards as motivated by personal neuroses: Starusch's desire to reform society stems from his failure to come to terms with the loss of Linde, Scherbaum's revolutionary zeal from an incident in early childhood when he saw his father naked.

The dentist is a self-confessed stoic – but so is Krings, the general who refused to accept the facts of the arctic winter. He cannot therefore be regarded as the mouthpiece of the text, however wise some of his words may appear. At the end of the novel his treatment has failed, Starusch has developed an abscess and the carefully constructed dental bridge has to be demolished. Whether Starusch can be regarded as the victor, however, is less clear.[12] The increasing violence of his personal vendetta against Krings puts his motivation in doubt; he and his generation remain tainted and unsure of themselves. Moreover, in *örtlich betäubt* it is, for once, the teacher who learns from the pupil.

Starusch himself had been a member of a teenage gang described in *Die Blechtrommel*, which wrought havoc to property in Danzig in the closing months of the Third Reich, resistance of a kind, but hardly politically motivated. It is his pupil Scherbaum who points out to him the active resistance to Hitler shown by the teenager Hellmuth Hübener, who had been caught distributing anti-Nazi leaflets and executed in Plötzensee prison on 27 October 1942. Starusch realises not only the juvenility of his anarchist past, but also that Hübener's actions might be a more relevant model for contemporary Germans than the botched last-minute attempt to assassinate Hitler by army officers on 20 July 1944.

örtlich betäubt is a more complex text than *Ansichten eines Clowns*. Its narrator, Starusch, is even less reliable than Schnier, to the extent that it is often impossible to tell what is 'fact' and what 'fiction' in his account of his own biography. Early reviewers were irritated by this; Hellmuth Karasek regarded it as modish imitation of Max Frisch's technique in *Mein Name sei Gantenbein*.[13] Starusch knows 'only stories', believes in 'stories' (p. 201). Ultimately the truths of *örtlich betäubt* are the truths of fiction. By thematising the act of writing Grass is stressing the primacy of the imagination in the writer's relation to society and by implication offering a counter-model to that of literature as documentation. To this extent the didacticism of the Scherbaum story is softened.

In *Die Ästhetik des Widerstands*, too, as we shall see, writing is thematised, but in a different way. It is a novel which sums up and develops many of the themes treated in *Ansichten eines Clowns* and *örtlich betäubt*.[14] Here, too, coming to a proper understanding of fascism is the precondition for political progress in the present – there can be no progress without a clarification of the past, as Weiss wrote in his notebooks.[15] Model figures for the young people of the 1970s are present once more. Heilmann, Coppi and the anonymous narrator, whom we encounter in the Pergamon Museum in pre-war Berlin at the opening of the novel, are eighteen-year-olds; the synthesis between bourgeois intelligentsia, represented by Heilmann, and industrial proletariat, represented by the other two, is something that the German student movement sought but never achieved. The involvement of Heilmann and Coppi, the equivalents of *örtlich betäubt*'s Hellmuth Hübener, in the Schulze–Boysen–Harnack resistance group is the theme of much of the final section of the novel. The text as a whole, however, as its title implies, centres on the theme of resistance: 'resistance' is equated with socialism, the one political ideology with the potential to combat the repression of the weak by the mighty, of the many by the few. Accordingly, the 'aesthetic' of resistance is a socialist one: the attempt to understand the cultural artefacts of the past in Marxist terms and the search for inspiration from these works in order the better to resist.

The novel follows the efforts of the left to resist the fascist dictators of Europe: in direct action in Spain, in underground activities in Germany. Two themes accompany this movement. The first of these is the imperative of left-wing unity with the concomitant question of the extent to which the individual must submit to the will of the collective. The second is the relationship between the political and the artistic avant-garde; it is linked to the first via the role of subjectivity. In both these domains Stalin, although like Hitler he is never named, and the distortions of socialism carried out under his leadership are declared responsible for the failures which led to the catastrophe of fascism.

There are, however, significant differences between Weiss's text and those of Böll and Grass. The action of Böll's novel is compressed into a couple of hours and its location is almost entirely Schnier's claustrophobic flat; Grass's novel covers a few months and is set in West Berlin, much of it in a dentist's surgery. Both introduce elements of the past and alternative locations through the extensive use of flashback. Weiss's novel, in three substantial volumes, starts in September 1937 and ends in 1945, and moves from Berlin to Czechoslovakia, Spain, France and Sweden and back to Berlin. Unlike the other texts it presents the fascist period directly and therefore avoids confronting head-on the question of how far postwar German society is a continuation of the previous one; it avoids also the awkwardness that so many of the bogeymen of the 1960s apostrophised by Böll and Grass have sunk into oblivion, unlike Hitler fascism which remains the ultimate reference for political evil. Here, too, however, flashback and reminiscence expand the historical time back to the beginning of the century, and at numerous points we read implicit references to events later than 1945. The detailed investigations of the development of art from the Pergamon altar down to Picasso expand this time scale even further to embrace a totality of human history seen in terms of humanity's struggle against oppression and exploitation. There is a sense in which Weiss's novel is truly 'epic' in scale, making it look almost old-fashioned in the landscape of the postwar German novel. *Die Ästhetik des Widerstands* has more in common with the prewar philosophical novels of Robert Musil and Hermann Broch than with most texts by Weiss's contemporaries. For all the profusion of historical events in the period covered by the text, external action is largely absent; excitement, tension in the traditional sense is concentrated at the end of the third volume, as the narrator describes the conspirators seeking ever more desperately to avoid arrest, and furnishes uniquely horrific accounts of their executions. One role of the numerous descriptions of works of art is to add colour and excitement in the otherwise densely abstract mass of theoretical discussion. Weiss's origins in the visual arts are recalled in echoes of the techniques of abstract painting in his novel: the isolated 'stories' might be compared to blobs of bright colours in a mass of grey tones.

In *Die Ästhetik des Widerstands* there is no generation conflict – always a middle-class phenomenon, whether in German Expressionism or in the texts by Böll and Grass. Weiss's narrator is of working-class origins, and although his politics are significantly different from those of his father, who remains staunchly devoted to social democracy, this does not cause a break between them. He respects his father, and especially his mother, of whom he paints one of the most moving pictures in the novel. On the trek fleeing from the Nazis she witnesses atrocities committed on Jews, mothers and children, and as a result literally becomes speechless and subject to recurrent horrific visions. Schnier's mother, we remember, was a collaborator.

The novel can be read as a variant of the German *Bildungsroman* (discussed by Russell Berman in chapter 6 above). There too, there was rarely a conflict between generations; rather representatives of the older generation acted as mentors to the young protagonist, whose personal development was usually accompanied by the development of insights into works of art and literature. But whereas, as the narrator puts it, 'from Wilhelm Meister down to the Buddenbrooks the world which set the tone in literature was seen through the eyes of those who possessed it' (1, 134), the world of this novel is largely a proletarian one. The narrator of *Die Ästhetik des Widerstands* is describing his own development in both political and aesthetic terms. He overcomes his initial hesitations and joins the Communist

Party, and at the same time he discovers his true vocation, that of writer; this latter development is signalled by the increasing complexity of his narrative technique. That he himself remains a somewhat shadowy, undefined figure is equally characteristic of the *Bildungsroman* tradition: it is not Hans Castorp in Thomas Mann's *Der Zauberberg* (*The Magic Mountain*) whom we afterwards can easily visualise but other characters such as Settembrini or Naphta. *Der Zauberberg* is actually discussed at one point, dismissed by the Swedish writer Karin Boye as an example of anti-feminist writing. Boye is one of a host of historical figures whom the narrator encounters, all of whom contribute to his development. Far and away the most important of these is Hodann, the ailing, liberal Marxist, but vivid pictures emerge of people such as Rosalinde Ossietzky and Bertolt Brecht. The narrator becomes an important intermediary for the communists working illegally in the Swedish underground, Wehner, Rosner, Stahlmann. There is thus in *Die Ästhetik des Widerstands* also something of the pattern of the historical novel as described by Georg Lukács: the (fictitious) 'mediocre' character in interaction with 'world-historical personages'.

However, although *Die Ästhetik des Widerstands* has a personalised narrator, the narrative strategy is not conventionally uniform. The voices of the innumerable alternative narrators, both protagonists and antagonists, leave the reader with a sense of openness, of unanswered questions. As already mentioned, one of Weiss's aims was to reclaim the aesthetic avant-garde for Marxism, and although his novel does not exploit all the possibilities illustrated by, for example, Joyce's *Ulysses*, one of the models invoked by the young workers (I, 79), it does use a number of internal focalisers, as does another canonical modernist author Kafka, whose novel *Das Schloß* is discussed in some detail (I, 171ff). The most important of these is the figure of Bischoff, whose experiences, first in Sweden, where she is trying to avoid deportation, later in Germany, where she is the only member of the underground communist organisation to survive, are recounted entirely as seen through her eyes. Bischoff's final plans are programmatic: after the war had ended she wished to become a teacher, 'to explain to the pupils what it had been like' (III, 236), a teacher who, unlike Grass's Starusch, will have the self-confidence and authority to do so. Bischoff is a woman – Weiss ignores the sexist conventions which insist that only men should be called by their surname. Other women in the text have already been mentioned; to them should be added Marcauer, who attacks Stalin's show trials not only for their manifest injustice but also as examples of repressive patriarchy, and is herself subsequently arrested. In its portrayal of women *Die Ästhetik des Widerstands* is more progressive than either *Ansichten eines Clowns*, whose Marie allows herself to be seduced first by Schnier and then by her church,

or *örtlich betäubt*, whose women never advance beyond the status of stereo-
types. The world described by Weiss is largely a male world; but it is also
one in which women have a voice and an active role, and are prepared to
call in question male attitudes. Coppi's mother, for example, has pertinent
observations to make on Heilmann's interpretation of the frieze on the Pergamon altar, reminding them of the price that had to be paid in labour terms
in order that these works of art might come into being.

Of the three novels analysed, Weiss's is the most explicitly left-wing. In the
light of the collapse of European communism less than a decade after its final
volume appeared, one may ask what relevance it still has today. Have not
the interminable debates on socialist strategies and on Marxist revisionism
become to the present-day reader as unfathomable as medieval theology? The
answer will inevitably depend on the reader. In any case a profound sense
of melancholy pervades *Die Ästhetik des Widerstands*. These were, after all,
battles which were lost. Again and again we read of advances which became
setbacks: Courbet, for example, destroying the Victory column on the Place
Vendôme only to have to pay for its subsequent re-erection. The severed
heads portrayed by Géricault anticipate in the second volume the fate of the
resistance at the end of the third. Nothing seems to have been learned: the
suppression of libertarian socialism in Czechoslovakia in 1968 was to repeat
what happened in Spain in the 1930s.

Melancholy is, indeed, perhaps the keynote of all the novels discussed.
Böll's clown repeatedly describes himself as a 'melancholic'; the defiance of
his final act of resistance cannot conceal the fundamental hopelessness of
his situation. In *örtlich betäubt* the capitulation of Scherbaum is not an occasion for rejoicing but for sadness; Starusch cannot suppress a feeling of
sorrow that his pupil is now 'grown up', that his idealism has been 'broken'
(p. 227). In Grass's *Tagebuch einer Schnecke* Albrecht Dürer's engraving
Melencolia is a central motif, representing everything that runs counter
to the snail of progress. The engraving is evoked by Hodann, too, in *Die
Ästhetik des Widerstands*. While earlier the narrator had found in the works
of Géricault evidence that the visions of the artist contributed to the overcoming of melancholy (II, 33), Hodann suggests that the experience of art can
be both ecstatic and melancholic, and the latter tends more frequently to be
the case (III, 132). Nevertheless, he ends his exposition with a more positive
assertion:

> It was Mneme, protected by the goddess Mnemosyne, who guided us towards
> our artistic acts, and the more we had absorbed of the phenomena of the world,
> the richer the combinations we should be able to create, the variety, in short,
> which was the criterion for the status of our culture.   (III, 134)

This position could scarcely be further removed from that of those who had proclaimed the 'death of literature' in 1968. Moreover, in his invocation of Memory as the inspiration of art, Hodann touches on the supreme motivating force of so much postwar German writing, not least of Böll, Grass and of Weiss himself.

NOTES

1. 'Befehl und Verantwortung. Gedanken zum Eichmann-Prozeß', in *Essayistische Schriften und Reden*, vol. I, ed. Bernd Balzer (Cologne, 1979), pp. 451–4.
2. Peter Weiss, *Notizbücher 1971–1980*, vol. II (Frankfurt am Main, 1981), pp. 730–1.
3. 'Kein Schreihals vom Dienst sein', in *Interviews*, ed. Bernd Balzer (Cologne, 1978), pp. 60–8 (p. 62).
4. *Werkausgabe in zehn Bänden*, vol. IV, ed. Volker Neuhaus (Darmstadt, 1987), p. 339.
5. 'Werkstattgespräch mit Horst Bienek', in *Interviews*, pp. 13–25 (p. 23).
6. 'Vom mangelnden Selbstvertrauen der schreibenden Hofnarren unter Berücksichtigung nicht vorhandener Höfe', in *Werkausgabe*, vol. IX, ed. Daniela Hermes, pp. 153–8. Böll, Grass and Weiss all signed a resolution in 1979 protesting against the GDR's treatment of the dissident Robert Havemann, the only occasion, I believe, on which they shared a platform (*Die Zeit*, 27 April 1979, p. 48).
7. Theodor W. Adorno, 'Engagement', in *Noten zur Literatur*, vol. III (Frankfurt am Main, 1965), pp. 109–35.
8. Cf. Michael Butler, '"Ansichten eines Clowns": the fool and the labyrinth', in Michael Butler (ed.), *The Narrative Fiction of Heinrich Böll: Social Conscience and Literary Achievement* (Cambridge, 1994), pp. 132–52, esp. pp. 145–7.
9. Cf. Ralf Dahrendorf, 'Die Intellektuellen und die Gesellschaft', *Die Zeit*, 29 March 1963.
10. On the relationship between *Ansichten eines Clowns* and the short-lived journal *Labyrinth*, which Böll helped to edit, see 'Im Gespräch: mit Heinz Ludwig Arnold', in *Interviews*, pp. 135–76 (pp. 159–60).
11. Cf. Böll's characterisation of Schörner in his 'Brief an meine Söhne', in *Die Fähigkeit zu trauern. Schriften und Reden 1983–1985* (Bornheim-Merten, 1986), p. 110.
12. Cf. Manfred Durzak, 'Abschied von der Kleinbürgerwelt. Der neue Roman von Günter Grass', *Basis*, I (1970), 224–37 (pp. 231–2).
13. 'Zahn gezogen', in *Die Zeit*, 5 September 1969, p. 20.
14. Böll castigated the neglect of Weiss's novel in West Germany and described it as a corrective to 'certain tendencies towards a hostility to art', in 'Der fragende Reporter', *Essayistische Schriften und Reden*, III, 429–33 (p. 429).
15. *Notizbücher 1971–1980*, I, 225.

PRIMARY TEXTS

Page references in the text are to the following editions:

Böll, Heinrich, *Ansichten eines Clowns. Roman*, in *Romane und Erzählungen*, vol. IV, ed. Bernd Balzer (Cologne, 1978)

Grass, Günter, *örtlich betäubt. Roman*, in *Werkausgabe in zehn Bänden*, ed. Volker Neuhaus, vol. IV (Darmstadt, 1987)

Weiss, Peter, *Die Ästhetik des Widerstands. Roman* (Frankfurt am Main; vol. I, 1975; vol. II, 1978; vol. III, 1981)

FURTHER READING

Blamberger, Günter, *Versuch über den deutschen Gegenwartsroman. Krisenbewußtsein und Neubegründung im Zeichen der Melancholie* (Stuttgart, 1985)

Bond, D. G., 'Aesthetics and politics: Peter Weiss, *Die Ästhetik des Widerstands* as a chronicle of horror', *Journal of European Studies*, 19 (1989), 223–44

Kane, Martin, 'Culture, political power and the aesthetics of resistance: Peter Weiss's *Die Ästhetik des Widerstands*', in Keith Bullivant (ed.), *After the 'Death of Literature': West German Writing of the 1970s* (Oxford, 1989), pp. 361–77

Lukács, Georg, *Der historische Roman*, in *Probleme des Realismus III* (Darmstadt, 1965), pp. 14–429

Mitscherlich, Margarete and Alexander, *Die Unfähigkeit zu trauern. Grundlagen kollektiven Verhaltens* (Munich, 1967)

Pischel, Joseph, 'Peter-Weiss-Lektüre nach der "Wende": noch einmal zum Verhältnis von Kunst und Politik in *Die Ästhetik des Widerstands*', in Axel Goodbody and Dennis Tate (eds.), *Geist und Macht: Writers and the State in the GDR* (Amsterdam and Atlanta, 1992), pp. 104–16

Poore, Carol, 'Mother earth, melancholia, and Mnemosyne: women in Peter Weiss's *Die Ästhetik des Widerstands*', *German Quarterly*, 58 (1985), 68–86

Reid, J. H., *Heinrich Böll: a German for His Time* (Oxford, New York and Hamburg, 1988)

Stolz, Dieter, *Vom privaten Motivkomplex zum poetischen Entwurf. Konstanten und Entwicklungen im literarischen Werk von Günter Grass (1956–1986)* (Würzburg, 1994)

14

ANTHONY WAINE

The *kleiner Mann* and modern times: from Fallada to Walser

The term *kleiner Mann* ('little man') is not a strictly defined sociological category. It is, rather, a loose expression used both in the everyday world of colloquial exchanges and also in more formal discourse to evoke associations with, and sympathy for, the lot of ordinary people in a world in which important decisions are taken by a small and powerful but largely invisible group of people 'up above'. The *kleiner Mann* is the underdog who feels the odds are stacked against him. The sense of being insignificant or helpless has of course been a widespread one in the mass society of the industrial age: the *kleiner Mann* is not a marginal creature but a very representative figure – 'the man on the street', 'the ordinary guy', or, in older parlance, 'the common man', 'Everyman'. Furthermore, his predicament has been articulated not only by writers but by artists from a variety of national and ethnic backgrounds, and working in a range of media and genres, who, in the midst of the confusing modern world of factories, machines, cities, bureaucracies, commercial entertainment and mass politics, have collectively created a 'culture of the little man'. Embracing both 'popular' and 'high' art, it includes phenomena as diverse as the cinema's iconic 'little man', Charlie Chaplin; the Czech novelist Jaroslav Hašek's good soldier Švejk, whose half-feigned stupidities effectively subvert the authority of his Austro-Hungarian superiors; the lonely individual lost in the monolithic cityscapes of the Flemish woodcutter Frans Masereel; and the spirituals, jazz and blues that gave a voice to America's oppressed black minorities, and lent their experiences an increasingly universal resonance (the title of one of the novels examined in this chapter, Böll's *Und sagte kein einziges Wort*, alludes to a line from a spiritual heard on the radio). My focus here is on the way in which modern German literature, particularly the novel, has foregrounded the theme of the *kleiner Mann*.

There are two overlapping German terms to consider before we embark on a comparative analysis of novels that feature the 'little man' as their (anti-)hero. The terms are *Kleinbürger* (lower-middle-class citizen, petit bourgeois) and *Angestellter* (white-collar worker). *Kleinbürger* refers to a segment of society lodged between the traditional working class and the comfortably off, cultured, privileged middle class. It is, however, used less as an objective socio-economic designation than as a somewhat pejorative label (*kleinbürgerlich*) invoking the typical mentality of this social stratum – a varying combination of narrow-mindedness, status-consciousness, materialism and conformism.

Whilst the *Kleinbürger* is hard to pin down objectively, the term *Angestellter* is more specific: it refers to an employee working in public or private industry, commerce or administration, but not enjoying the status or, more crucially, the security of that other uniquely German professional grouping, the *Beamte* (officials employed by the state). From having a relatively exclusive status in the nineteenth century, not dissimilar to that of the *Beamte*, the *Angestellte* became a mass phenomenon in the twentieth century. Often clinging to *kleinbürgerlich* values, they are characterised by an identity which is more fragmented than that of the blue-collar working class with its collectivism, and more amorphous than that of the class of employers and other professional elites who enjoy varying degrees of wealth, education and social influence. What has attracted the attention of a succession of German writers during the last century is the very precariousness of the lower-middle-class white-collar worker's existential situation. In an era of such profound social changes, and, moreover, in a country that has witnessed so many political and economic upheavals, his behaviour and his fate tell us more about modern Germany than those of almost any other single type of individual.

German novelists who venture into the realms of ordinary people in this period are therefore dealing with topics of great social, political and historical significance. But as one prominent sociologist pointed out in 1929 in a ground-breaking survey of Berlin white-collar workers, male and female, it is too simple to rail against the extreme threats to their lives, such as war, capitalism, miscarriages of justice in the courts, however well founded (and humane) such critiques are. Rather, argued Kracauer, the intelligentsia should 'assess the imperceptible, terrifying quality of their normal existence', because it is 'the succession of little occurrences out of which our normal social lives are composed'; only then will it be possible to 'transform our everyday life' ('der Alltag').[1] This is not only a challenge to Berlin's 'young, radical intelligentsia'. It also identifies with great succinctness problems that confront realistic novelists writing about the *kleiner Mann*.

For example, from the point of view of the writer wishing to generate narrative interest and suspense, ordinary people's lives may not be inherently dramatic, let alone heroic. Their pleasures and tastes may also tend to be conventional and therefore lacking in the artistic depth and richness which many highbrow or serious writers prefer to explore. Indeed there is the ever-present danger, for writers who choose this milieu, of their stories being labelled *trivial* and *populär*, two epithets which in the great German tradition of *Bildung* (acquired culture, erudition and taste) invite particular opprobrium. A twin challenge, therefore, confronts the serious writer: to situate his subject in a historical context, revealing how his mind is conditioned by it, and to give a realistic yet engaging portrayal of his everyday existence both at the workplace and within the four walls of his private life.

In the dying days of the Weimar Republic Hans Fallada (born in 1893) took up the gauntlet and placed the insignificant white-collar worker Johannes Pinneberg centre stage. Not only did he foreground him in the narrative but, as if to headline his symbolic social importance, he actually addressed him in the title of his novel. *Kleiner Mann – was nun?*, published in 1932, was an enormous success, on an international as well as a national scale (an abridged translation, *Little Man, What Now?* appeared in 1933),[2] and was lauded by several of Weimar's most respected authors, including Hermann Hesse, Lion Feuchtwanger, Thomas Mann, Robert Musil and Carl Zuckmayer. Set in the early 1930s the story focuses exclusively on the fortunes and misfortunes of one young German couple, the Pinnebergs. Expecting a baby, the couple have to adjust to this event emotionally, psychologically and financially. The first, relatively light-hearted part of the story is set in a small north German town, whilst the second and progressively more unsettling part is enacted in the metropolitan maze of Berlin. The central theme of the novel is the ever-encroaching social isolation and material insecurity of ordinary lower-middle-class folk in a hard-hearted capitalist society. It is also a capitalist society in deep crisis, manifest in the impoverishment of the masses, large-scale unemployment and widening political schisms. Lacking the close-knit ties of a working-class community and temperamentally unattracted to the aggressive ideology of the Nazis, the young Pinneberg and his expectant wife find themselves socially marginalised and excluded, especially in the big city.

If Fallada's protagonist epitomises the fate of the little man at the penultimate moment in the short-lived first German republic, then Heinrich Böll (born in 1917) shows in his novel *Und sagte kein einziges Wort* (1953; *And Never Said a Word*, 1978) an ordinary German family on the breadline in Cologne at a key moment in postwar West German history (1952), when the aftermath of war is still acutely present but the contours of a consumer society are beginning to become visible. Though one of the themes of this novel, material insecurity, vividly echoes Fallada's work, the central focus of the narrative is the marital estrangement experienced by the Bogners. Though Fallada was certainly sensitive to the deep psychological impact made on

Pinneberg by the threatening external forces, the marital relationship was basically secure and the crisis was perceived as being external to their private world. The crisis in Böll's work on the other hand takes place in the very heart and soul of the individual, as his faith in everything, including the Catholic religion, appears to disintegrate. Nevertheless looking back in 1959 over Böll's first decade of writing, Wolfdietrich Rasch emphatically places the writer's figures from this era in a tradition which Fallada would appear to have inaugurated: 'they are always simple, average people, without power, influence and important positions'.[3]

This description is certainly applicable to many of the characters portrayed in the radio and stage plays as well as the novels of Martin Walser (born in 1927). The work which has been chosen for inclusion in this survey is *Seelenarbeit* (*The Inner Man*), which on its appearance in 1979 moved the reviewer for the *Frankfurter Rundschau* to claim that the novel 'provided a kind of further development of the perspective of the little man'.[4] It remained in the *Spiegel* bestseller lists for several months and garnered almost unanimous praise from Germany's critics, who had often expressed major reservations with most of Walser's previous books. *Seelenarbeit* gave another twist to the tale of the little man by approaching it from the perspective of a master–servant relationship. Of course this was done in a thoroughly modern guise by having the 'servant' Franz Xaver Zürn play chauffeur to his 'master', Dr Gleitze, boss of an engineering firm employing nearly five hundred people. The material and social traumas which so affected the lives of the Pinnebergs in *Kleiner Mann – was nun?* and the Bogners in *Und sagte kein einziges Wort* have almost entirely receded, but it is now the immaterial consequences of capitalist class divisions which fill the servant's mind, soul and body with so many contradictory sensations and feelings that he becomes sick and unstable. Walser diagnoses the pathological symptoms of self-estrangement and of self-rejection in the *Kleinbürger*.

Following this brief introduction to the topic and to the selected novels exemplifying it, I will look at three aspects of the novels relating to the life of the 'little man': firstly, I will compare the social and political conditions under which he lives and discuss the importance of his working relationships in this context; secondly, I will evaluate the import of the private domain, the characterisation of the woman sharing his life, but also his self-understanding as a *Mann* and concomitant gender roles. Finally, the analysis will highlight the authors' deliberate and effective exploration of the psychology, emotions and culture of their subjects, and assess the way in which these contribute to the realism of the works. The aim of such an approach will be to establish continuities in the fate of ordinary people living in German society between the late 1920s and the mid 1970s, but also to identify their differing responses to changing historical constellations and, of course, to differentiate between the authors' own individual perspectives on the common man in the modern world.

The social and political conditions are shown in all three works not to be benevolent towards the 'little man'. They overwhelm him, paralyse him, and even deform him. This negative development is portrayed most radically by Fallada, who charts the relentless decline of a relatively good-natured, well-intentioned young man into a pariah. Pinneberg's fall is not the result of psychological ineptitude or moral failings. The reader constantly admires his fundamental decency, honesty and modesty. He is a diligent and loyal employee, and, furthermore, a devoted, faithful husband and committed father. But he is powerless to determine the social conditions of his life because – and this is perhaps where Fallada is indirectly levelling some criticism against him – he is motivated by a desire to be an individual and to acquire the trappings of social success. His *kleinbürgerlich* (petit-bourgeois) mentality thus divorces him very clearly from the working class, a fact which Fallada comically reinforces in the episode where Pinneberg meets the unashamedly working-class family of his wife-to-be. Their rootedness in the culture and politics of the proletariat give them a self-confidence which the feuding and self-interested white-collar workers seemingly can never attain. The latters' anti-collectivist principles are ruthlessly exposed both in the small-scale business of Kleinholz in Ducherow and in the large departmental store of Mandel in Berlin.

Pinneberg's sense of impotence does not just result from his pursuit of individualism in a hostile world of massed social and political forces. It is exacerbated by economic factors which are also largely beyond his control. Fallada pays scrupulous attention to the role played by money in the public and especially the private life of his central character. One of the very first episodes is entitled 'A nocturnal natter about love and money', as if to emphasise that even the most intimate sphere of human relations is not protected from the insidious invasion of economic forces. In fact that particular heading might just as easily have been encountered in Heinrich Böll's novel, had he chosen to entitle his chapters. The opening sentences of *Und sagte kein einziges Wort* focus on a crucial economic scenario:

> After work had finished I went to the bank to collect my pay. A lot of people were standing at the paying out counter, and I waited half an hour, handed over my cheque and saw how the cashier gave it to a girl wearing a yellow blouse. The girl went over to the pile of account file-cards, found mine, gave the cheque back to the cashier, said 'OK' and the clean hands of the cashier counted out the notes on to the marble counter dish.   (p. 7)

This opening sentence is not only quintessential early Böll. It is almost a symbolic scene-setting of the place of the little man in the mid-twentieth-century world: the identity-determining routine of work; the dependence on money; the impersonal world of *Angestellte* ('cashier' and 'girl'); the bureaucratisation of human intercourse ('account file-cards'). The narrator of this sequence, Fred Bogner, however, is a much more complex individual than the rather naive Pinneberg. Böll has given him a spiritual and philosophical dimension which recalls French existentialism. He is nomadic. Estranged from his wife and three children, with a string of different jobs behind him, he roams fairly aimlessly around the city of Cologne, calling in at hot-dog stalls, corner pubs, churches and cemeteries, whenever he is not working as a telephone operator at a Catholic administrative headquarters. But there are three further factors which have contributed to the marital and existential crisis which lies at the heart of the novel. Firstly, he and his family have been forced to share one room owing to the acute shortage of accommodation in cities such as Cologne which had been badly bombed – typically the housing shortage hits the vulnerable ordinary people most. Secondly, Fred had fought as an ordinary soldier in the war and that experience would seem to have left him with a sense of futility and a cynical indifference towards life. And, finally, he feels estranged from the customs and rituals of his church and from the faith which he has shared so far with his wife. Böll's narrative style, like Fallada's, enables the reader to share his protagonist's feelings and reflections on an intimate level and thus to empathise with the subjectivity of the ordinary man as it interacts with the external historical and social conditions.

Walser achieves a similar feat, though he uses a different narrative technique. The third-person narrator of *Seelenarbeit* remains fixed on the central figure's intense inner life from the opening to the closing pages, but with an ironic filter permitting narrator and reader a therapeutic and critical distance. This is crucial for Walser's particular treatment of the little man. He is at pains not to take a fatalistic and therefore pessimistic view of the lives of ordinary people, no matter how deep the crisis is in which they are enmeshed. The very fact that Xaver Zürn has reached a crisis point means that realities which he has been denying and repressing for years are now appearing in the form of psychosomatic ailments, emotional disturbances and obsessive thought patterns. Unlike the crises of Xaver's literary predecessors his has nothing directly to do with his economic situation. He and his family live a relatively affluent life. It is his personality, as well as his family history and his socially acquired values and attitudes which are at the core of his problem, a problem which only he can resolve. He is almost pathologically dependent on approval from his social superiors; he has a petit-bourgeois obsession with social advancement for himself and his family; and he has thoroughly internalised the ethic of hard work, self-sacrifice and efficiency. He has become mechanical in his behaviour and lost sight of his own unique human soul. Little wonder that he worships the beautiful Mercedes 450 in which he drives his boss: 'Not that he felt it essential to be taken for the owner. But everybody could see that this was his car. And it was his car . . . It was his, his, his car! And it was *the* best car in the world' (p. 25). This is one of the many fantasies of the little man Xaver Zürn, but the novel chronicles a period of three months during which Zürn learns to grasp the reality of his situation and ceases to operate functionally and mechanically.

Despite the fact that each novel is set in a different period of twentieth-century German history and despite the differing thematic foci adopted by the three novelists, their protagonists Pinneberg, Bogner and Zürn share some important common traits, which may well be typical of the *Volk* whom they represent. Each is, to a greater or lesser degree, passive. This is of course a concomitant of their powerlessness. They obey instructions, carry out orders, play the roles that higher authorities have prescribed for them. They are subservient, subordinated, forced into demeaning, dehumanising acts of servitude. Each suffers from low morale and a sense of inadequacy. Self-pity is often one of the few remaining emotions left for them. Pinneberg's self-portrait may be seen as typical here: 'He's a pathetic creature, he's stopped learning anything new, people can walk all over him' (p. 234). It is the perspective of the victim in history, whilst the victor continues to dictate the 'progress' of history. Walser's Zürn meditates ruefully yet critically on the precise nature of the relationship of victim to victor: 'After all, what is a victor? The difference between victor and vanquished is merely that the victor thinks of the vanquished only when he wants to, whereas the vanquished has to think of the victor whether he wants to or not' (p. 265).

How appropriate then is the surname of Walser's anti-hero Zürn! *Jemandem zürnen* means 'to be angry with somebody'. He finds himself in an almost constant state of rage, but because of his personality structure and his socio-economic situation the rage is impotent. It implodes and causes him agonising gut trouble. Or it is sublimated through his fetishistic collecting of knives and his passionate watching of Westerns on television. Zürn could just as easily be the surname of Fallada's and Böll's protagonists too. Both are subject to frequent sensations of ire. Böll's Bogner has expressed this ire by hitting his children, and one suspects that his drinking too is an attempt to neutralise his aggression. Fallada, for his part, captures perfectly the schizophrenia of the ordinary person who feels excessive anger, but has to suppress it and project a perfectly controlled exterior to a watching world: 'Pinneberg is thinking just one thing. "I'll smash your face. I'll smash your face. You bitch." But of course he made his little bow and kept smiling' (p. 182). What all three writers do is express how the ordinary person is prone to what today we call stress, and how a great deal of that stress is caused by the sense of not being in control of one's life, yet of having to control almost all one's emotions, especially the negative ones, in order to conform to the tacit and stated expectations and norms of 'die Welt', as Pinneberg invariably dubs the invidious system of oppression and inequality 'out there'.

In the preceding examples one can see a further aspect of the individuals' relationship to their environment. They are, in a sense, without a voice, either their own or a surrogate one which speaks on their behalf. They lack both a channel of communication as well as the confidence to communicate, though all three men possess an active and indeed critical mind. Their society's discourses sideline them. The epilogue in *Kleiner Mann – was nun?* is almost symbolic in this respect, for Pinneberg has been forced to live with his family on an allotment outside Berlin, and in the final scene he remains outside his hut unable to face even his loving wife. It is as if he had become mute. The very narrative structure of Böll's novel reinforces the sense of the man having lost his public voice and been compelled to tell his story to himself in an interior monologue. In his verbal isolation Bogner is nevertheless conscious of a symphony of external public voices, such as the announcer at the railway station, the sermons of the priests and the bishop, the advertisements on posters and in shop windows and the neon-lit slogan of the chemists' congress being held in the city: VERTRAU DICH DEINEM DROGISTEN AN (trust your chemist). Walser's Xaver too holds interminable monologues with himself because he believes that his servant status does not give him the right to initiate dialogues with his employers, and the very fact that his boss is invariably listening to music through his headphones whilst being chauffeured by Zürn symbolically reinforces the communication gulf in a hierarchical society between the powerful and the powerless.

There are many instances in all three novels where, as a result of his passivity and his distance from centres of power and influence, the central figure is reduced either to the role of listener and eavesdropper or to that of spectator, onlooker and voyeur. Fred Bogner, who works as a telephone operator, can almost be described as a professional eavesdropper, as the final chapter of the novel vividly illustrates. Zürn's occupation as a chauffeur also places him in a position where he listens to all manner of discussions, but ones from which he is excluded. And one of the most socially critical episodes in Fallada's novel has Pinneberg inadvertently overhearing the verbal and moral humiliation of a fellow *Angestellte*, Fräulein Fischer, accused of having had an affair at Mandel's with another employee, and then finding himself the hapless recipient of a sermon from his boss. And if the passive activity of listening and eavesdropping makes the individual feel excluded from the discourses of the powerful, then the cognate activity of looking and observing reinforces the feeling of not participating, of not being involved, of standing outside. At home Xaver is an avid watcher of Westerns on TV, and when killing time in towns where his boss is doing business he often goes to the red light areas and studies the pornographic displays. Likewise when Fred Bogner goes into a church it is not so much to participate in a religious act as to observe the other people there: 'It was strange that although I was in church I did not feel part of it' (pp. 33–4). In all three novels the main figure's sense of passivity in the public world generates a degree of alienation.

However, while Pinneberg, Bogner and Zürn find themselves (because of their lowly status) in the position of passive onlookers and listeners, they in turn are – more sinisterly – being observed and scrutinised by their superiors and other people in authority, recalling the Orwellian dystopia of *1984*. Pinneberg probably loses his job with Herr Kleinholz because he happens to be spotted one weekend relaxing with his wife in the countryside, after being asked by his boss to work extra hours on that day. Because Kleinholz wishes to marry off his daughter and sees Pinneberg as a potential husband, the latter has had to keep his marriage a secret – another example of the outside world intruding on the private life of the *kleiner Mann*. But while in this instance being spotted by Big Brother – albeit in the guise of the slightly caricatured Kleinholz – is a chance event, working in Mandel's department store in Berlin means that his every move and word are monitored. Indeed the surveillance of Pinneberg and the other salesmen is formalised when a time-and-motion consultant, Herr Spannfuß, is brought into the firm and each person's performance is subject to constant critical review. Possibly the most humiliating experience of being under observation is when the unemployed Pinneberg, window-shopping on a busy Berlin thoroughfare, is picked out by a suspicious policeman with many other people voyeuristically looking on. Bogner's private life too is the subject of gossip, rumour and speculation, both at his workplace and amongst his neighbours: 'They say that you drink and that your wife is pregnant – besides which you've been living apart from your wife for some time now' (p. 183). The loss of privacy, dignity and personal freedom by the little man at the hands of Big Brother is found in its most grotesque manifestation in Walser's *Seelenarbeit*. Xaver himself is often paranoid about the extent to which his superiors (and their clandestine allies such as his doctor) are monitoring and evaluating him. And not without justification. One day out of the blue he is informed by his boss's secretary that he is to go for a medical examination, which lasts five (!) days, after which it dawns on him that this investigation into his most inner self was the prerogative of the omnipotent boss: 'The boss sent him to Tübingen, to those machines, because he needs a man whose reliability has been scrutinised by every technological process . . . The boss was entitled to be informed about every square centimetre of his insides, that was quite obvious' (p. 156).

Little wonder then that the private sphere, the microcosmic world of wives, children, meals, bedrooms, sexuality, plays such an important role for these individuals. For it is here that, like their pathetic nineteenth-century counter-part, Woyzeck, in Büchner's dramatic portrait of have-nots, they too seek the affection, warmth and security and the sense of self which are denied them in the cut-throat, competitive world 'out there'. The bitter truth, however, is that there is no strict segregation of the public and the private worlds, at least not for the *Kleinbürger*. In *Kleiner Mann – was nun?* economics con-stantly intrudes into the private sphere; in *Und sagte kein einziges Wort* the Bogners' one-room flat gives them no sense of privacy, the thinness of the walls exposing them even to the ritualised love-making of their neighbours; and, finally, in *Seelenarbeit* the Zürns, reeling from one crisis after another, learn that they are to lose a significant portion of their beloved garden to enable a new road to be built. The petit-bourgeois idyll of 'my home is my castle' is unmasked as just another fantasy. The images of the Pinnebergs inhabiting a rented allotment hut and of Fred Bogner sleeping rough are trenchant social critiques.

It is, however, not so much the physical building, its location, its size, its decoration and furnishings, which represent the sense of *Heimat* (home) for the three males, but rather the three women, who personify the spiritual, emotional, sexual and maternal realities of the home. Despite differences in age, outlook and circumstances, Käthe in *Und sagte kein einziges Wort*, Lämmchen in *Kleiner Mann – was nun?* and Agnes in *Seelenarbeit* share a great many common characteristics. They are all very hard working, Käthe and Agnes almost pathologically so. None of them has a professional oc-cupation – though Lämmchen does do some menial work for upper-class households when her husband becomes unemployed – so that all their con-siderable energies are channelled into the rearing of children, the completion of domestic chores, the planning of the family budget (though not in the case of the materially better situated Zürns) and the caring for their husband. They have little time (or money) for leisure interests, make few demands on their husbands, give almost unconditional love. Their tolerance and pa-tience towards their husbands' idiosyncrasies, hang-ups, moods, and work-related stresses and strains, in fact verge on the heroic. Their male creators have, seemingly deliberately, portrayed them as the human antipodes to the depersonalising and dehumanising tendencies of the social and political system, serious malign symptoms of which are already quite apparent in their husbands.

It can of course be argued that this is a highly traditional portrayal of gender roles. In fact in the case of Käthe all three of the proverbially female 'K' activities apply to her situation: 'Kinder', 'Kirche' and 'Küche' (children, church and kitchen). Yet we should not be too censorious towards the writers in question. They are after all portraying *kleinbürgerlich* conditions where the status quo is probably more sacrosanct than in any other sphere of society; besides which Fallada's and Böll's stories are set in historical periods in which women's roles were certainly more clearly defined than they were to be after 1970, whilst the Zürns' origins are defiantly rural. Interestingly, it is the Zürns' eldest daughter who represents a new, younger generation of liberated, non-conformist, rebellious women, a fact which causes her parents endless headaches. Whilst the three male authors portray the central women figures traditionally and idealistically – Böll even permitting Käthe to counterpoint Fred's story and points of view with her own first-person narrative – they present a more challenging and critical view of male gender roles. The portrait of Pinneberg is perhaps the most fascinating. After Lämmchen becomes pregnant he is the breadwinner. But the combination of husband and father-to-be makes him a good deal more sensitive as well as critical towards the patriarchy of his fellow men, as encountered for example amongst the fathers waiting to collect their wives and new-born children at the maternity hospital. He openly expresses his feelings, is so devoted to the well-being of his wife and new-born son that he jeopardises his position at Mandels, and is prepared to make every kind of sacrifice on behalf of his dependents. His metamorphosis continues after his dismissal by Mandel when he actually swaps roles with his wife, as she goes out to work and he stays at home with their child. The headline of one chapter encapsulates this revolutionary gender-role reversal: 'The Husband as Wife'.

If there is something idyllic about the Pinnebergs' marriage, even in adversity, then Böll's portrait of this institution and especially of the male's role is distinctly pessimistic and critical. The story opens with the marriage in deepest crisis, owing in part to unremitting social, economic and psychological pressures but in no small measure also to the behaviour of the husband, Fred Bogner, who has abandoned his responsibilities and fled into alcohol and cigarette consumption, popular culture (frequenting corner pubs and playing the fruit machines) and vagrancy. He still provides the family income and has sexual intercourse with Käthe in rented rooms in third-class hotels or even public parks. His wife, not surprisingly, feels like a whore. Böll shows their marriage to be a charade and the husband to have been a failure – though he leaves it to the reader to apportion guilt, to the war, to

his society and to his gender code. In *Seelenarbeit* too Walser depicts a partially broken man, though once again one is aware of the degree to which his
social situation has contributed to his physical and mental malaise. Xaver's
masculine adult identity seems to be very shallow. Close to the surface lie a
number of infantile complexes. The most intractable is his longing for attention, approval, acknowledgment. His relationship to Gleitze is not only akin
to that of servant to master, but also of child to father. For his part, Gleitze
treats Xaver as if he were indeed a minor, always insisting on buying him
an ice cream whenever his chauffeur is in the same hotel restaurant. It is the
arrogant yet uncannily perceptive Doctor Meichle who hits the nail on the
head when he admonishes Xaver: 'The main thing is: kill that mother's pet
in you, accept the fact that you're an adult, and things will work out . . .'
(p. 100).

Despite the individual failings, the psychological pressures, the family dis-
cord, and the economic threats afflicting all three sets of little people, their
authors choose to end their novels on a note of hope, as if to reinforce the
message that whilst these individuals will never be the victors in the social
struggles, they are nevertheless adept at surviving. And their principal means
of survival is their union with wives who represent humane values. This is
the sole answer to the question posed in the title of Fallada's novel, as the
cowering speechless creature Pinneberg discovers at the very end: 'And suddenly the coldness has gone, an infinitely soft, green wave lifts her up and
him with her. They glide upwards, the stars twinkle close by; she whispers,
"but you can look at me. For ever and ever. You're with me, you know,
we're together, you know"' (p. 247). An almost identical sensation of this
mystical union between man and woman is experienced by the errant Fred
Bogner when he happens to see his wife on the street and is forced to admit
to himself: 'I saw her hands, saw her exactly, the woman with whom I shared
more things than with any other person in the world' (p. 188). And the final
poignant words of the story are 'Going home'. Home symbolising shelter,
security, love. A genuine pathos is also created at the very end of *Seelenarbeit*
where Zürn makes love to his wife and we are told: 'Like two fields under
the sun they now lay side by side' (p. 275).

The three authors concerned have of course been accused of trivialising
their art, of pandering to the popular demand for a happy ending, of in-
dulging in sentimentality. Such charges reveal the bigotry of critics who insist
on a clear divorce between art and entertainment, cerebral appeal and popular appeal, criticism and affirmation. These prejudices are particularly deeply
entrenched in the critical thinking of post-Enlightenment culture, which sets
such store by the privileging of the rational and the intellectual (immortalised
in the term *Geist*) over the irrational and emotional, painted so often as the

preserve of the philistine *Kleinbürgertum*. But it is precisely this class which engages all three writers, who do not merely feel a tenuous affinity with it but positively identify with it. Their accounts are written from the heart as well as from the head, and it is their sensitivity to the hopes, anxieties, longings and sufferings of their protagonists which makes all three works so compellingly readable and realistic. Furthermore it could be argued that all three works offer a critique of patriarchal, rationalistic and authoritarian values precisely by showing the devastating effects such values have on their characters' emotional lives. *Kleiner Mann – was nun?* for example excoriates an economic system which applies the principle of *Rationalisieren* in its drive for maximum profitability and leaves the little man so paralysed by angst that he can barely function. One of the most emotionally charged scenes in the book is the episode in which Pinneberg, desperate to meet his month's sales target, is sadistically manipulated by the actor, Schlüter, who in the end decides not to purchase anything and thus precipitates Pinneberg's downfall. The reader is not just moved by the drama but recognises its socio-economic determinants.

Und sagte kein einziges Wort counterpoints the dogma, the rites and the hierarchical structures of institutionalised Catholicism with the all-too-human realities of ordinary folk such as the Bogners. There are many instances of Böll's ability to create a powerful emotional rapport with the reader and even to incorporate overtly melodramatic and sentimental elements, though never gratuitously. Two scenes in particular stand out. One concerns the simple yet deep humanity of the family who run the hot-dog stall to which, by chance, both Fred and Käthe go, on the Sunday on which the story is set. The father, a war invalid, and his pious daughter embody genuinely Christian charity and compassion, showing concern both for the mentally handicapped son and for all their customers. The second example of Böll's instinctive sense of the *Volk*, their authentic pastimes and pleasures, is the episode at the fairground where Fred and Käthe sit on the animals of a stationary merry-go-round discussing their marriage. The ambience of traditional popular culture is entirely appropriate to their social and psychological situation. Käthe's nausea and swooning following one of the fairground rides are recognised by the reader as also being a symptom of her pregnancy, and the reader feels both deep sympathy for her and anger at the dogmatism of a church which discourages contraception.

Finally, in *Seelenarbeit*, whose very title locates those inner regions where instincts and emotions are co-active, Walser depicts an individual with a sensuous and sentimental attachment to his home region and its local culture, to his natural environs, to his immediate family and their ancestors (particularly his brother Johann who died in the war defending Königsberg – the various accounts of his death are amongst the most poignant passages in the book), and to music both popular and classical. His boss, Gleitze, the grand bourgeois individual with impeccable artistic tastes – he is writing a book on the production of Mozart operas – is driven in his daily life by the cold financial and industrial imperatives of the company he runs. Under the pretence of bonhomie he controls his employees such as Zürn with ruthless manipulative skill. One of the most emotionally powerful passages of the novel is the aforementioned week-long medical examination of Xaver, in which all the powers of science and technology are deployed to check the little man's functionality and usefulness for the wielders of power. Paradoxically, Xaver emerges from this high-tech torture chamber with a heightened sentimental attachment to himself and a more ambivalent, critical attitude towards his master. This attachment is expressed in the word 'Selbstgefühl' (feeling of self) which the narrator employs three times in succession like some existential mantra.

In conclusion one can say that Fallada, Böll and Walser plumb the subjective depths of their creations and reveal, in the process, structures of feeling with which a great many readers can sympathise and identify. But all three, whilst laying bare this subjectivity, succeed in uncovering those equally intangible ideological and cultural structures which shape the sense of self and implant in it the feelings of inferiority, inadequacy, insignificance, which are resonant in the epithet 'little'. Yet none of the authors patronises these representatives of the common people. They take them seriously, just as they take seriously the banalities, the pettinesses, and the pedestrian minutiae of their daily lives. These too belong to the structures of feeling already identified. They confirm too the validity of the now historical realisation that tragedy, pathos and passion are not dependent on the superior social status of individuals but can be experienced by ordinary people and can be empathetically felt by ordinary readers. Nor are the 'little women' of these male anti-heroes patronised. They are central to the narrative, both actively and passively, and influence perhaps more than any other factor the structures of feeling basic to their partners' identity and existential purpose. Ultimately it may be they who help to make their 'little' men feel greater and more human beings.

This chapter has indeed tried to portray the three authors as fired by what might be termed a democratic compassion. Their characters, male and female, are fellow human sufferers, and in uncovering and articulating that suffering these three writers may also be seen to be filling the void in our century left by declining religious belief, and also by the perception that the church has lost its significance as one *Heimat* for the excluded, the exploited and the exhausted, and aligned itself instead with the other established powers. Without the Heinrich Bölls, the Hans Falladas and the Martin Walsers, the Davids of their century would have few other chances of telling their story and of countering the Goliaths. These writers have taken up the fight and in the spirit of the New Testament have mobilised support for the weak against the strong, for the poor against the rich, for the humane against all forms of worldly power. And, as if to underline this secularised gospel of struggle and salvation, all three works conclude by demonstrating the human urge and capacity for love, and faith in love.

NOTES

1. Siegfried Kracauer, *Die Angestellten* (Frankfurt am Main, 1971), p. 109. Kracauer's book has been published in a translation by Quintin Hoare: *The Salaried Masses*, introduced by Inka Mülder-Bach (London and New York, 1998).
2. An unabridged translation by Susan Bennett was eventually published in 1996.
3. Wolfdietrich Rasch, 'Lobrede und Deutung', in *Der Schriftsteller Heinrich Böll* (Cologne and Berlin, 1959), p. 12.
4. Hugo Dittberner, 'Der abgeschmetterte Fahrer: Martin Walsers Roman *Seelenarbeit*', *Frankfurter Rundschau*, 24 March 1979.

PRIMARY TEXTS AND TRANSLATIONS

All translations, with the exception of those from Martin Walser's *Seelenarbeit*, are my own. Page numbers refer to the following editions:
Hans Fallada, *Kleiner Mann – was nun?* (Reinbek, 1950)
Heinrich Böll, *Und sagte kein einziges Wort* (Cologne, 1995)
Martin Walser, *The Inner Man*, trans. Leila Vennewitz (London, 1985)

FURTHER READING

Hans Fallada

Frotscher, Hans Jürgen, *Hans Fallada: 'Kleiner Mann – was nun?'*(Munich, 1983)
Heister, Marion, *'Winzige Katastrophen'. Eine Untersuchung zur Schreibweise von Angestelltenromanen* (Frankfurt am Main, 1989)
Liersch, Werner, *Hans Fallada. Sein großes kleines Leben* (Berlin, 1981)
Manthey, Jürgen, *Hans Fallada* (Reinbek, 1973)
Williams, Jennifer, *More Lives Than One: a Biography of Hans Fallada* (London, 1998)
Zachau, Reinhard K., *Hans Fallada als politischer Schriftsteller* (New York, Frankfurt am Main and Paris, 1990)

Heinrich Böll

Linder, Christian, *Heinrich Böll. Leben und Schreiben 1917 bis 1985* (Cologne, 1986)
Moeller, Aleidine Kramer, *The Woman as Survivor: the Evolution of the Female Figure in the Works of Heinrich Böll* (New York, 1991)

Nägele, Rainer, *Heinrich Böll. Einführung in das Werk und in die Forschung* (Frankfurt am Main, 1976)

Reid, James H., *Heinrich Böll: a German for His Time* (Oxford, New York and Hamburg, 1988)

Vogt, Jochen, *Heinrich Böll* (Munich, 1978)

Martin Walser

Pilipp, Frank, *The Novels of Martin Walser: a Critical Introduction* (Columbia, SC, 1991)

Pilipp, Frank (ed.), *New Critical Perspectives on Martin Walser* (Columbia, SC, 1994)

Schlunk, Jürgen E., and Armand E. Singer, *Martin Walser: International Perspectives* (New York, 1987)

Siblewski, Klaus (ed.), *Martin Walser* (Frankfurt am Main, 1981)

Waine, Anthony, *Martin Walser* (Munich, 1980)

Waine, Anthony, 'Productive paradoxes and parallels in Martin Walser's *Seelenarbeit*', *German Life and Letters*, 34 (1980–1), 297–305

15

PATRICIA HERMINGHOUSE

The 'critical' novel in the GDR

For many who watched them, the dramatic events that unfolded in the German Democratic Republic in the autumn of 1989 – the so-called *Wende* or 'turning-point' – seemed to confirm what Christa Wolf had asserted two decades earlier: 'The writer . . . is an important person.'[1] As one of the most acclaimed writers in the German Democratic Republic, Wolf's own importance was primarily an effect of the attention accorded to her as a critical voice by readers inside and outside the GDR – as well as by that state itself. For almost as long as the GDR existed, texts by Wolf and other critical writers were scrutinised on both sides of the East/West German border in order to discover how the writers' mastery of language was deployed in broaching taboo topics, expressing opinions contrary to the officially promulgated party line, or questioning the official code of form and content embodied in the notion of 'socialist realism'. For the purposes of this discussion, 'critical' novels are understood to be works written in the GDR, usually by convinced Marxists, who nonetheless distanced themselves from the rhetoric and expectations of those in power. This element of resistance can be located both in nonconformity to the party line in matters of content, such as pressure to depict 'positive socialist heroes', but also in regard to preferred aesthetic strategies. Well-known authors of such critical works usually managed to challenge the discursive limits of the system in which they were confined, while abstaining from the more adamant forms of dissidence that led to emigration, expulsion, or even imprisonment for some of their fellow writers.

Although they did not offer more radical forms of opposition directed at the system itself, these writers' resistance to the conservative aesthetic paradigms of 'socialist realism' was often understood to reflect deeper deviations from the party line, which called for unambiguous partisanship, ready comprehensibility, and optimism in art and literature. An assertion of aesthetic autonomy – be it in the employment of satire, fantasy, allegory, parody, or proscribed modernist forms – could be read as tantamount to a contradiction of the party's authority to control and delimit discussion of its policies and practices. Thus it is not surprising that censors, too, frequently couched their objections to particular texts in aesthetic terms. Although genuinely oppositional texts could be published only outside the state's borders, within the GDR itself, books of writers who were nonetheless perceived as critical sold out in a matter of hours. Deeply rooted belief in the power of the word to transmute abject reality, it may be argued, was one of the few shared articles of faith among the writers, the reading public and the state. The latter not only underwrote the literary enterprise (which was also reflected in subsidised prices that put books well within the financial means of all citizens), but also developed multiple bureaucracies to both coddle and control those who wielded this power.

In order to understand the centrality of literary culture in the GDR, it may be helpful to reflect briefly on the conditions of its production. Although many details of the process only became clear after German unification in 1990, it was well known that literature was subject to intensive and extensive scrutiny and censorship. This was true even after the older party conception of literature as a weapon in the class struggle yielded to a more flexible notion of literature as *Lebenshilfe* (help with life's challenges) – even, indeed, after the Honecker era began with his often-quoted 1971 pronouncement that there should be no taboos for the writer who is firmly grounded in socialism.[2] Both conformist writers, who accepted that their 'job' was the cultivation of socialist consciousness in their readers, as well as their more critical colleagues, for whom increased sales in the West were usually a corollary of an encounter with censorship in the East (the so-called 'dissident bonus'), depended in one way or another on the largesse of the state. Forms of subsidisation included relatively generous honoraria, as well as the salaries, stipends, well-endowed prizes and social perquisites provided by various cultural institutions of the state, such as theatres, publishing houses and the Writers' Union (*Schriftstellerverband*). But these writers were also confined within a tight network of control and censorship that extended from their editors in the publishing houses through the central publishing office of the Ministry of Culture (which also exerted a form of censorship through its control of paper allocations) and on up to the very highest echelons of the party. Sometimes even more insidious than institutionalised censorship were the forms of self-censorship against which Christa Wolf warned as early as 1974 because they 'internalise the kinds of demands that can prevent literature from being created, and bog writers down in a sterile and hopeless web of incompatible codes ordaining, for example, that they should write realistically and yet disregard conflict, that they should faithfully depict the truth and yet disbelieve what they see because what they see is "untypical" '.[3]

Ironically, this elaborate system itself contributed to the intensity of public interest in those works that appeared to have escaped the censors' control. The fact that critical literature was allowed to appear at all may seem paradoxical. Beyond the shifting levels of tolerance that can usually be traced to larger political developments, there were indeed differences in how much could be said in particular genres and by whom. There was, for example, a lively network of autonomous, unofficial journals that published poetry, essays and sketches; duplicated mechanically and circulated by hand, these publications evaded the censor, but lacked the technology necessary for longer works, such as novels. Yet whereas the party exerted direct control over newspapers, its relationship to literary publishing houses was more mediated. The literary sphere was generally accorded somewhat more freedom for the expression of 'constructive' criticism, as long as it did not constitute the dominant element of the text or appear to have been included just to titillate readers. As a genre intended for private consumption within one's own four walls, the novel seemed, in fact, to enjoy greater latitude than more public genres, such as theatre. And, of course, the decision-makers could not ignore the fact that both in their own country and abroad, censorship merely increased interest in the proscribed text. The censors may also have surmised that the demands made by the complexity and metaphorical allusions of many of these critical novels would deter many readers.

Faith in the importance of the writer reached its apogee in the famous 4 November 1989 demonstration of nearly half a million GDR citizens, who gathered on East Berlin's Alexanderplatz to hear the call for changes articulated by Wolf and other prominent critical voices, primarily from literature and the arts.[4] Although the *Wende* initially seemed to validate cherished beliefs in the role of critical literature as a force for reform, if not for revolution, what followed was not just reform but the end of the GDR. As ordinary citizens wrested back the power of language on their own behalf, often displaying great wit and imagination in the ubiquitous slogans and posters of the period, the special status of critical writers as representatives of 'the people' was quickly eroded. Those who had sought to ameliorate rather than to overthrow GDR-style socialism suddenly found themselves accused, especially by colleagues who had earlier left the GDR, of having actually helped to prolong the regime. The acrimonious debates of the following years demonstrated just how politically and historically contingent the meaning of the term 'critical' can be, conditioned not only by the content of the work in question but also by the context of its reception. In the absence of an unrestricted sphere for public discussion and debate (*Öffentlichkeit*), critical literature, especially in the form of novels, came to be regarded as a primary channel for the articulation of popular discontent and the airing of opinions that could not otherwise circulate publicly. Oppositional literature functioned, as Christa Wolf suggested early in 1990 when the very notion had already begun to seem obsolete, to point out contradictions that were otherwise never addressed, to produce or reinforce critical consciousness in its readers, and to give them the courage to speak out against lies, hypocrisy and resignation.[5] But as their fellow citizens began to voice their own quite divergent opinions on the question of German unification, the writers' claims for critical literature as an alternative public sphere (*Ersatzöffentlichkeit*), that articulated what neither ordinary citizens nor the state-controlled press could express publicly, were dismissed as arrogant illusions.

Even before German unification became a reality, the controversy aroused by the publication of Christa Wolf's *Was bleibt* (1990; *What Remains*, 1993) created a charged atmosphere of mistrust and accusations that ultimately led to one of the most bitter literary debates of the postwar era (see also the discussion by Dagmar Barnouw in chapter 12 above). Written in 1979 but not published until the demise of the GDR was imminent, the novel thematises the harassment and surveillance to which a well-known woman writer is subjected after she becomes identified as oppositional – an experience that Wolf herself underwent in the years after she became one of the leading signatories of a letter protesting against the GDR's expatriation in 1976 of its famous critical poet and songwriter, Wolf Biermann. The fact that Wolf did not attempt to publish the novel until 1990 gave rise to harsh criticism and heated debate about her motives and loyalty to the state. Accused of belatedly seeking to establish her credentials as a victim rather than acknowledging the privileges she might have been reluctant to risk in GDR times, Wolf was merely the best known of the many critical writers whose role was re-evaluated in the ensuing controversy about intellectuals and their complicity with the state system. Opinions remain divided on whether the charges of opportunism levelled at her are justified or whether Wolf became a convenient exemplar for an entire body of postwar literature that some critics began to attack in the ensuing *Literaturstreit* (literary debate). When it also became known that she (and indeed other authors who had previously enjoyed a positive reception by Western critics) had briefly collaborated with the State Security Service (Stasi) in the 1950s, the notion of critical writers as a challenge to the system was suddenly seen in a new light. Because they worked within the institutions of that state and contained their critique in 'tolerable' forms, they were accused of having helped to perpetuate the system. In this view their texts functioned as a safety valve that effectively vented popular dissatisfaction before it could reach the point of revolutionary explosion. Furthermore, it was now maintained, the acclaim that these writers enjoyed in the West provided the state with a measure of respectability and credibility that likewise retarded the advent of the peaceful revolution of 1989.

After completion of her university study of German literature in 1953, Christa Wolf herself appeared headed for a conformist career in the literary system of the GDR. Employed as a freelance writer in a publishing house in Halle, she also began working in a railway carriage factory in response to a party mandate (the so-called Bitterfeld Way) that charged intellectuals to become more involved in the sphere of production and labour. In 1963 Wolf came to public attention with her novel, *Der geteilte Himmel* (*Divided Heaven*, 1965), which reflects the Bitterfeld mandate in its depiction of a trainee teacher who spends her required period of practical experience in a railway carriage factory. But unlike most propagandistic factory novels of the period, Wolf's novel is related from the young woman's perspective as she recovers from a possibly suicidal accident after the building of the Berlin Wall separates her permanently from her lover, who has gone to the West. Despite the novel's hint that society may have failed the protagonist, the censors' objections were overcome by Wolf's positive portrayal of her protagonist's relationship to her mentors in the factory and her clear sympathies with the young woman's decision to remain in the East. (In 1989, this same commitment to socialism over capitalism led Wolf herself to oppose the move to German unification.) Despite a complex narrative style that enabled critics of the novel to condemn it on aesthetic grounds as 'formalist', *Der geteilte Himmel* garnered for Wolf two of the most important literary prizes of the GDR. In 1963 she also became a candidate member of the Central Committee of the Socialist Unity Party, a position that she lost in the wake of the Eleventh Plenum in 1965, where she had spoken out against repressive cultural policies.

In 'Reading and writing', a major poetological essay published in 1968, Wolf suggested the need to rethink what she simply called 'prose', stating that 'the need to write in a new way follows a new way of living in the world' (p. 20). This new prose, she argues, must achieve something more than the mere surface realism that she associates with film; it should try to be 'unfilmable' and not seek to offer a slice of 'reality cake' (p. 26). Drawing on the language of science, she insists on the possibility of a 'fourth dimension' in prose, the dimension of the narrator. 'This is the coordinate which supplies depth, contemporaneity, unavoidable commitment, which determines not only the writer's choice of subject but also its characteristic coloration' (p. 37). Contrary to what cultural policy-makers in the GDR had understood as the function of literature, such prose would touch the spirit of the reader most intimately, 'not to take control of it, but to free psychic energies whose power is comparable to those locked in the atom' (p. 40).

Wolf's essay, written before her 1968 novel, *Nachdenken über Christa T. (The Quest for Christa T., 1970)* appeared, reflects her own awareness of how controversial an attempt to break with the well-constructed fiction of socialist realism would be. To head off some of the resistance she knew her text would encounter, Wolf also published an 'Interview with myself' in 1968. Here she defends what she knew would be perceived as a withdrawal into subjectivity by attacking 'the ridiculous notion that socialist literature is not up to handling refined nuances of emotion, or individual differences of character: the idea that it depends on creating types who move along prescribed sociological paths'.[6] Here Wolf breaks decisively with many of the most firmly held conventions of form and content in a 'socialist' novel. The omniscient narrator who could lead the reader through a linear narrative about a positive socialist hero(ine) is abandoned in favour of one who is uncertain and questioning, who wants to confront the disparity between rhetoric and reality. In an interview with Hans Kaufmann published in 1976, the year that her equally controversial – and even more complex – novel *Kindheitsmuster (Patterns of Childhood)* appeared,[7] Wolf invoked the term 'subjective authenticity' to describe her ongoing attempt to write in a way that reflects a new reality:

> Things formerly taken as 'given' start to dissolve, revealing the reified social relations they contain and no longer that hierarchically arranged social cosmos in which the human particle travels along the paths preordained by sociology or ideology . . . It becomes more and more difficult to say 'I', and yet at the same time often imperative to do so.　　('Subjective authenticity', p. 22)

A landmark in the literary landscape of the GDR, *Nachdenken über Christa T.* appeared only in a timidly limited edition in 1968. It was reprinted in 1972, when a brief era of cultural liberalisation was ushered in by Honecker's 1971 assertion of greater freedom for writers who were genuinely committed to socialism. Far more autobiographical than *Der geteilte Himmel*, this novel focuses as much on the reflections of its first-person narrator regarding the act of writing as it does on its unorthodox title figure, who dies of leukemia, but, it is implied, also of alienation in her frustrated attempt at self-realisation and the effort to write honestly. In its refusal to offer a straightforward narrative of development with a clear political message, Wolf's text resists the expectation that the novel transmit the ideology of the state to the private sphere. With its firm insistence on the validity of individual subjective experience and its assertion of the claims of repressed subjectivity against the hegemonic ambitions of the party, *Nachdenken über Christa T.* represents a challenge to the party prescription for women's fulfilment in socialism. The narrator claims for herself 'the freedom and responsibility of invention. Just for once, for this once, I want to discover how it is and to tell it like it is: the unexemplary life, a life that can't be used as a model.'[8] No positive socialist heroine, no model for imitation, Christa T. is a nonconformist who 'shrank from stamping any name on herself, the brand mark which decided which herd you belong to and which stable you should occupy' (p. 35). Instead, she asserts defiantly, 'I am different' (p. 57). 'The most important thing about her', the narrator notes, 'is this: Christa T. had a vision of herself' (p. 117). In pursuit of this goal of self-realisation, Christa T. finds herself at odds with the hypocrisy that living in conformity with the ubiquitous slogans entails. In deliberately giving voice to feminine experience that did not fit the preordained mould, Wolf initiated a decisive turn away from the old prescriptions of form and content – albeit one that did not constitute a rejection of the project of socialism. Despite her critique of conformity, it should be noted, the feminine values that Wolf espouses are relatively traditional ones, including her tendency to cast women in the role of victims.

Nonetheless, as a critical writer who attempted to speak with a new voice precisely at a time of rising interest in the GDR and an incipient feminist movement in the West, Wolf attracted widespread attention. A new generation of critical GDR women writers also emerged in the 1970s, many of whom were clearly familiar with the new Western feminist discourse. Despite the positive reception they enjoyed in the West German women's movement, GDR women writers were quick and insistent in denying that they were 'feminist', a label that would have marked them in the GDR as championing the battle of the sexes over the class struggle. Unlike some of their male colleagues, who were marked as dissidents because their criticism appeared directed at the very foundations of GDR-style socialism, women writers addressed what were considered secondary (non-antagonistic) contradictions in their society: problems that were in fact capable of resolution in the context of socialism.

Foremost among the many women who emerged in this decade was Irmtraud Morgner, who, like Wolf, had actually begun publishing in a more conformist mode in the 1950s. She subsequently disavowed this work and by 1965 had so clearly broken with the conventions of socialist realism that her novel *Rumba auf einen Herbst* (Autumn Rumba) could not appear.[9] In 1969, however, she did manage to publish another unconventional work, *Hochzeit in Konstantinopel* (Wedding in Constantinople), a cycle of often fantastic stories related by an adventuresome modern-day Scheherazade,

who ultimately leaves her husband-to-be. Subsequently, Morgner imperti-
nently incorporated parts of *Rumba* as the seven 'Intermezzos' of her most
famous novel, *Leben und Abenteuer der Trobadora Beatriz nach Zeugnissen
ihrer Spielfrau Laura: Roman in dreizehn Büchern und sieben Intermezzos*
(1974; *The Life and Adventures of Trobadora Beatrice as Chronicled by Her
Minstrel Laura: a Novel in Thirteen Books and Seven Intermezzos*, 2000).
This complex work of nearly 700 pages recounts the friendship between
a twelfth-century woman troubadour awaking in 1968 after an 810-year
sleep (arranged with Persephone in order to escape life as a poet in the
male-dominated Middle Ages), and the tram driver Laura Salman, whose
life as a single working mother in the GDR, supposedly the 'promised land'
for women, embodies the contradictions that result from the persistence of
patriarchal values in socialist society. The *Trobadora* novel is discussed (together with its sequel *Amanda. Ein Hexenroman* (1983; Amanda: a Witch
Novel)) by Allyson Fiddler in chapter 17 below (pp. 256–60). Suffice it
here to point out that the novel's blend of fantasy, realism, humour and
feminism represents an achievement *sui generis* in GDR literature. Although
there are obvious points of tangency between Christa Wolf's assertion of
'subjective authenticity' and Morgner's literary experiment, which she calls
'the novel of the future', the *Trobadora* novel cannot really be equated with
the new 'prose' that Wolf sought to foster. For Wolf, validation of the inner
experiences of the individual is more fundamental to a new way of writing
realistically than 'facts', while Morgner seeks a form that is complex enough
to manifest not only the subjective perceptions, but also the concrete life
situation and experiences of real women.

Much more controversial than Morgner's was Volker Braun's critical
depiction of GDR reality in his 1985 *Hinze-Kunze-Roman* (Hinze–Kunze
Novel), a work that developed further the themes of his previous narratives *Das ungezwungne Leben Kasts* (4 parts, completed 1979; The Free and
Easy Life of Kast) and *Unvollendete Geschichte* (1975; Unfinished Story): the
yawning chasm between Marxist ideals and the economic and political alienation of 'actually existing socialism'; and the (ab)use of Marxist discourse to
both disguise and legitimate the unequal power relations between party elite
and the rest of the population. That it took four years for Braun's novel to
clear the hurdles of censorship is not surprising in view of the sharply satirical
tone of this work. Braun's narrator cites Honecker's famous assertion of no
taboos in art to justify the depiction of a lecherous party functionary (Kunze)
and the chauffeur (Hinze) who aids him in his conduct of business, official
and private, even when it includes Kunze's seduction of Hinze's wife: 'Dienst
war Dienst' (It was all part of the job).[10] In Braun's portrayal of the Hinze–
Kunze relationship as that of master and subordinate, however, it becomes

evident that things are not so straightforward as they might seem: Kunze is in many ways well-meaning and dedicated to his job and, by refusing to speak out, Hinze is complicit in his superior's unsavoury behaviour. The implicit ambiguous relationships that Braun establishes between Hinze and Kunze, the 'led' and the 'leader', the people and the politician, deliberately frustrate any attempt to think of them in dualistic terms as victim and perpetrator, as does the fact that the expression 'Hinz und Kunz' is the German equivalent of 'every Tom, Dick, and Harry'. After Kunze rapes a woman he has seen working in the fields while Hinze stands passively by, the narrator remarks in a laconic double entendre, 'Sie wurde gefördert zu ihrem Glück' (her happiness/good fortune has been fostered): through Kunze's action 'in the interests of society', she has been induced to take up a course of study! (pp. 39–40). Similarly advanced to happiness and fulfilment by the party functionary is (as already mentioned) Hinze's wife, Lisa, a sensual, earthy Berliner, who also becomes the object of Kunze's lust, as well as of his ambition for the 'improvement' and education of others. Retrained as a computer technician, Lisa gives birth to a child whom both Hinze and Kunze claim to have fathered – and severs her relationship with both of them, who are left in a homosexual embrace. Like others of Braun's female characters, Lisa bears utopian traces – 'eine fantastische Frau, eine utopische Körperschaft' (a fantastic woman, a utopian embodiment) – and her refusal to have anything more to do with the party functionary and his lackey can be read as reflecting something of the sentiment of many of her fellow citizens. At the end of this bizarre tale, the reader is left to think about the narrator's questions at the beginning of the text: 'Was hielt sie zusammen? Wie hielten sie es miteinander aus?' (What kept them together? How did they tolerate one another?) (p. 7). The seemingly unassailable answer to every such question, 'das gesellschaftliche Interesse' (the interests of society), grows more implausible with each repetition.

In addition to his allusion to Honecker's denial of taboos in literature, Braun's narrator taunts the practices of censorship in the GDR by referring to the likely fate of his text at the hands of the censors. He goes so far, in fact, as to parody the sort of review his text is likely to receive from the fictive Frau Professor Messerle, who can be expected to describe the sort of book he should have written – one like all the others, 'eine sichere Bastion gegen die unzuverlässige Wirklichkeit' (a safe bastion against an unreliable reality) (p. 147). If only he had stuck to what he was told, just followed the pattern! Readers familiar with the literary landscape of the GDR quickly recognised in the name of Prof. Messerle ('Messer' = knife) a play on that of the real-life Professor Anneliese Löffler ('Löffel' = spoon) who, in fact, did take on the task of writing a damning review in the party newspaper when the novel was finally allowed to appear in 1985!

By the mid 1980s, the emergence of *glasnost* in the Soviet Union began to have reverberations in the GDR. The increasingly bold allusions to institutionalised censorship that began to appear in texts in the aftermath of the 1976 Biermann affair gained further impetus following an interview that party ideologue Kurt Hager gave to the West German magazine *Stern*, in which he attempted to trivialise Soviet reform efforts as nothing more than a change of wallpaper.[11] At the Tenth Congress of the Writers' Union in November of that year, passionate discussion of the charged issue of *Öffentlichkeit* and censorship erupted in many of the sessions as writers expressed anger and frustration about the restrictions and controls that were placed on them. The most scathing comments were delivered by Christoph Hein, who not only dared to use the censored word 'censorship' publicly, but declared it 'überlebt, nutzlos, paradox, menschenfeindlich, volksfeindlich, ungesetzlich und strafbar' (outdated, useless, paradoxical, misanthropic, hostile to the people, illegal, and punishable by law).[12]

Only a few years earlier, Hein had published a devastatingly realistic novella about a modern GDR woman who avoids the coming-to-oneself, the admission of subjectivity that Wolf had already begun to advocate in the 1960s. Written in a detached, chillingly matter-of-fact first-person narrative that corresponds to the lifestyle of the protagonist, Hein's 1982 text, *Der fremde Freund* (*The Distant Lover*, 1989) portrays a female physician who, on the surface, could be mistaken for a model GDR career woman. Unlike Morgner's stressed-out tram driver Laura, Hein's over-achieving protagonist Claudia is startlingly independent, to the point of alienation. Hein depicts the relationship between Claudia, divorced and childless as a result of several abortions, and her lover Henry, a married man with little contact with his family, as one which is not merely characterised but indeed sustained by distance and a lack of commitment. For her, it is an ideal arrangement: 'I had no need to reveal myself completely to another person again. I enjoyed just caressing another's skin without wanting to crawl inside it.'[13] When her lover is killed by an adolescent in a bizarre altercation over a hat, she is not even sure that she cares to attend the funeral.

Proud of her good looks and health, self-confident in her work as a physician, Claudia rejects the customary model of caring femininity, leading the reader to engage in critical reflection on the etiology of such stark alienation: 'I can prescribe tablets and give injections. The rest isn't the responsibility of medicine. I'm not a priest, I don't dole out consolation. And I consider it presumptuous and dishonest to tell anyone to cheer up. I have my own problems'

(p. 98). As this last statement suggests, Claudia's repeated assertions of her own emancipation, her invincibility and thick skin, belie underlying trauma that has not been worked through, including abortions that she endured in a loveless first marriage, and her childhood betrayal of her dearest friend, the only person she ever really loved, for reasons of political and personal advantage. By the end the cause and cost of her present isolation become clear when she admits, 'I will die inside my invulnerable shell, I'll suffocate of longing for Katharina. I want to be friends with Katharina again. I want to get out of the thick hide of my fears and mistrusts. I want to see her. I want Katharina back' (p. 177). Like Christa Wolf, with *Kindheitsmuster*, Hein points to the deformities that can be caused by that which has been repressed and which lies, like so much radioactive waste, at the core of this hardened shell. Having learned to read Claudia's assured statements against the grain, the reader comes to recognise the depth of the despair and resignation behind her concluding self-estimate: 'I've achieved everything I could achieve. I can't think of anything I lack. I've made it. I'm fine' (p. 179).

Unlike Wolf, who was criticised for having never tried to publish her 1979 text *Was bleibt* before the *Wende*, her older colleague Stefan Heym became a symbol of the change when his novel *5 Tage im Juni* (*Five Days in June*), available since 1974 in the West, was finally published in the GDR with much fanfare and public signings at the beginning of 1990. Indicative of the paradoxes surrounding the notion of 'critical' literature, the publication history of this work spans almost the entire history of the GDR, beginning with an early manuscript version, *A Day Marked X*, written in English in the period 1954–8 and translated into German by Heym himself. His account of the days leading up to the GDR workers' revolt on 17 June 1953 was, in the eyes of the GDR authorities, an unwelcome reminder of their own egregious mistakes in the handling of this event. Even in the 'cultural thaw' period of the early Honecker years, Heym, still unable to publish a revised version of his novel in the GDR, resorted to the alternative of publishing it in West Germany (where he also faced some reluctance on the part of publishers); his own English rendering appeared in Great Britain in 1977.

Heym, who had come to the United States in 1933 as a Jewish refugee from Nazi Germany, served as a propaganda officer in the US army, beginning with the Normandy invasion of 1944. Travelling in Europe after the war, he decided not to return to the US and renounced his US citizenship because of the rise of McCarthyism and American involvement in the Korean War. Critical, too, of West Germany's inadequate attempts at de-Nazification, he ultimately decided to join other prominent returning socialist and communist exiles in the GDR, although not without a certain wariness of Stalinist-style socialism, occasioned by his witnessing the 1952 Slansky show trial in

Czechoslovakia. Although his books were banned in the GDR, he remained there as an uncomfortable, loyal but outspoken, voice for the nearly four remaining decades of its existence.

Heym's early work as a journalist in East Berlin as well as his critical position vis-à-vis both East and West Germany are reflected in both the content and form of *Five Days in June*, depicting in the microcosm of one industrial plant the unfolding of the 1953 workers' uprising that followed a government-decreed 10 per cent increase in the production norm. Detailing day-by-day, hour-by-hour developments in its individual chapters, the novel takes on documentary qualities through Heym's montage of authentic documents, ranging from the inflated language of excerpts from the constitution of the Socialist Unity Party of East Germany and speeches by party officials to the unvarnished anti-communist commentaries of West Berlin radio broadcasts expressing smug satisfaction at the course of events. In this, Heym reflects his own ambivalence, embracing East German theories of the involvement of Western *agents provocateurs* while exposing the Stalinist proclivities of a regime that relied on Red Army tanks to maintain its power. In the often preachy tone that characterises much of the novel, the central figure, head of the factory trade union committee, gives voice to the kinds of sentiments that made Heym vulnerable to accusations of deficient partisanship: 'The worst thing for us would be to try to throw the blame for our own incompetence and blunder on the enemy. In effect we'd be saying they're a bunch of supermen over there! . . . [O]nly those can turn their face to the future who have faced their past.'[14]

Like Christa Wolf, Heym played a prominent role in the much-publicised protest by GDR writers against the forced expatriation of the critical poet-singer Wolf Biermann. But unlike Wolf, who chose not to publish her 1979 manuscript version of *Was bleibt*, Heym did publish his 1979 novel *Collin* in West Germany. It, too, features a prominent socialist writer, who becomes ill in the course of trying to break down the self-censorship that blocks his own attempt to write his memoirs. As a result, he is confined in a hospital room with the Minister for State Security (the head of the Stasi, the secret police), who is also gravely ill. When the writer Collin dies, the loser of a bizarre competition between the two men to see who can outlive the other, the Stasi boss, with his 'heart of steel', carries on from his hospital bed. The fact that many characters in the novel were rather transparently counterparts of recognisable GDR political and cultural personages of course only made the novel more offensive – and enhanced its saleability as 'forbidden literature from the East' on the Western market. This, in the eyes of the GDR authorities, amounted to betrayal and led to the establishment of further legislation regulating authors' rights to publish their work abroad, declaring publication of critical statements about the GDR or distribution of materials without official approval to be a crime against the GDR, punishable by up to eight years in prison or a massive fine. The legislation, quickly dubbed 'Lex Heym', extracted a penalty of about ten thousand West German marks as punishment for what was viewed as Heym's illegal profit in hard currency for an attack on the state.

Undeterred, Heym refused to join the many GDR writers who were moving to the West, and continued to publish his work in West Germany and London. In the *Wende* of 1989, he was among those intellectuals, like Christa Wolf and Christoph Hein, who played a major role in the demonstration of 4 November on the Alexanderplatz and who argued for a reform of the GDR rather than immediate unification with West Germany. In an ironic reversal in the months following the *Wende*, Heym's *Collin* was widely disseminated in the still-existing GDR: prominently serialised in the pages of *Neues Deutschland* and issued in paperback format as well. While publication of this particularly notorious novel was clearly meant to signal the end of censorship and may well have been a marketing ploy to increase the dwindling circulation of the party newspaper, it also signalled that party leaders recognised that it had become politically expedient to end the taboo on allusions to the pervasive Stalinism of the past, thereby also implicitly dissociating themselves from it.

Ironically, after unification, Heym, as a member of the Party for Democratic Socialism (PDS), was elected to the first united German Bundestag, where, as the oldest member of that body, he gave the opening address. Nonetheless, until his death in 2001, he remained outspoken in his criticism of German unification. If he and the other critical novelists discussed here enjoyed respect and popularity as uncomfortable critics in the GDR, their abiding post-unification belief in the possibility of a better socialism also made them uncomfortable citizens in the new Germany, albeit with diminished popular resonance.

NOTES

1. Christa Wolf, 'Reading and writing', in *The Author's Dimension: Selected Essays*, trans. Jan van Heurck (New York, 1993).
2. Erich Honecker, quoted in *Neues Deutschland*, 18 December 1971.
3. Christa Wolf, 'Subjective authenticity: a conversation with Hans Kaufmann', in *The Fourth Dimension: Interviews with Christa Wolf*, trans. Hilary Pilkington (London, 1988), p. 28.
4. Three critical writers, in addition to Wolf, were invited to speak at this event: Christoph Hein, Stefan Heym and Helga Königsdorf.
5. Christa Wolf, 'Momentary interruption', in *The Author's Dimension*, p. 325.
6. Christa Wolf, 'Interview with myself', in *The Author's Dimension*, p. 18.

7. The translation published in 1980 at first bore the somewhat misleading title *A Model Childhood*.
8. Christa Wolf, *The Quest for Christa T.*, trans. Christopher Middleton (New York, 1970), p. 45.
9. After its non-publication in the wake of the Eleventh Plenum in 1965, the manuscript of the novel was presumed lost until after her death, when it was published posthumously in 1992. The *Trobadora* novel also contains another text, 'Die gute Botschaft der Valeska Kantus' (The Gospel According to Valeska Kantus), that had been rejected for an anthology of sex-change stories that appeared a year later (Edith Anderson (ed.), *Blitz aus heiterm Himmel* (Rostock, 1975)).
10. Volker Braun, *Hinze-Kunze-Roman* (Frankfurt am Main, 1985), p. 8.
11. Reprinted in *Neues Deutschland*, 10 April 1987.
12. Christoph Hein, in *X. Schriftstellerkongress der DDR. Arbeitsgruppen*, ed. Schriftstellerverband der Deutschen Demokratischen Republik (Berlin, 1988), p. 228.
13. Christoph Hein, *The Distant Lover*, trans. Krishna Winston (New York, 1989), p. 32.
14. Stefan Heym, *Five Days in June* (London, 1977), p. 347.

FURTHER READING

Bathrick, David, *The Powers of Speech: the Politics of Culture in the GDR* (Ithaca, NY, 1995)

Fox, Thomas C., *Border Crossings: an Introduction to East German Prose* (Ann Arbor, 1993)

Goodbody, Axel, and Dennis Tate (eds.), *Geist und Macht: Writers and the State in the GDR* (Amsterdam, 1992)

Grant, Colin B., *Literary Communication from Consensus to Rupture: Practice and Theory in Honecker's GDR* (Amsterdam and Atlanta, 1995)

Hallberg, Robert von, *Literary Intellectuals and the Dissolution of the State: Professionalism and Conformity in the GDR* (Chicago, 1996)

Hell, Julia, *Post-Fascist Fantasies: Psychoanalysis, History, and the Literature of East Germany* (Durham, NC, 1997)

Kane, Martin (ed.), *Socialism and the Literary Imagination* (Oxford, 1991)

Silberman, Marc (ed.), *What Remains? East German Culture and the Postwar Public*. American Institute for Contemporary German Studies Research Report (Washington, DC, 1997)

Torpey, John C., *Intellectuals, Socialism, and Dissent: the East German Opposition and its Legacy* (Minneapolis, 1995)

Williams, Arthur, et al., *German Literature at a Time of Change 1989–1990* (Bern, 1991)

Woods, Roger, *Opposition in the GDR under Honecker, 1971–1985* (London, 1986)

16

MICHAEL BUTLER

Identity and authenticity in Swiss and Austrian novels of the postwar era: Max Frisch and Peter Handke

> *This is no time for ego stories. And yet human life is fulfilled or goes wrong in the individual ego, nowhere else.*
>
> Max Frisch, *Mein Name sei Gantenbein* (1964)

> *I have only one theme: to achieve greater clarity about myself . . . in order to be able to communicate better with other people and get on better with them.*
>
> Peter Handke, 'Ich bin ein Bewohner des Elfenbeinturms' (1967)

The polemical tone of the above quotations is unmistakable. The slightly world-weary cadences of the established writer Frisch contrast sharply with the self-confident assertiveness of the young Peter Handke, but both were responding to the pressures brought about by the growing politicisation of literature in the 1960s, particularly in West Germany. The decade had opened with the controversial trial of Adolf Eichmann in Jerusalem (1961), and was dominated by the harrowing Frankfurt Auschwitz Trial (1963–5) and the powerful documentary theatre of Rolf Hochhuth, Peter Weiss and Heinar Kipphardt. The decade was to be even more politicised by increasing opposition to the Vietnam War, the formation of the *Außerparlamentarische Opposition* (Extra-Parliamentary Opposition) in the face of the threat to West German democracy posed by the CDU–SPD 'Grand Coalition' of 1966, and the rapid escalation of the anti-authoritarian student movement in West German universities. It is therefore perhaps understandable that at this critical moment *all* social activity, including literature and art, should have been seen in starkly political terms.

What unites Frisch and Handke is the fact that though they were by no means immune to German concerns, both of the past and the present, they were both writers on the neutral periphery: citizens of Switzerland and Austria. As such they tended to see such problems in more general, humanistic terms rather than with strict historical specificity. Such an attitude was clearly defined by the different cultural traditions of Switzerland and

Austria as they developed in the twentieth century and, more specifically, in the conditions that obtained in both countries in 1945.

For example, the concept of *das Jahr Null* (Year Zero) – as morally convenient as it was perhaps psychologically necessary after the end of the Nazi nightmare in Germany – did not apply to Switzerland. Despite murky aspects of Swiss policy during the war – for example, the country's economic collaboration with her fascist neighbours and the anti-Semitic colour of her refugee policy – bourgeois society remained intact, and with it a sense of cultural continuity which appeared so problematical in Germany. The case of Austria was different, but analogous. Despite the enthusiasm in the country for the *Anschluß* of 1938, and the prompt *Gleichschaltung* of the country's political and cultural institutions, Allied policy in the war against Hitler created the myth of Austria as German fascism's 'first victim' (Moscow Declaration, 1943). This led to the State Treaty of 1955 in which Soviet withdrawal was exchanged for permanent neutrality. Such political developments in European *Realpolitik* enabled Austria, like Switzerland, to avoid coming to terms with its support for National Socialism and thus to experience relatively little difficulty in maintaining cultural links with the past.

This is not to say, of course, that Swiss and Austrian writers were apolitical or did not explore the nature of guilt and complicity with fascism. The iconoclastic work of the Wiener Gruppe and, above all, the excoriating diatribes of Thomas Bernhard in Austria and the early plays of Frisch and Dürrenmatt in Switzerland are evidence enough of the often fierce sociocritical stance adopted by writers towards recent history in their respective countries. The point is that neither in Austria nor in Switzerland was the debate about the politicisation of literature conducted in the same black-and-white terms as in Germany. Indeed, their geographical and political marginality could be said to have helped Austrian and Swiss writers to avoid many of the crippling distortions which afflicted their German colleagues, typified by the discussion of the 'death of literature' initiated by Hans Magnus Enzensberger in his famous essay, 'Gemeinplätze, die neueste Literatur betreffend', published in *Kursbuch* 15 in 1968. On the other hand, writers in Austria and Switzerland, for all their fearless public utterances, never acquired the moral authority of their colleagues in West Germany, who frequently functioned as a kind of 'conscience of the nation', or in the German Democratic Republic, where they could claim to be standard-bearers of a new society. Nevertheless, the literatures of Austria and German-speaking Switzerland are intricately intertwined in German literature itself, and derive their vitality from similarly deep-rooted cultural antagonisms. Yet it can be argued that neither country suffered the savage political, economic and human caesura that was the fate of Germany and which led to the creation of two mutually hostile Germanys and two very different ideological versions of the past. Neutrality in both cases released them from playing a dominant role in postwar European politics.

The quotations from Frisch's novel *Mein Name sei Gantenbein* and Handke's essay 'Ich bin ein Bewohner des Elfenbeinturms' reveal the paradoxical tensions inherent in much modern German literature: the assertion of the primacy of individual experience and the implied claim of general validity. The fact that both Frisch and Handke, writers of different generations, one a father figure for numerous younger colleagues, the other an uncomfortable *enfant terrible*, have achieved enormous success despite – or perhaps because of – considerable controversy bears out the truth of their statements. In the case of Max Frisch, his position as one of the most significant European novelists of the twentieth century is secure. And that reputation owes much to the remarkable achievement of *Stiller* (1954; *I'm Not Stiller*, 1958).

The story of a young Zurich sculptor suddenly so horrified at society's expectations of his talent that he flees the country to fight in the Spanish Civil War would appear initially to be too trivially private to sum up a generation's frustrations or to provide a paradigm of individual malaise in modern society. Frisch's novel nevertheless has become the key work in the Swiss contribution to the theme of fractured identity which has dominated German fiction since the beginning of the twentieth century.

Anatol Stiller's dilemma is rooted in Frisch's own obsession, first articulated in his journal *Tagebuch 1946–1949* (1950), with a secularised version of the Second Commandment, 'Du sollst dir kein Bildnis machen' ('Thou shalt not make thee any graven image') (II, 369–74).[1] Frisch transfers the prohibition of attempting hubristically to define God to signalling the dangers of the tendency of human beings to fix graven images upon each other, thus denying the individual the opportunity to change and grow. The only antidote to this threat to human potential is love (II, 369). This cardinal principle in Frisch's understanding of human identity has major consequences for his presentation of personality in his narrative fiction. Since the individual, according to Frisch, is constantly evolving, his external figuration never more than an approximation to his internal sense of self, it follows that the nature of identity is fluid and, ultimately, inexpressible in words. This is the case with Stiller, and it is where Frisch connects to an older tradition of *Sprachskepsis* (suspicion of language), exemplified by Hofmannsthal, Rilke and Kafka. But as with these authors, the fear that language is inadequate to express our most fundamental feelings will be expressed, paradoxically enough, with brilliant articulacy.

In our civilisation the most urgent test of love is marriage, and *Stiller* is, among other things, an *Eheroman* of a quality to put beside Goethe's *Die Wahlverwandtschaften* (*Elective Affinities*), Fontane's *Effi Briest*, Tolstoy's *Anna Karenina* and Flaubert's *Madame Bovary*. With these great European novels it shares the creation of emblematic characters caught in the labyrinth of social constrictions and crippling role-expectations. Anatol Stiller's head-long flight from such pressures – after the failure of his Spanish adventure and the disaster of his marriage to Julika, a neurasthenic ballet dancer, he disappeared for seven years in America – culminates in an existential crisis: attempted suicide. The brush with death he names 'the encounter with my angel' (III, 436 and 726), a kind of rebirth which gives him the energy to return to Switzerland as 'Mr White'. This fiction is not a rediscovered or renewed identity, but rather a non-identity, a *tabula rasa* whose contours he proposes to delineate in a totally new existence. Recognised and arrested on the frontier – due to an ironic confusion of identity – Stiller spends his time on remand in prison obeying his exasperated defence counsel's naive request to write down his life-story, 'just the truth, nothing but the plain, unvarnished truth' (III, 362). The major part of the novel is thus the seven notebooks Stiller fills, partly with his musings on existential reality (the odd-numbered notebooks), and partly with Mr White's notes on the stories told to him by his visitors, including his wife Julika, former mistress Sibylle, and the strangely sympathetic prosecuting counsel, Rolf (the even-numbered note-books). Though it is clear to the reader at an early stage that Mr White and Anatol Stiller are one and the same person, the split identity is a subtle narrative device to balance the intense subjectivity of Stiller's crisis.

The stories that Stiller tells to his warder or to his defence counsel, Dr Bohnenblust, however far-fetched, are deeply symptomatic of his des-perate search for an adequate language in which to describe his encounter with his 'angel'. That Bohnenblust rejects them out of hand, accepting only the most banal biographical facts as the 'plain, unvarnished truth', is part of Frisch's polemic against the smug bourgeoisie of Switzerland. But equally the tales serve to illustrate the point that the oblique nature of literary invention – comic irony, parable, extended metaphor – is no longer able to underpin identity. Language itself has lost the power to capture reality. As Stiller cries poignantly: 'I have no words for my reality' (III, 436).

Stiller's basic problem is that he has perceived the need for a radical new start, but cannot find a way of rooting this new start in the ground of his old identity. He fails to realise that it is impossible to convince his wife and friends that his old life has been expunged, for that would imply the extinction of large sections of *their* lives which have impinged on Stiller's. Furthermore, his insistence on using Julika as the 'ultimate touchstone' (III, 752) for his *own* sense of personal reality denies her the freedom to be herself. The need for a 'Du' (specifically, Julika) against which to measure his own feelings and to guarantee his identity fatally sustains a graven image of his wife which would prevent her own development, even if, in her damaged psychological state, she saw any necessity to change. Not surprisingly, therefore, their attempt to start their marriage anew, chronicled by Rolf in his postscript, takes on all the negativity of entrenched attitudes which Stiller had feared during his stay in prison: 'My fear: repetition!' (III, 420). Language fails as a medium of understanding between Stiller and Julika because of its inherent ambiguity. As Stiller perceptively remarks: 'Every word is false and true, that is the nature of words' (III, 525). Rolf's account is thus a painful assessment of a marriage vitiated by mutual incomprehension.

However, the presentation of Stiller's dilemma is more sympathetic than that of Julika. For at one crucial level the opening words of the novel, 'I'm not Stiller!', are true. Until the abortive suicide attempt, the Stiller which the protagonist is intent on rejecting did *not* live, if living means leading an authentic, creative existence. Stiller's biography was indeed a non-life in the sense that he was forced into playing a variety of roles, not least that of forceful husband and lover. It is the limitations of the other characters, their circumscribed concept of selfhood, which prevent them from distinguishing between surface biographical reality and existential reality. It is Stiller's acute awareness of the chasm between the two notions of identity that make him, for all his absurd pretensions and overweening egocentricity (clearly noted by Mr White!), an oddly attractive figure.

Swiss society – and here it stands plainly for mid-twentieth-century bourgeois society as a whole – can only offer Stiller the paradoxical escape route back into the labyrinth. In this connection, Rolf's role is illuminating. Unlike Bohnenblust, the prosecuting counsel is presented as an individual who not only sympathises with Stiller's dilemma, but also understands much of its causes. Indeed, in the story of the parcel of 'flesh-pink cloth' *he* tells Stiller, Rolf illustrates his own crisis, brought on by the excessive demands he made on himself, which closely parallels Stiller's. The problem is that even in his objective-sounding postscript ('Nachwort des Staatsanwaltes'), there is no convincing evidence that Rolf has been able to solve the existential crisis of feeling through a renewed marriage with Sibylle. For example, he admits to dealing with the embarrassing parcel, symbol of the conflicting emotional life everyone carries with them, by throwing it down a railway station lavatory. On the surface, the pair appear successful and well-integrated – indeed, they have started a family – but Rolf's frequently puzzled words in his postscript, his confession of helplessness in the face of Stiller's despair, tell a different, more ironically nuanced story. In a novel which raises as a central issue the problem of authenticity in an 'age of reproduction' where individuals are reduced to mass consumers of secondhand experience – 'televiewers, telehearers, teleknowers' (III, 535) – Stiller's withdrawal to his kitsch 'schwyzerhüsli' with its ironical name 'Mon Repos' carved in fake marble, where his artistic gifts have shrunk to the repetitive manufacture of pottery for tourists, clearly indicates repressed individuality and the kind of social conformity of which Rolf's own accommodation with reality is merely a superficially more rational version.

It is perhaps a moot point whether the reader can accept that Stiller's mental journey, marked by much existential anguish, culminates in any true rediscovery of self. Frisch's placing of quotations from Kierkegaard's *Either/Or* at the front of Stiller's notebooks certainly indicates that identity is a permanent struggle for authenticity, not a fixed state the individual arrives at. The ironic cast of the novel, however, removes any temptation to clutch at any Kierkegaardian key to unlock the text's complexities. The search for God's grace in the ground of subjective being, which is the impetus of Kierkegaard's philosophy, is not shown as a convincing concept for Stiller, and certainly not for Rolf who gives the copy of *Either/Or* to Stiller but admits: 'I was never an expert on Kierkegaard' (III, 737). The final sentence of the novel – 'Stiller remained in Glion and lived alone' – with its distinct echo of the bleak closing rhythms of Goethe's *Die Leiden des jungen Werthers* and Georg Büchner's *Lenz* – points to a resigned stasis, not to a breakthrough to an authentic identity.

If Anatol Stiller recognised his spiritual dilemma to be located in a loss of articulacy and thus creative contact with the world, Walter Faber, the protagonist of *Homo Faber* (1957; trans. 1959) – subtitled 'ein Bericht' ('a report') – asserts a sense of self firmly rooted in everyday reality, mediated not least by a blunt use of language which is, in his view, neutral and factual, uncontaminated by relativity and paradox. The novel, constructed in two 'Stationen' ('stops'), is a first-person narrative cast predominantly in a retrospective mode. In other words, Walter Faber is engaged on a kind of autobiography aimed at constructing a version of events that will uphold his identity by proving his view of life to be valid and his guilt non-existent. What begins as an exercise in self-justification, however, ends in painful self-judgment. This ironic reversal is caused by the very phenomenon he felt so confident about: language. In recounting his stay in Cuba, cut off from his native language, Faber remarks on his halting command of Spanish: 'I don't say what I want to say but what the language wants' (IV, 179). In the same way, the report that he sets out to write – instead of a letter to Hanna, his youthful love and mother of his child, Sabeth, with whom he inadvertently sleeps and whose death he accidentally causes – slowly turns against its author's conscious intention. Far from illustrating the cruel nature of chance (Hanna had not told Faber before they parted twenty years previously that she had borne their child), the text paradoxically documents with every dishonest twist and turn the life-style of an individual who – to quote Frisch – 'lives in ignorance of himself'.[2]

What this marvellously taut novel demonstrates is the reverse of Anatol Stiller's predicament: Walter Faber lives an inauthentic existence, moving from one anonymous international airport and hotel to another, content to sink his energies in the technical minutiae of his job as an engineering consultant for UNESCO. His attenuated emotional needs are catered for by a series of meaningless relationships with empty-headed women – or at least with women he deems to be so. In other words, Walter Faber has created a graven image of himself with all the loss of spontaneity and love which that implies in Frisch's philosophy. His constant criss-crossing of continents is merely the outward indication of a personal rootlessness.

Such a refusal to reflect on life can only be sustained by prodigious energy; once this fails – technically, in the emergency landing in the Tamaulipas desert, personally, with the onset of stomach cancer – Faber is thrown out of his routine and onto his own pathetically thin resources. His text unwittingly reveals how his impoverished emotional life and over-reliance on rational calculation prove inadequate to the task of dealing with the string of 'Zufälle' ('coincidences') which led him to fall in love with his own daughter, as if age were merely an abstract, mechanical matter of addition rather than a biological process that shapes all experience and feeling. The way Frisch deconstructs his protagonist's increasingly threadbare linguistic subterfuges is one of the great successes of the novel. Particularly in the 'hand-written' passages inserted into the ongoing report in the 'Second Stop', the reader can see how Faber himself, once deprived of his typewriter, that is, his protection against the immediacy of feeling, slowly comes to see through his own doomed enterprise. His puzzled comments in conversations with Hanna, as both have to confront the fact that their daughter is dead and that their respective life-styles have been deeply flawed, are beautiful modulations of gentle irony.

It is in these final poignant scenes of the novel, when Faber issues the telling instructions: 'Arrangements in case of death: all written evidence of my existence such as reports, letters, loose-leaf notebooks are to be destroyed, none of it is true' (IV, 199), that he comes close to rediscovering the humane side of his identity which he has so wilfully suppressed for most of his life. For the destruction of his professional papers ('reports, loose-leaf notebooks') must also include the destruction of *this* 'report' which, although not untrue in its surface detail, simply does not hang harmoniously together – the

German has 'es stimmt nichts' – in the light of his belated reconciliation with Hanna, the only woman with whom, he once admitted, sexual intimacy was 'never absurd' (IV, 100). Humility and openness are shown to be better preconditions for approaching the 'Du' than violent manipulations of language to impose an egocentric view on the world.

One of the remarkable features of *Homo Faber* is the remorseless unmasking of male arrogance and male-chauvinist attitudes a considerable time before the feminist movement began and such undertakings became commonplace in literature. If the damaged marriage between Stiller and Julika had foundered on mutual incompatibility – the conjunction of male fears of impotence and female sexual frigidity – the depiction of male attitudes to personal relationships in *Homo Faber* is devastating. Admittedly Hanna does not escape censure in her attempt to keep her daughter for herself in a world hermetically sealed off from men – indeed, she clearly recognises her guilt in having her child without informing the father and in exploiting men for her own purposes with no thought for their emotional needs. Above all, however, the text pins down that kind of male inadequacy which refuses responsibility, whether for genuine human relationships or for the natural environment. As so often, Max Frisch deals critically with social and political issues years before they surface in common debate.

If in *Stiller* Frisch portrayed an individual who from the start was aware that he had lost the ability to orientate himself in language, in *Homo Faber* he delineated the contortions of a character who claimed to be totally comfortable in a world where words were stable and transparent. In both cases, the novels relate clearly to a crisis in modernity in the sense that they portray human beings caught up in the inimical pressures that distort or destroy identity. Both novels employ complex irony to articulate the need for authentic existence, and both novels posit at least the fictive reality of their characters in a recognisable world. With *Mein Name sei Gantenbein* (1964; *A Wilderness of Mirrors*, 1965), Frisch moves in a radically new direction. Whereas in the two earlier novels characters were presented as fictive entities operating within and against a concrete fictive environment, in *Mein Name sei Gantenbein* (roughly translatable as 'Let's suppose my name is Gantenbein') Frisch presents an anonymous narrator who spins out stories, plays with fictive possibilities, in order to reveal a pattern of experience ('Erlebnismuster') which is the sole point of the exercise. In one sense Anatol Stiller had recognised this key function of stories – and his storytelling could be seen as an attempt to explore such fluidity – but, unlike the protagonist of *Mein Name sei Gantenbein*, his increasingly desperate strategy was driven by a desire to build a coherent, stable identity. In the later novel, the radical consequences of language scepticism are drawn: the narrating consciousness is not interested in convincing an outside world of its own authenticity, but merely in finding some way of articulating patterns which it can recognise as uniquely expressive of itself. Despite the gravity of the crises the narrator delineates, the novel thus possesses a postmodern playfulness which marks it off from the serious irony of its predecessors.

In an imaginary interview, 'Ich schreibe für Leser' (1964; I write for readers), Frisch indicated the basic narrative strategy of his new novel: 'To show the reality of an individual by having him appear as a blank patch [weißer Fleck] outlined by the sum of fictional identities congruent with his personality . . . The story is not told as if an individual could be identified by his factual behaviour; let him betray himself in his fictions' (v, 325). And indeed the anonymous narrator does remain 'a blank patch' at the heart of the text, a Pirandellian non-character searching for a reflected identity in the fictions he narrates: 'I try on stories like clothes!' (v, 22). The joke, both painful and funny at the same time, is that such stories 'protect' his vulnerable nakedness against the predations of the external world, but like clothes have the tendency to fall into the same existential creases. Two episodes appear to underpin the narrator's drive for stories to express his experience: the vision of a horse's head straining to penetrate the rigidity of an imprisoning wall of granite – a symbol of the narrator's desire to escape the banalities of bourgeois existence – and the melancholy portrayal of a man sitting in his empty apartment after being abandoned by his wife. Such images of petrifaction and desolation are clearly unbearable unless they can be explored in stories where identities can be swapped and experimented with until the underlying experience is thoroughly, if not totally, articulated. Thus the dizzying play with identities – Gantenbein, Enderlin, Svoboda – explores the narrator's sensibility from various directions, held in their ellipses only by the energy of authenticity: 'Only the variations reveal the constant factor' (v, 327).

Although the game the narrator plays is a deadly serious one – personality is shown to be deeply fragmented, reality to be as consistent as shifting sands – *Mein Name sei Gantenbein* differs sharply from Frisch's other novels in its freedom from conventional fiction and its mimetic devices. Scepticism towards the traditional claims of language to structure the world is now seen not as a threat to identity but as liberating the ego from premature restriction. The very creativity involved in constructing stories that can be tried on 'like clothes' is itself perceived as evidence of an authentic connection with life. Frisch's shadowy protagonist can thus be made to declare at the end of his complicated odyssey towards his self: 'Life appeals to me' (v, 320). Paradoxically, this novel of identity-crisis, of jealousy and broken relationships, concludes on a warm note of *carpe diem* and, significantly, without the finality of a full-stop. What appeared to begin as a postmodern exercise in narrative irony turns into the acknowledgment that happiness can only be won within the confines of empirical reality.

What is striking about all three novels is that their protagonists, in their radically different ways, are trying through *writing* to get to grips with themselves and their surroundings. Their efforts are marked by the realisation, from the beginning in the cases of Anatol Stiller and the narrator in *Mein Name sei Gantenbein*, at the bitter end in the case of Walter Faber, that surface reality must be resisted, that social roles and demands distort rather than fulfil human potential.

It is now clear that the so-called 'Tendenzwende' of the early 1970s with its associated fashion of 'New Subjectivity' had much deeper roots than is often assumed. Indeed, such terms as 'New Subjectivity' or 'New Inwardness' were not particularly new at all, but a development of certain modes of writing in the late 1950s and 1960s. Though it is true that the disillusionment which followed the disintegration of the student movement and the revolutionary fervour of 1968 led certain writers to 'retreat' into melancholy introspection (well documented, for example, in Peter Schneider's *Lenz* (1973) and Nicholas Born's *Die erdabgewandte Seite der Geschichte* (1976; The Side of History Hidden from Earth)) as a reaction to the deflated hope that literature might effect political change, the 'Tendenzwende' (change of emphasis), as far as it is applied to literature, can best be seen as precisely that: a change of emphasis, not a radical new departure. The decade opened, after all, with the foundation of the Werkkreis Literatur der Arbeitswelt (Literature of the Workplace Writers' Group); it continued with Frisch's explosive dismantling of the national myth, *Wilhelm Tell für die Schule* (1971; William Tell for Schools), and his *Tagebuch 1961–1971* (1972), Günter Grass's *Aus dem Tagebuch einer Schnecke* (1972; *From the Diary of a Snail*, 1974), Max von der Grün's *Stellenweise Glatteis* (1973; Black Ice in Places) and more hard-hitting 'Industriereportagen' from Günter Wallraff, *Ihr da oben, wir da unten* (1973; You Up There, Us Down Here). The decade was also the period during which Peter Weiss began and completed work on his mammoth *Die Ästhetik des Widerstands* (1975–81; The Aesthetic of Resistance), discussed by J. H. Reid in chapter 13 above. All these texts illustrate the continuing obsession of German-speaking writers with the relationship between politics and literature. However, while it is clearly exaggerated to assert that a wholesale retreat to private themes took place in the 1970s, it is true that there was at this time a return by a large number of established and new writers to more self-reflective narratives, with strong autobiographical emphases – for example, Max Frisch's own *Montauk* (1975) or Karin Struck's *Die Mutter* (1975). Nowhere is this trend better exemplified than in three narratives produced by Peter Handke in the 1970s, *Der kurze Brief zum langen Abschied*

(1972; *Short Letter, Long Farewell*, 1977), *Wunschloses Unglück* (1972; *A Sorrow beyond Dreams*, 1974) and *Die linkshändige Frau* (1976; *The Left-handed Woman*, 1978).[3]

Leaving aside the now legendary outburst at the meeting of the Gruppe 47 in 1966 in Princeton, during which Peter Handke berated his senior colleagues for what he witheringly termed their 'puerile literature of description',[4] the Austrian tyro first came to more general notice with his controversial plays, *Publikumsbeschimpfung* (1966; *Offending the Audience*, 1969) and *Kaspar* (1968; trans. 1969), which were closely related to the linguistic experimentation of the Wiener Gruppe and the younger writers associated with the Forum Stadtpark in Graz, of whom Handke was one. In his fiction of the 1970s, however, the exploration of the crippling effects of linguistic structures on human personality was widened to encompass explorations of the propensity of *any* system to restrict and undermine identity – work which brings Handke very close to Frisch's 'Bildnis' theory. In *Der kurze Brief zum langen Abschied*, for example, the occasion of Handke's marital breakdown serves as a starting-point not just for a critique of language but for the delineation of a fundamental existential crisis. The book is constructed as a parody of the archetypal American 'road novel', such as Kerouac's romanticised version of the Beat Generation in *On the Road*. At the same time, Handke's text draws overt parallels with earlier fictive protagonists who undertake spiritual journeys in search of an authentic identity: Heinrich Lee in Gottfried Keller's *Der grüne Heinrich* (second version 1879–80) and Karl Philip Moritz's eponymous hero in *Anton Reiser* (1785–90). What is not so often remarked, however, are the more subtle echoes of Goethe's *Die Leiden des jungen Werthers* (1774). In particular, the narrator's trajectory across America is defined by the same schizophrenic split that characterised Werther's flight from *his* problems: moments of intense happiness flash across a backcloth of fear and existential nausea.

Two key episodes illustrate the point. Pausing briefly at the beginning of his journey, Handke's narrator notices two young girls in a telephone kiosk in New York – a moment of everyday banality that suddenly takes on a magical glow: 'It was a sight which liberated me and lifted my spirits. With a light heart, I gazed as if in paradise where seeing is all and seeing is perception' (*KB*, p. 36).[5] This Yeatsian epiphany or glimpse of *Präexistenz*, to quote Hofmannsthal, is by its ephemeral nature problematic, for the narrator is otherwise constantly threatened by a world on the verge of overwhelming the individual: 'Once again, as in my childhood, I felt as if the world around me could suddenly explode and be transformed into something quite different, for example, into a monster's mouth' (*KB*, p. 96). The parallel with Werther's idyllic encounter with the little boy and his baby brother whom he sketches in total harmony with nature (Book I, 26 May) and the terrifying dichotomy expressed in the famous letter of 18 August, in which nature is transmogrified from a human paradise to an 'ever devouring, ever ruminating monster', could not be more marked. Indeed, in both cases of identity-crisis, the key question is one of *memory*.

It is clear from the opening page that this journey, freeing the narrator from all ties, is to be used as a means of coming to terms with repressed memories, dreams and unresolved experience: 'As far back as I can remember, horror and terror have been second nature to me' (*KB*, p. 9). Such primal fear – that could have come straight from Thomas Bernhard – is associated, as it was for Bloch in *Die Angst des Tormanns beim Elfmeter* (1969; *The Goalie's Anxiety at the Penalty Kick*, 1972), with a sense of being imprisoned in a world of incomprehensible signs which began the moment the narrator realised that he was a vulnerable individual alone in a hostile world. This existential insight is encapsulated in his earliest memory: his fear as a small child when, after a bath, he saw the water gurgling down the plughole (*KB*, p. 88). The narrator recalls this defining moment when he takes a bath in his New York hotel: the water slowly disappears 'as if I too was gradually growing smaller, flowing towards a final dissolution' (*KB*, p. 16). Such disintegration of personality can only be prevented by entry into 'A DIFFERENT TIME' (*KB*, p. 25), a vague alternative state of perception which clearly echoes Musil's similar notion of 'a different state of existence'. As a kind of objective correlative, the narrator is accompanied across America by an old girl-friend and her small daughter. Claire, the opposing double to his wife Judith, and her child act as a surrogate family whose non-threatening presence prevents the narrator's collapse into solipsism. Mother and child are fixed points in the shifting mental landscape traversed by the narrator and point to the possibility of creative human relationships despite the disastrous failure of the protagonist's own marriage.

In contrast to Stiller who returns from America as a would-be 'new man' in order to 'pursue' a completely fresh life with Julika (see III, 768), Handke has *his* narrator pursued across the New World by a vengeful wife. This brings a welcome note of humour to a text which otherwise is dominated by such dark nouns as 'terror', 'panic' and 'nausea'. However, the final reconciliation of narrator and wife, crowned by a visit to John Ford in his Eden-like garden, remains unconvincing. Though Handke's prose here achieves a lightness of touch which indicates at least the possibility of spiritual progress, the meeting and discussion with Ford have much the same sense of reality as the latter's film-sets. This 'Paradise' in the ironically named Bel Air recalls the fragility of Stiller's 'ferme vaudoise' in Glion. Moreover, Ford can only offer the 'American' solution to the problem of identity – retreat from subjectivity into the collective 'wir': 'Ego stories only exist where one individual stands for all the others . . . Here in America there is no sulking, and no one retreats into himself' (*KB*, p. 188). Such advice is familiar enough: Werther received it from Wilhelm, Anatol Stiller from Rolf; it is the message of social conformity – the retreat back into the very societal repression from which Handke's protagonists are continually attempting to escape. Despite this problematic conclusion, however, the story offers a fascinating exploration of the crucial significance of memory in the shaping of identity. The book, like *Stiller*, underlines the vital need to learn to remember, not destroy, the past in order to achieve 'a feeling of attachment, a feeling of existence, security, a feeling of being alive . . . That is true moral strength.'[6] The secret is to master not succumb to introspection, to connect the fleeting moments of happiness into a creative continuum. The indication in *Der kurze Brief zum langen Abschied* that such a possibility even exists, if not yet realised, marks a significant 'Tendenzwende' for Handke. The new perceptions achieved through its composition were put severely to the test in his next work, *Wunschloses Unglück*.

His mother's suicide triggered in Handke the appalled realisation that this unhappy woman was a stranger; his reaction to her death was, significantly, an 'apathetic speechlessness' (*WU*, p. 7).[7] The compulsion to fight such apathy by reconstructing a plausible identity for Frau Handke was thus a paradoxical undertaking. On the one hand, Handke could see his mother in purely objective terms, on the other, writing about her inevitably involved a subjective journey into painful areas of his own distant past. Indeed, in a central section set in parentheses which discusses the pitfalls of turning the untidiness of a real person into a neatly pleasing 'artificial character' (*WU*, pp. 44–8), Handke recognises that only via the exploration of his 'dream world' will he begin to grasp his mother's reality, 'because by doing so her feelings will become so concrete that I will experience them as a "Doppelgänger" and be identical with them' (*WU*, p. 48).

To get at this truth, Handke starts with the clichés that determined his mother's existence. Each of her attempts to break out of the systems which deformed her, above all the rigid role-expectations inflicted on women by the stultifying social environment of Austrian village life, failed. The only experience she had of 'communal life' was after the Nazi *Anschluß* in 1938, and that was merely a cleverly staged illusion. Social conformity was the only available structure for such an uneducated woman, its narrow conventions interrupted only by 'moments of speechless terror' (*WU*, p. 47) which Handke relives as he attempts to piece together the fragments of his mother's monotonous life.

The individual could not survive such sterility; authenticity was negated by oppressive routine, particularly for women. The point was underlined when one day Maria Handke began to read. Though she claimed this activity had a rejuvenating effect, in fact Handke sees how she used literature to illuminate the past and never as an emancipatory tool to change the future. Even the girls of the village were wont to play out their fate in a macabre game, 'Tired / Weak / Ill / Seriously Ill / Dead' (*WU*, p. 17). Such fatalism is underpinned by language, custom, and above all the fear of change. To that extent, the mother's life appears emblematic of social conditions in the backward provinces of Austria after the Second World War.

Nevertheless, Maria Handke did ultimately seek a radical solution to her dilemma, and for her son this breakthrough won her a significant degree of individuality. Thus he records with extraordinary honesty his euphoria on receiving the news of her death and his pride in her decision to reject the world she lived in. The momentary feeling of authenticity does not last. The depersonalising effect of the ritual of funeral and burial merely unleashes the desire to write about his mother. But at the end of his most autobiographical text Handke is forced to admit that the creative process has not in fact helped: 'Writing was not, as I had initially still believed, a process of recalling a finished period of my life, but simply a constant affectation with memory in the form of sentences which merely asserted a distancing had taken place' (*WU*, p. 99). The mechanisms that entrapped his mother still threaten her son. All that remains of Maria Handke are fragments of childhood memory and 'the *horror vacui* in consciousness' (*WU*, p. 105). As Max Frisch discovered in *Montauk* (1975), autobiography is no antidote to the slippery nature of fiction. Both forms of expression are subject to the elusive and distorting demands of the subconscious. To write exactly – the declared aim of *Wunschloses Unglück* – a synthesis of both subjective and objective modes of perception is essential. Characteristically, the story presents an open end: the decision to continue the search for identity elsewhere.

If the story of Handke's mother illuminates obliquely the subservient role of women in a patriarchal system, *Die linkshändige Frau* relates more directly to concerns of such feminist novelists as Elfriede Jelinek and Karin Struck, although without their fiery controversy. However, the protagonist Marianne's decision to take responsibility for her life and end her marriage is not overtly 'feminist'; it is not presented as the result of logical analysis, but as a sudden, inexplicable moment of spontaneity in the face of her husband's smug contentment. It is clear that Marianne's dilemma is another version of Handke's central theme of violated individuality. Bourgeois family life is suddenly robbed of the patina of normality expressed in the quotation from Goethe's *Die Wahlverwandtschaften* which is placed as an ironic coda to the text.

Not only does Marianne suddenly see her family life as a cliché, but she also experiences social relationships in a similar way. Her friend Franziska's women's group, for example, appears as mechanically predictable in its behaviour as the men in her life. Her attempt to earn money through translation sharpens these insights, for the text she works on contains a quotation from Baudelaire that revolt is the only effective form of political action: 'I suddenly thought: the only political action I understand is running amok' (*LF*, p. 83). Although the narrative imitates society's obliteration of female identity by the constant use of the term 'die Frau' rather than the protagonist's first name, such literary moments of emancipation are crucial in underpinning Marianne's newly won independence. Indeed, paradoxically, the very distancing effect of such depersonalisation could be said to be a precondition for Marianne's desire to refashion her identity.

A striking feature of the story is that Marianne has no past; indeed, in stark contrast to Frisch's novels, no character is given psychological depth. The effect is to stress the abstract power of the social system in which they are all embroiled. The initial stages of Marianne's emancipation thus result from her confrontation with her own inner emptiness, after which she resolutely frees herself from all male definitions of herself as represented by father, husband, employer and lover. The cost of such resistance is intense loneliness. After a party in her flat, she feels she has passed a self-imposed test of hiding her new sense of identity from the pressures of the outside world: 'You have not betrayed yourself. And no one will humiliate you any more!' (*LF*, p. 130). Whether such an assertion can be taken at face value is a moot point. Open endings by their nature are ambiguous, but Handke's closing cadences do suggest a positive development has taken place.

The criticism often levelled at Handke that his extreme espousal of the tenets of 'New Subjectivity' endangers the accessibility of his narratives, is contradicted by the immense popularity of precisely these intensely 'subjective' texts. In fact, both Frisch and Handke reject that radical category of subjectivity which would deny the self-determination of the individual. Ultimately, they both continue to subscribe to the Enlightenment's faith in personal integrity, however difficult it is to sustain authentic modes of living against the corrosive influence of postmodern relativities.

Neither Max Frisch nor Peter Handke deluded himself that literature could change the world. What their work demonstrates, however, is that, despite articulated scepticism towards the traditional claims of language to be a reliably neutral system by which to orientate the individual in the world, literature still exerts a positive power. By challenging systems and 'graven images' of whatever provenance, literature can change our perceptions. It thus continues to perform its emancipatory function and retains, inevitably, a political dimension.

NOTES

1. All references to Frisch's work are taken from the standard Suhrkamp edition in seven volumes, *Gesammelte Werke in zeitlicher Folge* (Frankfurt am Main, 1976/86). Roman numerals refer to the volume, arabic to the page.
2. Quoted in Walter Schmitz, *Max Frisch. 'Homo Faber'. Materialien, Kommentar* (Munich and Vienna, 1977), p. 16.
3. A comprehensive survey of postwar German literature describes Handke as the 'Trend-Figur' of the 1970s. See Wilfried Barner (ed.), *Geschichte der deutschen Literatur von 1945 bis zur Gegenwart* (Munich, 1994), p. 626.
4. 'Läppische Beschreibungsliteratur.' Quoted in Volker Bohn, *Deutsche Literatur seit 1945* (Frankfurt am Main, 1993), p. 255.
5. References to Handke's work are to the following editions: *KB = Der kurze Brief zum langen Abschied* (Frankfurt am Main, 1972); *WU = Wunschloses Unglück* (Frankfurt am Main, 1974 = suhrkamp taschenbuch 146); *LF = Die linkshändige Frau* (Frankfurt am Main, 1976).
6. Handke to Manfred Durzak in the latter's *Gespräche über den Roman* (Frankfurt am Main, 1976), p. 343.
7. A fear of losing articulacy and a stubborn defence of the writer's existence are central themes of Handke's story, *Nachmittag eines Schriftstellers* (1987).

FURTHER READING

Frisch

Bircher, Urs, *Max Frisch 1911–1955. Vom langsamen Wachsen eines Zorns* (Zürich, 1997)

Bircher, Urs, *Max Frisch 1956–1991. Mit Ausnahme der Freundschaft* (Zürich, 2000)

Butler, Michael, *The Novels of Max Frisch* (London and New York, 1975)

Pender, Malcolm, *Max Frisch: His Work and its Swiss Background* (Stuttgart, 1979)

Schmitz, Walter, *Max Frisch. Das Werk (1931–1961). Studien zu Tradition und Traditionsverarbeitung* (Bern, Frankfurt am Main and New York, 1985)

Schmitz, Walter, *Max Frisch. Das Spätwerk (1962–1982). Eine Einführung* (Tübingen, 1985)

White, Alfred D., *Max Frisch: the Reluctant Modernist* (Lewinston, 1995)

Handke

Arnold, Heinz Ludwig (ed.), *Peter Handke. Neufassung, Text+Kritik* 24 (Munich, 1999)

Fellinger, Raimund (ed.), *Peter Handke* (Frankfurt am Main, 1985)

Firda, Richard Arthur, *Peter Handke* (New York, 1993)

Fuchs, Gerhard, and Gerhard Metzler (eds.), *Peter Handke. Die Langsamkeit der Welt* (Graz, 1993)
Pütz, Peter, *Peter Handke* (Frankfurt am Main, 1982)
Schlueter, June, *The Plays and Novels of Peter Handke* (Pittsburgh, 1981)

Regularly updated overview articles on both authors can be found in: Heinz Ludwig Arnold (ed.), *Kritisches Lexikon zur deutschsprachigen Gegenwartsliteratur (KLG)*

17

ALLYSON FIDDLER

Subjectivity and women's writing of the 1970s and early 1980s

Thanks to committed and painstaking work by feminist literary historians and academics, it is now widely accepted that women did not first pick up their pens in the twentieth century but that they have always written. Many reasons have been put forward to explain the scarcity of writing by women in previous centuries: sanctions were placed on such activities not deemed suitable for women, and even when women found the time and private space to write, their finished work struggled to be accepted by publishers and the reading public. In any case, women, it was suggested, had little to write about given their supposedly limited 'domestic sphere'.

The patriarchal nature of the publishing industry was one of the obstacles which women writing in the 1970s still had to overcome. At the same time previously 'private' or domestic matters were beginning to find heightened political and literary treatment, as exemplified in the feminist slogan, 'the personal is political' ('das Private ist politisch'). It is not my intention to suggest that all writing by women in the 1970s and 1980s reflected or was informed by the concerns of the post-1968 women's movement, nor indeed that there are not many important works of literature by women which have little in common with feminist issues. Nevertheless, the texts chosen for discussion in the present chapter – Verena Stefan's *Häutungen*, Elfriede Jelinek's novels *Die Liebhaberinnen*, *Lust*, and *Die Klavierspielerin*, Irmtraud Morgner's *Trobadora Beatriz* and *Amanda*, and Ingeborg Bachmann's *Malina* – represent merely a handful of the highly acclaimed novels by women in this period which either deal with issues concerning women's social situation or whose aesthetic concerns exemplify the debate surrounding the existence of a feminine aesthetic.[1] Such issues and concerns extend to the novels of GDR author Irmtraud Morgner, although the socio-political context in which she was writing was very different from that of the Austrians Bachmann and Jelinek, and from Verena Stefan who was born and brought up in Switzerland but has lived most of her life in the FRG.

Women's writing of the 1970s in West Germany and Austria has many characteristics in common with the contemporaneous literature of 'New Subjectivity' discussed by Michael Butler in the preceding chapter. That it has not been subsumed under this label by literary criticism in part reflects the distinct focus and political agenda of many texts by women writing in the aftermath of the student movement. Like the works of New Subjectivity, much early 'women's writing' also sees the individual reassessing her position in society, but this early women's writing is often expressly concerned with the female body politic or with a feminist agenda and is arguably less about redefining the self than with establishing or discovering the female self, with staking out a right to occupy this position in the first place. This difference of focus may account for the fact that while Verena Stefan's first work, *Häutungen* (1975; *Shedding,* 1994), was received as one of the first and most important manifestations of *Frauenliteratur*,[2] Karin Struck's novel *Klassenliebe* (1973; Class Love) was mostly written about as a work of New Subjectivity, in which the concerns of the first-person 'narrator' centre mainly on her explorations of her class status and her sense of not belonging to either the working class into which she was born or the middle class (the 'bourgeoisie') to which her education has allowed her access. Nevertheless, both works have elements in common. The most important points of reference are the foregrounding of 'man's' relationship with nature, the autobiographical style of the writing, and the journey of discovery or voyage of self-exploration which the texts contain.

Häutungen charts the development of the first-person narrator as she looks back on her acculturation as a woman and uncovers the power imbalance in heterosexual relationships. The narrator leaves her cohabitation with boyfriend Samuel to live with a community of women with whom she collaborates on feminist projects, and enjoys a loving relationship with another woman. The book does not end with lesbian coupledom having replaced heterosexual relationships, however – in many ways the narrator is concerned that the old dependencies might simply be replaced – but with the narrator's growing sense of her own subjectivity: she has developed from sexual object into a self-aware woman who respects and loves her own, natural body. The title metaphor of 'shedding' indicates the peeling off of layers of woman's inauthentic and oppressed, or 'man'-made self, which the narrator undertakes.

Verena Stefan's book, published by the newly founded Munich-based feminist publisher, Frauenoffensive, was phenomenally successful. Its first print run sold out in a matter of months. That this success was achieved without the marketing machinery of a large publisher is partly a testimony to the directness of its appeal. The subject matter of *Häutungen* is radical enough:

it ranges over issues such as menstruation, contraception, homosexual love, sexual harassment and rape. As an autobiographically based text it is set against the background of the political campaigns of the 1970s: for the provision of childcare or women's centres; against the anti-abortion laws (Paragraph 218), or against violence to women, to name but a few. In political terms, Stefan's deliberations are also radical. Her conception of woman is a radical feminist's view of women as a class, a class whose defining feature is sex. Having been verbally and physically harassed by two *Ausländer* (foreigners), she analyses this as follows: 'I probably have a nicer apartment, more social contacts, better working conditions, than most of the foreign workers in West Berlin. But every man – foreign or native – can, regardless of living or working conditions, mistreat me at any time he pleases' (p. 12). Radical feminists might accuse liberal and Marxist feminist colleagues of adopting and internalising male culture and norms. As Alison Jaggar explains, 'radical feminists, by contrast, challenge the values of the male culture. They do not want women to be like men. Instead, they want to develop new values, based on women's traditional culture.'[3]

One aspect of women's traditional culture which the author sets out to explore and redevelop is that of woman's relation to nature, a relationship which has been destroyed by patriarchy and which must be examined anew (foreword to the first edition). In her new physical understanding of her own body, the narrator coins new, often lyrical terms for parts of the female body:

I glide and fall with Fenna through meadows of blossoming labella
(only a man could
have named one of these erotic feminine flowers *snapdragon*).
From now on we'll just call them vulva-flowers, Fenna decides.
I set the scene: Hello, I'd like a
bunch of vulva-flowers –
What do you want? Get out of here!
Fenna and I convulse with laughter.
(*Shedding*, p. 61; Stefan's emphasis)

It is for this aspect of her work that Stefan has been most vehemently criticised. The neologisms and poetic address to a mythical wood nymph or *ur*woman – 'I am quite sure / that you used to dwell in trees / as I in lakes and rivers. / In my glittering hair of moss / solar energy erupted' (*Shedding*, p. 56) – seem to replicate a kind of biological determinism which many feminists then and now reject. For some readers, Stefan's mystical rewriting of woman's affinity with 'mother' nature merely reaffirms gender characteristics as innate and not, as the unnamed narrator herself had been at pains to point out, culturally acquired – the title metaphor of 'shedding' itself suggests a personal journey towards an essential core of womanhood. The final and shortest section of Stefan's text, 'Gourd Woman', is, however, more ambiguous. The narration is in the third person and now names its character as 'Cloe', a woman who is either finally in control and in full knowledge of her own body, or breaking up into another feminine myth of chaos and hysteria, depending on one's reading.

One final, but in a sense the most important, radical dimension of Stefan's text is its aesthetic agenda. *Häutungen* does not describe itself as a novel but as 'autobiographical notes, poems, dreams, analyses', and the author sets herself the task of examining existing language and developing a new language with which to write about her new experiences. Stefan writes in her foreword to the first edition that after the work on her book she could now begin to work systematically on sexism in language, on a feminine language, a feminine literature. The use of lower-case letters is estranging if nothing new, but Stefan combines this with linguistic experiment to expose hidden sexism and to promote a more conscious understanding of a word's meaning. Practising a kind of 'theoretical reformism',[4] Stefan instates 'frau' (woman) for the generic pronoun 'man' (one) and deliberately spells the latter with 'nn', 'mann' (man), when she wishes to expose the masculine assumptions behind its use. Additionally, she divides words up into meaningful units to expose what she sees as the hidden sexual politics – 'er fahren' (experience; 'er' = 'he')) (*Häutungen*, p. 22), 'herr schaft' (domination; 'herr' = 'master') (p. 35) – or to emphasise the constituent units of meaning – 'liebes geschichte' (love story) (p. 94), 'körper bewusst sein' (body consciousness) (p. 10). *Häutungen* may be seen as an experiment in the feminine writing, or 'écriture féminine', which, according to its theorists, is resistant to phallic, patriarchal culture and represents a writing of the body. Stefan's writing can be seen as subversive in this sense, undermining in a thought-provoking and at times witty way the normal assumptions of language and of gender identity. The text thematises women's lack of access to and control over existing language as the narrator laments that she is left sitting on the floor trying to piece letters together to forge a meaning (*Shedding*, p. 5) whereas men's use of language is self-confident and unquestioning. This exclusion of women from language and from the wider 'symbolic order' of laws and social institutions is something which has been posited by the French psychoanalyst Jacques Lacan and been given wider feminist meaning by philosophers and theorists such as Hélène Cixous, Julia Kristeva and Luce Irigaray.[5]

Stefan, through her narrator's exploration of female history and the creative feminine subconscious, could be seen to be making steps towards countering women's exclusion. On the other hand, her text could be seen as too theoretical and detached from the material conditions that determine women's oppression and the oppression of other groups in society. *Häutungen* is in any case a more sophisticated and complex text than many critics have allowed. Its mixture of modes represents several strands in women's cultural projects of the 1970s. The documenting of women's personal experiences in relationships with men which Alice Schwarzer collected and published in the West under the title *Der kleine Unterschied und seine großen Folgen* (1975; The Small Difference and Its Large Consequences), or the experiences of women in East Germany published by Maxi Wander as *Guten Morgen, du Schöne* (1977; Good Morning, Beautiful), are just two famous examples of the fact-finding and consciousness-raising aspect of feminist culture. The pronounced autobiographical trend in women's writing is unsurprising as women wanted to exercise their new confidence in speaking and writing about themselves, but it undoubtedly led to some degree of stereotyping on the part of publishers and literary critics who did not expect women to write in the abstract but rather to reveal something of their own identity and personality in their writing. This narrow limitation of 'the market' is something to which Elfriede Jelinek has drawn attention on many occasions.

Although many of her novels and plays do not concentrate on women's issues, Elfriede Jelinek has become widely known as a feminist writer, most controversially through her much publicised attempt to write feminine pornography in the best-selling novel, *Lust* (1989). Jelinek's critique of culture originates not from a radical-feminist position like Stefan's but from a Marxist-structuralist understanding of the material workings of capitalist culture and the stabilising myths of its media and cultural products. Published the same year as *Häutungen*, Jelinek's third novel *Die Liebhaberinnen* (1975; *Women as Lovers*) was her first to foreground the theme of women's social oppression. Whereas her compatriot Brigitte Schwaiger's *Wie kommt das Salz ins Meer* (1977; *Why is there Salt in the Sea?*, 1994), with its autobiographically inspired story of the breakdown of a marriage and the central character's exploration of the influences on her gendering, might be described as an Austrian counterpart to Stefan's *Häutungen*, Jelinek's novel adopts a completely different strategy.

The central characters of *Die Liebhaberinnen*, brigitte and paula (there are no capital letters in the novel, apart from the occasional emphatically capitalised word) are, as in most of Jelinek's novels, two-dimensional figures with none of the psychological detail or emotional depth of a traditionally 'realist' depiction. Just as Schwaiger's or Stefan's characters function as mouthpieces for a certain message, Jelinek's figures act as representatives of an idea, not as authentic characters. The reality which Jelinek is at pains to expose is that of the material and social structures of life for these rural women. In mock-didactic tone, Jelinek constructs a satirical anti-romance to debunk some of the myths of love and marriage. With heavy ironical nods to the reader, the narrator describes brigitte's and paula's paths to marriage, constructing brigitte as 'good example' and paula as 'bad example'. The two teenagers do get married, but paula is forced to turn to prostitution in order to make ends meet and feed her child, as her handsome but stupid husband, erich, spends his woodcutter's wages on drink. Paula is found out and is forced to take a job in the brassière factory on her divorce from erich, and the circle is completed with paula having to work in the same factory from which brigitte, at the opening of the novel, was trying to escape, to a 'better' life as housewife and mother. Whereas paula feeds her imagination with cinematic images and with thoughts of becoming a seamstress so as to be able to sew her own wedding dress for her marriage to a handsome 'Mr Right', brigitte calculates that a pregnancy by heinz will force the trained electrician (who will have his own shop and house) to conform to middle-class expectations by marrying her and securing her future.

The Marxist–feminist corrective delivered by Jelinek's *Die Liebhaberin-nen* is clear: the author's intentions are not to point forwards to a putative mutual bonding and understanding between women but to analyse the prevailing mechanisms of competition at play within the sexual economy and to argue that women's oppression is not just to do with their sex but with their material circumstances. Indeed, one of the most uncomfortable, and yet most important, achievements of Jelinek's writing is precisely that she exposes women's complicity in defining and perpetuating the patriarchal status quo.

Linguistic manipulation and experimentalism are key features of Jelinek's entire oeuvre. Satire is Jelinek's favoured mode and in *Lust* the discourse of love is given a new focus in the author's debunking of pornographic writing. Far from creating the language of a feminine eroticism which Jelinek claims to have set out to achieve, the final effect is part harrowing imitation of porn's repetitive abuse of women, part witty lampoon of bourgeois marriage. Psychoanalytic theories about women's lack of access to or role in the symbolic order are put into practice here, too. Gerti, a housewife, is abused by her husband, the director of the local paper works. Religious discourse is used to colour this proto-typical or highest representative of the male sex as the 'eternal Father. This man dispenses truth as readily as he breathes out air' (p. 7). 'When he returns home at the end of the day he has earned the right to set his signature to life', we are told. Gerti's attempts to speak, to acquire the power of language, on the other hand, are in vain, she can merely write 'characters in the air with her hand' (p. 54). In her writing Jelinek does not start out like Stefan from a nervous and uncertain female subjectivity, campaigning for a more 'authentic' language. Instead she draws attention to women's social and artistic oppression, articulating views that her characters are unable to express.

Erika Kohut, the protagonist of *Die Klavierspielerin* (1983; *The Piano Teacher*), is another woman who has failed to achieve full artistic and social 'mastery'. Erika is not good enough to have fulfilled her mother's dreams of her becoming a concert pianist and works instead as a piano teacher at the conservatory. In her late thirties, Erika still lives with, indeed shares a bed with, her elderly mother. The first part of Jelinek's novel shows the repressive nature of the daughter's upbringing. Erika's mother controls her life, feuds with her if she spends any of 'their' money on clothes and punishes her for any misdemeanours by forbidding her to watch their favourite television programmes. When Erika does escape her mother's control, she visits peep shows or watches couples fornicating in the woods of the Prater. The second part of the novel deals with Erika's sexual relationship with Klemmer, one of her pupils. Her inability to establish a 'normal', loving relationship is evidently a product of her mother's over-zealous protection of her and of the brutality of the sexual images to which she has acted voyeur.

Erika tries to take the initiative with Klemmer, writing him a letter with strict instructions and a gruesome list of her sado-masochistic fantasies. Klemmer is disgusted, but more importantly, his masculinity is threatened as Erika tries to dictate to him how he should behave. Klemmer fails to recognise that Erika is not serious about her demands, in fact 'instead of torturing her, she wants him to practise love with her according to Austrian standards' (*The Piano Teacher*, p. 231). It is significant that Jelinek should choose to have her protagonist *write* down her sexual demands: the act of fixing words on paper stands metaphorically for women's attempts to express their desire, however contradictory, unpalatable, or 'un'-feminist this might be. In keeping with the overwhelmingly negative vision of Jelinek's work, Erika is doomed to failure. As Klemmer puts it: 'There's nothing worse than a woman who wants to rewrite Creation' (p. 263).

Die Klavierspielerin was the novel which brought Jelinek widespread acclaim and international acknowledgment. Due to the author's statements in interviews that the novel had incorporated autobiographically based ideas, it was also the text which seemed to endorse biographical readings of her work. The novel has received much critical attention as a 'mother–daughter' novel. Novels which thematise a mother–daughter or father–daughter relationship, sometimes inspired by the author's own family relationships, were abundant in the 1970s and 1980s. In some cases the relationship is scrutinised for the father's association with National Socialism (Ruth Rehmann, *Der Mann auf der Kanzel. Fragen an einen Vater* (1979; *The Man in the Pulpit: Questions for a Father*, 1997); Brigitte Schwaiger, *Lange Abwesenheit* (1980; Long Absence)). Other novels, like Jelinek's, deal with the powerful mother and with an exploration of the childhood of the first-person narrator (Helga Novak, *Die Eisheiligen* (1979; The Ice Saints); Anna Mitgutsch, *Die Züchtigung* (1987; *Three Daughters*, 1987)). In Jutta Heinrich's *Das Geschlecht der Gedanken* (1977; The Gender of Thoughts) the first-person narrator probes the brutality and control of her father over her mother. Both Karin Struck and Verena Stefan went on to write in praise of their mothers, in, respectively, *Die Mutter* (1975; The Mother) and *Es ist reich gewesen. Bericht vom Sterben meiner Mutter* (1993; There were Riches: On the Death of My Mother).

Jelinek has cited her own reluctance to say 'I' in her writing as a reason why she left it to this, her fifth novel, to rework ideas from her own life. Her satire has been criticised as cruel and patronising, though one cannot but wonder whether these characteristics are so vilified in male writers. Humour is an excellent means of underpinning a political point, and Jelinek's bleak settings and negative picture of human relations serve to open our eyes. Jelinek's writing concurs with Ingeborg Bachmann's assertion that 'people really can be told the truth', even if she presents this 'truth' in a concentrated and exaggerated form.[6]

Irmtraud Morgner was acutely aware of the need to develop her own subjectivity as a writer and of the desirability of investing something of her 'self' in her work. Indeed, she discounted her first prose text, the *Erzählung* 'Das Signal steht auf Fahrt' (1958; The Signal Is at 'Go'), stating: 'lacking in self-confidence, I didn't dare enter into my first book directly or indirectly. Accordingly, it wasn't a book at all.'[7] Morgner's break in the 1960s with the GDR's conventions of socialist realism has been discussed by Patricia Herminghouse in chapter 15 above (p. 224); my focus here is on the two quite remarkable later works on which her international reputation is founded. Although they doubtless do incorporate experiences, ideas, facts and events from the author's own life, it is not an authentic correlation between reality and fiction or between the characters of a novel and the life of the author which Morgner strove to achieve in her writing. The fantastic component is as integral to Morgner's novels as the 'real' settings: the late 1960s and early 1970s in the case of *Leben und Abenteuer der Trobadora Beatriz nach Zeugnissen ihrer Spielfrau Laura* (*The Life and Adventures of Trobadora Beatrice as Chronicled by Her Minstrel Laura*, 2000), and the early 1980s in the case of *Amanda. Ein Hexenroman* (Amanda: a Witches' Novel). These two novels were planned as the first two parts of a trilogy. Sadly, the reader can only speculate on how Morgner might have concluded her accounts of the life of the GDR citizen Laura Salman – and much else besides – since the third part had not been completed on the author's death in 1990.[8]

What Morgner had in mind with her aesthetic principle of 'entering into' her writing, was, I think, twofold – first, she is criticising the programmatic nature of her own early work in its compliance with the norms of 'good writing' and socialist realism which, in her job as assistant editor with the journal *Neue deutsche Literatur*, she was absorbing and helping to inculcate; second, the phrase underscores Morgner's need to *engage* politically with the world in and through her writing. Although the author repeated her support for GDR socialism on many occasions, she did not accept it unquestioningly, especially with regard to its sexual politics. Morgner's commitment, in this regard, was towards the 'Menschwerdung' (becoming human) of woman- and mankind alike. To paraphrase the much-quoted dictum from *Trobadora Beatriz*, Morgner's desired objective was not patriarchy, nor matriarchy, but humanity (*Trobadora Beatriz*, p. 27).

Both *Trobadora Beatriz* and *Amanda* are extensive and structurally complex novels. The first describes itself as a 'novel in thirteen books and seven intermezzos', and the second, which simply denotes its genre as a 'witches' novel', is split into 139 numbered and titled chapters and is framed by a 'Greek Prologue' and a 'New Year's Eve Epilogue'. The 1974 novel describes the adventures of the female troubadour, Beatriz de Dia, who is awoken from her 810-year sleep in May 1968 and sets out in pursuit of her profession – the writing of poems to set to music. Beatriz's travels take her to the GDR, the 'Promised Land' (p. 131), where she enlists the help of the tram driver, Laura Salman, as her assistant or minstrel. As Laura's mobility is restricted – she is pregnant and she is a GDR citizen – they swap roles, and Beatriz goes off on her travels to collect observations and material for Laura. Although Laura and Beatriz are contrasted with each other both physically and in their attitudes, they gravitate towards and take on characteristics of each other. When the left-wing parties seem to have made gains in the French elections, Beatriz celebrates by cleaning the windows. Laura sees this as a rather domestic reaction, and it is during the window cleaning that Beatriz 'loses her balance' and falls to her death. In the final book of the novel Laura is co-opted in Beatriz's place onto the 'round-table committee', a committee which since 1918 has been composed of equal numbers of men and women (p. 655).

In the second novel of the trilogy, Beatriz returns as a siren in the body of a bird and is told by Arke (daughter of Gaea, goddess of the earth) that, like all the other sirens in the world, she too must work at the process of remembering and thus help to ward off war and preserve the planet. Having lost her voice, Beatriz trains her memory by dipping her claw in ink and writing down Laura's life story in the form of a novel called *Amanda*. This she intends as a good 'extracurricular' read for Laura's son Wesselin. *Amanda* tells the story of Laura's childhood, her marriages, her problems of combining her job as a tram driver with looking after her son. When her second husband dies and Laura has to take on a night-shift the strain becomes unbearable and Laura brews up a poison to help her end it all. Instead, the potion summons up Laura's 'other half' Amanda. Amanda is one of the leaders of the three witches' factions and wants Laura to assist her in overthrowing the regime which rules the Blocksberg. Laura breaks with Amanda and seeks to supplement her own capabilities with the help of another woman, Vilma Tenner. Ultimately, Laura's attempts to brew up a sleep-replacement potion fail, but there is better news for the siren. Beatriz's stolen tongue is retrieved and stitched back on by the witches on New Year's eve.

The reviewer from the *Frankfurter Rundschau* was right to describe the liberating potential of Morgner's writing as residing as much in the *style* of her writing as in the theme of emancipation itself. Although the individual chapters of Morgner's books are generally episodic and complete units in themselves, the plot structures are highly interwoven and multilayered. In the first novel there are many different shifts of location; in the second the author draws on a number of different temporal references including Laura's childhood, her past during Beatriz's own lifetime as a troubadour, Beatriz's own present time as a siren, and mythical or ancient Greek temporality. Morgner's writing abounds in intertextual references, quotations and allusions. Goethe and E. T. A. Hoffmann are two of the key influences, but scholars have detected more than one hundred explicit literary references in *Amanda* alone.[9] Morgner's novels are also strongly self-referential – there are several references to or appearances of 'the author Irmtraud Morgner', whose novel *Trobadora Beatriz* is denounced in *Amanda* as not telling Laura's story properly. Morgner thus not only undercuts or rewrites existing stories, philosophies, myths, she also reworks and rewrites her own characters and authorial identity.

In *Trobadora Beatriz* Beatriz had been sensitised in her investigation of women's lot in contemporary society by her discovery of the Marxian rule that 'the progress of society can be measured exactly by the status in society of the weaker sex' (*Trobadora Beatriz*, p. 93). In *Amanda* Marx is embellished and improved and his eleventh Feuerbach thesis turned into the observation that 'until now, philosophers have only interpreted the world in a masculine way. What matters now is to interpret it in a feminine way in order to change it in a human way' (p. 253).[10] In fact both novels represent a plea by the author for the inclusion of women in historiography. Morgner's corrective appropriation of the figure of the troubadour – a traditionally male role – and her celebration and rewriting of witchcraft as a positive resource are but two humorous and creative examples. After the West German publication of *Trobadora Beatriz* in 1976 Morgner was hailed as 'the GDR feminist' and her novel taken to be something of a feminist bible. But this assertion is humorously denounced in *Amanda* and the various wings of the West German feminist movement brilliantly parodied in the names and beliefs of the witches' factions.

As a socialist state, the GDR fully acknowledged the necessity and desirability of sexual equality – which its citizens enjoyed on paper – but at the same time omitted to engage in the discussion of women's 'double burden'. There, as in capitalist systems, it was women who took on most of the domestic work in addition to their own paid employment. But it is not just this superficial if important sense of 'women's issues' that informs Morgner's writing. The idea of trying to interpret the world in a feminine way comes into its own in *Amanda*. Published the same year as Christa Wolf's *Kassandra*, Morgner's novel is also a reaction to the escalating militarism and nuclear threat of the period. Both works criticise war as a traditionally masculine means of trying to solve disputes and both authors have questioned the value of scientific reason as the dominant principle of human progress.

In addition to the setting of her novels in GDR reality, there are a number of possible allegorical references to the GDR in Morgner's work. The very fact that women have to resort to magic potions and flying broomsticks to make their lives bearable is, of course, a hilarious indictment of the GDR's official policy that women's full participation in the labour force guaranteed their equality. In the GDR, literature and aesthetics were matters for political debate and proscription, and the question of the right *way* to write thus had a heightened relevance for writers of both sexes. The publication of *Trobadora Beatriz* was due for 1972, but the publisher insisted on various cuts and amendments. The political climate had, however, changed sufficiently for Morgner to be able to incorporate material from her earlier, unpublished novel *Rumba auf einen Herbst* (Autumn Rumba, scheduled for 1964) into the intermezzi of the novel.

It would be wrong to read the divided subjects in Morgner's work merely as expressions of the divided Germany and to see their longing to be reunited with their other halves as a kind of nostalgia for a whole and unified Germany. Alison Lewis points out parallels between Morgner's conception of subjectivity and poststructuralist theories of subjectivity derived from psychoanalysis, linguistics and philosophy. She comments that 'the female subject in Morgner's works is conceived as radically split, non-unified, and decentred' and that 'increasingly, the reliance on a double becomes essential for survival in everyday life, the double eventually becoming a surrogate for a whole range of activities the subject is precluded from enjoying'.[11] There is, however, more than just a 'residual humanism' in Morgner's divided subjectivity. Like the plea to think in neither a patriarchal nor a matriarchal fashion, the desire to find fusion with one's other half is a dialectic expression. Morgner's split characters – male and female – are manifestations of the desirability but also the problems of trying to reconcile differences and produce new and better understandings. In terms of forging a new human subjectivity, Morgner's writing is not arguing for an androgynous or de-sexed identity politics. It is rather a celebration of female qualities and of love between the sexes. Morgner seems to be arguing that it is only by in-corporating women's perspectives and life experiences into the historical and political process that mankind – I should perhaps say humanity – can prosper.

Ingeborg Bachmann's *Malina* (1971; *Malina*, 1990) is also a novel about the struggle between 'masculine' and 'feminine' modes of existence and qualities, but where the tone of Morgner's writing might be said to be predomi-nantly upbeat and her ideas projected onto the lives and adventures of her characters, the text of *Malina* largely reflects the anguished, internalised world of its unnamed, first-person narrator, 'because all dramas take place on the inside'.[12] Bachmann's novel also ends with a death, here of the fe-male narrator who disappears into a crack in the wall, and the narration is taken up by a third-person narrator who pronounces that 'it was mur-der' (p. 225). On the whole, *Malina* was not received positively when it first came out, and it was not until the 1980s that feminist critics rediscov-ered it as a novel 'about' the oppression of woman. Later critics inspired by theories such as poststructuralism or psychoanalytic criticism have shown that the gender politics of this novel are more complex than this, but it would be fair to say that in comparison with Morgner's novels Bachmann's prose texts are the result of a less optimistic view of male–female relations. They reflect the author's own opinion that 'fascism is the first thing in a relationship between a man and a woman, and I have tried to say that here, in this society, it's always war. There isn't war and peace, there is only war.'[13]

Malina charts the first-person narrator's relationships with her lover, Ivan, with her male flatmate Malina, and – via her dreams and memories – with her father, or, as one of the three chapter titles describes him, 'the third man'. Although head over heels in love with Ivan, the narrator finds it difficult to talk to her lover and hides from him the results of her intellectual and creative work as a writer. The lovers can only develop fragmented groups of words for different subjects and tellingly they have no group of words for emotions. Ivan admonishes her for producing such gloomy writing when he discovers the pieces of paper on which she has written the words 'Notes from a Morgue' and 'Death Styles' (p. 30).[14] The narrator's relationship with Ivan is not embedded in a concrete political or historical context as in many of the new texts by women writing in the 1970s (see the discussion of Stefan's writing above), nor does the female narrator represent a woman whose growing political awareness allows her to make sense of and rebel against her socialisation or 'victimisation', as many critics chose to read the first-person narrator's plight. Ingeborg Bachmann was not aiming to produce an authentic 'account' of one woman's inner turmoil, neither, however, did she eschew historico-political realities as many of her critics have claimed. Bachmann's novel reflects a highly differentiated and complex picture of (female) subjectivity even though it is the earliest of the novels discussed here. Again, the author's own reflections on the nature of the individual subject in modern society and in literature provide a key to understanding her novel. Bachmann says of the subject ('das Ich'), that: 'it no longer resides *in* history; latterly, history resides *in* the subject' ('es sich nicht mehr *in* der Geschichte aufhält, sondern daß sich neuerdings die Geschichte *im* Ich aufhält'). Bachmann goes on to explain that the subject used to be considered as integral, unitary, trustworthy, but that since the subject has been reconsidered and is now seen as fragmentary, its history and the stories that it tells are no longer 'guaranteed' ('Das schreibende Ich' (The writing self), *Werke*, IV, 230). It is worth noting that there are close parallels between reflections such as these and the thinking of the Swiss writer Max Frisch, in particular his novel *Mein Name sei Gantenbein* (discussed by Michael Butler in chapter 16 above, pp. 239–41).

The first-person narrator embodies this view of subjectivity as something which is fragmentary and non-unitary. It becomes clear to the reader that Malina is not so much a separate entity, an independent subject, but part of the narrator's own subjectivity, a kind of alter ego. A fortune-teller confirms that 'it's really not a picture of one person but of two people standing in extreme opposition to one another, it must mean that I am constantly apt to be torn in two' (p. 163) and pities her for having to try constantly to reconcile the masculine and the feminine, reason and emotion, productivity and self-destruction. For the most part this is how the two 'characters' are portrayed: the narrator is sensitive, emotional, distracted, anguished, whereas Malina is rational, focused, practical and phlegmatic. Nevertheless, there are character qualities which do not fit into this neatly polarised scheme. Malina, for example, is distrustful of science and feels that the narrator's threat that she will gain power and reverse the traditional gender roles can only lead her out of one sort of madness and into another (p. 206). For her part, the narrator seems to be almost androgynous. She wonders if she is not 'something dimorphic? Am I not entirely female – what am I, anyway?' (p. 183).

When the narrator's relationship with Ivan breaks down, she loses her ability to use language, she can no longer even communicate with Ivan using the trusty telephone and after her disappearance into the wall, Malina even denies that she has ever existed, telling a telephone caller that 'there is no woman here. I'm telling you, there was never anyone here by that name' (p. 224). Opinions differ over how to interpret the conclusion of the novel, with some critics seeing the narrator's murder as the proof of men's denial or suppression of women's voice. In these terms, Bachmann would seem to underline the feminist critique of patriarchy which sees the male pole in any binary pair seeking to conquer the female pole.[15] Other readers see in the narrator's death her refusal to live life according to the male law or the symbolic order of masculine rules, institutions and power, indeed her refusal to accept a polarised value system. Thus the narrator's final act of disappearance is seen not as an act of resignation but as one of defiance. Moreover, the incompatibilities of gender are not to be seen as universal and eternal but rather as the 'expression of the experiences of a woman living "today"'.[16] The narrator may be living 'today', but the past is stored up inside her. She has nightmare visions of deportation, of being gassed to death by her father, of having her books destroyed by him; indeed she has died numerous deaths at the hands of her father before she is finally 'murdered'. It is not made clear whether the father image is to be read as a real person and the atrocities and abuse to be taken as manifestations of the daughter's own childhood experience. It is more likely that the father should be seen as an embodiment of an exaggerated universal principle of patriarchal destruction or as a metaphor for fascism.

This chapter began by recalling the very real sanctions placed by society on women's writing and creativity, in effect, on their subjectivity, by restricting how they should relate to their world. It is an issue which continues to be thematised and problematised in novels by women, as here in Bachmann's *Malina*. Many of the narrator's dreams involve her father trying to steal her voice or tear out her tongue. Just as Morgner's Beatriz has to record her memories with her claw since her absent tongue will not allow her to sing her story, the narrator of *Malina* struggles to articulate her experiences, her love, her fears and her hopes. Stefan's novel is bound up with the attempt to develop a new language with which to express her narrator's developing new consciousness and sexuality. Jelinek's characters Gerti and Erika Kohut also seek a means to express themselves and to take control of their own lives, and the novel *Die Liebhaberinnen* is the author's attempt to give a political *voice* to the subject of women's oppression. The four novelists considered here may all be said to engage with the problem of women's subjectivity and with the wider problem of women's status. In doing so they develop distinctive and powerful styles of writing which, in varied and thought-provoking ways, challenge and subvert those very restrictions on women's creativity that form both the context and the major (though by no means the only) theme of their novels.

NOTES

1. Verena Stefan, *Häutungen* (Munich, 1975), English translation by Johanna Steigleder Moore and Beth E. Weckmueller, in Verena Stefan, *Shedding and Literally Dreaming* (New York, 1994); Elfriede Jelinek, *Die Liebhaberinnen* (Reinbek, 1975), translated by Martin Chalmers as *Women as Lovers* (London, 1994); *Die Klavierspielerin* (Reinbek, 1983), translated by Joachim Neugroschel as *The Piano Teacher* (New York, 1988); *Lust* (Reinbek, 1989), translated by Michael Hulse (London, 1992); Irmtraud Morgner, *Leben und Abenteuer der Trobadora Beatriz nach Zeugnissen ihrer Spielfrau Laura* (Weimar, 1974), quotations here are my translations from the dtv paperback edition (1994); *Amanda* (Weimar, 1983), quotations here are my translations from the Luchterhand paperback edition (1992); Ingeborg Bachmann, *Malina* (Frankfurt am Main, 1971), translated by Philip Boehm (New York, 1990).
2. As a term, *Frauenliteratur* was discarded early on by many women writers and theoreticians since it carries strong connotations of a form of light fiction (*Trivialliteratur*), specifically, as Sigrid Weigel points out, 'the nineteenth-century tradition of women's sentimental and often serialised popular novels'. The term *Frauenliteratur* is thus less acceptable than the English terms 'women's writing', 'feminine aesthetics', or the theoretically charged French term *écriture féminine*. See editorial note to '"Woman begins relating to herself": contemporary German women's literature (part one)', *new german critique*, 31 (1984), 53–94 (p. 53).
3. Alison M. Jaggar, *Feminist Politics and Human Nature* (Brighton, 1983), p. 251.
4. For a critique of this approach, see chapter 5 'Making changes: can we decontaminate sexist language?', in Deborah Cameron, *Feminism and Linguistic Theory* (Basingstoke, 1985).
5. For a clear explanation of these psychoanalytic theories, see chapter 3 'Feminist poststructuralism and psychoanalysis' in Chris Weedon, *Feminist Practice and Poststructuralist Theory* (Oxford, 1987), pp. 43–73.
6. Ingeborg Bachmann, 'Die Wahrheit ist dem Menschen zumutbar', *Werke*, 4 vols. (Munich, 1978), IV, 277.
7. Irmtraud Morgner, 'Apropos Eisenbahn' (1973), in Marlis Gerhardt, *Irmtraud Morgner. Texte, Daten, Bilder* (Frankfurt am Main, 1990), p. 23.
8. Fragments of this final part have been published posthumously: *Das heilige Testament. Ein Roman in Fragmenten*, ed. R. Bussmann (Hamburg, 1998).

9. See, for example, Hildegard Pietsch, 'Goethe as a model for feminist writing? The adaptation of a classical author in Irmtraud Morgner's *Amanda. Ein Hexenroman*', in Gertrud Pickar and Sabine Cramer (eds.), *The Age of Goethe Today: Critical Reexamination and Literary Reflection* (Munich, 1990), pp. 212–19.

10. Marx's original statement is: 'The philosophers have only *interpreted* the world in different ways; the point is to change it.' T. B. Bottomore and Maximilien Rubel (eds.), *Karl Marx: Selected Writings in Sociology and Social Philosophy* (Harmondsworth, 1964), p. 84.

11. Alison Lewis, *Subverting Patriarchy: Feminism and Fantasy in the Works of Irmtraud Morgner* (Oxford, 1995), p. 271.

12. Preface to Ingeborg Bachmann, *Der Fall Franza*, in *Werke*, 4 vols. (Munich, 1978), III, 342.

13. Ingeborg Bachmann, *Wir müssen wahre Sätze finden: Gespräche und Interviews*, ed. Christine Koschel and Inge von Weidenbaum (Munich, 1983), p. 144.

14. 'Todesarten' was the intended title for a cycle of novels which Bachmann had planned, but only the first, *Malina*, was completed and published before Bachmann's death in 1973. The two uncompleted fragments *Der Fall Franza* and *Requiem für Fanny Goldmann* were published posthumously in the *Werke*, 4 vols. (Munich, 1978), III, 339–482 and 483–524.

15. Hélène Cixous's idea and criticism of 'patriarchal binary thought' is explained in Toril Moi, *Sexual/Textual Politics* (London, 1985), pp. 104–5.

16. Sigrid Weigel, 'Der schielende Blick. Thesen zur Geschichte weiblicher Schreibpraxis', in Inge Stephan and Sigrid Weigel (eds.), *Die verborgene Frau. Sechs Beiträge zu einer feministischen Literaturwissenschaft*, *Argument* Sonderband (Berlin, 1983), 83–137 (p. 123).

FURTHER READING

Abel, Elizabeth, Marianne Hirsch and Elizabeth Langland (eds.), *The Voyage In: Fictions of Female Development* (Hanover, NH, 1983)

Bammer, Angelika, *Partial Visions: Feminism and Utopianism in the 1970s* (New York, 1991)

Bartsch, Kurt, and Günther Höfler (eds.), *Elfriede Jelinek* (Graz, 1991)

Dietze, Gabriele (ed.), *Die Überwindung der Sprachlosigkeit. Texte aus der neuen Frauenbewegung* (Darmstadt, 1979)

Fiddler, Allyson, *Rewriting Reality: an Introduction to Elfriede Jelinek* (Oxford, 1994)

Gerhardt, Marlis (ed.), *Irmtraud Morgner. Texte, Daten, Bilder* (Frankfurt am Main, 1990)

Gürtler, Christa (ed.), *Gegen den schönen Schein. Texte zu Elfriede Jelinek* (Frankfurt am Main, 1990)

Johns, Jorun B., and Katherine Arens (eds.), *Elfriede Jelinek: Framed by Language* (Riverside, CA, 1994)

Koschel, Christine, and Inge von Weidenbaum (eds.), *Kein objektives Urteil – nur ein lebendiges. Texte zum Werk von Ingeborg Bachmann* (Munich, 1989)

Lennox, Sara, 'The feminist reception of Ingeborg Bachmann', *Women in German Yearbook*, 8 (1993), 73–112

Linklater, Beth, '*Und immer zügelloser wird die Lust.*' *Constructions of Sexuality in East German Literatures (with special reference to Irmtraud Morgner and Gabriele Stoetzer-Kachold* (Bern, 1998)

Scherer, Gabriele, *Zwischen 'Bitterfeld' und 'Orplid'. Zum literarischen Werk Irmtraud Morgners* (Bern, 1992)

Schmidt, Ricarda, *Westdeutsche Frauenliteratur in den 70er Jahren* (Frankfurt am Main, 1982)

Weedon, Chris (ed.), *Postwar Women's Writing in German* (Oxford, 1997)

Wigmore, Juliet, 'Ingeborg Bachmann', in Keith Bullivant (ed.), *The Modern German Novel* (Leamington Spa, 1987), pp. 72–88

18

PAUL MICHAEL LÜTZELER

The postmodern German novel

In his study of the mechanics of scientific revolutions, Thomas Kuhn demonstrated that scientific researchers operate at any given time within a widely accepted paradigm, which determines the prevailing theories until the moment when a consensual crisis causes the old paradigm to be discarded in favour of a new one. In the humanities, paradigm shifts do not take place with such revolutionary abruptness, with such definitive breaks as in the sciences. Here the prevalent paradigms are more difficult to identify; one finds a codominance of older, renewed and new schools of thought that operate alongside, together with, or against one another.

Despite this, one particular paradigm has nevertheless attained clear preeminence in discussions of cultural theory during the past decades: that of the postmodern. Arising out of sporadic attacks during the 1960s against the conventions of modern literature and art, the postmodern debate has expanded into a general cultural critique and has affected practically all areas of the humanities. Important contributions to the postmodern theme came initially from the United States, then from France and Italy, and finally – somewhat belatedly – from Germany. Contributions to the discussion on postmodernism have come equally from philosophers (Jean-François Lyotard, Richard Rorty, Gianni Vattimo), architects (Charles Jencks, Robert Venturi), cultural critics (Leslie Fiedler, Jean Baudrillard, Mattei Calinescu, Ihab Hassan, Ingeborg Hoesterey), intellectual historians (Peter Koslowski, Perry Anderson, Fredric Jameson, Wolfgang Welsch), feminists (Sandra Harding, Alice Jardine) and literary historians (Douwe Fokkema, Linda Hutcheon, Brian McHale).

Theoreticians of postmodernism describe the current cultural factors, conditions and circumstances that differentiate it from the modernist culture of earlier decades. Although the studies on the subject are diverse and distinct, there exist certain tendencies and characteristics that mark the differences between modernism and postmodernism. Much of what is defined as being typically postmodern was actually already contained in modernism; that is to say, the advent of postmodernism enabled the breakthrough of many an inspiration from modernism. Lyotard speaks of the hidden postmodern in the modern, and Welsch gave his book the appropriate title of 'Our Postmodern Modernity'. Certainly not every element of postmodernism is an explicit counter-movement against modernism. Mediating concepts such as development and transformation are more helpful than strict oppositional thinking in analysing the postmodern. At best, the differences between modernism and postmodernism may be viewed as movements *from* one state *towards* another, as movements in which processes of democratisation and individualisation are reflected. Accordingly, the changing circumstances can be characterised by 'from–to' formulations.

In the area of politics and society the changes are from 'either–or' ideologies demanding decisive battles, to a readiness for carefully thought-out compromise; from debates in terms of strict opposites like right and left or progress and reaction, to an acceptance of composites and transitions; from a belief in technological progress to a cognisance of the fragility of the environment; from a trust in unlimited economic growth to an awareness of the exhaustibility of natural resources; from a male-dominated society to a social structure in which women play an increasing role; from a western or Eurocentric attitude to a multiculturalist and postcolonial identity; from a dominant and centristic cultural bent to polycentristic worldviews encompassing an understanding of other civilisations and the cultures of minorities. In the field of philosophy and *Weltanschauung* the movement is from emphasis on the general to a preference for the specific; from an overview of perspectives of totality to a focus on the local and regional; from monistic explanations to a plurality of attempts at interpretation; from striving for uniformity to a diversity of thought and lifestyles; from universalistic metanarratives to a multitude of language games or biographically mediated experience; from a belief in historical continuity to a conviction of historical discontinuity; from a predominantly utopian idealism to a dialogue with history.

In the sphere of architecture, the shift is from an infatuation with merely functional beauty to a delight in a plurality of styles, and to the return of the ornament; in art, it takes us from a resolute earnestness of intent to manifestations of the playful and the ironic-parodistic; from a privileging of elitist art and a fixation on towering cultural achievements to a preference for popular forms or a cultural mix; from a desire for constant innovations to attempts at synthesising traditional styles; and from a preference for uniqueness and purity of style to a renewed esteem for eclecticism. Finally, in the closely related area of literature we find – in addition to many of the above – a move from monologic discourse to dialogic interaction; from definitive categorisations to double and multiple codes; from an avantgardist fixation on the future to an interest in the past; from the intention to grasp social totality in the novel, to a description of the personal and autobiographical; from the demand that the hero of a novel represent an era, a generation, a class, or a utopian idea, to the elimination of the hero as a central figure altogether.

In short, while in the case of modernism we were often dealing with conflicting utopias and high-minded manifestos, postmodernism in contrast presents itself as an honest admission of uncertainty, of compromise, of scepticism towards utopian thinking, involving a dialogue with history, and a view of the future that is characterised by unpredictability. With respect to postmodern literature, one can say that it is not striving for totality, that its heroes are disempowered, that it is not as bent on utopias or as constrained by aesthetic declarations, not as ideologically decisive, not as hermetic or obscure, not as referential or representative and not as highbrow as was the literature of modernism. In contrast, freer expression is given to the playful, the eccentric and peripheral, the parodistic – frequently in the form of criticism of the canon – the self-referential and self-reflexive, as well as to intertextual pastiche, to the synthesis of elitist and popular culture, to the historical and the autobiographical.

Georg Lukács's *Theory of the Novel*, first published in 1916, was both the swan song of the aesthetics of German idealism and the herald of the modern novel (see chapter 6 above, pp. 78–9). Lukács was still thinking in the categories of early Romanticism when he declared that in the age of 'transcendental homelessness' the novel would have to create the new totality of meaning that used to be established by myth and religion. The classical modern novel written during the following three decades by Joyce, Gide, Kafka, Thomas Mann, Döblin, Musil and Broch could not possibly meet Lukács's expectations, but their monumental oeuvre expressed the same sadness about the loss of central values that had been articulated in the *Theory of the Novel*. The novel of classical modernism has thus been characterised by Hassan and Lyotard as a document of mourning. According to them, however, the end of this grieving period has arrived with the advent of postmodernism. A characteristic of the postmodern condition is its insight into the irretrievability of closed ideologies based on beliefs that pretend to encompass and explain all segments of a culture. Postmodernism stands for a pluralism that can no longer lament the disappearance of a cultural centre. Postmodern novelists do not see themselves as would-be creators of meaning but as part of a literary discourse that is competing with other discourses in a pluralistic society. Thus there will not be a Lukács of the postmodern novel who would be able to define its one and only mission. A fixed definition of the poetics of the postmodern novel would be a contradiction in terms. A postmodern aesthetics can formulate a number of characteristics but it cannot execute gestures of totality of the sort that we find in Lukács's *Theory of the Novel*.

Contemporary German novelists themselves have openly confessed this new modesty in matters regarding their literary intentions. Their lectures in poetics (*Poetikvorlesungen*) – important and respected events, held at the universities of Frankfurt am Main, Munich, Mainz, Graz and Paderborn – have become an important part of the postmodern literary scene. The first of them – Ingeborg Bachmann's *Poetikvorlesung* in Frankfurt am Main – more or less coincided with the beginnings of postmodern aesthetics (Leslie Fiedler's essays) in the early 1960s. Considering the more personal and autobiographical nature of the postmodern novel, professors of German literature reacted appropriately in inviting the authors to explain their individually different poetics. These lectures (as is shown in my volume *Poetik der Autoren*) demonstrate again that the contemporary German novel is less ambitious and tense, less totality-oriented, less utopian, less decisive, less hermetic, less representative and less highbrow than the modernist novel. Some of these lectures (at least in part) even take on the form of autobiographies; Ortheil's *Das Element des Elefanten* (1994; The Element of the Elephant) is the most extreme expression of this general trend.

Owing to their critical approach to the literary canon of the past, postmodern authors have a more open attitude to popular culture. While a modernist like Hermann Broch identified 'kitsch' as the incarnation of evil within the value system of the arts, postmodernists have no problem in adapting genres that previously were considered to be outside the realm of high culture (such as the Gothic novel, detective fiction and adventure stories). Mass culture has also received revalorisation by critics like Leslie Fiedler and Susan Sontag. Examples of a successful fusion of highbrow and popular German literature are Patrick Süskind's *Das Parfum* (1985; *Perfume*, 1986), Sten Nadolny's *Die Entdeckung der Langsamkeit* (1983; *The Discovery of Slowness*, 1987), Christoph Ransmayr's *Die Schrecken des Eises und der Finsternis* (1984; *The Terrors of Ice and Darkness*, 1991) and Josef Haslinger's *Opernball* (1995; Opera Ball).

Just as important as the synthesis of so-called high and low culture is the preference for the periphery versus the centre. 'Things fall apart; the centre cannot hold', wrote W. B. Yeats in his poem 'The Second Coming'. As a modernist he could not cope with the disintegration of values and, like Broch, he was convinced that an imminent new religion or myth would bring an end to a chaotic cultural situation. With regard to form and theme, the postmodernists have given up this preference for the centre. A decentred, non-linear narration is becoming more and more popular, for which the images of the labyrinth and the rhizome have been invoked (Deleuze, Guattari). Key examples are Herta Müller's *Der Fuchs war damals schon der Jäger* (1992; Then the Fox Was the Hunter), Andreas Neumeister's *Salz im Blut* (1990; Salt in the Blood), Peter Weber's *Der Wettermacher* (1994; The Weather Maker) and Urs Richle's *Mall oder Das Verschwinden der Berge* (1993; Mall or The Disappearing of the Mountains). The opposition between the eccentric and the centre is the theme in Handke's *Langsame Heimkehr* (1979; *Slow Homecoming*, 1985) as well as in Ransmayr's novels. Handke's Sorger never reaches the centre of the imagined Europe, and in Ransmayr's *Die letzte Welt* (1988; *The Last World*, 1990) the plot moves away from the centre (Rome) to the periphery of the empire. Broch's *Der Tod des Vergil* (1945; *Death of Virgil*, 1945) functions as the intertext in Ransmayr's novel. The difference is obvious: in Broch's novel the hero moves from the colonial periphery back to Rome, and his meeting with the emperor is seen as the book's centre of the centre. Marginalised artists in a rigid society are the topic in Christa Wolf's *Kein Ort. Nirgends* (1979; *No Place on Earth*, 1982). Jurek Becker's *Bronsteins Kinder* (1986; Bronstein's Children), Edgar Hilsenrath's *Der Nazi & der Friseur* (1977; *The Nazi & the Barber*, translated from the manuscript 1975) and *Das Märchen vom letzten Gedanken* (1989; *The Story of the Last Thought*, 1990), Gert Hofmann's *Veilchenfeld* (1986), and Ulla Berkéwicz's *Engel sind schwarz und weiß* (1992; *Angels are Black and White*, 1997) deal with the most inhuman marginalisation: that of anti-Semitism, the Holocaust and genocide.

In contrast to the situation in the late 1960s, the aesthetics of postmodern writing does not proclaim the death of literature as such. But one does encounter numerous references to the demise of the author, the subject and the hero. To paraphrase Mark Twain, news concerning the death of these aesthetic concepts is not greatly but somewhat exaggerated. Roland Barthes, in his 1968 essay 'La mort de l'auteur' ('The death of the author') was among those theoreticians who devalued the idea of the author's originality. It is a fact that the relationship between the author and the reader has changed. According to Barthes, the reader is challenged to participate more actively in the creation of the text; not the author but the reader is the creator of the literary text, since it is the act of reading that initiates the game of codes and meanings. This sounds exaggerated but it was indicative of the reader-oriented aesthetics of the early 1970s (Jauss, Iser) that Barthes anticipated. In the meantime novelists and critics have left behind this one-sided view of the author–reader relationship. Sten Nadolny, in his lecture 'Das Erzählen und die guten Absichten' (Narration and good intentions) has pointed out that he imagines the reader as a critical friend who has a voice during the creative process of writing a novel and who is the third partner in the author–narrator–reader triangle. Once the novel is finished this imagined reader ceases to exist and is replaced by a multitude of dissonant voices of 'real' readers who express their views in reviews, letters, discussions, telephone calls. It is obvious that the relation between the author and the reader has changed: the reader is asked to participate more actively in the novel, since the old authorial narrative that tells a story with a beginning, a middle and an end is disappearing. This becomes all the more obvious when one looks more closely at the role the hero plays (or rather, no longer plays) in the postmodern novel.

Three different kinds of hero have emerged in the postmodern novel: first, the hero as explorer, discoverer, wanderer and detective; second, the hero as an eccentric and marginal figure; and third, the hero who is missing from the narrative altogether. The first kind of hero has an exploring, inquiring, curious and examining mind, and is ready to change things. In the books of Umberto Eco, Italo Calvino, Sten Nadolny and Thomas Pynchon, the reader accompanies this hero on an adventurous quest for meaning, only to find that life is a conglomeration of coincidences, unpredictable developments and incalculable constellations. Ortheil concentrated on the specifically postmodern viewpoint of this hero in his essay collection *Schauprozesse* (1990; Show Trials). In my opinion, the allegory of the postmodern novel is Hermes or Mercury who, in his inconstancy, is on his way with ever new messages, and who – in his role as a novelist – would enjoy eclecticism, pastiche, imitation, citation and its formal correspondences of collage and bricolage. It was only a question of time until Hermes showed up as the hero of a postmodern novel. This happened when Sten Nadolny published *Ein Gott der Frechheit* (1994; A God of Insolence), in which the ancient gods experience a rebirth. The gods appear to be immortal, except now they no longer live on Mount Olympus but rather among the people on earth. As is true for humans, much has changed for the gods, who are also subject to historical alterations. Zeus is disempowered, and Hephaestus, the god of volcanoes, has become the new ruler over gods and men. He has evolved from the blacksmith of old into the commander of human technology, the god of a world driven by computers. Hephaestus had imprisoned Hermes for two thousand years. But now Hermes – the god of insolence, chaos, turmoil, fertility, thievery, erotic freedom and sleep – is free again. He appears just in time, so that – with his infusion of life, his love of mankind – he is able to avert the devastation of the earth and the self-destruction of mankind. *Ein Gott der Frechheit* is the most humorous novel of contemporary German literature.

The second kind of hero is the eccentric one. Whereas the main characters of classical modern novelists such as Proust, Joyce, Thomas Mann, Musil, Döblin and Broch are found in major cities like Paris, Dublin, Venice, Vienna, Berlin, Rome – that is, in the cultural centres of Europe – the heroes of Nadolny, Ransmayr, Thomas Bernhard (*Auslöschung. Ein Zerfall* (1986; *Extinction*, 1996)), Günter Grass (*Zunge zeigen* (1988; *Show Your Tongue*, 1989)), Barbara Frischmuth (*Über die Verhältnisse* (1987; How Things Are)) and Gerold Späth (*Barbarswila*, 1988) appear in such locations as the polar regions, Third World countries, the outskirts of the Roman Empire, and the provinces of Austria and Switzerland. The off-centre perspective forces a change in viewpoint and leads to a questioning of convention and tradition. This kind of hero encompasses the figure of the outsider, whom Hubert Winkels (*Einschnitte. Zur Literatur der 8oer Jahre*, 1988) and Thomas Anz (*Gesund oder krank?*, 1989) have analysed in their studies of the postmodern scene in contemporary German literature.

The third kind of hero is actually a non-type. Here we find reduced to absurdity every representation of the hero from the beginnings of the novel tradition to the present. In the twentieth-century modernist novel, we already find a destabilisation of the protagonist, an abandonment of the idea of a hero who develops as a unified subject. But the hero in the modernist novel is still a representative type, is still a synthesis of the commonalities and the peculiarities of a particular era. In the postmodern novel one finds an absence of the teleological development and the so-called typical qualities of the hero or heroine. In Handke's *Langsame Heimkehr* the narrator and the protagonist start out as separate entities, but a synthesis is achieved through the transformation of the hero Sorger from the third through the second to the first person. During the course of the narrative process, Sorger himself becomes an example of his own insight that form is not static but rather is subject to constant metamorphoses. The merging and the ultimate disappearance of the narrator and the hero is also apparent in Hildesheimer's *Tynset* (1965) and *Masante* (1973) as well as in the absolute prose of Heißenbüttel (*Textbücher* 1–6, 1980). The metamorphosis *is* the actual hero in Ransmayr's *Die letzte Welt*. Its laws are sustained by protagonists who do not develop as people but evaporate, as is implied by some of their names like Echo and Fama. Even Cotta – who at first glance appears to be the main character of the book – is composed of multiple 'selves' and disintegrates as a subject, hears himself from afar, and observes himself from a bird's eye view. The relativisation of the meaning of the hero is also revealed in Grass's *Kopfgeburten oder Die Deutschen sterben aus* (1980; *Headbirths, or, The Germans are Dying Out*, 1982) as well as in his *Die Rättin* (1986; *The Rat*, 1987) (where one finds a doubling and multiplication of the narrator as well as the metamorphosis of the author into a fictional figure) and in Michael Krüger's *Das Ende des Romans* (1990; The End of the Novel). In a meta-poetic fashion, these novelists show to what degree the depicted figures are merely fictional constructs of the narrator. Thus the reader is inspired to do more productive work on the text, in which more questions are raised than answers given. Murnau in Bernhard's *Auslöschung* exposes the process of the disintegration and the 'extinction' of the subject, actually appearing as a sort of non-subject. Gerold Späth in *Commedia* (1980) and Andreas Neumeister in *Salz im Blut* manage without any central hero or heroine whatsoever. Späth's title already indicates that his work has no 'hero' as the main character. First he lines up brief biographical sketches of common people, then he sends a group of tourist protagonists into a museum, where they disappear in a dungeon. It would be hard to imagine a clearer metaphor for the termination of the hero in the novel. However, one female tourist escapes the museum trap, thus subverting to some extent the idea of the abolition of the protagonist. As for Neumeister's novel, one can start reading it at the beginning, in the middle, at the end, or at any point because there is no commencement, centre or conclusion. Autobiographical memories, historical reminiscences, surreal scenes, plays on words and critical reflections are freely interchanged. No effort is made to construct a main character as the pivotal point of a coherent story.

The problematising, the splitting, the weakening and the disappearance of the main character of the novel can be seen within the context of present-day discussions concerning the subject. Descartes's subject-theory was the seed from which sprouted Enlightenment ideas on the autonomy of the subject, the ethics of the individual, and the emancipation of the person from religious and secular authorities. In idealistic philosophy, the subject was perceived as the locus of all significance and character formation, as the mediator of a universal spirit, as a sort of monad endowed with the attributes of freedom, reason, consistency, justice, harmony, totality and perfectibility. Nietzsche's attacks on the claims to universality of Hegelian reason resulted in the decentralisation, demystification and relativisation of the subject. He undertook the task of annulling the traditional subject in an attempt to prove the fictionality of its constructs. Equally powerful were the attacks launched by theorists ranging from Marxists through psychologists to poststructuralists against the idealistic concept of the subject. Marx, Mach, de Saussure, Husserl, Freud, Jung, Heidegger, de Beauvoir, Habermas and Foucault made sure that the formerly solid nucleus of the subject was dissolved in the acid solutions of their diverse discourses – social, empiriocritical, structural, logical, psychoanalytical, archetypical, existential, gender-specific, communicational and poststructural. The poststructuralist theory of the subject, which got its major impetus from Foucault (who, in turn, owes a great deal to Nietzsche) maintains that a subject constituted by language cannot be autonomous. Foucault, Barthes, Deleuze, Guattari, Lyotard, Lacan, Derrida and Kristeva describe the subject as diffuse and undecided, since it is part of a constantly changing stream of discourse. The discourse defines the subject's view of the world; its perception is prestructured in the discursive formation of the era. Therefore the subject (unlike Descartes) does not define itself by means of the 'cogito ergo sum' but perceives itself through the mirror of the other, at whom its (ever unfulfilled) desire is directed. This does not imply a declaration of the subject's death, but rather the questioning of its autonomy, the emphasis of its historisation, the analysis of its conditioning, its fragmentation, its flexibility and its readiness for metamorphosis.

Scepticism towards utopian thinking is a common characteristic of postmodern culture. It plays a significant role in contemporary literature as well. The strong preference for entropy, chaos, carnival and history leaves little room for utopias. Herein lies the main contrast to the cultural climate of the 1960s. Utopias project an improved future order against the deficient order of the present. Carnival and entropy dissolve existing structures without proposing alternative models. The concept of entropy was borrowed from thermodynamics to denote increasing disorder and was first designated by the American author Thomas Pynchon as the hallmark of postmodern writing. It can also be used to describe contemporary German literature. This is manifest in the works of the 1980s, which are marked by an increasing tendency to anarchy, such as Grass's *Kopfgeburten*, Späth's *Barbarswila*, or Weber's *Wettermacher*. In novels like Nadolny's *Ein Gott der Frechheit* the carnivalesque (as a non-aggressive revolt against petrified conventions and institutions) is openly espoused. The notion of the carnivalesque developed by Mikhail Bakhtin in his Dostoevsky study was taken up, discussed and popularised on an international scale. Bakhtin portrayed carnival as an episodic suspension of a hierarchically structured social system, accompanied by a temporary renunciation of fear, timidity, piety and social conventions. In the postmodern novel entropy and carnival are treated as alternatives to a paranoid delineation of order with its associated over-technical, over-organised, over-perfected industrialised civilisation, a civilisation that is nevertheless subject to catastrophic events.

Contemporary novelists distrust modern utopias in both their scientific and their social forms. The two world wars, the Holocaust, ecological disasters like Chernobyl, the terror of the communist systems – all this is reflected in the contemporary novel. In his epic poem *Der Untergang der Titanic* (1978; *The Sinking of the Titanic*, 1981) Enzensberger lets this dinosaur of a technical utopia drown anew, sinking into a sea of ineffective blueprints for the future. Ransmayr's *Die Schrecken des Eises und der Finsternis* can also be read as a symbol of the end of modern civilisation. The subject of this book is an Austrian polar expedition that takes place towards the end of the last century; their destiny is an icy death. In Handke's *Langsame Heimkehr* one finds the insight that modern science belongs to a culture of the past. Like Enzensberger's Titanic, Bernhard's fortress Wolfsegg in *Auslöschung. Ein Zerfall* is a metaphor for the erroneous direction of the modern. The monstrous aspects of the modern utopias are criticised in Gabriele Wohmann's *Der Flötenton* (1987; The Sound of the Flute) and Christa Wolf's *Störfall. Nachrichten eines Tages* (1987; *Accident. A Day's News,* 1989), their respective literary contributions to the debate on Chernobyl. In Wolf's book, Joseph Conrad's *The Heart of Darkness* (1902) functions as an example of a text from colonial times in which the inhuman aspects of western 'progress' are taken to task. Grass's *Die Rättin* is written from a similar critical point of view. A comparable theme is dealt with in Max Frisch's *Der Mensch erscheint im Holozän* (1979; *Man in the Holocene,* 1980). It tells the story of the 73-year-old Herr Geiser who, living in a village in the Swiss Alps, is watching the unusually heavy rainfalls. He suddenly becomes convinced that they are indicators of a worldwide ecological crisis. He falls victim to his own *Angst,* and the novel ends with his personal catastrophe – his death – and not with the destruction of the world that he had anticipated. Frisch develops a complex structure of apocalyptic visions in which Geiser's story has an exemplary quality.

Similarly critical viewpoints are prevalent in novels about life in Third World countries, like Born's *Die Fälschung* (1979; basis of Volker Schlöndorff's film *Circle of Deceit,* 1981), Gert Hofmann's *Vor der Regenzeit* (1988; Before the Rains), Bodo Kirchhoff's *Zwiefalten* (1983; Folds) and *Infanta* (1990), Jeannette Lander's *Jahrhundert der Herren* (1993; Century of the Masters), Adolf Muschg's *Baiyun oder Die Freundschaftsgesellschaft* (1980; Baiyun or The Friendship Society) and Uwe Timm's *Der Schlangenbaum* (1986; *The Snake Tree,* 1990). In particular Grass's *Zunge zeigen (Show Your Tongue)* has to be mentioned here. Grass uses Calcutta both as a parallel to Germany's fascist past and as a projection screen for the imagined future of the First and Third worlds. Depicted as an escape from contemporary events in Germany and Europe at the end of the 1980s, Grass's trip to India serves as a way to come to terms with a troubled past and an equally distressing outlook for the future, a future in which – according to the author – only the migrant can save the West. These books are part of the postmodern postcolonial discourse, dealing in a critical manner with the colonisation and imperialisation of European identity. Their authors try to adopt the perspective of another culture and thus their vision of western industrialised society is, in a literal sense, estranged.

Scepticism towards utopian thinking corresponds to a new and growing interest in history on the part of the authors. With respect to the new fascination with history, one must distinguish three aspects: *first*, the adoption or integration of themes from literary history, historical genre models, and narrative forms; *secondly*, a preoccupation with the problems of fictional and historiographic narration; and *thirdly*, the thematisation of historical events.

Upon entering the archives of literary history we encounter the theme of intertextuality and interdiscursiveness. The form and manner of the intertextual and interdiscursive references tend to differ in modernist and postmodern literature. For example, when T. S. Eliot refers to Dante in *The Waste Land* (1923) or when Hermann Broch cites the Roman author Virgil in *The Death of Virgil*, their intention is to establish a connection in the sense of carrying on a tradition. They feel that their appropriation of a parallel historical situation justifies this notion. Postmodern literature gives no expression to direct connections with past historical phases. Rather, authors like Thomas Bernhard, Gert Hofmann, Patrick Süskind, Elfriede Jelinek (*Die Ausgesperrten* (1980; Locked Out)) and Christoph Ransmayr use intertextual allusions to highlight the differences rather than the similarities, the discontinuity instead of the continuity. They want no part of historical models or historical analogies, but rather in their allusions they point up ironic breakdowns, proofs of distance and alienation. The past – even the literary past – can be viewed only with irony, not with innocence, as Eco asserts in his *Postscript to 'The Name of the Rose'* (1984). The postmodern relationship to tradition is characterised not by longing, inclination, affirmation, continuation, but rather by concepts such as correction, rebuttal, revocation, disintegration and parody. Instead of meaningful bridges to the past, subversive allusions are the goal. The intent is not to celebrate the original text being cited but rather to question the idea of canonical works.

Hayden White, in *Metahistory* (1974), has studied the relation between history and fiction, quoting examples from nineteenth-century philosophy of history and historiography. Here it becomes obvious that neither a clear-cut distinction between nor a simple identification of these two narrative forms is possible. Given the historical interest articulated in the postmodern novel, Linda Hutcheon has characterised contemporary narrative as 'historiographic metafiction'. According to her the literary narrative is designated, first of all, as genuinely fictional; secondly, as historiographic, owing to its retention of historical themes; and thirdly, as self-reflexive, addressing the meta-level. The present is understood as a complex conceptual structure of various presences, while the past is seen as a network of different recollections. Illustrative of the problematising literary approach to history in the German domain are Alexander Kluge's *Schlachtbeschreibung* (1964; *The Battle*, 1967), Dieter Kühn's *Ich Wolkenstein* (1971), Günter Grass's *Kopfgeburten*, Christa Wolf's *Kassandra* (1983; *Cassandra*, 1984), Christoph Ransmayr's *Die Schrecken des Eises und der Finsternis*, and, in particular, Peter Handke's *Mein Jahr in der Niemandsbucht* (1994; *My Year in the No-Man's-Bay*, 1998). In this narrative Handke does what other authors reflect on in their lectures on poetics: he writes an autobiographical aesthetics, shedding light on the interrelation of his biography and his subjective poetics. Here he describes in detail the forms and principles of his poetic perception, discussing today's condition of narration by writing about writing, trying to regain a new basis for the great epic by way of the great epic.

History is also thematised in a number of contemporary novels that centre on the discussion of cultural identities. In Germany as in Western Europe in general, the migration of workers, which has been taking place for decades, and the emigration from Eastern Europe, which has gained strength since 1989, have created a society that is trying to cope with the multicultural facts of life. In a number of large cities the proportion of foreigners constitutes about a quarter of the inhabitants. People in the German-speaking countries – as in the rest of Europe – are seldom ready to perceive themselves as a segment of a culturally fragmented society, to initiate a dialogue about the new situation, to urge the majority to promote the acculturation and assimilation of the minority, to practise tolerance towards the culturally different, the stranger.

Underdeveloped as it may be, the multicultural discourse has nevertheless been initiated in the German-speaking countries and novelists have made important contributions to it. These novelists are border-crossers and intermediaries between cultures and they have shown that literature is an appropriate instrument for initiating discussions on multiculturalism. Barbara Frischmuth, who had spent a few years as a student in Turkey, demonstrated in several of her narrative works (especially in *Das Verschwinden des Schattens in der Sonne* (1973; *The Shadow in the Sun Disappears*, 1998)) what is involved in crossing cultural borders. She showed what positive aspects the Islamic and Christian cultures owe to each other, and she also demonstrated that intercultural dialogue brings out the fact that we must live and deal with our own prejudices as well as with those of strangers. The Swiss author Paul Nizon, in his autobiographical narratives *Das Jahr der Liebe* (1981; The Year of Love) and *Die Innenseite des Mantels*

(1995; The Inside of the Coat) has shown – somewhat paradoxically – that home is always a foreign country. Accordingly, he has lived in Paris for most of his life, studying the international and multicultural conditions of this European metropolis. Sten Nadolny and Peter Schneider also belong to those authors with multicultural influences. Like Frischmuth and Nizon, Nadolny reflects on the process of overcoming prejudices towards the cultural other. In choosing a Turk as the hero of his novel *Selim oder Die Gabe der Rede* (1990; Selim or The Gift of Speech) Nadolny lets the reader see through the eyes of a foreigner. Like Nadolny, Schneider too is influenced by the experience of Berlin's multiculture, constantly present in his novel *Paarungen* (1992; Couples).

Barbara Honigmann – along with Robert Schindel, Ralph Giordano and Robert Menasse – belongs to the youngest generation of Jewish novelists who write in German. She grew up in East Berlin and rediscovered her Jewish heritage. In her novels *Roman von einem Kinde* (1986; A Child's Story) and *Eine Liebe aus nichts* (1991; Love Made out of Nothing, 2002) she reflects – as does Robert Schindel in *Gebürtig* (1992; Born Where, 1995) – on identity problems as well as on the tragic fate of the Jews in Germany. Robert Menasse's educational novel *Selige Zeiten, brüchige Welt* (1991; Wings of Stone, 2000) also shows the search for identity on the part of a young Jew of the postwar generation whose parents emigrated to Brazil during the Nazi regime. Finally, Ralph Giordano wrote on his Shoah experience in his novel *Die Bertinis* (1982). His book is simultaneously a critical discussion of how the Germans are coping with their Nazi past.

Arabic, Turkish and Iranian authors are also part of the contemporary multicultural literary scene in the German-speaking countries. Rafik Schami is the most prominent author from the group of Arabic-German authors. At the beginning of his career he was a teller of folktales and fairy tales, but now his novels *Eine Hand voller Sterne* (1987; A Hand Full of Stars, 1992), *Der ehrliche Lügner* (1992; The Honest Liar) and *Erzähler der Nacht* (1989; Damascus Nights, 1993) are found on the German bestseller list. He utilises the narrative traditions of his culture by taking *The Arabian Nights* as a model; that is, he uses the technique of the framework story into which he weaves numerous fantasy tales without abandoning the realm of reality. Similar fusions of oriental and occidental narrative traditions can be found in Emine Sevgi Özdamar's *Mutterzunge* (1990; Mother Tongue, 1991) and *Das Leben ist eine Karawanserei* (1992; Life Is a Caravanserai, 2000) as well as in the books of the most prominent Turkish-German novelist Aysel Özakin (*Die Leidenschaft der Anderen* (1983; The Passion of Others), *Die Vögel auf der Stirn* (1991; The Birds on the Forehead), *Die blaue Maske* (1989; The Blue Mask), *Die Preisvergabe* (1982; The Prizegiving, 1988), *Der fliegende Teppich. Auf der Spur meines Vaters* (1987; The Flying Carpet: on the Trail of My Father)). Among the Iranian writers living in Germany, one should mention the female author TORKAN and her book *Tufan. Brief an einen islamischen Bruder* (1988; Tufan: Letter to an Islamic Brother), another example of an intercultural narrative. All the texts mentioned challenge the reader to rethink his or her perspectives on 'Otherness' in the interlocking realms of contemporary German aesthetics, culture and politics.

FURTHER READING

Bakhtin, Mikhail Mikhailovich, *Problems of Dostoevsky's Poetics*, trans. Carl Emerson (Minneapolis, MN, 1984)

Barner, Wilfried (ed.), *Geschichte der deutschen Literatur von 1945 bis zur Gegenwart* (Munich, 1994)

Barthes, Roland, 'The death of the author' (1968), in Barthes, *Image–Music–Text*, ed. and trans. Stephen Heath (London, 1977), pp. 142–8

Briegleb, Klaus, and Sigrid Weigel (eds.), *Gegenwartsliteratur seit 1968* (Munich, 1992)

Bullivant, Keith, *The Future of German Literature* (Oxford, 1994)

Deleuze, Gilles, and Félix Guattari, *Rhizome: introduction* (Paris, 1976)

Fiedler, Leslie, *Collected Essays* (New York, 1971)

Hoesterey, Ingeborg, *Verschlungene Schriftzeichen. Intertextualität von Literatur und Kunst in der Moderne/Postmoderne* (Frankfurt am Main, 1988)

Horrocks, David, and Eva Kolinsky (eds.), *Turkish Culture in German Society Today* (Providence, RI, and Oxford, 1996)

Hutcheon, Linda, *A Poetics of Postmodernism* (New York and London, 1988)

Lützeler, Paul Michael (ed.), *Spätmoderne und Postmoderne* (Frankfurt am Main, 1991)

Lützeler, Paul Michael (ed.), *Poetik der Autoren* (Frankfurt am Main, 1994)

Lützeler, Paul Michael (ed.), *Schreiben zwischen den Kulturen* (Frankfurt am Main, 1996)

Lützeler, Paul Michael (ed.), *Räume der literarischen Postmoderne* (Tübingen, 2000)

Lyotard, Jean-François, *La condition postmoderne* (Paris, 1979)

Renner, Rolf Günter, *Die postmoderne Konstellation* (Freiburg im Breisgau, 1988)

Saariluoma, Lisa, *Der postindividualistische Roman* (Würzburg, 1994)

Welsch, Wolfgang, *Unsere postmoderne Moderne* (Weinheim, 1988)

Wittstock, Uwe (ed.), *Roman oder Leben. Postmoderne in der deutschen Literatur* (Leipzig, 1994)

Zeyringer, Klaus, *Österreichische Literatur seit 1945* (Innsbruck, 2001)

INDEX

Adorno, Theodor W. 174, 190
aestheticism 84
Anderson, Perry (intellectual historian) 266
Angestellte (white-collar workers) 203
Anz, Thomas, *Gesund oder krank?* 272
The Arabian Nights 278
Auschwitz trials (Frankfurt, 1963–5) 188, 232
Austria 15
  Allied occupation after Second World War 25
  Anschluß (annexation by Third Reich 1938) 233, 244
  conservatism in 6, 9
  First World War and 18
  Habsburg Empire 3, 9, 15, 16, 18
  identity (cultural/national) of 8–9, 28, 232–3
  National Socialism (Nazism) in 24, 233
  and Nazi past 9, 233
  Republic of (1918–34) 18
  Republic of (1945–present) 233; novel in 232–3, 242–7, 253–6, 260–3; political–cultural situation after 1945 233; State Treaty (1955) 233; women, situation of 244–5; writers and politics in 233–4
  Vienna Secession (modernist art movement) 17
  Viennese culture 17–18
autobiography, *see* novel; novel, postmodern

Baader–Meinhof group 27, 189
Bachmann, Ingeborg 249, 256
  fragmentary subject in 261–2
  Der gute Gott von Manhattan (The Good God of Manhattan) 111–12

Malina 249, 260–3; and critique of patriarchy 262; reception of 260
  'Poetikvorlesung' (lecture on poetics) 269
  'Das schreibende Ich' (The writing self) 261; parallels with Max Frisch 261
  'Todesarten' (Death Styles) (projected novel-cycle) 261, 264
Bakhtin, Mikhail (notion of carnivalesque) 274
Balzac, Honoré de 31, 94, 119, 144
Barthes, Roland 273–4
  'La mort de l'auteur' ('The death of the author') 270
Baudelaire, Charles 115, 119
Baudrillard, Jean (cultural critic) 266
Baum, Vicki 6, 124, 125
  Menschen im Hotel (*Grand Hotel*) 125–7; cosmopolitanism in 125; filmic elements in 125–6; montage in 125; 'New Objectivity' in 125, 127; 'New Woman' in 127
  stud. chem. Helene Willfüer 124–5, 128; 'New Woman' in 125; sexual morality in 124–5; 'vamp' type in 125; women and modernity in 124
Beamte (state-employed officials) 203
Becker, Jurek, *Bronsteins Kinder* (Bronstein's Children) 270
Benjamin, Walter
  on Paris 111–12, 115
  'The Storyteller' 5–6, 7
  on time 84
  'The work of art in the age of mechanical reproduction' 90
Bergengruen, Werner, *Der Großtyrann und das Gericht* (*A Matter of Conscience*) 8, 153, 159

CAMBRIDGE COMPANIONS TO LITERATURE

The Cambridge Companion to Greek Tragedy edited by P. E. Easterling

The Cambridge Companion to Old English Literature edited by Malcolm Godden and Michael Lapidge

The Cambridge Companion to Medieval Women's Writing edited by Carolyn Dinshaw and David Wallace

The Cambridge Companion to Medieval Romance edited by Roberta L. Krueger

The Cambridge Companion to Medieval English Theatre edited by Richard Beadle

The Cambridge Companion to English Renaissance Drama, second edition edited by A. R. Braunmuller and Michael Hattaway

The Cambridge Companion to Renaissance Humanism edited by Jill Kraye

The Cambridge Companion to English Poetry, Donne to Marvell edited by Thomas N. Corns

The Cambridge Companion to English Literature, 1500–1600 edited by Arthur F. Kinney

The Cambridge Companion to English Literature, 1650–1740 edited by Steven N. Zwicker

The Cambridge Companion to Writing of the English Revolution edited by N. H. Keeble

The Cambridge Companion to English Restoration Theatre edited by Deborah C. Payne Fisk

The Cambridge Companion to British Romanticism edited by Stuart Curran

The Cambridge Companion to Eighteenth-Century Poetry edited by John Sitter

The Cambridge Companion to the Eighteenth-Century Novel edited by John Richetti

The Cambridge Companion to the Gothic Novel edited by Jerrold E. Hogle

The Cambridge Companion to Victorian Poetry edited by Joseph Bristow

The Cambridge Companion to the Victorian Novel edited by Deirdre David

The Cambridge Companion to Crime Fiction edited by Martin Priestman

The Cambridge Companion to Science Fiction edited by Edward James and Farah Mendlesohn

The Cambridge Companion to Travel Writing edited by Peter Hulme and Tim Youngs

The Cambridge Companion to American Realism and Naturalism edited by Donald Pizer

The Cambridge Companion to Nineteenth-Century American Women's Writing edited by Dale M. Bauer and Philip Gould

The Cambridge Companion to the Classic Russian Novel edited by Malcolm V. Jones and Robin Feuer Miller

The Cambridge Companion to the French Novel: from 1800 to the Present edited by Timothy Unwin

The Cambridge Companion to the Spanish Novel: from 1600 to the Present edited by Harriet Turner and Adelaida López de Martínez

The Cambridge Companion to the Italian Novel edited by Peter Bondanella and Andrea Ciccarelli

The Cambridge Companion to the Modern German Novel edited by Graham Bartram

The Cambridge Companion to Jewish American Literature edited by Hana Wirth-Nesher and Michael P. Kramer

The Cambridge Companion to the African American Novel edited by Maryemma Graham

The Cambridge Companion to Contemporary Irish Poetry edited by Matthew Campbell

The Cambridge Companion to Modernism edited by Michael Levenson

The Cambridge Companion to Australian Literature edited by Elizabeth Webby

The Cambridge Companion to American Women Playwrights edited by Brenda Murphy

CAMBRIDGE COMPANIONS TO CULTURE